Lecture Notes in Energy

Volume 28

Lecture Notes in Energy (LNE) is a series that reports on new developments in the study of energy: from science and engineering to the analysis of energy policy. The series' scope includes but is not limited to, renewable and green energy, nuclear, fossil fuels and carbon capture, energy systems, energy storage and harvesting, batteries and fuel cells, power systems, energy efficiency, energy in buildings, energy policy, as well as energy-related topics in economics, management and transportation. Books published in LNE are original and timely and bridge between advanced textbooks and the forefront of research. Readers of LNE include postgraduate students and non-specialist researchers wishing to gain an accessible introduction to a field of research as well as professionals and researchers with a need for an up-to-date reference book on a well-defined topic. The series publishes single- and multi-authored volumes as well as advanced textbooks.

More information about this series at http://www.springer.com/series/8874

Jale Tosun · Sophie Biesenbender
Kai Schulze
Editors

Energy Policy Making in the EU

Building the Agenda

Springer

Editors
Jale Tosun
Institute of Political Science
Heidelberg University
Heidelberg
Germany

Kai Schulze
Faculty of Economics and Social Sciences
University of Potsdam
Potsdam
Germany

Sophie Biesenbender
Institute for Research Information
and Quality Assurance (iFQ)
Berlin
Germany

ISSN 2195-1284 ISSN 2195-1292 (electronic)
Lecture Notes in Energy
ISBN 978-1-4471-6644-3 ISBN 978-1-4471-6645-0 (eBook)
DOI 10.1007/978-1-4471-6645-0

Library of Congress Control Number: 2014957135

Springer London Heidelberg New York Dordrecht

Printed on acid-free paper

Springer-Verlag London Ltd. is part of Springer Science+Business Media (www.springer.com)

Acknowledgments

This edited volume originates from a workshop held at the University of Mannheim's Center for European Social Research (MZES) in Germany, during 30–31 May 2013. We gratefully acknowledge funding from the Fritz Thyssen Foundation for the organisation of the workshop as well as the research project *Agenda Definition in European Energy Policy: Actors, Preferences and Strategies*. We thank Cornelius Eich, Frederic Neuendorf, Christine Stegmann and the MZES for their support in the organisation of the workshop. Marc Debus, Johann Köppel and Shaun Bevan did a terrific job in commenting on the draft versions of the chapters. This project was inspired by the workshop "Intra-institutional Politics of EU Energy Policy-Making: Landscape-Level Shifts, Discourses and Organizational Cultures" organised by Luigi Carafa and held at Robinson College, Cambridge University, 27–28 April 2012. The volume as a whole additionally benefitted from the seminal discussion at the Workshop "Energy Policy in Europe: Understanding Agenda-Setting Dynamics" held at the International Conference on Public Policy, 26–28 June 2013, Institute of Political Studies, Grenoble. We thank Nazmiye Balta-Ozkan, Andrei Belyi and Tina Hunter for participating in the workshop and providing us with valuable suggestions for further improving this project. Finally, we want to express our gratitude to Andreas Fleig for a final set of comments, Sophie Dolinga, Frederic Neuendorf and Simon Schaub for formatting the chapters and James Ferrell for language-editing.

Heidelberg, October 2014 Jale Tosun
Berlin Sophie Biesenbender
Potsdam Kai Schulze

Contents

Contributors

Petya Alexandrova Institute of Political Sciences, Leibniz University of Hannover, Hannover, Germany

Sophie Biesenbender Institute for Research Information and Quality Assurance, Berlin, Germany

Stefan Bouzarovski SEED, University of Manchester, Arthur Lewis Building, Manchester, UK; Department of Economic Geography, University of Gdańsk, Gdańsk, Poland

Elina Brutschin International Relations Department, Webster University Vienna, Vienna, Austria

Andrea Ciambra Institut de Dret I Tecnologia, Universitat Autònoma de Barcelona Campus UAB–Edifici B, Bellaterra (Barcelona), Spain

Robert Henry Cox Walker Institute for International and Area Studies, University of South Carolina, Columbia, SC, USA

Mariam Dekanozishvili Department of Politics and Geography, Coastal Carolina University, Conway, SC, USA

Gerhard Fuchs Institute for Social Sciences, Sowi VI, University of Stuttgart, Stuttgart, Germany

Nicole Herweg Institute of Political Science, University of Heidelberg, Heidelberg, Germany

David Jacobs Department of Political and Social Sciences, Environmental Policy Research Centre (FFU), Freie Universität Berlin, Berlin, Germany

S. Petrova SEED, University of Manchester, Arthur Lewis Building, Manchester, UK

Kai Schulze Faculty of Economics and Social Sciences, University of Potsdam, Potsdam, Germany

Israel Solorio Environmental Policy Research Centre, Freie Universität Berlin, Berlin, Germany

Arco Timmermans Institute of Public Administration, Campus the Hague, Leiden University, The Hague, The Netherlands

Jale Tosun Institute of Political Science, Heidelberg University, Heidelberg, Germany

Chapter 1
Building the EU's Energy Policy Agenda: An Introduction

Jale Tosun, Sophie Biesenbender and Kai Schulze

Abstract When are energy issues likely to be placed on the political agenda of the European Union? Which actors are influential in agenda shaping and what are their strategies? When does agenda shaping lead to legislative action? These are the research questions that guide the contributions to this edited volume. This introductory chapter gives an overview of the key concepts and research themes, and explains why the field of energy policy is useful for gaining an understanding of agenda shaping in the European Union. Furthermore, it outlines the structure of the book and summarises the contents of the individual chapters.

1.1 Introduction: Why Study Agenda Shaping?

It is the principal objective of this collection of case studies to provide insights into the shaping of the European Union's (EU) political agenda. This research focus is promising for several reasons. First of all, political attention to social problems is scarce and yet also consequential (Green-Pedersen and Walgrave 2014, p. 6). Policy makers are constantly confronted with resource constraints, which prevent them from addressing the practically infinite number of social problems. Therefore,

J. Tosun
Institute of Political Science, Heidelberg University,
Bergheimer Strasse 58, 69115 Heidelberg, Germany
e-mail: jale.tosun@ipw.uni-heidelberg.de

S. Biesenbender (✉)
Institute for Research Information and Quality Assurance,
Schützenstraße 6a, 10117 Berlin, Germany
e-mail: biesenbender@forschungsinfo.de

K. Schulze
Faculty of Economics and Social Sciences, University of Potsdam,
August-Bebel-Str. 89, 14482 Potsdam, Germany
e-mail: kai.schulze@uni-potsdam.de

J. Tosun et al. (eds.), *Energy Policy Making in the EU*,
Lecture Notes in Energy 28, DOI 10.1007/978-1-4471-6645-0_1

only a small share of the entirety of social problems is given political attention and ends up on the political agenda. However, without making it to the political agenda, a social problem cannot be addressed, which indicates why this step is consequential for the subsequent policy-making process. As a result and as acknowledged by the literature, agenda shaping represents an important source of political power (see, e.g. Shepsle and Weingast 1987; Baumgartner and Jones 1993; Rochefort and Cobb 1993; Tallberg 2003, 2006; Baumgartner et al. 2006; Jennings 2011; Engeli et al. 2012; Green-Pedersen and Walgrave 2014).

Studying agenda shaping in the EU is particularly insightful for the following two reasons. First, selecting and placing issues on the agenda of this political system is challenging because further to gaining attention, national governments need to be convinced that an issue requires an EU-wide solution (Princen 2011). This process is often mediated through epistemic communities especially in uncertain decision-making environments (Dunlop 2012, 2014). Second, the interaction of many and different types of actors in varying institutional constellations with a vertical division of powers between the EU institutions and the member states and a horizontal division among the different EU institutions offers multiple institutional access points, which should facilitate agenda shaping (see, e.g. Peters 1994; Pollack 2003, 2010; Young 2010; Princen 2007; Heinelt and Knodt 2011; Alexandrova et al. 2012; Alexandrova and Timmermans 2013; Tosun 2013). Thus, the EU's institutional set-up allows for two classes of competing expectations about agenda shaping: one emphasising the political challenge and the other stressing the extensive opportunities.

In any political system, there usually exists a multitude of agendas, and so it is important to state in which of them one is interested in. The literature on public policy usually distinguishes between the discussion agenda and decision agenda (Cobb and Elder 1972; Cobb et al. 1976), but it should be noted that several discussion and decision agendas coexist in any polity. The discussion agenda refers to all kinds of issues debated in society, whereas the decision agenda is about issues that are up for serious consideration by decision-makers. Thus, issues must reach the decision agenda before they can be addressed by policy-making institutions. The decision agenda is often times not only motivated and influenced by the discussion agenda but also constrained by existing agendas (see Peters et al. 2005). Items on the decision agenda are usually well-defined, some being encompassing and some referring to technical details. The discussion agenda, by contrast, usually consists of rather broad concepts and ideas. The contributions to this volume are interested in both types of agendas to which they uniformly refer to as the 'political agenda', which can be defined as "the set of issues that are the subject of decision making and debate within a given political system at any one time" (Baumgartner 2001, p. 288).

We presume that there is a relationship between the discussion and the decision agenda, but it is not our objective to explore it in greater detail here, in particular because the absence of a 'European' public makes establishing a direct link difficult (for analyses of individual countries see, e.g. Walgrave et al. 2008; Green-Pedersen and Stubager 2010; Jennings 2011; Tresch et al. 2013). Nonetheless, the EU context is useful—adding to the two aforementioned reasons for having chosen it—for learning about both successful and unsuccessful agenda-shaping efforts. This book defines successful agenda shaping as a process that culminates in the adoption of binding or non-binding rules by the EU legislative organs.[1] Unsuccessful agenda-shaping efforts refer to a process where no rules are adopted by the EU legislative organs. In national political systems, governments are eager to downplay and de-emphasise unsuccessful attempts for reasons of party competition (see, e.g. Manow and Burkhart 2007). In the EU-context, quite the opposite is the case since the EU is in a much greater need to legitimise both its actions and non-actions (see, e.g. Tosun 2013, p. 36). As a result, agenda-shaping efforts and their outcomes in terms of legislative initiatives are well documented, which forms an important advantage for understanding the causal mechanisms at work.

We use the terminology 'agenda shaping' in accordance with Tallberg (2003, p. 5), who utilises it as a generic term for three forms of agenda influence that are "distinct and mutually exclusive in logical and conceptual terms": agenda setting, agenda structuring and agenda exclusion. *Agenda setting* is about placing (new) issues on the political agenda. *Agenda structuring* happens if issues that are already on the agenda are emphasised or de-emphasised. *Agenda exclusion* is about the active barring of issues from the political agenda; as hinted at above, this type of agenda shaping is the one that is empirically most difficult to observe. Most contributions to this book are interested in illuminating agenda-setting processes, but some chapters also explore activities that can be regarded as agenda structuring and agenda exclusion. In fact, as will be shown in the remainder of this book, the role of individual EU institutions for agenda shaping can be better understood by differentiating between these three forms.

The common thread through this volume is the analysis of agenda-shaping activities with regard to EU energy policy. In order to understand how energy issues are placed on the EU's political agenda or not, this volume poses three research questions:

- When are energy issues likely to be placed on the EU's political agenda?
- Which actors are influential in agenda shaping and what are their strategies?
- When does agenda shaping lead to legislative action?

The remainder of this chapter outlines the characteristics of EU energy policy and explains why this field was chosen as the motif for this edited volume. The chapter then continues to sketch the agenda-shaping powers of the EU institutions. Finally, the chapter details the rationale of the book and gives an overview of the individual contributions.

[1] Binding rules in the EU are Regulations, Directives and Decisions, while Recommendations and Opinions represent non-binding instruments of European law (Tosun 2013, p. 30).

1.2 Energy Policy: A Cross-sectoral Field

In this section, we pursue three objectives. First, we illustrate how EU energy policy has developed over the last decades. Second, we present our rationale for choosing energy policy as the overarching topic for this volume. Third, we explain why it is promising to approach EU energy policy from the perspective of agenda shaping.

For a long time, joint rules in the field of energy policy could only be defined because of voluntary and horizontal cooperation between EU member states (Egenhofer et al. 2011). This was the result of the member states' reluctance to transfer decision-making powers to the European Commission (henceforth: Commission)—especially with regard to energy security (Pointvogl 2009; Youngs 2009). Since the mid-1980s energy issues have acquired an increasingly important role on the EU's political agenda, which has led to a rather comprehensive body of rules that address the security, economic and environmental dimensions of energy policy (Buchan 2010).

The first area of EU energy policy to evolve was the one on energy security. In reaction to crises related to the supply of oil from the Middle East, the EU—or at that time, the European Community—adopted legislation specifying the level of emergency oil stocks in the late 1960s (Tosun 2011). With the recent enlargement rounds and the Central and East European states' dependence on Russian energy supplies, concerns about energy security have received even more attention and the member states are increasingly willing to strengthen the Commission's role in securing energy supply (Belyi 2003; Youngs 2009; Le Coq and Paltseva 2009; Buchan 2010; Tosun and Solorio 2011; Kuzemko et al. 2012).

An important stimulus for the further development of energy policy was the 1987 Single European Act and the subsequent Single Market Programme. This opened up the second avenue along which energy policy became institutionalised at the EU level, namely harmonised rules related to the creation of the internal market and the regulation of competition. The result was the adoption of three packages of Directives in 1996, 2003 and 2007 that pursued the liberalisation of the energy market (see, e.g. Eising 2002; Eberlein 2008; Buchan 2010; Eikeland 2011; Pollak and Slominski 2011).

The institutionalisation of environmental policy through the Single European Act and the signing of the Treaty on European Union (TEU) in 1992 opened up a third avenue for promoting EU energy policy as a means to attain environmental policy goals. Compared to the first two avenues, the environmental dimension has provided the most effective means for advancing energy policy at the European level (Buchan 2009, 2010). In this regard, there is broad consensus in the literature that the EU's concern for climate change is one of the main drivers of the formal strengthening of the Commission's competence to take action in the area of energy policy (see, e.g. Buchan 2009, 2010; Tosun and Solorio 2011; Da Graça Carvalho 2012; Morata and Solorio 2012; Wettestad et al. 2012; Collier 2013; Maltby 2013; Calvin et al. 2014). As a result of these developments, the Commission began to push forward the energy debate with the paramount goal of laying down the foundations of a new energy policy of global character as a step towards effectively tackling climate change (see, e.g. Jordan et al. 2010; Helm 2014).

EU energy policy today comprises rules concerning energy sources, technology and innovation, renewable energy, energy efficiency, the single market for gas and electricity, energy from abroad, energy infrastructure and environmental aspects of energy production, consumption and transit (see, e.g. Talus 2013). Even in the area of nuclear energy, the EU has adopted rules which ask the member states to present national programmes, indicating when, where and how they will construct and manage final repositories guaranteeing the highest safety standards (see Council Directive 2011/70/Euratom). This was made possible by the Lisbon Treaty entering into force in December 2009. It introduced for the first time an energy title to the EU's treaty framework (Buchan 2010; Tosun and Solorio 2011; Kuzemko et al. 2012; Talus 2013). Compared to its origins, EU energy policy has developed into a fully-fledged policy field with the Commission having achieved more and more competencies in the course of time (Maltby 2013). Even more astonishingly, not only has EU energy policy developed in a remarkable fashion internally, but it has also been extended to non-member states through external action like the Energy Community (Göler and Kurze 2009; Prange-Gstöhl 2009; Renner and Trauner 2009; Tosun 2012; Carafa 2013; Tosun and Schulze 2015).

So why is EU energy policy a promising field for the analytical purposes of this book? First off, energy policy spans across sectoral boundaries, including economic policy, environmental policy, security policy, more generally international relations and—as it will be shown in this book—social policy. In the EU context, the linkage between energy policy and other policy areas is particularly strong since before the Lisbon Treaty entered into force in 2009 the EU had no legal competence for formulating energy policy. Instead, policy making had to be based on the provisions of the internal market, competition or environmental protection (Tosun and Solorio 2011). This cross-sectoral nature of energy policy is analytically useful as it allows us to draw more generalisable conclusions. In particular, studying agenda shaping in such boundary-spanning policy fields should entail variation in four elements that are essential for such processes: attention, actors, framing and venues (Engeli et al. 2012, p. 10; see also Princen 2011). Since there are a large number of actors coming from different sectors who interact in an attempt to formulate energy policy, the analysis of how the EU energy agenda is shaped appears to be particularly rewarding.

The second reason for choosing energy policy is that it is a relatively dynamic field subject to intense public and political debate. On the one side, this stems from the only recent formalisation of this field, which provides many opportunities for new legislative initiatives. On the other, energy issues are heavily affected by developments at the international level such as climate summits or armed conflicts within or between states.

The third motivation relates to Tallberg's (2003) argument that successful agenda setting—one of the three types of agenda shaping analysed here—requires a policy entrepreneur, a 'skillful leader' (Weible 2007), who raises the awareness of a problem by providing information and a specific definition—or framing (see

Daviter 2007)—of the problem at hand. Several studies have argued that the Commission acts as a policy entrepreneur in an increasing number of policy areas (see, e.g. Wettestad 2005; Maltby 2013). So it will be interesting to see to what extent this observation can be confirmed for the case of EU energy policy as a whole.

The fourth and final motivation for studying EU energy policy from the agenda-shaping perspective is that there is already an implicit claim in the literature about how energy issues are brought onto the EU's political agenda. Following Buchan (2010, p. 371), EU energy policy—at least the energy-security part—can be conceived as being 'driven by events'. As a result, one expects that energy issues are placed on the European policy makers' agenda when there is a specific 'triggering event' or 'focusing event' (Birkland 2004). The importance of events for agenda shaping in EU energy policy is a theoretical expectation we seek to test empirically in this edited volume.

Paraphrasing the four motivations above, we expect the contributions to this volume to advance the state of research by illuminating three aspects: First, whether the cross-sectoral nature of energy policy has implications for the attention paid to energy issues on the European level, which types of actor constellations evolve around them, what policy images the individual actor groups create and through which institutional venues energy issues enter the EU's political agenda. Second, the case studies will assess the role of the Commission as a policy entrepreneur. Third, the chapters address the role of events for explaining agenda shaping in EU energy policy.

1.3 The EU Institutions' Agenda-Shaping Powers

This volume aims to shed light on agenda-shaping processes and their outcomes in the EU. Having said this, one must keep in mind that there exists not only one EU political agenda but several. Most importantly, each EU institution has its own political agenda, which can then influence the political agenda of the EU as a whole. When speaking of this overall political agenda, we mean that an issue is debated by the EU's legislative and executive organs in an attempt to propose EU legislation.

One EU institution that is influential in shaping the overall political agenda is the European Council, which consists of the heads of state or government of the member states, together with its President and the President of the Commission. The High Representative of the Union for Foreign Affairs and Security Policy (henceforth: High Representative) also takes part in the European Council's work. In the absence of legislative power, Article 1(16) of the Lisbon Treaty charged the European Council with the definition of "general political directions and priorities". Thus, even though the formal monopoly to initiate legislation belongs to the European Commission (see below), the European Council has obviously the power to shape the EU's political agenda by deciding to address certain issues. Princen and Rhinard (2006) refer to this process as agenda shaping through the 'high-politics route'. Issues reaching the EU's political agenda through this route are often shared political problems that may also be associated with extraordinary events. In the high politics route, issues are usually outlined in a broad way and details left to lower level institutions. This division of work is plausible since the high-politics route corresponds to agenda shaping by political leaders while the 'low-politics route'—to which we will turn immediately—emphasises the role of bureaucrats and technical knowledge.

However, agenda shaping by the European Council most times goes beyond the setting of informal political guidelines. It often comprises surprisingly detailed and clear-cut agenda-setting activities. The existing and arguably growing agenda-shaping power of the European Council is both surprising and plausible at the same time. On the one hand, it is surprising since this EU institution does not formally possess any legislative functions (Bocquillon and Dobbels 2014). On the other hand, it is quite straightforward that the European Council is influential since it brings together the EU's top political elites. Without taking into consideration their voice, EU policy making simply might not be feasible at all. This assessment corresponds with anecdotes that highlight the influence of the heads of state or government of the member states for agenda shaping. For example, at the 2005 informal meeting of the leaders of the EU member states in Hampton Court, United Kingdom, it was concluded that work in the energy sector needs to be taken forward.[2] Based on this conclusion, the other EU institutions started to discuss how to develop further EU energy policy, which eventually culminated in the passage of the Commission's green paper entitled "A European Strategy for Sustainable, Competitive and Secure Energy" in March 2006.

The Commission and the Council of the EU (henceforth: Council) can either react to how the European Council prioritises problems or make its own attempts for shaping the EU's political agenda by making use of their decision-making competencies in the boundaries of treaty law. Princen and Rhinard (2006) refer to processes in which issues are placed on the agenda by bureaucrats working in the Commission or the Council's Committee of Permanent Representatives (COREPER) and Working Parties as the low-politics route of agenda shaping. However, it should be noted that agenda shaping through the Commission or the Council can also be driven by political considerations (and therefore the high-politics route as well), which will become clear when taking a closer look at the functions of these institutions in EU politics.

The Commission is the EU's cabinet government with a currently 28-member College of Commissioners. In addition, the Commission also includes an administrative body of civil servants who are split into departments called Directorates-General and Services. Article 17 TEU assigns the Commission the responsibility to "develop medium-term strategies". In terms of agenda-shaping powers, the

[2] Until 2009, the European Council was an informal body. It was only formalised as an institution upon the entry of force of the Lisbon Treaty.

Commission enjoys a special role in the EU political system: it has the formal monopoly on agenda setting since it possesses the exclusive right to initiate legislation.[3] Without a proposal from the Commission, the Council cannot preside over Community legal acts. Along with that, the Commission can withdraw its proposals and stop the process at any time during the legislative process (Knill and Tosun 2011, p. 176). This turns the Commission into an EU organ that enjoys powers of both agenda setting and exclusion. It can therefore be considered the key actor at this policy-making stage (see, e.g. Larsson and Trondal 2006; Blom-Hansen 2008; Young 2010; Häge and Toshkov 2011; Hartlapp et al. 2013). Yet, it should be noted that EU scholars are divided over whether the Commission's right of initiative constitutes a drafting power or an agenda-shaping power (Bauer 2008, p. 692)—an important debate indeed to which we will return in the concluding chapter.

However, the Council and the European Parliament are able to request legislative initiatives and in most cases the Commission acts upon their requests and initiates legislation. Furthermore, a number of studies have shown that the governments of the member states have been influential for the Commission's agenda-shaping activities because the Commission anticipates member states' opposition to its plans (see, e.g. Börzel 2002; Pollack 2003; Häge and Toshkov 2011)—as are interest groups (see, e.g. Bouwen and McCown 2007; Baumgartner and Mahoney 2008; Klüver 2013). Finally, one of the innovations of the Lisbon Treaty is that EU citizens are now also able to request the Commission to legislate in an area through a petition carrying one million signatures, which must come from at least 7 out of the 28 member states. If the formal requirements are met, the Commission either adopts a formal response stating what actions it will propose or specifies the reasons for not doing so (see, e.g. De Clerck-Sachsse 2012 for an overview).

The Council—together with the European Parliament—is part of the bicameral EU legislature and consists of the member states' governments. It meets in ten different configurations, which vary according to the topic under consideration. With regard to agenda shaping, the literature concentrates on two aspects of the Council. The first one is the role of the rotating Council Presidency, which has led to intensive academic debate on whether or not the incumbent has agenda-shaping powers (see, e.g. Tallberg 2003; Pollak and Riekmann 2007; Warntjen 2007). In this context, Vandecasteele et al. (2013) show that the Council Presidency allowed Poland to influence to a certain extent the political agenda with regard to the EU's Eastern Partnership but not on the contents of the actual decisions made on these policies. The second perspective taken up in the literature refers to the Working Parties and the COREPER—i.e. the bureaucratic components of the Council—and their role for agenda shaping via the low-politics route (see, e.g. Princen and

[3] As Vanhoonacker and Pomorska (2013, p. 1320) outline, an important exception is foreign policy, where the High Representative can put forward proposals together with the member states (Article 30(1) TEU). In the other areas of EU external action, the High Representative can submit joint proposals together with the European Commission (Article 22(2) TEU).

Rhinard 2006). Thus, in the relevant strands of literature the Council is associated with both agenda-setting and agenda-structuring powers.

The European Parliament represents the second legislative branch of government and is the only EU organ that is legitimised by direct elections. Initially, the European Parliament had very limited possibilities to shape the political agenda. The extension of co-decision powers has given the European Parliament increased agenda-shaping powers (Hix et al. 2006). However, it should be noted that this power to influence the agenda predominantly concerns the "power to make proposals that others find easier to adopt than to amend" (Burns 2013, p. 139). When defining agenda shaping more broadly—as it is done in this volume, the European Parliament is not perceived as a key player by EU scholars. Nonetheless, the European Parliament can still be important for agenda shaping by means of agenda structuring. This point is illustrated by Natorski and Surrallés (2008), who show that in the past the European Parliament succeeded to sustain the political discourse on energy policy and to even bring in new aspects into the debate such as the social dimension.

Finally, the Court of Justice represents the judicial branch of the EU's political system. It interprets European law and in this way facilitates its uniform application in all member states. Another important task of this institution is the enforcement of EU law together with the Commission. The Court of Justice has used its rulings to claim authority over national law, judicial activities law and the interpretation of the EU treaties. This authority has allowed this institution to bring issues onto the political agenda "independent of those of the member states and counter to their interests" (Carrubba et al. 2008, p. 436). In fact, a range of actors such as interest groups address the Court of Justice strategically in order to obtain a ruling that will force other EU institutions to react (Princen 2007, p. 23). Thus, while the Court of Justice cannot initiate legislation itself—since it is obviously a judicial organ—it must still be seen as an institution with vested agenda-setting powers (see, e.g. Garrett and Weingast 1993; Pollack 2003).

Summing up, in the EU's political system the Commission has the exclusive right of legislative initiative, which turns it into the most important formal agenda shaper, which possesses both agenda-setting and agenda-exclusion powers. Of course, when referring to the individual EU institutions' agendas, exclusion can also be practiced here. However, when talking about the EU's overall political agenda, the Commission only can decide to abstain from addressing an issue. The Commission does not act in a vacuum, and the formal right of initiative is no guarantee for a successful policy proposal—that is, one that eventually becomes an EU rule. Therefore, the literature has highlighted a number of other factors as discussed earlier—e.g. institutional rules and the preferences of other players—that co-determine the outcome of the Commission's agenda-shaping activities. In this context, with the formalisation of the European Council as an EU organ by the Lisbon Treaty, the 'competitive cooperation' (Bocquillon and Dobbels 2014) between the Commission and the European Council has moved to the forefront of studies on EU politics. Overall, given the EU's particular institutional set-up, Princen (2012, p. 207) expects agenda-shaping processes to "show a number of regularities and recurring dynamics". It is the objective of this edited volume to empirically assess this expectation for the case of agenda shaping in EU energy policy.

1.4 Structure of the Book and Overview of the Contributions

This book brings together scholars in EU energy policy in an attempt to provide an improved understanding of agenda-shaping activities. The individual contributions are comparative or single case studies that aim to illustrate how the EU's political agenda is shaped by the various actors. There are four main topics addressed by this edited volume. All chapters are varied in their use of theoretical underpinnings, and their assignment to the individual topics stems from the emphasis they place on specific aspects. The use of a wide range of theoretical frameworks is encouraged and expected to provide a particularly encompassing understanding of agenda-shaping dynamics.

The covered topics focus on (a) the relationship between agenda shaping and subsequent decision-making, (b) the role of the Commission as the formal agenda-setting power, (c) the impact of member states' attempts to shape the EU agenda and (d) the way in which the framing of issues determines agenda-setting processes and their success.

The first topic is about agenda-shaping patterns and how these translate into legislative activities. Chapter 2 by Sophie Biesenbender sets out to depict how EU energy policy developed in the last six decades. In doing so, she compares agenda-shaping patterns and framing strategies in different EU institutions over time. Her analysis reveals that the development of EU energy policy is influenced by both regulatory legacies in political institutions and external events or factors. In this context, the chapter shows that the European Council and the Commission have increasingly dominated agenda shaping in this field.

This finding fits very well with that provided by Petya Alexandrova and Arco Timmermans in Chap. 3. The authors analyse the appearance of energy-related issues on the agenda of European Council meetings and find that the attention to these issues was initially limited, but is constantly growing. Furthermore and in line with the literature (see, e.g. Bocquillon and Dobbels 2014), the mentioning of energy-related issues in fact often does lead to policy proposals, thus underlining the political weight of the European Council.

Kai Schulze in Chap. 4 also takes a comparative approach to the legislative activities that can be witnessed in response to the political agenda. His analysis differs from the previous two since he concentrates on the EU's agenda-shaping powers from an 'outward perspective'. For this purpose, the chapter assesses the role of the Energy Community for the adoption of four major EU energy policies across the member and observer states to the Energy Community, i.e. non-member states of the EU. The analysis shows that the EU has been successful in placing energy issues on the political agenda of EU non-member states, albeit to varying degrees. According to the analysis, success also depends on how EU energy policies are framed.

All three chapters are innovative in their own way. Chapter 2 presents the broad lines in the development of EU energy policy and engages in theorisation. In a similar vein, Chap. 3 contributes to the state of research by illustrating the political attention paid to energy policy issues by the EU political elites over time and relative to other policy issues. It is rigorously embedded in the theoretical literature on policy punctuations as put forward by Baumgartner and Jones (1993) and also most recently by Jones and Baumgartner (2012). The main strength of Chap. 4 is that it approaches the Energy Community from the perspective of agenda shaping. This perspective is promising for disentangling the mechanisms by which agenda shaping affects energy policy outside the EU (see also Tosun 2012; Tosun and Schulze 2015). Together, these chapters help to increase our understanding of when agenda shaping leads to legislative action and when it does not.

The second topic concerns the empirical assessment of the Commission's role as a policy entrepreneur and agenda shaper. In Chap. 5, Nicole Herweg presents a rigorous analysis of the agenda-shaping process leading to the first out of three gas directives using Kingdon's (1984) multiple streams framework. The analysis shows that the liberalisation issue entered the EU's political agenda because the Commission skillfully managed to frame energy matters as an integral part of competition policy, which opened a window of opportunity.

Chapter 6 by David Jacobs also provides an in-depth analysis of the Commission's agenda-shaping role in furthering the use of renewable energy sources. The major strength of this analysis consists in depicting how the Commission acts when confronted with two contradictory goals: one being the promotion of low-carbon energy and the other focusing on the liberalisation of the electricity sector. In fact, being torn between these two objectives the Commission has failed to present a promising supranational strategy. Instead, the Commission is now trying to influence national policy decisions indirectly via state-aid guidelines. This is indeed an important finding since it shows that not all agenda-shaping efforts by the Commission are successful.

Chapter 7 by Stefan Bouzarovski and Saska Petrova complements this group of studies by illustrating how the Commission can place an issue onto the agenda by actually aiming to further a completely different goal. This happened in the case of the EU energy poverty and vulnerability agenda, which was created because the Commission was eager to implement the Third Energy Package. Without having a clear idea of how to tackle the issue of energy poverty and being confronted with resistance by some powerful EU member states such as Germany, the Commission's initial efforts to establish a pan-European energy poverty policy failed.

In sum, Chap. 5 makes a genuine theoretical contribution to the literature since the author presents a revised version of the multiple streams framework that systematically distinguishes between agenda shaping and decision-making. In this way, some of the flaws attributed to the original version of this approach become rectified. The empirical richness turns Chap. 6 into a very instructive piece that contributes to the literature by providing insights into bureaucratic politics inside the Commission (see also, e.g. Bauer 2008; Hartlapp et al. 2013). Chapter 7 then represents an almost ideal test case for the multiple streams framework as revised by Herweg (Chap. 5), even though it is theoretically embedded in a different strand of literature. Another major achievement of Chap. 7 is that is draws attention to the social dimension of energy policy by testing the expectation that agenda shaping in this field is driven by events.

The next group of chapters consists of two contributions that address the importance of certain member states for the occurrence and success of EU agenda-shaping processes. In Chap. 8 Andrea Ciambra and Israel Solorio make a compelling case for the role played by the United Kingdom for bringing the liberalisation of the internal energy market onto the EU's political agenda. This study is particularly insightful as it combines the 'uploading'-perspective of Europeanisation research with agenda shaping (see, e.g. Radaelli 2003; Jordan and Liefferink 2004). In this context, Chap. 8 takes a particular approach that focuses on the discourse of EU energy policy.

In Chap. 9, Robert Henry Cox and Mariam Dekanozishvili also concentrate on the influence of one particular member state for explaining how Directive 2009/28/EC on the promotion of the use of energy from renewable sources was proposed. The authors convincingly argue that Germany was responsible for bringing this issue on the EU's political agenda. What is particularly instructive in this analysis is that the determinants of Germany's agenda-shaping power are discussed. In this context, the authors highlight the importance of a broad consensus in member states for successful agenda shaping. National consensus then also shapes the ability of individual EU member states to act as policy entrepreneurs and to affect the design of the policy proposals resulting from the agenda-shaping process.

Chapter 10 by Elina Brutschin links the fourth group of papers on the role of framing strategies for agenda-shaping success to the previous set of analyses that study the influence of member states. Her chapter focuses on the role of Eastern European countries in bringing the specification of a 'Gazprom clause' on the agenda. Yet, her study stresses the importance of the framing strategies of the Eastern European countries. Her chapter illustrates very well how the overall perception of the third gas directive changed following the invoking of a security-related image for this piece of legislation.

In Chap. 11, Gerhard Fuchs outlines agenda-shaping processes in situations of high scientific and technological uncertainty. In so doing, this chapter also links to the third group of papers since it was the positive Norwegian experience that brought Carbon Capture and Storage on the EU's political agenda. Altogether, this chapter brings in considerations of risk and uncertainty in the literature of agenda shaping. Finally, the importance of framing as well as the definition and re-definition of policy images highlighted in Chap. 10 speaks very well to Chap. 12 by Jale Tosun. This study shows how differently hydraulic fracturing was framed by the actors involved. While the policy image created by the European Council was a positive one, which linked shale gas production with the security of energy supply, the resulting policy process developed around a different policy image that highlighted the uncertain risks related to hydraulic fracturing in regard to human health and the environment. This re-definition of the policy image was primarily the result of the European Parliament's involvement in the policy process as well as the expansion of the political conflict over this issue. In the end, however, the European Parliament was unsuccessful in bringing about stricter EU-wide rules addressing hydraulic fracturing.

These three contributions speak very much to the literature on agenda shaping by assessing the impact of policy or issue images (see, e.g. Engeli et al. 2012). At the same time, each chapter individually helps to further this literature. Chapter 10 does so by asking whether the success of framing and re-framing policy images depends on the political power of states. Chapters 11 and 12 help to develop the literature further by showing how risk-related issues are framed and re-framed by different actor and interest groups.

In the closing chapter, Jale Tosun, Sophie Schmitt and Kai Schulze summarise the key findings of the case studies and discuss them in light of the research questions outlined above. In a second step, the authors elaborate on a research agenda for future theoretical and empirical work on both agenda setting and energy policy making in the EU.

References

Alexandrova, P., Carammia, M., & Timmermans, A. (2012). Policy punctuations and issue diversity on the European council agenda. *Policy Studies Journal, 40*(1), 69–88.

Alexandrova, P., & Timmermans, A. (2013). National interest versus the common good: The presidency in European Council agenda setting. *European Journal of Political Research, 52*(3), 316–338.

Bauer, M. W. (2008). Diffuse anxieties, deprived entrepreneurs: Commission reform and middle management. *Journal of European Public Policy, 15*(5), 691–707.

Baumgartner, F. R. (2001). Agendas: Political. In N. J. Smelser & P. B. Baltes (Eds.), *International encyclopedia of social and behavioral sciences: Political science* (pp. 288–290). New York: Elsevier.

Baumgartner, F. R., & Jones, B. D. (1993). *Agendas and instability in American politics*. Chicago: University of Chicago Press.

Baumgartner, F. R., & Mahoney, C. (2008). The two faces of framing. Individual-level framing and collective issue definition in the European union. *European Union Politics, 9*(3), 435–449.

Baumgartner, F. R., Green-Pedersen, C., & Jones, B. D. (2006). Comparative studies of policy agendas. *Journal of European Public Policy, 13*(7), 959–974.

Belyi, A. (2003). New dimensions of energy security of the enlarging EU and their impact on relations with Russia. *European Integration, 25*(4), 351–369.

Birkland, T. A. (2004). "The World changed today": Agenda-setting and policy change in the wake of the September 11 terrorist attacks. *Review of Policy Research, 21*(2), 179–200.

Blom-Hansen, J. (2008). The origins of the EU comitology system: a case of informal agenda-setting by the commission. *Journal of European Public Policy, 15*(2), 208–226.

Bocquillon, P., & Dobbels, M. (2014). An elephant on the 13th floor of the Berlaymont? European council and commission relations in legislative agenda setting. *Journal of European Public Policy, 21*(1), 20–38.

Börzel, T. A. (2002). Pace-setting, foot-dragging, and fence-sitting: Member state responses to Europeanization. *Journal of Common Market Studies, 40*(2), 193–214.
Bouwen, P., & McCown, M. (2007). Lobbying versus litigation: political and legal strategies of interest representation in the European Union. *Journal of European Public Policy, 14*(3), 422–443.
Buchan, D. (2009). *Energy and climate change: Europe at the crossroads*. Oxford: Oxford University Press.
Buchan, D. (2010). Energy policy: Sharp challenges and rising ambitions. In H. Wallace, W. Wallace, & M. Pollack (Eds.), *Policy-making in the European Union* (pp. 357–380). Oxford: Oxford University Press.
Burns, C. (2013). The European Parliament. In A. Jordan & C. Adelle (Eds.), *Environmental policy in the EU: Actors, institutions and processes* (pp. 132–151). London/New York: Routledge.
Calvin, K., Edmonds, J., Bakken, B., Wise, M., Kim, S., Luckow, P., & Graabak, I. (2014). EU 20–20–20 energy policy as a model for global climate mitigation. *Climate Policy, 14*(5), 581–598.
Carafa, L. (2013). EU energy cooperation in the neighbourhood: Tailoring the rules of the game? In A. Boening, J. Kremer, & A. van Loon (Eds.), *Global power Europe: Policies, actions and influence of the EU's external relations* (pp. 93–109). New York: Springer.
Carrubba, C. J., Gabel, M., & Hankla, C. (2008). Judicial behavior under political constraints: Evidence from the European Court of Justice. *American Political Science Review, 102*(4), 435–452.
Cobb, R. W., & Elder, C. D. (1972). *Participation in American politics: The dynamics of agenda building*. Boston: Allyn and Bacon.
Cobb, R. W., Ross, J.-K., & Ross, M. H. (1976). Agenda building as a comparative political process. *American Political Science Review, 70*, 126–138.
Collier, U. (2013). The EU and climate change policy: The struggle over policy competences. In U. Collier & R. E. Löfstedt (Eds.), *Cases in climate change policy: Political reality in the European Union* (pp. 43–64). Oxon: Earthscan.
Da Graça Carvalho, M. (2012). EU energy and climate change strategy. *Energy, 40*(1), 19–22.
Daviter, F. (2007). Policy framing in the European Union. *Journal of European Public Policy, 14*(4), 654–666.
De Clerck-Sachsse, J. (2012). Civil society and democracy in the EU: The paradox of the European Citizens' initiative. *Perspectives on European Politics and Society, 13*(3), 299–311.
Dunlop, C. (2012). Epistemic communities. In E. Araral, S. Fritzen, M. Howlett, M. Ramesh, & X. Wu (Eds.), *Routledge handbook of public policy* (pp. 229–243). New York: Routledge.
Dunlop, C. (2014). The possible experts: How epistemic communities negotiate barriers to knowledge use in ecosystems services policy. *Environment and Planning C: Government and Policy, 32*(2), 208–228.
Eberlein, B. (2008). The making of the European energy market: The interplay of governance and government. *Journal of Public Policy, 28*(1), 73–92.
Egenhofer, C., Behrens, A., Tol, R. S. J., Berthélemy, M., Lévêque, F., & Jansen, J. C. (2011). Does Europe need a comprehensive energy policy? *Intereconomics, 46*(3), 124–142.
Eikeland, P. O. (2011). The third internal energy market package: New power relations among member states, EU Institutions and non-state actors? *JCMS: Journal of Common Market Studies, 49*(2), 243–263.
Eising, R. (2002). Policy learning in embedded negotiations: Explaining EU electricity liberalization. *International Organization, 56*(1), 85–120.
Engeli, I., Green-Pedersen, C., & Larsen, L. T. (2012). Theoretical perspectives on morality politics. In I. Engeli, C. Green-Pedersen, & L. T. Larsen (Eds.), *Morality politics in Western Europe* (pp. 5–26). Basingstoke: Palgrave Macmillan.
Garrett, G., & Weingast, B. (1993). Ideas, interests, and institutions: Constructing the European Community's internal market. In J. Goldstein & R. O. Keohane (Eds.), *Ideas and foreign policy: Beliefs, institutions, and political change* (pp. 173–206). Ithaca: Cornell University Press.

Göler, D., & Kurze, K. (2009). Die EU als transnationaler Polity-Shaper. Über die Schaffung sektoraler Governance-Strukturen am Beispiel der Energiegemeinschaft. *Österreichische Zeitschrift für Politikwissenschaft, 38*(4), 423–436.

Green-Pedersen, C., & Stubager, R. (2010). The political conditionality of mass media influence. When do parties follow mass media attention? *British Journal of Political Science, 40*(3), 663–677.

Green-Pedersen, C., & Walgrave, S. (2014). Political agenda setting: An approach to studying political systems. In C. Green-Pedersen & S. Walgrave (Eds.), *Agenda setting, policies, and political systems: A comparative approach* (pp. 1–18). Chicago: University of Chicago Press.

Häge, F., & Toshkov, D. (2011). Anticipating resistance: The effect of member state preferences on the European Commission's agenda-setting activity. University of Limerick PPA Working Papers.

Hartlapp, M., Metz, J., & Rauh, C. (2013). Linking agenda setting to coordination structures: Bureaucratic politics inside the European commission. *Journal of European Integration, 35*(4), 425–441.

Heinelt, H., & Knodt, M. (Eds.). (2011). *Policies within the EU multi-level system*. Baden-Baden: Nomos.

Helm, D. (2014). The European framework for energy and climate policies. *Energy Policy, 64*(1), 29–35.

Hix, S., Noury, A., & Roland, G. (2006). Dimensions of politics in the European parliament. *American Journal of Political Science, 50*(2), 494–520.

Jennings, W., Bevan, S., Timmermans, A., Breeman, G., Brouard, S., Chaques-Bonafont, L., et al. (2011). Effects of the core functions of government on the diversity of executive agendas. *Comparative Political Studies, 44*(8), 1001–1030.

Jones, B. D., & Baumgartner, F. R. (2012). From there to here: punctuated equilibrium to the general punctuation thesis to a theory of government information processing. *Policy Studies Journal, 40*(1), 1–20.

Jordan, A., & Liefferink, D. (Eds.). (2004). *Environmental policy on Europe: The Europeanization of national environmental policy*. London: Routledge.

Jordan, A., Huitema, D., Van Asselt, H., Rayner, T., & Berkhout, F. (Eds.). (2010). *Climate change policy in the European Union: Confronting the dilemmas of mitigation and adaptation?*. Cambridge: Cambridge University Press.

Kingdon, J. W. (1984). *Agendas, alternatives, and public policies*. Boston: Little, Brown.

Klüver, H. (2013). *Lobbying in the European Union*. Oxford: Oxford University Press.

Knill, C., & Tosun, J. (2011). Environmental policy. In H. Heinelt & M. Knodt (Eds.), *Policies within the EU multi-level system* (pp. 171–188). Baden-Baden: Nomos.

Kuzemko, C., Belyi, A. V., Goldthau, A., & Keating, M. F. (Eds.). (2012). *Dynamics of energy governance in Europe and Russia*. Basingstoke: Palgrave Macmillan.

Larsson, T., & Trondal, J. (2006). Agenda setting in the European commission: How the European commission structure and influence the EU agenda. In H. C. H. Hofmann & A. H. Türk (Eds.), *EU administrative governance* (pp. 11–43). Cheltenham: Edward Elgar.

Le Coq, C., & Paltseva, E. (2009). Measuring the security of external energy supply in the European Union. *Energy Policy, 37*(11), 4474–4481.

Maltby, T. (2013). European Union energy policy integration: A case of European commission policy entrepreneurship and increasing supranationalism. *Energy Policy, 55*, 435–444.

Manow, P., & Burkhart, S. (2007). Legislative self-restraint under divided government in Germany, 1976–2002. *Legislative Studies Quarterly, 32*(2), 167–191.

Morata, F., & Solorio, I. (2012). *European energy policy: An environmental approach*. Cheltenham: Edward Elgar.

Natorski, M., & Surrallés, A. H. (2008). Securitizing moves to nowhere? The framing of the European Union's energy policy. *Journal of Contemporary European Research, 4*(2), 70–89.

Peters, B. G. (1994). Agenda-setting in the European community. *Journal of European Public Policy, 1*(1), 9–26.

Peters, B. G., Pierre, J., & King, D. S. (2005). The politics of path dependency: Political conflict in historical institutionalism. *Journal of Politics, 67*(4), 1275–1300.
Pointvogl, A. (2009). Perceptions, realities, concession. What is driving the integration of European energy policies? *Energy Policy, 37*(12), 5704–5716.
Prange-Gstöhl, H. (2009). Enlarging the EU's internal energy market: why would third countries accept EU rule export? *Energy Policy, 37*(12), 5296–5303.
Pollack, M. (2003). The engines of European integration. Delegation, agency and agenda setting in the EU. New York: Oxford University Press.
Pollack, M. A. (2010). Theorizing EU policy-making. In H. Wallace, M. A. Pollack, & A. R. Young (Eds.), *Policy-making in the European Union* (pp. 14–43). Oxford: Oxford University Press.
Pollak, J., & Riekmann, S. P. (2007). The Austrian presidency: Pragmatic management. *JCMS: Journal of Common Market Studies, 45*(s1), 7–16.
Pollak, J., & Slominski, P. (2011). Liberalizing the EU's energy market: Hard and soft power combined. In G. Falkner (Ed.), *The EU's decision traps: Comparing policies* (pp. 92–110). Oxford: Oxford University Press.
Princen, S. (2007). Agenda-setting in the European Union: a theoretical exploration and agenda for research. *Journal of European Public Policy, 14*(1), 21–38.
Princen, S. (2011). Agenda-setting strategies in EU policy processes. *Journal of European Public Policy, 18*(7), 927–943.
Princen, S. (2012). Agenda-setting. In A. Jordan & C. Adelle (Eds.), *Environmental policy in the EU: Actors, institutions and processes* (pp. 191–208). London/New York: Routledge.
Princen, S., & Rhinard, M. (2006). Crashing and creeping: Agenda-setting dynamics in the European Union. *Journal of European Public Policy, 13*(7), 1119–1132.
Radaelli, C. M. (2003). The Europeanization of public policy. In K. Featherstone & C. M. Radaelli (Eds.), *The politics of Europeanization* (pp. 27–55). Oxford: Oxford University Press.
Renner, S., & Trauner, F. (2009). Creeping EU membership in Southeast Europe: The dynamics of EU rule transfer to the Western Balkans. *European Integration, 31*(4), 449–465.
Rochefort, D. A., & Cobb, R. W. (1993). Problem definition, agenda access, and policy choice. *Policy Studies Journal, 21*(1), 56–71.
Shepsle, K., & Weingast, B. (1987). The institutional foundations of committee power. *American Political Science Review, 81*(1), 85–104.
Tallberg, J. (2003). The agenda-shaping powers of the EU council presidency. *Journal of European public policy, 10*(1), 1–19.
Tallberg, J. (2006). *Leadership and negotiation in the European Union*. Cambridge: Cambridge University Press.
Talus, K. (2013). *EU energy law and policy: A critical account*. Oxford: Oxford University Press.
Tosun, J. (2011). When the grace period is over: Assessing the new member states' compliance with EU requirements for oil stockholding. *Energy Policy, 39*(11), 7156–7164.
Tosun, J. (2012). Emergency oil stocks in Southeastern and Eastern Europe: What explains variation in convergence towards the EU model? *Energy Policy, 46*(1), 417–426.
Tosun, J. (2013). *Risk regulation in Europe: Assessing the application of the precautionary principle*. New York: Springer.
Tosun, J., & Schulze, K. (2015). Compliance with EU biofuel targets in South-Eastern and Eastern Europe: Do interest groups matter? *Environment and Planning* C, forthcoming.
Tosun, J., & Solorio, I. (2011). Exploring the energy-environment relationship in the EU: Perspectives and challenges for theorizing and empirical analysis. *European Integration online Papers, 15*(7). http://eiop.or.at/eiop/texte/2011-007a.htm.
Tresch, A., Sciarini, P., & Varone, F. (2013). The relationship between media and political agendas: Variations across decision-making phases. *West European Politics, 36*(5), 897–918.
Vandecasteele, B., Bossuyt, F., & Orbie, J. (2013). Unpacking the influence of the council presidency on European Union external policies: The polish council presidency and the Eastern Partnership, *European Integration online Papers*. 17(Special Issue 1). http://eiop.or.at/eiop/texte/2013-005a.htm.

Vanhoonacker, S., & Pomorska, K. (2013). The European external action service and agenda-setting in European foreign policy. *Journal of European Public Policy, 20*(9), 1316–1331.
Walgrave, S., Stuart, S., & Nuytemans, M. (2008). The mass media's political agenda-setting power: A longitudinal analysis of media, parliament, and Government in Belgium (1993 to 2000). *Comparative Political Studies, 41*(6), 814–836.
Warntjen, A. (2007). Steering the Union: The impact of the EU presidency on the legislative activity in the council. *Journal of Common Market Studies, 45*(5), 1135–1157.
Weible, C. M. (2007). An advocacy coalition framework approach to stakeholder analysis: Understanding the political context of California marine protected area policy. *Journal of Public Administration Research and Theory, 17*(1), 95–117.
Wettestad, J. (2005). The making of the 2003 EU emissions trading directive: An ultra-quick process due to entrepreneurial proficiency? *Global Environmental Politics, 5*(1), 1–23.
Wettestad, J., Eikeland, P. O., & Nilsson, M. (2012). EU climate and energy policy: A hesitant supranational turn? *Global Environmental Politics, 12*(2), 67–86.
Young, A. R. (2010). The European policy process in comparative perspective. In H. Wallace, M. A. Pollack, & A. R. Young (Eds.), *Policy-making in the European Union* (pp. 45–68). Oxford: Oxford University Press.
Youngs, R. (2009). *Energy security: Europe's new Foreign policy challenge*. London: Routledge.

Part I
Patterns of Agenda Building and Legislative Activities

Chapter 2
The EU's Energy Policy Agenda: Directions and Developments

Sophie Biesenbender

Abstract This chapter deals with the emergence and development of energy policy agendas in European institutions. The first part of the chapter identifies the broad lines in the development of energy policy in the EU over the last six decades. It starts out with a description of how energy policy making as well as its institutional framework have evolved since the foundation of the EU. In this context, the focus is on policies dealing with the generation and provision of energy. Hence, it addresses issues of energy mixes, energy security and energy infrastructure. The second part of the chapter offers an analysis of the patterns of agenda shaping regarding the development of a comprehensive EU energy policy that has been on the political agenda of the EU since the mid-2000s. The aim of the qualitative analysis is to assess the impact of situational factors (e.g. problem perception and framing) and institutional determinants (e.g. perceived authority) on the inter-institutional and internal energy policy agendas of different European institutions.

2.1 Introduction: The Context of EU Energy Policy

In times of increasing environmental and climate challenges or diplomatic crises, energy issues have repeatedly entered the agendas of policy makers, researchers and society in the European Union under a number of different frames. During the last 60 years, EU environmental policy has taken place under changing institutional, environmental and societal conditions. These conditions have influenced both agenda shaping and decision making with regard to the regulation of energy issues. During the first decades of the European integration process, the main motivation was to secure energy provision in an emerging community of nation-states. Moreover in the 1960s, 1970s and 1980s, several attempts were made to design a

S. Biesenbender (✉)
Institute for Research Information and Quality Assurance, Schützenstraße 6a, 10117 Berlin, Germany
e-mail: biesenbender@forschungsinfo.de

J. Tosun et al. (eds.), *Energy Policy Making in the EU*,
Lecture Notes in Energy 28, DOI 10.1007/978-1-4471-6645-0_2

comprehensive energy policy and to transfer national capacities with regard to energy security to the EU (Correljé and van der Linde 2006)—a topic that has recently gained renewed attention. However, in the absence of any concrete primary law to empower the EU institutions to regulate the energy sectors prior to the mid-1980s, these attempts failed because they did not reach consensus among the member states. Finally in the 1990s, the EU was successful in liberalising the electricity market (see Ciambra and Solorio in Chap. 8). However, despite its implications for the common market, energy policy was not defined as an area of priority action by primary (i.e. treaty) law until the passage of the Treaty of Lisbon (Braun 2011). Since then, energy policy has ranked high on the EU's political agenda, which has also led to the passage of concrete regulatory decisions. This process was also motivated and shaped by concerns for environmental and climate change. In addition, the mid- and long-term security of energy supplies has been a main driver of the EU's energy policy agenda (Piebalgs 2009).

Altogether, the emergence of EU energy policy decisions and their agenda-shaping processes have been strongly linked to developments in the international energy markets, the evolution of EU primary law, national policy targets and decisions as well as developments in the environment and climate. Changes in treaty law and problem perception along with new framing opportunities have therefore paved the way for the development of a comprehensive energy policy since the mid-2000s. Shortly thereafter, regulations were passed to extend the agenda-shaping power of the European public through the introduction of the European Citizens' Initiative thereby laying the legal foundations for a smooth interaction between the systemic and the EU's political agendas (see Tosun et al. in Chap. 1).

The following chapter seeks to draw a systematic and coherent picture of these processes by contrasting the agenda-shaping processes with subsequent decision making in energy policy in EU institutions. More precisely, it will provide a review of the legal documents on energy policy issued by different EU institutions since 1960. By considering and evaluating agenda-related documents (e.g. green papers or recommendations by the Commission), I assess the degree of attention that has been devoted to a certain issue or sub-aspect over time. I will then turn to the legislative output and describe when European institutions have been most active in regulating these matters. The gathering and presentation of information lays the ground for a detailed follow-up analysis of agenda-shaping patterns in different European institutions following the European Council meeting in 2005 (Hampton Court), which marks the beginning of the development of a comprehensive EU energy policy.

This chapter is structured thus. First, I briefly describe the evolution of the institutional framework for energy policy making in the EU since its foundation. Then, I provide an overview of the main dynamics and developments in agenda shaping and regulation with respect to energy policy in the Commission and the Council. After that, I discuss how current institutional rules and recent developments in energy demand, technology, problem perception and framing have influenced recent agenda-shaping patterns and attempts to develop a comprehensive EU energy policy since 2005.

2.2 Evolving Institutional and Legal Conditions of EU Energy Policy

The impact of institutional and legal conditions on energy policy making in the EU has been of interest to a number of scholars. They assess how primary law and institutional conditions determine the content, pace and direction of energy policy making in the EU (Schmitt and Schulze 2011). In this context, scholarly interest has been widespread with respect to the environmental dimension of EU energy policy, especially in the context of the principle of Environmental Policy Integration (EPI; see e.g. Collier 2002; Lenschow 2002; Tosun and Solorio 2011).

Energy issues were part of the EU's political agenda already in the first steps of the European integration process (Lucas 1977; Matláry 1997). The foundation of the European Coal and Steel Community (ECSC) in 1951 and the European Atomic Energy Community in 1957 was to guarantee the supply of energy in an emerging community of nation-states. Notwithstanding the initial significance attached to energy issues, attempts to extend EU policy beyond the ECSC and Euratom were seldom made (Egenhofer et al. 2011). This was mainly due to the limits of primary law that confined the Commission's room for manoeuver in energy issues to the provisions established through ECSC and Euratom (see Article 16 of the TFEU 1957).

Over the years, the European Commission (henceforth: Commission) backed by the European Parliament (EP) made several attempts to modify treaty law by including an energy chapter. These attempts repeatedly failed due to the resistance by member states that were reluctant to transfer further competencies in energy matters to the EU (see also Ciambra and Solorio in Chap. 8). The Treaty of Maastricht (or Treaty on EU; TEU 1992) underscored the role of energy security and policy for the functioning of the EU by specifying that "measures in the spheres of energy, civil protection and tourism" (TEU 1992: Article 3t) constitute priority matters for the Community. According to treaty law, this refers specifically to energy infrastructure and networks. Already five years earlier, the Environmental Policy Integration principle had been included into treaty law (by means of the Single European Act (SEA 1987: Article 130r); see Tosun et al. in Chap. 1).

This change in treaty law allowed EU policy makers to frame energy initiatives as environmental policies. This principle was further strengthened in the Treaty of Amsterdam (1997: Article 6) (see Mahmoudi 2000). Altogether, from the late 1980s onward EU decision makers have been able to couple energy policy objectives with a number of other policy goals (with e.g. common market interests or energy security; see Lenschow and Zito 1998). This diversification increased the importance of agenda shaping as the stage of the policy cycle in which problems are defined and framed.

In sum, energy policies in the EU in the first decades took mostly the form of broad policy objectives. In addition, energy issues have repeatedly been brought on the political agenda along with several attempts to extend the EU's legal capacities for energy policy. However, the EU still lacked a consistent European energy policy. As a consequence at the European Council meeting in Hampton Court in

Table 1 Energy policy and treaty law in the European Union

	First stage	Second stage	Third stage
Time frame	Mid-1950s to late 1980s	Late 1980s to mid-2000s	Since mid-2000s
Legal framework	• European Coal and Steel Community (1951)	• Single European Act (1987)	• Treaty of Lisbon (2007)
	• Atomic Energy Community (1957)	• Treaty of Maastricht (1992)	
Focus of EU energy policy	• Energy security	• Environmental policy integration (EPI) principle	• Functioning of energy markets
	• Common market	• Energy as a priority matter	• Energy supply
			• Energy efficiency
			• Renewable energy
			• Interconnection of energy networks

Source Own elaboration based on TFEU (1957), SEA (1987), TEU (1992), Treaty of Amsterdam (1997), Treaty of Lisbon (2007)

October 2005, heads of state formally agreed to develop a comprehensive European energy policy. This initiative was followed by the Commission in spring 2006 that published the green paper "A European Strategy for Sustainable, Competitive and Secure Energy" in which the Commission proposed concrete measures to concretise a common European energy policy.

The Treaty of Lisbon (2007) finally provided a more specific frame for energy policy activities in the EU. Policy making should be designed to (1) support the functioning of energy markets, (2) secure energy supply, (3) promote energy efficiency, (4) support the development and exploitation of renewable energy sources and to (5) advance the interconnection of energy networks. Treaty law hence provided a broad mandate for energy policy making, which enabled decision makers not only to enact comprehensive regulation of the policy field as a whole but also to pursue a number of different (or even conflicting) energy-related policy goals. These developments have had effects not only on agenda-shaping dynamics in different European institutions. Treaty law has also consistently influenced decision-making procedures in the EU. Table 1 summarises the different stages of EU energy policy over the last decades.

On top of these changes and following a regulation of the EP and the Council in 2011, European citizens have been given the possibility to submit citizens' initiatives—a right that was granted to them by the Treaty on EU and the Treaty of Lisbon. Since spring 2012, a total of 13 successful or open initiatives have been registered with the goal to request the Commission to initiate or adjust legislation on different topics.[1] The European Citizens' Initiative enables the public to shape the Commission's and hence the EU's overall political agenda also but not only in terms of energy policy. In August 2012, a citizens' initiative was started to suspend the 2009 "Energy and Climate Change" package of the EU hence moving this issue again from the systemic to the political agenda of the Commission (Cobb and Elder 1972, 1991; Cobb et al. 1976).

2.3 The Evolvement of Energy Policy Agendas in EU Institutions

Changing institutional and legal conditions over the last six decades have led to evolving agenda-shaping and decision-making processes in different EU institutions. In order to illustrate the developments in attention for energy issues, this section will provide a descriptive account of the amount of official documents issued in the context of these processes. On the one hand, I assume the degree of attention and decision-making activity for certain issues to be reflected in the number of *legislative documents* in force on the different dimensions of energy policy. On the other hand, there are also situations, in which political attention for certain issues does not last beyond the agenda-setting stage of an institution either because agenda setting is unsuccessful and the issue is dropped altogether from the agenda or because the issue is being delegated to other institutions for further decision making. In order to address these cases, the analysis also includes the number of *preparatory documents* on the different energy topics issued by EU institutions over time.

I look at the developments in the issuance of preparatory and legal documents in two different European decision-making bodies, which are the Commission and the Council of Ministers (or Council). Such a perspective seems fruitful as it allows me to compare two institutions that have repeatedly been the target for delegated action in energy policy by the European Council (see Chap. 3 by Alexandrova and Timmermans). Moreover, it allows for comparing the institution with the formal monopoly for agenda setting (the Commission) with an institution that has contingent or indirect agenda setting powers (the Council) through its ability to request legislative initiatives from the Commission.

The following sections assess how and at what pace the overall degree of agenda activity has evolved over time in the two institutions. In this context, I compare regulation and agenda shaping surrounding different dimensions of energy policy

---

[1] Successful initiatives refer to closed initiatives that were not withdrawn and that received sufficient support by European citizens (this is true for 9 out of 25 initiatives since 2012 with 4 initiatives that are still ongoing). See also http://ec.europa.eu/citizens-initiative/public/initiatives/ongoing (last accessed 16 October 2014).

(i.e. general principles, electricity as well as coal, oil and gas, nuclear energy or renewable energy) in the Commission and the Council. This prepares the ground for the subsequent section, in which I take an in-depth look at the agenda-shaping cascade in European institutions following the European Council meeting in Hampton Court in 2005 and in the wake of the Treaty of Lisbon.

2.3.1 The Energy Policy Agenda of the Commission

In order to understand agenda-shaping priorities in energy policy in the EU, the following paragraphs compare the development in the number of preparatory acts and legislative documents for different issues of energy policy over the last decades. Figures 2.1 and 2.2 graphically depict how "densely" energy production from different sources (coal, nuclear, oil, gas, renewables, etc.) has been addressed in the Commission from 1960 to 2010 (see Knill et al. 2011 for an overview of conceptual alternatives for measuring policy change). They also approximate the role that internal market considerations have played over time (e.g. through the regulation of the electricity market) and how often general principles and programmes were subject to the agenda-shaping or decision-making processes. The figures illustrate the cumulative number of documents (that is preparatory acts and legislative documents respectively). They do not report the content, bindingness, extent or the number of issues addressed in the different provisions. Therefore, the counts can only serve as rough proxies for the development in attention and regulation over

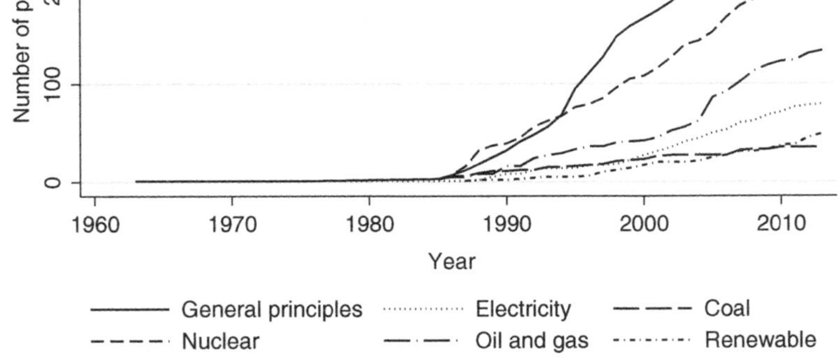

Fig. 2.1 Number of preparatory acts on energy issued by the Commission. *Source* Own illustration based on EUR-Lex (2013)

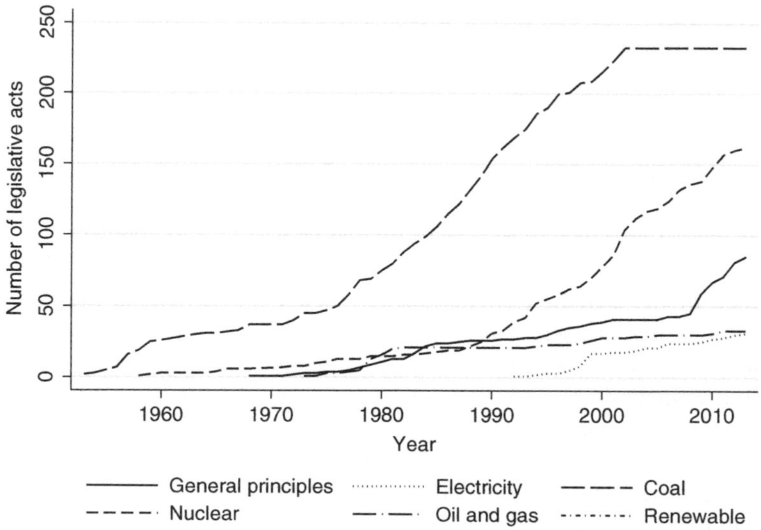

Fig. 2.2 Number of legislative acts on energy issued by the Commission. *Source* Own illustration based on EUR-Lex (2013)

time. Furthermore, the comparison between the two figures (preparatory versus legislative documents) allows for assessing if issues that have been on the agenda actually translate into concrete regulation.

Attention in the Commission has been traditionally high with regard to general principles and programmes in energy policy (Fig. 2.1). Since the mid-1980s, the energy policy agenda of the Commission has constantly dealt with overall objectives of EU energy policy. Nevertheless, political attention has often not translated into concrete policy decisions (Fig. 2.2), which is in part explained by limited decision-making competencies of the Commission in this area. Another focus of the Commission's preparatory documents has been on the regulation of nuclear energy based on the Euratom treaty. In this context, the Commission has repeatedly brought the issue (nuclear energy) also back to the Council's policy agenda by proposing Council decisions or by reporting on past activities in this area of regulation. In fact, several attempts have been made in the Commission to shape the Council's agenda and to encourage legislative action (through proposals, draft regulations or directives, communications as well as green papers and reports). This is also true for the Commission's agenda in the area of oil and gas—at least as it concerns the years from 1985 to the mid-1990s. During this period, most of the preparatory acts were directed to the Council with the explicit request to address certain issues related to the regulation of oil and gas in the EU. These agenda-shaping activities were successful if we look at the Council's legislative record in these areas (see Fig. 2.4).

However, also the Commission's policy agenda has also been shaped by the political agendas of other EU bodies. Since the mid-1990s, the European Council has increasingly requested the Commission to regulate energy matters by means of delegated action (see Alexandrova and Timmermans in Chap. 3). As the case studies of this volume illustrate, the Commission has prioritised certain energy issues over others, which is why the success of these requests in terms of concrete policy outputs varies over issues.

The policy priorities are broadly reflected in the Commission's legislative activity with regard to energy policy (see Fig. 2.2). As outlined above, regulation in the area of coal usually took the form of approving aids from different member states to the national coal-mining industry, which were usually granted for a period of one year. Since the turn of the millennium, activity in this area has stopped altogether. In line with the Commission's agenda, much regulation was also passed in the area of nuclear energy. This has come in the form of Commission Decisions but also Commission Opinions with respect to national policy decisions in this area (e.g. on decommissioning or dismantling of nuclear facilities in member states or the disposal of radioactive waste).

Finally, especially since the mid-2000s, the Commission has increasingly become involved in the regulation of general principles and programmes in the energy sector. This may be due to the increasing complexity of energy policy, technological progress and the diversification of energy generation. This finding also reflects the complex interrelationship between energy, climate and environmental policy making, which has not sufficiently been addressed by past legislation. All in all, it shows how the framing of energy policy as a horizontal policy issue (Egenhofer et al. 2011) has increased the perceived need of policy actors for a coherent approach in EU energy policy. Altogether, the broad overview of agenda shaping and decision making illustrates that the development of a comprehensive EU energy policy has gradually become a priority on the Commission's energy policy agenda in times of growing environmental challenges (Oberthür and Pallemaerts 2010; Schmitt and Schulze 2011; Solorio 2011).

2.3.2 The Energy Policy Agenda of the Council

The picture is slightly different for the Council. Figure 2.3 shows that attention in the Council has changed over time. From 1975 to 1990 the Council mainly published preparatory acts on energy generation based on coal. By issuing a number of assents, it empowered the Commission to grant support to the European coal industry or to support research in this area. The Council hence directly structured the Commission's policy agenda and regulatory activity with regard to energy production from fossil fuels (i.e. coal, see Fig. 2.2).

The picture became more diverse in the beginning of the 1990s. The Treaty of Maastricht (1992) meant a diversification in the Council's approach towards energy policy in the EU. From then on, the design of general principles and programmes became more important and has influenced the energy debate in the Council until today. This is reflected in different publications of Council positions on a number of issues such as energy networks, energy mix, the role of different sources therein and

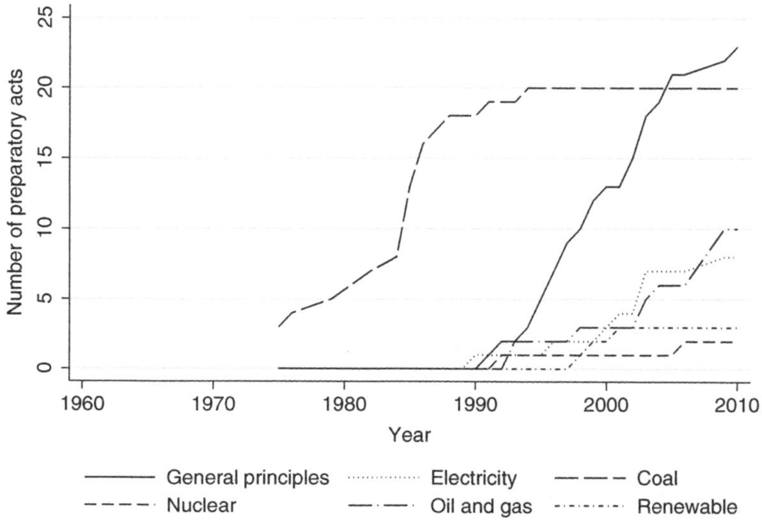

Fig. 2.3 Number of preparatory acts on energy issued by the Council of the EU. *Source* own illustration based on EUR-Lex (2013)

energy efficiency. In addition, internal market considerations (electricity) and external energy relations (oil and gas) have repeatedly been on the Council's policy agenda since the mid-1990s, which was in part prompted by the Commission.

This picture roughly corresponds to the actual regulatory activity in the Council. Apart from Euratom's activities in regulating nuclear energy provisions and structures in the EU, the Council has mainly and constantly acted to specify the broad lines of energy policy (general principles and programmes, see Fig. 2.4).

Moreover, policy making in Council reflects the energy policy agenda of the European Council (i.e. the heads of state or government of the member states), which is also due to the institutional linkage of the two EU bodies. Until the early 2000s, the Council was the main target for delegated action in energy policy by the European Council (see Alexandrova and Timmermans in Chap. 3). By means of mostly recommendations, resolutions, directives and decisions, the Council has therefore worked among other things on an energy policy strategy for the EU, financial issues as well as research and demonstration projects. Since the mid-1990s, a number of these policies on general principles have been developed in cooperation with the EP based on the co-decision procedure that was introduced by the Treaty of Maastricht. Another area of regulatory involvement of the Council is external energy relations and internal market issues with regard to the provision with oil and gas. Due to the EU's import dependency in this area, most of the initiatives regulate external trade and internal market aspects with regard to energy production from and imports of oil and gas. Compared to these fields of action, the Council has paid relatively little but even attention to the regulation of the remaining aspects of energy policy (that is coal, electricity and renewable energy).

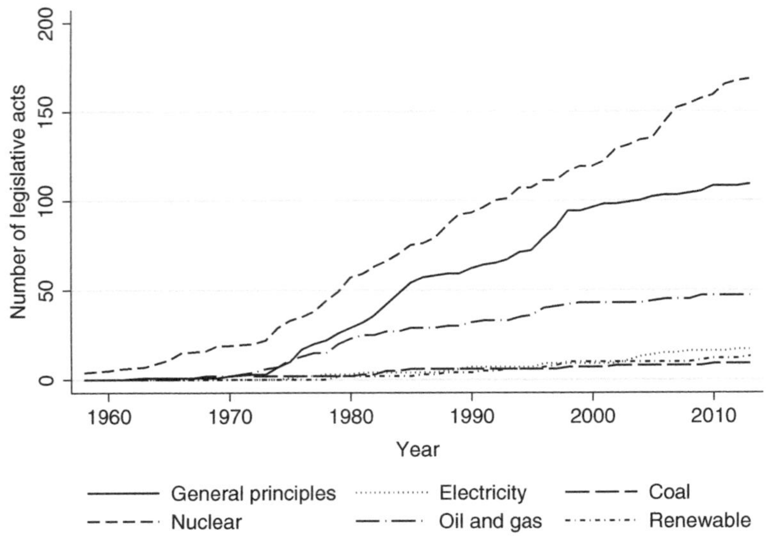

Fig. 2.4 Number of legislative acts on energy issued by the Council of the EU. *Source* own illustration based on EUR-Lex (2013)

This section illustrated patterns of EU agenda shaping and regulation in two institutions—the Commission and the Council. Agenda-shaping dynamics were roughly approximated with the number of preparatory acts for a given issue. The number of legislative acts was used to reflect the priority of regulation and the legal competences to do so. By focusing on the field of energy policy only, the figures do not allow for any conclusions with regard to the relative attention that is paid to the area of energy policy as compared to other fields of regulation (but see Alexandrova and Timmermans in Chap. 3 for an assessment of the distribution of attention over different policy fields in the European Council).

The broad lines of agenda shaping and decision making as illustrated in Figs. 2.1, 2.2, 2.3 and 2.4 allow for different conclusions. First, they show that agenda shaping in an institution usually corresponds to the overall subsequent regulatory or legislative output. Second, they draw the overall changes in EU energy policy as a consequence of technological developments, different priorities and changing policy problems. Third, there is also evidence for inter-institutional dynamics (i.e. the transfer of attention and priorities), which will be explored in more detail in the next section. Finally, the figures showed that the idea to fundamentally adjust or develop EU energy policy has increasingly been on the political agenda of both the Commission and the Council (but also of other European institutions). This pattern suggests that the idea to develop a comprehensive EU energy policy was not motivated exclusively by external factors or events but that it was also promoted from within EU institutions (see also Princen 2007, p. 24ff).

2.4 Patterns of Inter-institutional Agenda Shaping and the Emergence of a Comprehensive EU Energy Policy

The previous sections showed that agenda shaping and energy policy making in different areas were for a long time singular and constituted rather a series of single decisions. This is for instance true for the EU's regulatory approaches in the areas of nuclear energy (see Egenhofer and Behrens 2011). These developments reflect the structural and institutional conditions in which the decisions were made. Notwithstanding, as outlined in Sect. 2.2, energy policy has increasingly become a policy field on its own with strong links to neighbouring fields such as environmental, climate or technological policy. As a result since the mid-2000s, European institutions and actors have worked towards the development of a comprehensive European energy policy (or the EU energy union), which had been on the political agenda of different EU institutions for a while (see Sect. 2.3). An approach was needed to adequately accommodate current challenges in the generation, use and distribution of energy by incorporating developments in related areas of regulation such as climate, environment, technology and research. The following subsections shed light on this process. The subsequent part 2.4.1 identifies the structural determinants of agenda shaping. Section 2.4.2 assesses the impact of the European Council and the Commission on the development of a comprehensive EU energy policy. Section 2.4.3 highlights the role of the EP in shaping the EU's energy policy agenda and the resulting legislative process.

2.4.1 Structural Determinants of the EU's Energy Policy Agenda

The recent development of a comprehensive European energy policy is embedded in a policy discourse that has evolved over the past six decades. By creating the frame for the policy-making process, this discourse shapes the political and policy agendas in the following dimensions.

First, institutional and legal conditions have always defined the procedure for policy actors (see above Sect. 2.2). With the fourth Environmental Action Programme (1987–1992) for instance, environmental considerations have become a core element of the EU's energy policy agenda (Hey 2005; Lenschow 1999; Schmitt and Schulze 2011; Tosun and Solorio 2011) simultaneously to the formal inclusion of the Environmental Policy Integration principle into treaty law (i.e. in the Single European Act 1987; see also Barnes and Hoerber 2013).

Second, economic and trade-related developments have constantly impacted EU energy policy considerations due to the EU's dependence on energy imports (in particular oil and gas). As a consequence, energy security has increasingly become a priority within the EU's overall energy policy approach (Correljé and van der

Linde 2006; Jong and van der Linde 2008)—especially after the oil crisis of the 1970s and again so in the context of the Russia-Ukraine crisis.

Third and related to the previous aspect, there is a manifested problem, which is due to human-induced deterioration of the environment and climate. This situation has created an ever-growing need to adjust energy policies on all administrative levels (including the EU) and to further technological innovation. As a consequence, energy efficiency and renewable energies have become crucial components in the EU's energy policy (see Collier 2002; see also Jacobs in Chap. 6 for a detailed description of the Commission's take on renewable energy since 2000). These developments are illustrative of the hybrid nature of the field of energy policy. During the first decades, the regulation of energy issues was legitimated by its contribution to the EU's common market and European integration in general. In recent years however, attention has also been paid to aspects like climate change, environmental protection and security and their relationship with energy policy (see e.g. Ciambra and Solorio in Chap. 8 and Cox and Dekanozishvili in Chap. 9).

Finally, the debates on a comprehensive EU energy policy are contingent on the institutional framework in which the EU institutions are embedded. These structures most likely affect not only the selection of issues to come on the EU political agenda but also the way in which they are framed and eventually addressed (Princen 2007). Moreover, institutional rules mediate the transfer of issues to the inter-institutional policy agenda and influence agenda-shaping patterns across different EU institutions (see Tosun et al. in Chap. 1). Treaty law crucially determines the degree to which EU institutions manage to claim authority for regulating an issue at all (Princen 2011). In addition, legal rules (e.g. the co-decision procedure) along with the building of relevant capacities in institutions also impact the way in which issues then come to the policy agenda in order to be taken up in subsequent decision making (see Herweg in Chap. 5 for a similar analytical distinction).

2.4.2 Developing an Inter-institutional Agenda for a Comprehensive EU Energy Policy: The Role of the European Council and the Commission

Institutional changes have facilitated the work on a comprehensive European energy policy since the mid-2000s by providing a common frame for the debates. This process involved a number of European institutions. This section outlines how the European Council and the Commission defined the targets and principles of a future European energy policy thereby shaping the EU's energy policy agenda. This analytical perspective seems fruitful in order to assess agenda-shaping dynamics in a contested policy field, for which the European Council has increasingly claimed political interest and authority (see Chap. 1 by Tosun et al. as well as Chap. 3 by Alexandrova and Timmermans; cf. Bocquillon and Dobbels 2014).

The following paragraphs will focus on the development of the institutions' agendas on energy policy and assess whether inter-institutional communication has led to a harmonisation of these agendas. The decision to design a comprehensive energy policy was made at the European Council meeting in 2005 in Hampton Court and has since then been on the political agenda of most European institutions (for a discussion of the role of the European Council in shaping the 'high-politics' route see Alexandrova and Timmermans Chap. 3). Shortly thereafter, the Commission shaped the EU's energy policy agenda by publishing its "Green paper on a European strategy for sustainable, competitive and secure energy" in March 2006. This document opened up the inter-institutional debate on a formulation of a comprehensive EU energy policy. The Commission's green paper was centred on achieving ambitious climate policies (sustainability) and on finalising the internal energy and gas market (see Herweg in Chap. 5 as well as Brutschin in Chap. 10) with an emphasis on energy security (competitiveness and security of supply). In addition, it called for a broad debate on the future European energy policy thereby putting the topic also on the public agenda. At the same time, the European Parliament debated its own initiative (entitled "A European strategy for sustainable, competitive and secure energy"). The subsequent resolution was passed in December 2006. The goal of the EP's initiative was to harmonise energy policy agendas across institutions by proposing a common approach. Essentially, the EP reinforced the Commission's objectives by further stressing the need for a comprehensive approach.

The initiatives by the Commission, the European Council and the EP were accompanied and influenced by the newly emerging gas dispute between Russia and the Ukraine, which culminated in the crisis of January 2006 and subsequent gas shortages. With the EU depending on Russian gas (40 % share of total gas imports) the periodical flaring of tensions raised in particular questions of energy security and strategic policy responses (see Finon and Locatelli 2008; Stern 2006). As 'focusing events', these tensions shaped the general debate by demonstrating not only the need to agree on a common energy policy as such but also the focus of a future policy strategy (see Cox and Dekanozishvili in Chap. 9; Egenhofer et al. 2011). Energy security, energy networks as well as external energy relations became central issues in the debate.

Subsequently in January 2007, the Commission published a communication to the European institutions entitled "An energy policy for Europe". The document not only summarised the current energy situation in the EU but most importantly specified avenues for future strategic policy making. In order to implement the policy objectives as outlined in the green paper, the communication focused on among other things promoting the internal energy market, securing future energy supply, reducing atmospheric pollution, new energy technologies, energy efficiency and the use of low-carbon energy sources.

Interestingly, the Commission's action plan put particular emphasis on the realisation of the internal energy market as the key target to solve most of the current policy challenges—that is, in particular to address concerns of energy security (see also Jacobs in Chap. 6 for a similar observation). This strategy might be explained by the fact that the liberalisation of the internal energy market had been on the Commission's policy agenda since the 1980s (see Herweg in Chap. 5 and Ciambra and Solorio in Chap. 8). This framing of the issue (the development of a comprehensive energy policy) as a competition or market problem also reflects institutional and constitutional legacies. As Princen (2007, p. 32) puts it, in order to successfully address issues on the EU's political agenda "actors have to argue not only that certain substantive aspects of an issue are more important than others but also that European action is needed to address it". Thus, framing energy regulation as an internal market problem represented an effective agenda-shaping strategy (see Princen 2011: p. 936ff). In addition, ongoing tensions in the gas dispute as well as the EU's authority in transnational and market issues influenced the direction of the EU's energy policy agenda since the mid-2000s.

The framing of issues on the EU's inter-institutional policy agenda slightly changed with the 2007 spring European Council by the heads of state (see Cox and Dekanozishvili in Chap. 9). At this meeting, particular emphasis was laid on linking the issues of climate and energy policy in order to concretise the policy priorities outlined in the Commission's previous communication. In fact, the debate of the spring European Council was guided by the aim to simultaneously address energy and climate challenges. The European Council committed itself to reduce overall greenhouse gas emissions in the EU (by 20 % by the year 2020 compared to 1990). Moreover, energy efficiency should be increased by 20 % until 2020 in relation to previous estimates and the share of renewable energy of total energy consumption should be extended by 20 %. As a result, the "20-20-20 targets" contained binding commitments with respect to the reduction of emissions of greenhouse gases, the consumption of primary energy (as a result of increased energy efficiency) and the share of renewables in the overall energy mix. In order to implement these targets, the resulting "Energy Action Plan" of March 2007 passed by the European Council contained a number of measures for European institutions and nation-states. The plan shaped the EU's energy policy agenda by identifying five areas for priority action. In addition to promoting the internal energy market, the Council highlighted the issues of energy security, the development of an effective international energy policy, energy efficiency and renewable energy as well as the development of a European "Strategic Energy Technology" plan. As a reaction, the Commission published a proposal in January 2008 (entitled "Energy for a Changing World"), which again highlighted the role of renewable energy in achieving the defined EU's climate goals (see also Jacobs in Chap. 6).

Altogether, the framing of the EU's energy policy agenda has become more diverse since the late 2000s (or the 2007 spring European Council) with different institutions focusing on different policy frames. Problem perception did not remain centred on the internal market but increasingly linked the debate to issues of climate change and considerations of environmental policy. In this context, European institutions played different roles with regard to the agenda for a comprehensive EU energy policy. By formulating mid- and long-term policy goals (through the development of such a policy since 2005 and the specification of integrated climate and energy targets in 2007), the European Council put energy policy on the EU's political agenda by means of the high-politics route and linked energy and climate-change issues. The Commission in turn was an important player in identifying key and priority areas of political action. By continuing to frame energy problems and challenges in the EU as internal market problems (see Ciambra and Solorio in Chap. 8, Jacobs in Chap. 6 or Brutschin in Chap. 10), the Commission also influenced the policy agendas of the Council and the EP (see Tosun in Chap. 12 or Bouzarovski and Petrova in Chap. 7).

2.4.3 The Role of the European Parliament in the Development of a Comprehensive EU Energy Policy

The European Council and the Commission defined a broad agenda with a focus on general principles and the elements of a future comprehensive EU energy policy. The debate created the framework for the energy policy agenda of the Council and the EP. I argue that the "macro-institutional change from formal sequential to informal simultaneous negotiations" (Farell and Héritier 2004, p. 1186) that was implemented with the co-decision procedure (introduced by the Treaty of Maastricht 1992 and refined by the Treaty of Amsterdam 1997) not only changed the bargaining power and decision-making patterns of the Council and the EP. I expect institutional conditions to also affect the agenda-shaping processes both within and across collective actors. On the one hand, the co-decision procedure defined the patterns of negotiation between the Council and the EP. On the other hand, it changed processes within organisations and strengthened the degree of influence of single individual actors (i.e. Members of European Parliament (MEP); see Farell and Héritier 2004).

This process was accompanied by the continuous differentiation of the committee system in the EP and the increasing specialisation of MEPs (Neuhold 2001). By the start of the sixth legislature (in 2004), the EP included as many as 20 standing committees. Energy policy has long been dealt with in the Industry, Research and Energy (ITRE) committee, which has traditionally been made up of experts or representatives from industry in recent parliamentary periods (McElroy 2006). Environmental issues have been debated in a separate group (i.e. the committee for Environment, Public Health and Food Safety, ENVI). It has been argued in the literature that the committee structure of the EP favouring specialisation in different policy areas inhibits horizontal policy coordination (Jordan and Schout 2006) and tends to concentrate the agenda on particular issues. As the following discussion shows, this structure has indeed gone along with a fragmentation of the energy policy agenda in the EP. While issues of energy security and the energy market have been debated in the ITRE committee, horizontal environmental legislation and policy making touches upon the competences of the ENVI group. As the energy policy example shows, the committee structure has led to separate and issue-specific political agendas in the EP.

In the process of developing a comprehensive energy policy, the ITRE committee of the EP sought to shape EU's energy policy agenda in particular prior to the resulting legislative procedures (in co-decision with the Council). In this context, two lines of attention have emerged since the early 2000s.

On the one hand, focus was on achieving the internal energy market. The realisation of the internal energy market was framed as favouring other goals such as energy efficiency, energy security and sustainability. In the EP's resolution on the "Prospects for the internal gas and electricity market" (2007/2089(INI)), emphasis was put on the need of ownership unbundling at the transmission level (i.e. separation of production and network operation) in order to stimulate investments in energy networks and grids. Further, the resolution called for closer cooperation between regulators on the national level to allow for harmonised and more effective regulation in particular with respect to trans-national issues. With this resolution, the EP shaped the policy agenda for the subsequent "Third Gas and Electricity Market" package, which was presented by the Commission in September 2007. This legislative package was the result of the co-decision process involving the EP and the Council. It consisted of two draft directives and three regulations with the goal to further liberalise and to work towards a common EU energy market (gas and electricity). In this context, the policy proposal aimed to develop an integrated transmission network in the EU, to facilitate third-party access and to promote an appropriate level of interconnections in the network (see Brutschin in Chap. 10 for further details).

On the other hand, the EP focused on the regulation of renewable energy generation in the EU thereby dealing with environmental implications and challenges of energy. The issue had been on the policy agenda already prior to the "Energy and Climate Change" package as presented by the Commission in January 2008 and the "Energy Action Plan" by the European Council of March 2007. By that time members of the ITRE committee had already initiated a number of resolutions that broached the issue of renewable energy in terms of both political targets and preparatory legislation. These preparatory acts were then incorporated in the Directive on the "Promotion of the use of energy from renewable sources" (Directive 2009/28/EC), which in turn became part of the "Energy and Climate Change" package. The directive was developed by the two involved committees (ITRE and ENVI) following the enhanced cooperation rules. As a consequence of the inter-committee cooperation, the EP's policy agenda contained both a focus on enhanced sustainability (e.g. for biofuels) and the overarching energy policy goals as specified by the European Council (see above Sect. 2.4.2). In addition, the package comprised three further legislative acts: a directive to reform the EU emission trading system, a decision to meet the Community's greenhouse gas emission reduction commitments and a regulation to limit CO_2 emissions from passenger cars. All fell under the responsibility of the ENVI committee.

Altogether, the comprehensive EU's energy policy agenda mainly shaped by the European Council and the Commission in the mid-2000s has found its way into the subsequent policy agenda of the EP and the Council. Through the "Third Gas and Electricity Market" package, decisions were made to strengthen the European energy market along the lines of the Commission's green paper. The fact, however, that the EP had dealt with the topic already at an early stage (e.g. by means of its resolution on the internal energy market) illustrates that it was not the Commission to shape the policy agenda of the EP (see Princen 2007). Further, issue framing in the EP and the Council (regarding energy policy) seems to differ from the approaches initially advocated by the European Council and the Commission (see Alexandrova and Timmermans in Chap. 3 for similar observations). Since the beginning of the sixth term (2004), agenda-shaping activities in European Parliament had focused on the regulation of renewable energy as an integral part of a future comprehensive energy policy. The debate was marked by strong emphasis on the environmental and climate-related aspects of energy policy. It is not least for this reason, that the Council and the EP fully supported the 20-20-20 targets (advocated by the European Council in 2007) when passing the "Energy and Climate Change" package.

These findings illustrate that the policy agendas of different EU institutions have become more and more intertwined. In the development of a comprehensive European energy policy, the EP has indeed made use of its "conditional agenda-setting power" (Burns 2013, p. 139; see also Earnshaw and Judge 1997) in the decision-making procedures of the Council and the Commission. Further, agenda-shaping processes have become more complicated with the introduction of the European Citizens' Initiative in 2012. Since then, citizens have made use of their right to request the temporary stop the "Energy and Climate Change" package and its regulation until the signing of a comprehensive international climate treaty. As a consequence of this instrument of participatory democracy, the organised public has gained access to the agenda of the Commission. The ongoing initiative demonstrates that the public is indeed willing to make use of its right to shape the EU's energy policy agenda.

2.5 Conclusion: Towards a Comprehensive EU Energy Policy

This chapter illustrated patterns and principles of agenda-shaping processes in the EU with respect to the field of energy policy. In so doing, it started out with an assessment of the institutional framework for energy policy making in the EU and how these rules have changed during the last six decades. The subsequent part presented a descriptive analysis of the emergence and development of energy policy agendas in two European institutions (i.e. the Commission and the Council). In this context, particular emphasis was on tracing agenda-shaping activities for policies on the generation and provision of energy. The third section of the chapter dealt with the recent attempts to design a comprehensive European energy policy—a process that started shortly after the turn of the millennium. It provided an analysis of how the 'problem' or challenge to pass a comprehensive energy policy has been approached and how this was taken up on the subsequent policy agendas of different EU bodies (i.e. the selection of issues that made it to the Council's and the EP's debates). The aim of the analysis was to assess the degree to which agenda shaping in different EU institutions influenced (inter-) institutional policy agendas and subsequent decision-making processes.

Another focus of this qualitative study was to analyse how situational factors (e.g. problem perception or framing strategies) and institutional determinants (e.g. allocation of decision-making power or perceived authority for different policy issues) have shaped the energy policy agenda in the EU. The findings suggest that the idea to develop a comprehensive European energy policy has increasingly been on the political agendas of different EU institutions over a long period. The Commission and the Council have worked on general principles and overarching issues of energy policy since the 1970s. This laid the groundwork for the subsequent development of a comprehensive energy policy, which started with the 2005 spring European Council. The broad agenda-setting patterns reveal an increasing focus in different EU institutions on general principles in energy policy. This finding suggests that the issue (the idea to develop a comprehensive EU energy policy) was formed and promoted, at least in part, from within the EU institutions (Princen 2007). It was then further accelerated by external factors and events that allowed different institutions to pursue their preferred policies by adjusting their framing strategies.

These processes were facilitated by adjustments in treaty law and subsequent changes in the institutional framework that shaped the patterns of communication and influence of different EU institutions. With energy policy becoming a priority matter for EU policy making (with the Treaty of Maastricht 1992 and more explicitly with the Treaty of Lisbon 2007), the foundations were laid for policy actors in the EU to move the issue to the EU's inter-institutional policy agenda. In this context, institutional factors also shaped the framing opportunities for policy entrepreneurs (including the ability to link different issues; see also Cox and Dekanozishvili in Chap. 9).

Furthermore, the exploratory analysis showed how the agendas of different institutions) relate to one another (see also Alexandrova and Timmermans in Chap. 3). In addition, it illustrated how different institutions tend to rely on specific framing strategies for perceived problems or policy issues. While the Commission considered the internal energy market as the main instrument to realise the stated targets of a comprehensive EU energy policy (see e.g. Jacobs in Chap. 6), agenda-shaping activities by members of the EP repeatedly focused on the environmental and climate-change implications of energy policy (see also Tosun in Chap. 12 for the role of the EP in agenda shaping). This interpretation is underscored by the inter-committee cooperation in the European Parliament in its consideration of the renewable energy directive.

These findings open up several avenues for systematic research on agenda shaping in EU energy policy. For example, how do institutional and external factors shape or constrain framing opportunities for policy entrepreneurs in different institutional venues? Which frames will win over others given environmental and climate-change challenges? What is the impact of international developments (e.g. the failure to find an international agreement)? What is the prospect for EU energy policy given extended competencies in a number of areas in the light of limited resources? And finally, in what way does inter-institutional communication shape the EU's energy policy agenda? In order to answer these questions, further theoretical and empirical work will be needed. The following chapters and case studies will lend first insights into these issues.

References

Barnes, P. M., & Hoerber, T. C. (2013). Linking the discourse on sustainability and governance. In P. M. Barnes & T. C. Hoerber (Eds.), *Sustainable development and governance in Europe: The evolution of the discourse on sustainability* (pp. 19–33). London: Routledge.

Bocquillon, P., & Dobbels, M. (2014). An elephant on the 13th floor of the Berlaymont? European Council and Commission relations in legislative agenda setting. *Journal of European Public Policy, 21*(1), 20–38.

Braun, J. F. (2011). *EU energy policy under the treaty of lisbon rules: Between a new policy and business as usual.* Brussels: EPIN Working Paper No. 31.

Burns, C. (2013). The European Parliament. In A. Jordan & C. Adelle (Eds.), *Environmental policy in the EU: Actors, institutions and processes* (pp. 132–151). London/New York: Routledge.

Cobb, R. W., & Elder, C. D. (1971). The politics of agenda-building: An alternative perspective for modern democratic theory. *The Journal of Politics, 33*(4), 892–915.

Cobb, R. W., & Elder, C. D. (1972). *Participation in American politics: The dynamics of agenda building*. Boston: Allyn and Bacon.

Cobb, R. W., Ross, J.-K., & Ross, M. H. (1976). Agenda building as a comparative political process. *American Political Science Review, 70*, 126–138.

Collier, U. (2002). European Union Energy Policy in a Changing Climate. In A. Lenschow (Ed.), *Environmental policy integration: Greening sectoral policies in Europe* (pp. 175–192). London: Earthscan Publications.

Correljé, A., & van der Linde, C. (2006). Energy supply security and geopolitics: A European perspective. *Energy Policy, 34*(5), 532–554.

De Jong, J., & van der Linde, C. (2008). EU energy policy in a supply-constrained World. *European Policy Analysis (Swedish Institute for European Policy Studies), 11*, 1–9.

Earnshaw, D., & Judge, D. (1997). The life and times of the European union's co-operation procedure. *Journal of Common Market Studies, 35*(4), 543–564.

Egenhofer, C., Behrens, A., Tol, R. S. J., Berthélemy, M., Lévêque, F., & Jansen, J. C. (2011). Does Europe need a comprehensive energy policy? *Intereconomics, 46*(3), 124–142.

EUR-Lex (2013). Access to European Union Law. Brussels.

Farell, H., & Héritier, A. (2004). Interorganizational negotiation and intraorganizational power in shared decision making: Early agreements under codecision and their impact on the european parliament and council. *Comparative Political Studies, 37*(10), 1184–1212.

Finon, D., & Locatelli, C. (2008). Russian and European gas interdependence: Could contractual trade channel geopolitics? *Energy Policy, 36*(1), 423–442.

Hey, C. (2005). EU Environmental Policies: A short history of the policy strategies. In S. Scheuer (Ed.), *EU environmental policy handbook: A critical analysis of EU environmental legislation* (pp. 17–30). Brussels: European Environmental Bureau.

Jordan, A., & Schout, A. (2006). *The coordination of the European union: exploring the capacities of networked governance*. Oxford: Oxford University Press.

Knill, C., Schulze, K., & Tosun, J. (2011). *Measuring environmental policy change: Conceptual alternatives and research implications*. Working Paper Political Science Series 125. Institute for Advanced Studies, Vienna.

Lenschow, A. (2002). *Environmental policy integration: Greening sectoral policies in Europe*. London: Earthscan Publications.

Lenschow, A. (1999). Transformation in European environmental governance. In B. Kohler-Koch & R. Eising (Eds.), *Transformation of governance in the European Union* (pp. 37–58). London: Routledge.

Lenschow, A., & Zito, A. (1998). Blurring or shifting of policy frames? The institutionalization of the economic-environmental policy linkage in the European community. *Governance, 11*(4), 415–441.

Lucas, N. J. D. (1977). *Energy and the European communities*. London: Europa Publications.

Mahmoudi, S. (2000). Protection of the European environment after the Amsterdam treaty. *Scandinavian Studies in Law, 39*, 123–137.

Matláry, J. H. (1997). *Energy policy in the European union*. New York: San Martin's Press.

McElroy, G. (2006). Committee representation in the European parliament. *European Union Politics, 7*(1), 5–29.

Neuhold, C. (2001). The "Legislative Backbone" Keeping the Institution Upright? The role of European parliament committees in the EU policy-making process? *European Integration online Papers (EIoP), 5*(10), 1–23.

Oberthür, S., & Pallemaerts, M. (2010). *The new climate policies of the European union: internal legislation and climate diplomacy*. Brussels: VUB Press.

Piebalgs, A. (2009). *How the European union is preparing the third industrial revolution with an innovative energy policy*. EUI Working Papers RCAS 2009/11.

Princen, S. (2007). Agenda-setting in the European Union: a theoretical exploration and agenda for research. *Journal of European Public Policy, 14*(1), 21–38.

Princen, S. (2011). Agenda-setting strategies in EU policy processes. *Journal of European Public Policy, 18*(7), 927–943.

Schmitt, S., & Schulze, K. (2011). Choosing environmental policy instruments: An assessment of the 'environmental dimension' of EU energy policy. In J. Tosun & I. Solorio (Eds.), *Energy and environment in Europe: Assessing a complex relationship? European Integration online Papers (EIoP)*, Special Mini-Issue 1, Vol. 15, Article 9.

Single European Act (SEA) (1987) OJ L169/01.

Solorio, I. (2011). Environmental policy integration (EPI) and the Europeanisation of the energy governance. In F. Morata & I. Solorio (Eds.), *European energy policy: The environmental dimension* (pp. 75–94). Barcelona: IUEE.

Stern, J. (2006). The Russian-Ukrainian gas crisis of January 2006. *Oxford Institute for Energy Studies, 16*, 5–12.

Tosun, J., & Solorio, I. (2011). Exploring the energy-environment relationship in the EU: Perspectives and challenges for theorizing and empirical analysis. In J. Tosun & I. Solorio (Eds.), *Energy and environment in Europe: Assessing a complex relationship*? *European Integration online Papers* (EIoP), Special Mini-Issue 1, Vol. 15, Article 7.

Treaty Establishing the European Economic Community (EEC) (1957) [hereinafter Treaty on the Functioning of the European Union (TFEU)].

Treaty of Amsterdam amending the Treaty on European Union, the Treaties establishing the European Communities and certain related acts (1997) OJ 97/C 340/01 [hereinafter Treaty of Amsterdam].

Treaty of Lisbon amending the Treaty on European Union and the Treaty establishing the European Community (2007) OJ C306/01 [hereinafter Treaty of Lisbon].

Treaty on European Union (TEU) (1992) OJ C191/01 [hereinafter Treaty of Maastricht].

Chapter 3
Agenda Dynamics on Energy Policy in the European Council

Petya Alexandrova and Arco Timmermans

Abstract Policy issues can arrive on the agendas of political institutions following two routes: a low and a high politics one. In the first case, involvement of experts and working groups is envisaged. In the latter, the power of top institutions is emphasized with their tasks of drawing overall strategies, acting as final arbiters or decision-makers and delegating policy proposals downwards. A high politics institution in the multilevel system of the EU is the European Council, whose role in shaping the Union agenda has increased over the years. Analysing the Conclusions issued after meetings of this body, we find that energy is a topic with relatively little overall attention and sensitive to drastic shifts over time. Energy-related issues appearance on the agenda was sometimes the result of focusing events but also represented strategic discussions in the form of policy planning and review. Classifying the statements in the Conclusions of the European Council in categories, we find that the text can be almost equally divided between evaluations or positions, setting of targets and concrete actions. In short, while attracting on average rather limited attention, energy has the power to become salient in times of critical events or strong need of strategic guideline provision. And its appearance on the agenda often results in new initiatives and delegation of action to lower levels of policy making.

P. Alexandrova (✉)
Leibniz University of Hannover, Institute of Political Sciences, Schneiderberg 50, 30167 Hannover, Germany
e-mail: p.alexandrova@ipw.uni-hannover.de

A. Timmermans
Institute of Public Administration, Campus the Hague, Leiden University, Schouwburgstraat 2, 2511 VA The Hague, The Netherlands
e-mail: a.timmermans@cdh.leidenuniv.nl

J. Tosun et al. (eds.), *Energy Policy Making in the EU*,
Lecture Notes in Energy 28, DOI 10.1007/978-1-4471-6645-0_3

3.1 Introduction: A Punctuated Equilibrium Perspective on the Policy Agenda

As the scope of policy-making institutions across the Western world expanded, these institutions have come to experience constant pressure to prioritise widely different problems. National governments and international or supranational institutions, such as those in the European Union (EU), address multiple issues. They are expected to formulate and deliver policies on issues after these issues have passed what Wilson (1979) called the 'legitimacy barrier'. As Jones (2012) shows for the United States, the scope of the government agenda widened when it became clear and accepted that no other organisations would take up issues such as unemployment, environmental pollution and white collar crime. During this period of government agenda expansion between the 1950s and 1980s, the administrative apparatus for processing policy relevant information also expanded. In the EU, the broadening and increasing specialisation of Directorates-General (DGs) of the Commission reflect this development. The DGs function together to address multiple issues at the same time. This is possible since much of the daily business in government organisations consists of routine and adaptive behaviour. Such routine issues are addressed in specialised 'policy subsystems' below the level where the political agenda is set and disruptions in attention may occur (Baumgartner and Jones 1993).

The key condition to such institutional multi-tasking is thus that issues are limited in scope and remain insensitive to focusing events and political drama. But this condition is not always met. The environment of policy-making institutions is undisciplined with interest organisations, public opinion, the media, competing political parties and even partners in office trying to disrupt stable policy programmes and challenge the status quo. This may happen at electoral intervals, but often agenda changes occur at any time during institutional life cycles of policy-making organisations. Intrusion of new information can alter views on which problem is most urgent and what matters can be placed on the waiting list. In turn, policy programmes and carefully scheduled consultations may be undermined and policy makers pressed to respond. This is why politics is by definition a constant battle over attention to issues and policy decisions on them, not just about their content but also over their prioritisation and timing. If the Eurocrisis and the economic recession are a top priority, other matters come next in the attention ranking even if indicators do not show they have become less serious problems.

Since the early political agenda-setting studies of Schattschneider (1960), Bachrach and Baratz (1962), Downs (1972) and Cobb et al. (1976), the appearance and disappearance of issues from government consideration has been a central element in accounts of the policy process. While these studies helped to better understand political agenda-setting, it was the subsequent work by Kingdon (1984) and in particular by Baumgartner and Jones (1993) and Jones and Baumgartner (2005) that provided the theoretical and empirical elements for drawing up the bigger picture of political agenda-setting and its policy consequences. Baumgartner and Jones have pointed to the importance of information signals and limits to the information processing capacity of institutions in addressing problems. While functionally designed organisations can help policy makers in dealing with many issues in parallel and keep the policy making and delivery machineries active, bottlenecks become visible when issues rise to the top of the agenda. Topics that are sensitive to focusing events and involve urgency, drama and controversy then drive out other problems. The implication of this is that political institutions address major matters serially, one or a few at a time, rather than simultaneously. Following Herbert Simon's theory on bounded rationality (1985), Baumgartner and Jones argue that cognitive and organisational limits within policy making institutions lead them to suppress or ignore information about new problems as long as possible and maintain the steady state until the flow of new and alarming information is so strong that a response is inevitable. This is the central element in the theory of punctuated equilibrium: the policy agenda shows stability or incremental change but also major shifts in attention that spark policy change (Jones and Baumgartner 2005). As institutions and interconnections between them become more complex, the alternation over time between agenda continuity and change may also be affected. Recent empirical work on countries on both sides of the Atlantic has shown that punctuations in the policy agenda become more pronounced as institutions contain higher thresholds for change. Such change becomes less frequent but when it occurs its intensity is stronger (Baumgartner et al. 2009; Jones and Baumgartner 2012). This type of dynamic involving all kinds of policy topics also applies to institutions in the EU such as the European Council (Alexandrova et al. 2012).

The punctuated equilibrium perspective on agenda-setting is a systemic view in which attention to one problem is contingent to how much other problems attract the interest and concern of policy makers in another manner than just being business as usual. Problems are at the centre in an ongoing competition for attention, and this competition is driven not only by preferences and strategies but also by the information flow that forces policy makers to make choices about priorities. Complex political systems with separated powers and different tiers of government involve more thresholds and friction before issues reach the top of the agenda. The EU is such kind of a complex system of multilevel governance sensitive to attention punctuations. With its institutional architecture of policy-making organisations with no equivalents in other parts of the world, the EU makes an intriguing and important case for understanding agenda dynamics.

There are different ways in which problems and issues can reach the agenda of policy-making institutions. It is important to note that agendas of different institutions do not necessarily follow the same logics or patterns. Depending on the institutional characteristics and the background of the involved actors, sensitivity or attention to events may vary. This chapter elaborates thereon and applies the theoretical distinction to the empirical case of energy policy in the EU with a focus on the European Council as a major venue in which problems with relevance to the EU are signalled, informally delegated to other policy-making bodies or settled politically.

Bringing together the EU's Heads of State or Government, the European Council sets the broad political priorities and serves as the overall agenda setter for the Union. In addition, it constitutes the link between member states and EU institutions. With its horizontal and vertical dimensions of power distribution, there are multiple routes for agenda access. Whether these routes are avenues of opportunity for policy entrepreneurs or roads full of obstacles and veto points is not only a matter of theory but is first and foremost an empirical question. Issues may enter the scope of concern or move upward on the agenda, but the time and space for top priority is always limited. The degree of controversy over an issue can prolong its stay high on the agenda, however, not all issues have similar capacity to remain there until they are settled. Issues are sacrificed to make space for other points of great concern. Core themes of government such as the economy, international affairs and the structure and operation of government appear to condition the space for other matters (Jennings et al. 2011; Alexandrova et al. 2012). Agenda space and the intensity of issue competition also depend on what specific policy-making institution we consider. Again, this brings us at the different possible routes of agenda access.

In the following sections, we elaborate on the theoretical perspective on attention dynamics and the ways of agenda access in the EU, and provide empirical data on attention to energy in the European Council (see Biesenbender in Chap. 2 for an assessment of the energy agenda in the Council of the European Union and the Commission). Building on earlier work, we show the pattern of attention over time and provide the first large-scale content analysis of the policy statements on energy issues produced by the European Council. Mentions of problems can be symbolic or substantive, meant to show rhetorical responsiveness or to initiate or delegate real policies. We also compare the pattern of rise and decline of attention to the relative position of energy issues on national government agendas in a number of EU member states. The data allow us to draw some preliminary conclusions about the nature of attention to energy issues in the EU and the conditions under which this theme and the specific issues belonging to it consolidate on the agenda or are dropped again when other matters of concern emerge.

This chapter is structured as follows. Sections 3.2–3.5 deal with different theoretical perspectives on political attention and agenda-setting. Sections 3.6–3.8 present the empirical analysis of attention tracks in energy policy in the European Council. And finally, the chapter concludes with a discussion and an outlook on avenues for further research.

3.2 Attention Tracks and Policy Consequences in the EU

Though expressly not a federal political system, the EU has features that make it in some ways similar to federal polities. There are power separations between institutions at the EU level and the transfer of sovereignty and use of the subsidiarity principle distribute powers between the EU, national and regional levels. The institutional set up provides multiple access points for policy actors who seek to influence the course of public policy or call for attention to a new problem (Peters 1994, 2001; Princen 2009). Since the concept multilevel governance was introduced for the EU context in the mid-1990s (Marks et al. 1996), we have seen an increasing volume of work dealing with policy issues in this respect (see, e.g. Hooghe and Marks 2001; George 2004). For example, actors in EU member states attempt to influence the agenda upwards when trying to overcome domestic opposition as Guiraudon (2000) has shown for the case of internal security and migration policies. Recently, we witnessed how Northern Eurozone member states successfully tried to set the topic and tone in the European Council and empower the Commission to enforce budget discipline in all Eurozone countries (see Tosun et al. 2014). The success of this enforcement in both Southern member states and Northern ones is not guaranteed as political actors within these countries may use alternative venues for weakening the effects of EU fiscal consolidation pressures (see Cox and Dekanozishvili in Chap. 9 for an analysis of the case of Germany and its attempts to shape the European energy agenda and Ciambra and Solorio in Chap. 8 for an assessment of the British impact on the liberalisation of the internal energy market).

Peters (1994, 2001) has argued that with its multiple venues, the EU is still in search of its 'policy equilibrium' in those areas where it obtained competencies and is developing initiatives. The boundaries of policy jurisdictions are moving, and this is not just because each enlargement of the Union creates another Commission portfolio. Moving jurisdictional boundaries are themselves products of the politics of attention. They indicate shifts in 'legitimacy barriers' resulting from the interaction between member states and EU institutions. The widening and deepening of European integration involves constantly shifting loci of attention and policy initiatives. Such shifts have come with the successive European treaties, but multilevel governance and agenda shaping as a crucial part of it do not only follow such formal institutional pathways. This is why Peters stressed the still unconsolidated nature of the European policy-making system at the turn of the century. The years since have shown developments in which despite increasing complexity some institutional settlements at the EU level took place.[1]

The European Council became more prominent in agenda-setting (Werts 2008; Puetter 2014) and, following Tallberg (2008) and the terminology set in the introductory chapter in this volume, in agenda shaping. Further, the co-decision procedure institutionalised, and the tools repertoire of the European Parliament stabilised (Rittberger 2012). In the same past decade, European integration became less a process by stealth (Majone 2005) and more a political issue, involving contestation within most of the member states. For the purpose of this chapter, the

[1] After Croatia entered on 1 July 2013, there are 21 more member states than at the time when Peters wrote his essay.

key message is that the connection between institutional and political conditions in the EU has not led to uniformity in agenda shaping, but has sustained different routes towards agenda access.

3.3 High and Low Politics Avenues in the EU

The two main possible routes to reach the political agenda in the EU are from below or from above (Princen and Rhinard 2006). This distinction relates to the concepts of 'uploading' and 'downloading', but it is important to acknowledge that in this chapter we deal with agenda shaping, not with policy implementation. While practically all policy topics travel up and down on the agenda and thus have high times as well as periods of low key importance and invisibility, they may enter the agenda in different ways.

The low politics route is via experts, specialised officials in the administration who detect issues, organise information and develop policy initiatives. This approach includes what Hogwood and Peters (1983) have called 'inside initiatives', proposals generated within the administration itself. On the low politics route, it is crucial to build support and critical political mass in order to move forward. But often, the travel upward of issues follows a difficult path. As Kingdon (1984) described in his multiple streams model of agenda-setting, solutions need to get connected to problems that are actually identified by political decision-makers and are considered urgent enough to be attended to. Windows of opportunity usually open just shortly (see Herweg in Chap. 5). In the EU context of multilevel governance, a route from below may mean a point of origin in a specialised arena of experts and other actors within a policy community, but it can also refer to the level of member states in which actors or even national governments themselves try to place a problem on the agenda of an EU institution. In parallel processing organisations, many issues can be on the route from below, but bottlenecks at the political top prevent that they all are given political consideration. As we noted, attention scarcity means that problems compete for getting addressed, and some must stay long on the waiting list.

The other route, from above, is the opposite not only in terms of its way through the EU institutions but is also different in the dynamics at play. Here, problems enter the political agenda as matters of high urgency, and the driving forces are less directly expert concerns or policy production routines and initiatives within administrative organisations. Instead, they involve necessity to respond to issues and events in the social and political environment. The high politics route often involves a 'focusing event' (Birkland 1997), but this is not a necessary condition. Issues may also have become a matter of concern in the social environment before they are taken up by policy makers. In this regard, Polsby (1984) speaks of problems and policy changes that are incubated as opposed to changes that are acute. High politics can also involve making major choices about issues of strategic interest for the future. Within the EU, the key arena where the high politics avenue begins is the European

Council, which is composed of the Heads of State or Government of all member countries. It has gained increasing prominence as the institution setting the parameters for EU policies (Eggermont 2012; Foret and Rittelmeyer 2014) and making the fundamental decisions, including those about treaty change. The position of the European Council in EU agenda shaping is thus at the top of the pyramid where matters are delegated to lower levels, or where topics come up for political conflict resolution. This also means that the European Council must be highly selective in attending to problems. Usually, it considers matters of substantial urgency in order to show responsiveness, and it deals with the most politically controversial issues in the EU for final settlement (see Chap. 12 by Tosun).

3.4 Problem Definition and Policy Entrepreneurship

Policy topics may have objective attributes, but these do not make them intrinsically matters for exclusively the low politics or the high politics route in agenda shaping. Information about a topic may involve an 'alarmed discovery', as Downs (1972) has called it, but as he has shown for environmental problems signalled by experts such alarm may take a long time to resonate among policy makers. This adds to the dynamics of agenda shaping. Not only do issues travel through institutions, but on their way they also change slowly or abruptly in definition and tone. This is what Baumgartner and Jones (1993) call 'interaction of image and venue'. In the same way as attention is not given and constant, the definition of problems can shift, and such shifts are themselves essential to strategies of agenda shaping (Rocheford and Cobb 1994; Rhinard 2010; Baumgartner 2013).

For matters to move up in the EU system, a technical problem definition will rarely suffice (see Bouzarovski and Petrova in Chap. 7 on the role of problem definition and recognition in agenda-shaping processes). Broadening the scope of debate and building up political endorsement requires a degree of emotion and drama. Riker (1996) referred to this connection when speaking of the 'strategy of rhetoric'. Such issue expansion often involves adding new dimensions to a problem and making linkages across issues. Energy problems, in particular, involve economic costs and benefits, innovative technology, precaution or coping with environmental impacts. And they often also incorporate geopolitical power or domestic social affairs in their definitions. In the EU, this expansion process features a specific type of framing: one of asserting the 'European' nature of an issue (Princen 2009, 2011), which helps push a matter beyond the legitimacy barrier in EU policy-making. But as attention to a problem widens and moves into the sphere of high politics, this problem then must be structured and downsized again in order for other institutions in a lower sphere to produce and deliver the policies that are expected. A problem which stays comprehensive, multidimensional and controversial will hardly entail viable policy solutions.

Scholars studying political agenda-setting or agenda shaping vary in their emphasis on rational strategising by policy entrepreneurs. Problem definitions may be changed to win the political game and stay in office, or policy tinkering may happen out of a deep conviction that a problem must be settled in order to achieve goals of social justice, sustainability or moral order. Likewise, actors may engage in extensive venue shopping to accomplish such goals, or they may actually stick to the channels of agenda access with which they are familiar and bring up the political transaction costs, as Pralle (2003) has argued.

In this book, the leading question is not why (for what specific underlying motivations) actors pursue policy goals, but how they do this and how we may recognise and understand the patterns of agenda access and their consequences. Our assumption is that actors involved in agenda shaping (and also actors not able to access the political agenda) are driven by substantive policy goals. We are thus oriented to the visible results of actor behaviour in agenda shaping: seeking to address policy issues and broadening or narrowing their definition.

3.5 Two Patterns of Longitudinal Problem Attention

One way in which these choices and dynamics become evident on the EU agenda is the pattern of attention to policy topics over time. As said, a systemic view places attention to specific problems in the context of attention to other problems. We distinguish two general patterns of attention to issues within a policy-making institution. It is important to appreciate the aforementioned point that issues travel through venues. We mean that the rise and decline in attention to one and the same problem may be quite dissimilar between institutions over time (see Biesenbender in Chap. 2). Empirical analysis of a range of venues of attention, including different policy-making institutions across countries, has shown that no single policy topic stays permanently at the top of the agenda (Baumgartner et al. 2009; Mortensen et al. 2011; Alexandrova et al. 2012). All problems decline at some point and for some period to lower status. But not all policy topics disappear entirely from the political agenda.

The first type of attention development to an individual topic on the political agenda is a smooth rise and decline over time, which follows the theoretical ideal type of attention waves (Downs 1972; Nisbet and Huge 2006). In terms of the punctuated equilibrium model, changes in attention in this case are relatively proportionate to information signals about the problem. Topics behaving in this way thus do not—or do rarely—disappear from the agenda. They may be prominent for some time but then decline to lower priority status until the next increase in salience.

The second possible pattern is when a problem stays low key on the political agenda most of the time or is absent, but it shows episodic and quite short upsurges to prominence. Problems belonging to this category of agenda dynamics may appear more sensitive to focus events. Information processing by policy makers in this case is also more disproportionate; such issues are mostly considered less crucial to the agenda and are ignored but after a period of neglect they suddenly rise to become a matter of major concern. Problems following this attention path experience more intense competition from other problems, and they are usually effectively delegated to policy subsystems in the sphere of low politics. There, the problem definition is often contained by experts and specific stakeholders not seeking expansion of the scope of debate.

The prevalence of either of these two possible attention patterns depends in part on the institutional properties and the information processing capacity of policy-making institutions, but both types occur together in all institutions. The dynamics of attention to specific problems are not determined only by institutional properties. They result from the interplay of such features and the way in which actors seek to change images of problems, and accordingly want to absorb issues into the policy-making institution, or rather have them addressed elsewhere. It is important to appreciate also that if a theme is not prominent on a signalling political agenda, this does not mean that policy production on it has come to a halt. More likely, the level of production may vary with attention rise and decline. In the following section, we illustrate these theoretical points about the dynamics of attention by focusing on the way in which the European Council has addressed energy matters in the past decades. Our focus is thus on the agenda of a high politics venue within the EU.

3.6 Episodic High Politics on Energy in the European Council

Empirical analysis of the European Council has shown that the agenda of this policy-making institution contains attention changes of all degrees (Alexandrova et al. 2012). The two aforementioned patterns of attention development are both present. One finding that stands out—compared to analyses of other political institutions—is that problems that are addressed during one Presidency semester (a half-year) or even during a whole year can be dropped entirely in the next semester or year. In the European Council, issues are sacrificed frequently in order to create agenda space for other matters (Alexandrova et al. 2012, pp. 76–79; Alexandrova et al. 2014a).

Energy is a topic that is sensitive to drastic shifts with low level of attention as a basis. If energy issues often travel as very technical matters through policy-making institutions, focusing events can add dramatic attributes to them (see Cox and Dekanozishvili in Chap. 9). This pattern matches the second theoretical type of attention dynamics as discussed in the above section. A content analysis of all issued Conclusions of the European Council since its first year in operation (1975) shows that on average energy received just over 3 % of the total attention. This estimate is based on a dataset of some 44,000 content coded statements in all Conclusions produced by the European Council until the end of 2012 (see Alexandrova et al. 2014b for a detailed explanation of the construction of the dataset). In the topic classification used for this content analysis, we distinguish 21 major policy fields and energy comes 11th in size ranking.[2]

---

[2] The dataset is publicly available at www.policyagendas.eu/data.

Table 3.1 displays the overall share of attention per policy topic as measured in (quasi-)sentences contained in the Conclusions. On average, energy is a medium-sized policy topic distant from international affairs (23 %), macroeconomic policy (15 %) and institutional matters of the EU (10 %). On the European Council agenda, energy features more prominently than agriculture and foreign trade but comes after defence and employment, on which the EU has quite limited competencies but which appear to be matters of political concern at the EU top. This also indicates that the European Council agenda often has an indirect relationship with policy production—this institution does not always make the policy decisions but often provides impulses for such decisions in the formal policy-making bodies of the EU. One of its functions is signalling, which involves stimuli for policy initiatives but, as said, policy initiatives also emerge in the route from below or from the internal policy machinery in the EU. Such plans and programmes need political endorsement and then emerge at the higher level.

Thus, while the EU has many formal competencies on agriculture and (until the Lisbon Treaty of 2009) very limited powers on energy policy, such issues may be signalled at quite different levels of attention in the European Council. Since this institution is also a major venue for engineering European treaty changes, attention to problems can lead to expansion in competencies at a later stage (see Biesenbender in Chap. 2 for an assessment of the institutional and legal foundations of EU energy policy over time). This is what happened with European energy policy between the 1970s and the present. While the average proportion of European Council policy talk devoted to energy is rather modest, this hides large variation over time. For the size of the issue, variation in salience is quite large—from no attention at all to about one-third of the attention devoted to all problems within a single year.

In Fig. 3.1, we see that the appearance of energy problems on the European Council agenda follows a pattern of low key salience most of the time (the theme disappeared from the agenda twice in the 1980s) but interrupted by some peaks in

Table 3.1 Average attention to topics on the European Council agenda, 1975–2012

Attention (%)	Topic (ranking in terms of overall agenda share)
23	International affairs (1)
15	Macroeconomics (2)
10	Governance (3)
7	Defence (4) and banking, finance and internal trade (5)
6	Employment (6)
5	Law and crime (7)
4	Environment (8), civil rights and liberties (9) and immigration (10)
3	Energy (11) and foreign trade (12)
2	Science and technology (13), social policy (14) and agriculture (15)
1 or less	Transportation (16), regional policy (17), education (18), health (19), culture (20) and lands and water (21)

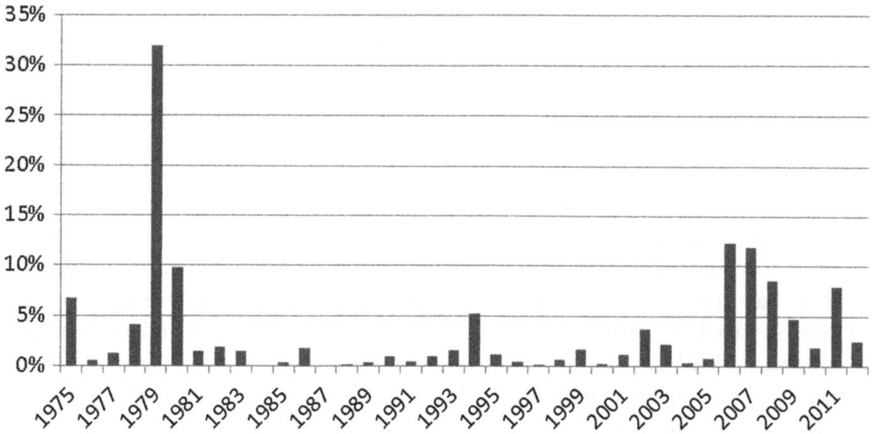

Fig. 3.1 Attention to energy as a share of the whole European Council agenda, 1975–2012

attention, most visible in the 1970s and in the past decade. The spikes in 1975 and 1979–1980 relate to the first and second international oil crisis and signified a sense of urgency to resolve problems with oil supply in the future. Another energy-related crisis provoked a rather tiny surge in attention in 1986. The Chernobyl disaster was noted but at that time the accident's location was still relatively distant from the territory of the Community. Notably in later years, this tragedy left a mark on the enlargement and neighbourhood policies of the EU. In 1999 the European Council promoted a broad partnership with Ukraine where a comprehensive energy sector reform was envisaged. Around the turn of the century some acceding member states had to comply with EU conditions for nuclear safety. A smaller-scale crisis which also emerged in the attention pattern was the disruption of Russian gas supply in late 2008–early 2009. While the EU had agreed on a comprehensive energy policy in preceding years, the disruption urged the government and state leaders to stress that security of energy supply remained a priority. Finally, an increase in attention occurred in 2011, part of which was triggered by the nuclear power plant disaster in Fukushima and another part related to matters of energy supply and sustainability.

Energy issues on the agenda of the European Council have also been aspects of more comprehensive policy initiatives in this domain, in which the Commission was involved since the 1990s with a series of white and green papers. One broader set of plans was the European Energy Charter, which was proposed in 1990 and signed in the end of 1991 by 51 signatories. It aimed at cooperation with other industrialised countries for securing energy supply. Eventually it resulted in the Energy Charter Treaty of 1994. Another significant example is the Energy Policy for Europe, which was initiated and discussed extensively in 2006–2007. It represented the EU's attempt to reduce energy consumption, maintain security of supply and undertake a shift towards a sustainable and competitive energy use. The climate change debate which entered the political agenda also played a major part in preparing an expansion of EU energy policy competencies in the next European treaty signed in Lisbon in 2007 and enforced in December 2009 (see Ciambra and Solorio in Chap. 8 for an analysis of the British government in shaping the EU energy-climate agenda). The priority actions of this recent EU policy included internal market for gas and electricity, energy efficiency and renewable energies, energy technologies or research in sustainable energies, security of supply and a common approach to external energy policy. A review of the policy was carried out in 2011 and new actions were announced. In May 2013 these energy policy issues recurred on the agenda.[3]

Thus, it seems that attention to issues within the energy domain in the European Council has come mostly in two forms: reaction to focusing events and 'high politics as usual' regarding issues requiring strategic attention and broader plan development. This finding provides empirical support for the claim by Buchan (2010) that energy policy in the EU is driven by focusing events. However, it shows that detailed designing and routine monitoring of large policy plans can also act as an attention propeller in the European Council in this policy field.

We note at this point that the attention pattern as we analysed it from year to year hides even more variation from one European Council summit to the next. With an increased number of data points (there are some five or seven meetings per year in recent times), we see an even more erratic pattern of low attention and prominence over time. For example, the European Council meeting of 22 May 2013 was devoted largely to energy issues, which followed a number of meetings where these issues were barely addressed. Such focused summits by the European Council may indicate how this institution of high politics processes problems serially—very few at a time. When issues are addressed, they are meant to set the policy-making machinery elsewhere in the EU in motion and endorse initiatives politically. It is likely that years of rising attention to energy on the European Council agenda are followed shortly by policy output (see Biesenbender in Chap. 2).

3.7 Multilevel Attention to Energy Policy

The European Council is the key venue of the high politics route. It is crucial for signalling and for endorsing attention to problems of broad EU concern, in which energy is an episodically occurring theme. In this role the institution interacts with other policy-making bodies at the EU level and with the governments of the member states. The horizontal link entails the policy-making traffic with the Commission and the Parliament as well as a specific body such as EURATOM. Before the European Council summit devoted in large part to energy policy in May 2013, a huge banner on the EU internal energy market on the Commission's

[3] Not shown in the figure.

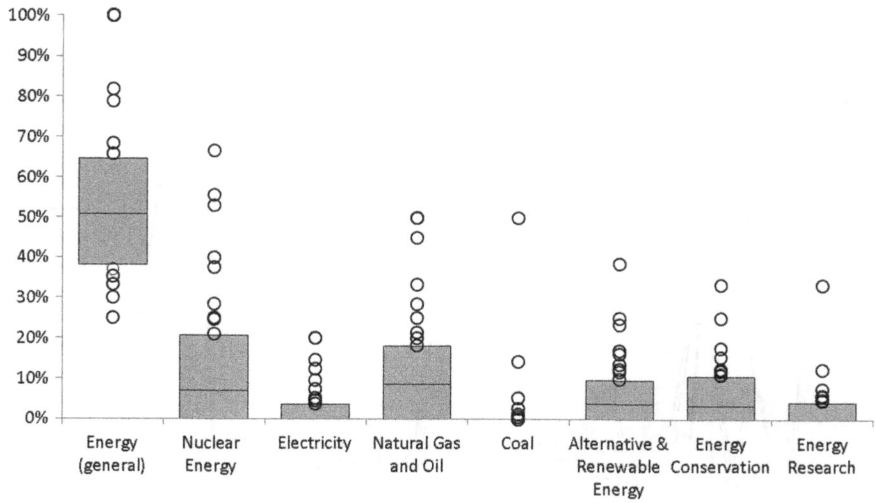

Fig. 3.2 Relative annual attention to energy-related issues in the European Council, 1975–2012. All coded statements per year to energy-related issues = 100 %

Berlaymont building in Brussels advertised plans under construction. The European Council Conclusions delegating this task to the Commission were thus testimony of a link between agenda shaping and the following steps in policy formulation (see Herweg in Chap. 5 for a comparative analysis of the processes of agenda shaping and policy formulation in the context of the European gas directive). This link was strengthened after the Lisbon Treaty, which included new EU responsibilities on energy policy.

More generally, the European Council agenda provides the basic and strategic pointers for more specific energy issues to be addressed within the other institutions where regulatory fine print is produced. This can be observed in Fig. 3.2 where we see that about half of the energy agenda normally is devoted to such broad policy talk. Nuclear energy and natural gas and oil are the two more specific energy topics addressed next to the general theme.

The other subtopics in this domain mentioned in Fig. 3.2 get less on average and also at times of rising salience they rarely dominate the energy policy part of the agenda. Energy conservation and alternative or renewable energy are not typical matters of high politics, and the same applies to electricity. Attention to them in the European Council is incidental. In this analysis, we have not considered linkages of energy policy issues to other topics such as environment, international security or the internal market and competition policy. Such linkages were crucial in the development of energy initiatives in the EU given the narrow limits of EU competencies in this area.

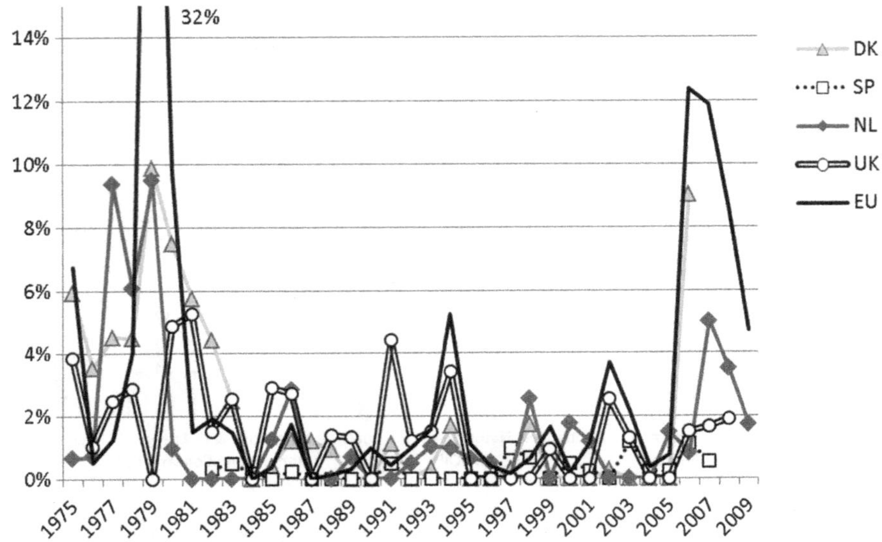

Fig. 3.3 Attention to energy on governmental agendas in four member states compared to the European Council, 1975–2009. Some national data are missing, 2007–2009 for Denmark, 1975–1981 and 2008–2009 for Spain, 2008–2009 for France and 2009 for the UK

Further, even with few formal competencies at the EU level, the international or supranational nature of this theme was emphasised. The first concerns about energy in the European integration process already related to international energy security (Tosun 2011). As the analysis of the period since 1975 suggests, the aim of securing supply or repercussions of foreign energy crises adds a strong international dimension to the attention devoted to energy. Likewise, eastern enlargement of the EU made the relationship with Russia on energy supply more prominent (see Brutschin in Chap. 10 and Tosun in Chap. 12). Thus, energy issues have travelled across levels within the EU and between the EU and the international environment. In the European Council Conclusions, only some 40 % of the overall energy agenda can be considered internal to the EU.

Figure 3.3 presents attention development on the governmental agenda in four member states compared to the European Council.[4] The oil crisis is visible in some countries, in particular the Netherlands, which already in the 1970s had a European main port function for oil import and refinery. And in the UK, attention to energy was at a higher level in the 1980s during the years of Margaret Thatcher, who set a course of emphasising privatisation.

Generally, however, attention levels in member states were below the level displayed in the European Council. In at least one-third of all the years analysed for

[4] The data on governmental agendas are based on executive speeches coded within the Comparative Agendas Project (www.comparativeagendas.info).

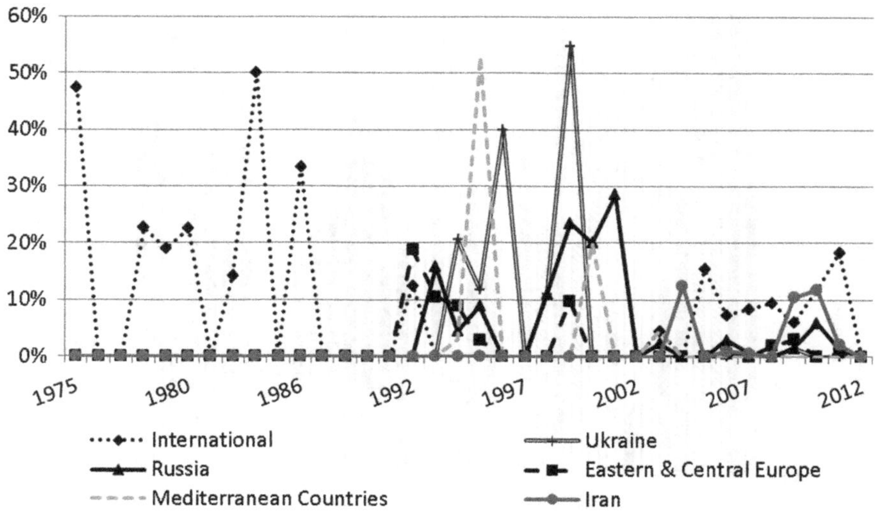

Fig. 3.4 Most common external references in the energy field as share of the total energy agenda in the European Council Conclusions, 1975–2012. Each unit of analysis (quasi-sentence) can contain more than one external reference

individual member states since 1945, energy issues were absent from the annual executive speech while such absence of energy talk was much rarer in the European Council. One reason for this difference may be the broader scope of the policy agenda in member states compared to European institutions (which have a smaller range of jurisdictions). Our findings may also indicate that attention to energy policy in the European Council is meant for signalling and driving initiatives on the substantive policy agenda elsewhere. We consider this delegation of policy tasks further below.

Figure 3.4 displays the relative frequency of references in statements on energy issues to the international environment. Until the early 1990s, such references were quite general. This can be interpreted as both an expression of the global nature of the two oil crises and the still weak state of development of a regional orientation in European energy policy. Such an orientation occurred in later decades. These instances of regional attention were followed by several agreements on energy supply or nuclear safety (the Mediterranean, Russia and Ukraine) or were about countries (including candidate member states) in Central and Eastern Europe. Besides the neighbours, Iran received attention mostly due to its contested nuclear programme. In recent years, the general international dimension again became the most relevant, which indicated renewed concerns about globalisation and its effects on energy security and sustainability.

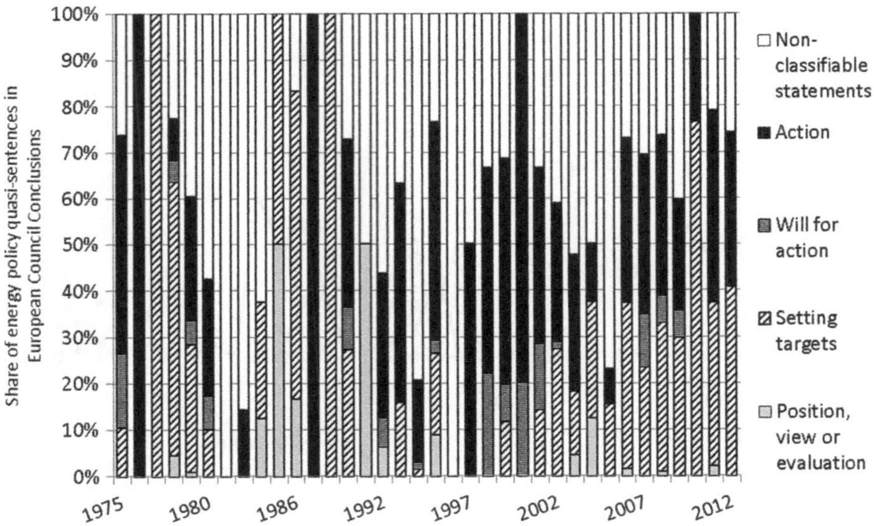

Fig. 3.5 Types of statements in the energy field, European Council Conclusions, 1975–2012. All coded statements per year to energy-related issues = 100 %. Action can refer to announcing, endorsing or delegating a decision

3.8 Types of Agenda Statements and Policy Delegation

The European Council endorses, gives impulses and delegates. In this role, it is located prominently in EU multilevel governance. In its Conclusions, we classified four types of statements on energy policy—each with different intended and more or less direct effects in the EU's multilevel governance system.[5] First, statements may contain evaluations and positions; second, they may set targets; third, points agreed between the Heads of State and Government may express will for action; finally, they may announce, endorse or delegate concrete policy actions.[6] In regard to the involvement of the EU with an issue, these four types represent a gradient: from a mere general view via fixing of goals and expression of political will to committing statements about upcoming actions.

In addressing energy problems, all of these types of statements have been used as displayed in Fig. 3.5. Views, targets and actions have taken each about a third of the whole agenda; will for action is expressed more rarely in just some 5 % of all cases. No clear trend over time can be distinguished. Figure 3.5 shows years of emphasis on action alternating with years where views or positions were the prevailing type of policy talk. When comparing these findings to the development of attention to energy over time (Fig. 3.1 and its discussion above), it becomes clear

[5] Such statements may or may not be followed by substantive policy proposals.

[6] An action can also be cancelled or withdrawn, but this happens just occasionally.

that the level of salience of energy issues on the European Council agenda is not related to the proportion of concrete actions. In years of lower attention, the share of actions often was high while attention spikes came with all kinds of policy statements. The varying mix of types of statements over time may indicate some sequence from views and targets to actions announced, but this pattern is not straightforward. Statement types rather seem to have come in cycles.

Agenda shaping in the European Council thus may be followed by a more concrete proposal on an energy issue, it may be left for later consideration or it even may entirely remain a matter of symbolic politics. This requires further investigation of specific energy policy issues as is done in the following chapters in this book. In cases where the European Council discussed a new action in the energy sector, this action often was delegated to another institution where it subsequently was linked to matters of formal policy-making competences such as internal market, competition or environment. The delegation entailed a request for further research or a concrete proposal, green light for a decision on an issue, etc. Figure 3.6 displays the spread of delegated action over time.

The institutions to which tasks were delegated most often were the Commission and the Council of Ministers (see Biesenbender in Chap. 2 and Tosun in Chap. 12). Very rarely other actors such as the European Parliament and the member states were

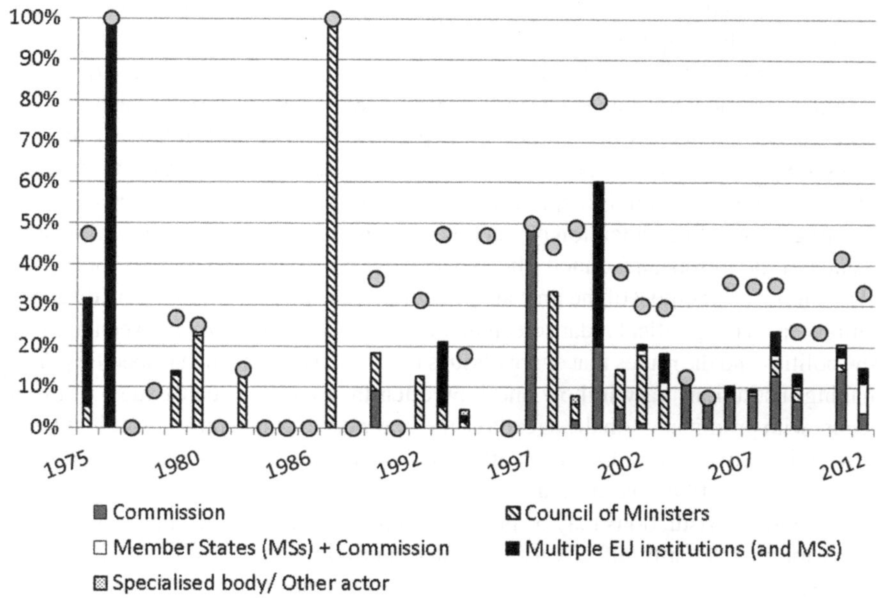

Fig. 3.6 Delegation of action to EU institutions and member states in the energy field, European Council Conclusions, 1975–2012. Total statements per year to energy-related issues = 100 %. Grey points indicate the total share of action-related statements out of all statements. *Bars* indicate the actor to which the European Council delegates an action. The *grey point* is located higher than the *upper end* of the bar when (part of) the action does not constitute delegation

the target of such requests. Thus, despite very limited formal competencies on energy policy until the Treaty of Lisbon and even though member states continued to be much in control of national energy policy-making, the signalling function of the European Council agenda had substantive effects on energy policy-making at the level of the EU. Figure 3.6 further indicates that delegation to the Commission became more frequent also in obtaining its portion of concrete actions on European energy policy.

3.9 Conclusion: Signalling and Delegating Energy Issues for EU Policy-Making

In this chapter, we presented two ways in which a policy theme may arrive on the agenda: from below in channels of low politics or from above via the high politics route. Attention to problems first may be signalled by experts or be part of routine policy-making in a subsystem devoted to a set of connected issues. Alternatively, a focusing event or major political development may create a sense of urgency among political leaders at the top and spark an expanding debate. Issues travel through policy-making institutions, and they may go up and down between these two spheres of agenda shaping: one more hidden and the other exposed to the media and the public. These different venues also alter the shape of problems; they are narrowed down and given technical definitions or take a much more dramatic load in order to mobilise support or opposition.

Policy problems however do not all follow the same route. The rise and decline in attention and the tone connected to it can be smooth or be steep and drastic. Energy policy in the EU travels up and down the political agenda, with relatively low key status as its base point. At times of normality, energy issues do not feature prominently on the European agenda. But spikes in attention occur, and often these are driven by focusing events. Such attention bursts however are rather short-lived. Looking at the agenda of the European Council (the venue at the top of the high politics route in the EU), energy issues most of the time are low priority even though they rarely disappear entirely from the political radar screen in this arena. The distinction between high and low politics and the routes that energy issues may travel also mean that specific policy-making institutions vary in how and how often they address such issues. If a topic occurs with prominence on the agenda of the European Council only episodically, this may indicate two things. One possibility is that the topic is mostly unattended in the EU and is in institutional no-man's land. New issues and those belonging to weak formal policy jurisdictions may be prone to such fuzzy status. The other possibility is that a topic is actually effectively delegated and addressed resulting in EU policy actions. On energy policy, such actions have involved constant linkages to other policy themes on which the EU developed strong formal competencies early in its existence, such as the internal market, competition and the environment. These initiatives were not substitutive to domestic energy policies in member states as the latter have much primacy in energy policy-making. Initiatives at the EU level were rather complementary and functioned to underline the need for shared strategies and harmonisation in confronting challenges from the international environment.

Analysis of the statements on energy formulated at summits by the European Council since 1975 showed that attention in this field of limited formal powers was not just symbolic. Delegation and policy action followed. Thus, if energy, in competition with other major policy topics, often stayed at the margin of the scope of attention of the Heads of State and Government in the EU, this did not mean it was left unattended. The different types of statements made in the European Council have functioned—and continue to function—to re-route energy policy issues to other policy-making arenas within the EU. This process in building and elaborating the different components of the EU energy policy agenda requires a more in-depth analysis of specific issues. Such analysis is provided in the following chapters that deal with more substantive energy policy developments, the working and regulation of the European energy market as well as with particular issues such as nuclear power and renewable energy. The studies in this volume also show how the two theoretical routes of agenda shaping and policy making co-occur in the energy policy domain.

References

Alexandrova, P., Carammia, M., & Timmermans, A. (2012). Policy punctuations and issue diversity on the European Council agenda. *Policy Studies Journal, 40*(1), 69–88.

Alexandrova, P., Carammia, M., & Timmermans, A. (2014a). EU high politics: The policy agenda of the European Council, 1975–2011. In F. Foret, & Y. Rittelmeyer (Eds.), *The European Council and European Governance. The commanding heights of the European Union* (pp. 53–72). New York: Routledge.

Alexandrova, P., Carammia, M., Princen, S., & Timmermans, A. (2014b). Measuring the European Council agenda: Introducing a new approach and dataset. *European Union Politics, 15*(1), 152–167.

Bachrach, P., & Baratz, M. S. (1962). Two faces of power. *The American Political Science Review, 56*(4), 947–952.

Baumgartner, F. R. (2013). Ideas and policy change. *Governance, 26*(2), 239–258.

Baumgartner, F. R., Breunig, C., Green-Pedersen, C., Jones, B. D., Mortensen, P. B., Nuytemans, M., et al. (2009). Punctuated equilibrium in comparative perspective. *American Journal of Political Science, 53*(3), 603–620.

Baumgartner, F. R., & Jones, B. D. (1993). *Agendas and instability in American politics*. Chicago, IL: University of Chicago Press.

Birkland, T. A. (1997). *After disaster: Agenda setting, public policy, and focusing events*. Washington: Georgetown University Press.

Buchan, D. (2010). Energy policy: Sharp challenges and rising ambitions. In W. Wallace & M. Pollack (Eds.), *Policy-making in the European Union* (pp. 357–380). Oxford: Oxford University Press.

Cobb, R., Ross, J., & Ross, M. H. (1976). Agenda building as a comparative political process. *American Political Science Review, 70*(1), 126–138.

Downs, A. (1972). Up and down with ecology: The "Issue-Attention Cycle". *Public Interest, 28*, 38–50.

Eggermont, F. (2012). *The changing role of the European Council in the institutional framework of the European Union: Consequences for the European integration process*. Mortsel: Intersentia.

Foret, F., & Rittelmeyer, Y.-S. (2014). *The European Council and European Governance. The commanding heights of the EU*. London: Routledge.

George, S. (2004). Multi-level governance and the European Union. In I. Bache & M. Flinders (Eds.), *Multi-level governance* (pp. 107–126). Oxford: Oxford University Press.

Guiraudon, V. (2000). European integration and migration policy: Vertical policy-making as venue shopping. *Journal of Common Market Studies, 38*(2), 251–271.

Hogwood, B., & Peters, G. B. (1983). *Policy dynamics*. New York: St. Martin's Press.

Hooghe, L., & Marks, G. (2001). *Multi-level governance and European Integration*. Maryland: Rowman & Littlefield Publishers.

Jennings, W., Bevan, S., Timmermans, A., Breeman, G., Brouard, S., Chaqués-Bonafont, L., et al. (2011). Effects of the core functions of government on the diversity of executive agendas. *Comparative Political Studies, 44*(8), 1001–1030.

Jones, B. D. (2012). The dynamics of agenda expansion and contraction in the U.S. *Perspectives on Europe, 42*(2), 22–28.

Jones, B. D., & Baumgartner, F. R. (2005). *The politics of attention. How government prioritizes problems*. Chicago: University of Chicago Press.

Jones, B. D., & Baumgartner, F. R. (2012). From there to here: Punctuated equilibrium to the general punctuation thesis to a theory of government information processing. *Policy Studies Journal, 40* (1), 1–20.

Kingdon, J. W. (1984). *Agendas, alternatives and public policies*. Boston: Little, Brown & Co.

Majone, G. (2005). *Dilemmas of European integration*. Oxford: Oxford University Press.

Marks, G., Hooghe, L., & Blank, K. (1996). European integration from the 1980s: State-centric v. multi-level governance. *Journal of Common Market Studies, 34*(3), 341–378.

Mortensen, P. B., Green-Pedersen, C., Breeman, G., Chaqués-Bonafont, L., Jennings, W., John, P., et al. (2011). Comparing government agendas: Executive speeches in the Netherlands, United Kingdom, and Denmark. *Comparative Political Studies, 44*(8), 973–1000.

Nisbet, M. C., & Huge, M. (2006). Attention cycles and frames in the plant biotechnology debate: Managing power and participation through the press/policy connection. *The Harvard International Journal of Press/Politics, 11*(2), 3–40.

Peters, B. G. (1994). Agenda-setting in the European community. *Journal of European Public Policy, 1*(1), 9–26.

Peters, B. G. (2001). Agenda-setting in the European Union. In J. Richardson (Ed.), *European Union. Power and policy-making* (pp. 77–94). London: Routledge.

Polsby, N. (1984). *Political innovation in America: The politics of policy initiation*. New Haven: Yale University Press.

Pralle, S. B. (2003). Venue shopping, political strategy, and policy change: The internationalization of Canadian Forest Advocacy. *Journal of Public Policy, 23*(3), 233–260.

Princen, S. (2009). *Agenda-setting in the European Union*. Basingstoke: Palgrave Macmillan.

Princen, S. (2011). Agenda-setting strategies in EU policy processes. *Journal of European Public Policy, 18*(7), 927–943.

Princen, S., & Rhinard, M. (2006). Crashing and creeping: agenda-Setting dynamics in the European Union. *Journal of European Public Policy, 13*(7), 1119–1132.

Putter, U. (2014). *The European Council and the Council. New intergovernmentalism and institutional change*. Oxford: Oxford University Press.

Rhinard, M. (2010). *Framing Europe: The policy shaping strategies of the European commission*. Dordrecht: Martinus Nijnhoff Publishers.

Riker, W. H. (1996). *The strategy of rhetoric*. New Haven: Yale University Press.

Rittberger, B. (2012). Institutionalizing representative democracy in the European Union: The case of the European Parliament. *Journal of Common Market Studies, 50*(1), 18–37.

Rochefort, D. A., & Cobb, R. W. (1994). *The politics of problem definition: Shaping the policy agenda*. Lawrence, KS: University of Kansas Press.

Schattschneider, E. E. (1960). *The semi-sovereign people: A realist's view of democracy in America*. New York: Holt, Rinehart and Winston.

Simon, H. A. (1985). Human nature in politics: The dialogue of psychology and political science. *American Political Science Review, 79*(2), 293–304.

Tallberg, J. (2008). Bargaining power in the European Council. *Journal of Common Market Studies, 46*(3), 685–708.

Tosun, J. (2011). When the grace period is over: Assessing the new member states' compliance with EU requirements for oil stockholding. *Energy Policy, 39*(11), 7156–7164.

Tosun, J., Wetzel, A., & Zapryanova, G. (2014). The EU in crisis: Advancing the debate. *Journal of European Integration, 36*(3), 195–211.

Werts, J. (2008). *The European Council*. London: John Harper Publishing.

Wilson, J. Q. (1979). American politics, then and now. *Commentary, 67*, 39–46.

Chapter 4
Exporting the Energy Acquis: The External Agenda Shaping Power of the EU

Kai Schulze

Abstract The development of EU energy policy is facing resistance from different member states. At the same time, the EU is developing an external energy policy with a view to expand its regulatory reach to third states. The EU's main instrument of this process is the Energy Community (EnC), which establishes a legal and institutional framework for EU rule exportation. These developments raise important questions. Given the difficulties in developing its own energy policy agenda, how successful can the EU's efforts to shape the energy policy agendas of non-member states be? And how can we explain success and failure of the EU's efforts? This chapter discusses how the EU exerts external agenda shaping power from a governance and framing perspective. The empirical part examines EU external agenda shaping success with regard to four energy policy measures across EnC members and observers. The results show that the EU was indeed able to influence the energy policy agendas of third states, albeit to varying degrees. While EU membership provides a powerful incentive for third states to adopt EU energy policies, alignment with EU rules can also be witnessed in countries without such a perspective or ambition. The results also suggest that successful external agenda shaping is more likely if issues can be framed in multiple ways.

4.1 Introduction

The EU's energy policy consists of an economic, security and environmental dimension (Buchan 2010).[1] While all three dimensions of energy policy are now included in the Lisbon Treaty, this does not imply that they have always been equally

[1] Moreover, a social dimension is developing, but is still in its infancy (see Bouzarovski and Petrova in Chap. 7).

K. Schulze (✉)
Faculty of Economics and Social Sciences, University of Potsdam,
August-Bebel-Str. 89, 14482 Potsdam, Germany
e-mail: kai.schulze@uni-potsdam.de

J. Tosun et al. (eds.), *Energy Policy Making in the EU*,
Lecture Notes in Energy 28, DOI 10.1007/978-1-4471-6645-0_4

salient on the agendas of the EU and the member states (neither are they today). Rather, the saliency of each dimension or frame has alternated over time (see Tosun et al. in Chap. 1; Biesenbender in Chap. 2) and so has the degree of conflict between the member states, EU institutions and sectorial interests. Arguably, one of the most conflict-laden processes has been the creation of the internal energy market, which was, despite a strong preference of the Commission, for a long time blocked by the member states (Eikeland 2004; Eberlein 2008). And even after relevant EU legislation has been adopted, the internal energy market remains difficult to realise as national models of market organisation show high levels of persistence (Fernandez and Palazuelos 2014; Helm 2014). Such persisting conflict is the reason why EU energy policy was only formalised in 2007, even though the roots of the European integration process date back to energy issues and the foundation of the European Coal and Steel Community and the European Atomic Energy Community in the 1950s.

More recently, the EU's eastern enlargement in 2004 and 2007 has been an important catalyst for the development of EU energy policy. It led to a renaissance of security concerns due to the new member states' strong dependence on Russian energy (Natorski and Herranz Surrallés 2008). For example the first gas directive was enabled by the competition or market frame, whereas the making of the third gas directive was heavily influenced by reframing energy policy as a security issue (see Herweg in Chap. 5; Brutschin in Chap. 10). However, the eastern enlargement also produced new conflict. For example, the new member states were generally more sceptical about the EU's plans to fight climate change, because they feared increased costs for their energy-intensive economies. Indeed, the conflict was partly settled only after the central and eastern European member states received additional concessions from the European Emissions System (ETS) (Buchan 2010, p. 376).

At the same time that the EU managed the formalisation of energy policy and dealt with the interest of the new member states, it also started developing a comprehensive external energy policy in order to extend its regulatory reach to non-member states. In fact, the external dimension of energy policy has become one of the European Commission's key priorities for the coming years (European Commission 2011). The EU's main instrument of this externalisation process is the Energy Community (EnC), founded in 2006, which commits its members to adopting and implementing core EU energy and competition policies.

Formally, the EU's external energy policy pursues similar objectives as its internal rules and refers to all three dimensions of energy policy. How energy issues are understood and framed along these three dimensions has important consequences for the whole policy process (see, e.g. Rochefort and Cobb 1994). More precisely, the EU seeks to establish a stable regulatory and market-based framework in order to attract investments and to create an integrated energy market as well as to improve the security of supply and the environment (European Commission 2006; Correljé and van der Linde 2006; Mañé-Estrada 2006; Prange-Gstöhl 2009a).

These developments raise important research questions: Considering the difficulties in developing its own energy policy agenda, how successful can the EU's efforts to shape the energy policy agendas of non-member states be? And how can we explain success and failure of the EU's efforts? Finally, if frames have played such an important role in the development of EU energy policy, do different frames also determine whether the EU's energy polices end up on the agendas of non-member states?

This chapter addresses these questions. After a brief introduction to the Energy Community (EnC), it discusses how the EnC's institutional features, an external governance perspective, and a framing perspective can contribute to a better understanding of the EU's external agenda shaping success. The empirical analysis examines whether the EU has been successful in shaping the energy policy agendas of third states. The focus is on four specific EU rules and whether the EnC members and observers have aligned their domestic legislation with them. The results show that both external governance mechanisms and framing strategies can help to explain EU external agenda shaping success.

4.2 The Energy Community: The External Dimension of EU Energy Policy

The EnC is a multilateral institution established by the Energy Community Treaty (ECT) which entered into force in July 2006. The organisation is deliberately modelled after the European Coal and Steel Community (and thus the origin of the EU itself) and is meant to create a pan-European sectorial market on the basis of EU energy regulations including non-EU countries (Prange-Gstöhl 2009b, p. 441). The parties to the EnC are the EU and eight members (Albania, Bosnia and Herzegovina, Kosovo, the Former Yugoslav Republic (FYR) of Macedonia, Moldova, Montenegro, Serbia and Ukraine), also known as Contracting Parties. Bulgaria and Romania were members of the EnC until 2007 and Croatia until 2013. After ascending to the EU, these countries became participant countries, joining a group of currently 16 additional EU member states.[2] Participants have the right to attend all institutional meetings of the EnC, but unlike the members, they do not hold independent voting rights. States can also join the EnC as observers with the possibility to become members in a second step.[3] Observers are not bound to adopt EU regulations but they are allowed to attend the institutional meetings. The EnC members commit to implementing core EU energy directives as well as three articles of EU competition law. The members also commit to create independent regulators and transmitting institutions to decartelise energy markets and to fight corruption (see Renner 2009 for details).

[2] The 19 participants are Austria, Bulgaria, Croatia, Cyprus, Czech Republic, Finland, France, Germany, Greece, Hungary, Italy, Latvia, Netherlands, Poland, Romania, Slovenia, Slovakia, Sweden, and the United Kingdom. Latvia and Sweden were the latest EU members to become participants in September 2014.

[3] Armenia, Georgia, Norway, Turkey are currently observers. Moldova and Ukraine became full members in 2010 and 2011 after being observers since 2006. Georgia is now a candidate for full membership, negotiating with the European Commission about its accession since February 2014.

Initially, the EnC's geographic focus was on the Western Balkans. The goal was to stabilise war-torn South-Eastern Europe by providing a framework for financial aid in energy networks in a region that functions as an important hub for energy imports from the East and thereby to prepare the countries for eventual EU membership. Promoting the adoption of EU energy law and creating a market for energy amongst the South-Eastern and Eastern European countries was seen as a major way to achieve these goals. Instead of directly receiving these countries as EU members, the EnC offered a form of sectorial regional integration in order to prepare the countries either for full EU membership or to provide them with a medium-term alternative to full membership (Renner and Trauner 2009, p. 458). However, at the latest by accepting Moldova and Ukraine as members in December 2009, the EnC dismissed its initial regional focus and started to promote the export of EU energy policy to non-EU countries more generally.

4.3 EU External Energy Policy: Mechanisms of Influence

This section discusses the mechanisms that are available to the EU for promoting the export of its energy policies to non-member states. The focus is in turn on institutional attributes of the EnC, different aspects of third states' relations with the EU (external governance mechanisms), and on framing strategies. Domestic characteristics of third states such as their political systems or the composition of their energy sectors are not discussed. They have been analysed elsewhere (see, e.g. Padgett 2012; Tosun 2012; Tosun and Schulze 2015; Brutschin in Chap. 10). Dealing with them would require policy-specific data, whereas this chapter is interested in making a contribution to combining external governance and agenda shaping perspectives more generally.

4.3.1 The Energy Community Institutions

Promoting EU rule export to non-member states, the EnC relies on a comprehensive institutional setting. Its institutions comprise a Ministerial Council, which meets once a year and serves as the principal decision-making institution, a Permanent High Level Group (PHLG), meeting every three month to prepare the Council's work, a Regulatory Board (ECRB), consisting of the national energy regulators and advising the Ministerial Council, and the PHLG, as well as four advisory Fora which serve as discussion platforms for different stakeholders in the areas of electricity, gas, social issues and oil. Finally, the Secretariat seated in Vienna is the only permanently acting institution assisting and monitoring the Contracting Parties in implementing their obligations under the ECT. As this comprehensive list reveals, the EnC is institutionally well equipped for bringing together state and non-state actors. It combines EU rule extension with the organisational inclusion of non-member states, which is typical of network governance or horizontal flexible integration (Lavenex 2008).

Its strong and flexible institutional backing enables the EnC to develop its regulatory framework and to absorb new members. This ability of the EnC to adjust its policies and institutional rules to future developments is quite unique and can be an important resource. As Padgett (2012, p. 264) points out, it can lock in member states into dynamics they did not anticipate before joining the EnC (see also Göler and Kurze 2009).

The monitoring and assistance offered by the Secretariat is quite thorough. It includes the preparation and publication of annual implementation reports, which are submitted to the Ministerial Council. Further to producing implementation reports, the Secretariat also prepares detailed roadmaps, assists the member states in drafting and amending their legislation, and organises thematic workshops to exchange experience and best practise. The Secretariat is also supported by the European Commission in a number of ways on a regular as well as case-by-case basis.

Yet despite these detailed activities, compliance with the ECT cannot be ensured in particular because the legal status and enforceability of the ECT remains uncertain and sanctions are weak. As Padgett (2012, p. 272) notes, it is possible (but not guaranteed) that such rights can be used in domestic courts which could then bring infraction to the attention of the European Court of Justice. In such cases, there is a dispute settlement procedure, created by Articles 90–93 (Title VII) of the ECT, dealing with infractions. In case of infractions, any Party, the Secretariat or the Regulatory Board, may make a reasoned request thereof to the Ministerial Council. Private bodies can approach the Secretariat with complaints. There is a preliminary procedure managed by the Secretariat, which clarifies the legal circumstances of each case before it is brought before the Ministerial Council. This usually involves an exchange in which the Party concerned has the opportunity to justify its position or to comply with the requirements. Since the adoption of the dispute settlement rules in June 2008, the Secretariat has filed numerous cases upon complaints and on the Secretariats own motion. Currently, the Secretariat has 20 dispute settlement cases ongoing.

4.3.2 External Governance Mechanisms

If the EnC's institutions cannot provide for rule transfer, which alternatives does the EU have to shape non-member states' energy policy agendas? If such a mechanism is also to explain cross-country variance in policy responses, it must relate to differences in non-member states' relations with the EU. In other words, membership in the EnC must reward countries in different ways.

The most important difference across countries is their prospect for full EU membership. While some EnC members have a more realistic perspective, membership remains a far-off scenario for others. Accession conditionality is likely to offer important incentives to put EU energy policies on domestic agendas. In this view, incentives to align domestic energy policies with EU law are strong because compliance is a necessary condition in the accession process (Padgett 2011, p. 1078).

The relatively young literature on the EU's external governance has elaborated these arguments in greater detail, as it observed that the countries of the first Eastern enlargement had to comply with the acquis communautaire in order to qualify for membership (see, e.g. Schimmelfennig and Sedelmeier 2004; Lavenex and Schimmelfennig 2009). Governance by conditionality thus entails a strongly legalised and institutionalised asymmetric relationship between the EU and a third state, where the EU offers the reward of membership in exchange for rule transfer. In more abstract terms, hierarchical external governance resembles harmonisation at the level preferred by a hegemonic state power, in this case the EU (Simmons 2001; Knill and Tosun 2009).

At first sight, it looks like this governance mechanism can only be effective if the EU has legal force in the respective country (Börzel and Risse 2012, p. 6). This is usually the case in those countries that have a status as an accession candidate. But, the logic of hierarchical governance can also apply to countries that are not (yet) accession candidates. For example a country may want to join the EnC voluntarily in order to improve its reputation as a reliable contractual partners more generally, and eventually (though not necessarily) in the case of EU membership (Chayes and Chayes 1993, p. 177; Schulze and Tosun 2013, p. 585). Recall that the EnC's institutional flexibility means that such a country can even commit to unanticipated developments, not only ahead of accession, but also independent of a credible membership perspective. Therefore, in this argument, the credibility of the accession perspective is a decisive factor (Epstein and Sedelmeier 2008; Schimmelfennig and Scholtz 2008; Trauner 2009).

Even though the EU accession prospect is a sufficient condition for alignment with EU policies, it is not necessary for such developments (Schimmelfennig and Sedelmeier 2004, p. 673). EU external influence can also be exercised through markets and networks. These non-hierarchical mechanisms can coincide with accession conditionality, but they can also work independently and supersede the hierarchical exchange mechanism.

Markets and investments can offer important incentives for third states to comply with EU law (Bauer et al. 2007; Prange-Gstöhl 2009b; Lindstrom 2011; Tosun 2012; Schulze and Tosun 2013). If incentives are created through markets, this means that that under certain circumstances or for some actors, the trade-related benefits conferred by aligning energy policies with EU law may actually outweigh the costs.[4] This creates incentives for potential beneficiaries to lobby for placing EU energy policies on domestic agendas. The second mechanism, investments, speaks

[4] These benefits can relate to the possibility to sell energy or energy products on the EU's markets or to efficiency gains from opening up domestic markets for foreign competitors. The former scenario is arguably more likely for countries that make net sales in energy (or a certain types of energy) to the EU market (see Bradford 2012).

to one of the main reasons for establishing the EnC in the first place: the establishment of an investor-friendly framework in the Western Balkans. Accordingly, alignment with EU energy law promises to provide a more attractive environment for investors, raising the incentives for adopting EU energy policies in those countries in need of investments (Prange-Gstöhl 2009b). Third states can not only trade alignment for investments, but investments and technical assistance provided by EU institutions can also strengthen these states' capacity to implement EU energy legislation and thus reduce the costs of putting them on the agenda (Prange-Gstöhl 2009a, p. 5300; Fagan 2012). Investments can also relate to the environmental dimension of energy policy by bringing in required technologies to alleviate environmental problems (Perkins and Neumayer 2012). Finally, markets and investments can also contribute to improving the security of supply by diversifying the sources for energy imports and production or by bringing in technologies that improve energy efficiency (Tosun 2012).

In contrast to accession conditionality and markets, external governance through networks is characterised by more symmetrical exchange. Two closely related mechanisms of EU influence are possible: On the one hand, networks and communication can trigger rational processes of learning and persuade third states of the legitimacy of EU policies. On the other hand, communication can trigger socialisation processes where third states update their norms and beliefs as they start seeing EU policies as the appropriate rules (e.g. Eising 2002; Meseguer 2006; Börzel and Risse 2012; for a critical assessment see Noutcheva 2009). Of the EnC's institutions, the Board of Regulators (ECRB) as well as the advisory fora and thematical workshops are non-hierarchical venues, which are suited to influence national agendas via socialisation and/or persuasion.[5] Following Lavenex (2008, p. 943), the ECRB can be characterised as an implementation network of experts and technocrats (national regulators) with shared beliefs and special knowledge that may contribute to the de-politicisation of cooperation (see also Haas 1992). By contrast, the advisory fora involving different stakeholders and non-state actors rather represent information networks that share best practise, policy-relevant knowledge and ideas. Moreover, the EnC engages non-state actors not only in the advisory fora, but also gives them the possibility to wage complaints about non-compliance at the EnC Secretariat. Such arrangements are typical of network governance, which tends to blur the divide between public and private actors by offering new roles, opportunities, and shared responsibility (see, e.g. Héritier and Rhodes 2011).

Table 4.1 summarises the theoretical discussion so far. The framework distinguishes between a demand-side perspective (i.e. the perspective of the non-member states), which identifies the rewards offered to non-member states when joining the EnC; and a supply-side perspective, which identifies the resources and activities

[5] Padgett (2011, p. 1077) argues that the ECRB is more effective in prompting such processes than the fora.

Table 4.1 EU/EnC external governance mechanisms

	Governance mechanism	EnC rewards (demand-side perspective)	EnC reinforcement (supply-side perspective)
Accession	Coercion, hierarchy	Conditionality, cooperative reputation	Institutional evolvement (lock-in), monitoring and enforcement
Markets and investments	Competition, capacity building	Efficiency gains, market access, investments, financial aid, security of supply (diversification), sustainability (clean technology)	Investments, financial aid
Networks	Socialisation, persuasion	Expertise, norms and values	Regular communication, expertise and best practise, draft legislation

Source Own compilation based on Lavenex and Schimmelfennig (2009), Börzel and Risse (2012), Padgett (2012)

employed by the EnC in pursuit of its goals. We can see that the EU can effectively rely on a combination of different incentives, socialisation, and capacity building when trying to shape the energy policy agendas of third states.

4.3.3 Policy Frames

External governance mechanisms are particularly suitable for explaining third states' diverging responses to EU rules. But what about common patterns or variance across policies? This section contends that a framing perspective which identifies the frames that can be attached to policies can improve our understanding of such patterns or cross-policy variance.

The framing of issues is fundamental to the process of public policy making. It influences each stage of the policy process from issue initiation to final legislative enactment (Rochefort and Cobb 1994). Framing is about creating or changing the terms in which an issue or problem is defined or about emphasising or deemphasising certain aspects of problems in order lend them to particular solutions. Political actors can make strategic use of frames in order to structure the political conflict in their favour. More precisely, strategic actors can engage in framing by emphasising or reemphasising certain images in order to place issues on the agenda, to structure issues already on the agenda, or to keep certain issues off the agenda (Baumgartner and Jones 1991; Daviter 2007; Knill and Tosun 2012, pp. 102–103).

The relevant question for policy making is whether a frame can get enough attention and mobilise a sufficient number of actors to lift an issue on the institutional agenda and eventually to trigger a policy decision. Moreover, for issues to come onto the EU agenda, gaining attention is not enough. Actors also need to be convinced that the EU is the appropriate organisation to deal with the issue (Princen 2011). By contrast, EU external agenda shaping means that national policymakers in non-member states need to be convinced that an issue requires attention and that the EU's policies are appropriate solutions to these issues. This can be achieved by making reference to known policy priorities and commitments, by reference to focussing event (see further below) as well as by linking issues to already existing EU policies or by claiming that joint action with the EU will produce mutual gains (Princen 2011, pp. 933–938).

In EU energy policy, the most basic frames relate to the policy field's three dimensions, i.e. the economic, security, and environmental frame. As the salience of each frame has changed over time, it has given certain frames at times predominance over others and thereby left its mark on the EU energy policy agenda (see, e.g. Alexandrova and Timmermans in Chap. 3). For example the first successful steps towards the liberalisation of the European gas market were enabled by the competition frame, whereas the making of the third gas directive was heavily influenced by a reframing of energy policy as a security issue in the wake of eastern enlargement (see Herweg in Chap. 5; Brutschin in Chap. 10).

Issues or specific policies can also be framed in more than one way at the same time (see Tosun in Chap. 12). Frames do not exist in isolation but they can interact in meaningful ways. Successful policy adoption can therefore not only depend on the predominant frame but also on the number of different frames that are available in the process. Adding new dimensions to issues and establishing linkages across frames can thus be an important strategy to broaden the scope of debate and to increase the likelihood of successful agenda-setting and legislative action. The cross-sectional nature of energy policy offers plenty of opportunities for this (see Ciambra and Solorio in Chap. 8). For example, in the run-up to the 2007 spring European Council, the Commission has successfully aimed at 'selling' the completion of the internal energy market as a solution to both security and environmental problems (Eikeland 2011, p. 251). Di Lucia and Kronsell (2010) argue that EU policies are more likely to be implemented if the national frame matches the one at the EU level. Even though this study does not deal with implementation, the same argument can be made for policy adoption. Accordingly, the likelihood of successful external agenda shaping rises if the way(s) in which an EU policy is framed finds a correspondent in national discourse. Naturally, the likelihood of finding a correspondent should increase the more frames are attached to a given policy and linked with each other. All in all, we can expect that EU policies which can be framed in multiple ways will more likely end up on national agendas and lead to legislative action.

Closely related to the question about the role of frames for policy making is the question about the role of events. Extraordinary or "focussing" events (Birkland 2004) can offer new opportunities for actors to place issues on the agenda by defining a problem in a new or additional way, i.e. by emphasising or deemphasising an existing image or by adding other images to already existing ones. For example, the gas disputes between Russia and Ukraine mentioned earlier have contributed to successfully framing energy policy as a matter of security again (Buchan 2010). Of course, events can not only change agendas at the EU level, but they can also influence the way governments and other actors respond to EU policies. The security frame, for example, was particularly helpful for furthering compliance with EU energy policies in a number of Eastern member states (Tosun 2011).

4.4 Four EU Energy Policy Measures

Rather than focussing on the whole energy acquis or entire directives, this section examines whether third states have aligned their domestic energy legislation with four specific requirements from the EnC's acquis on oil, gas, renewables and energy efficiency. The selected measures are: requirements for the holding of emergency oil stocks, the establishment of third party access to national gas markets, and the setting of targets for the use of biofuels and for energy savings (see Table 4.2). Focussing on entire directives would be difficult because they have undergone too many important changes and contain too many rules for assessment in a single comparative study. The selection of the four aforementioned policy measures aims at representing different sectors of energy policy and to acknowledge the growing scope of EU energy policy (see, e.g. Kanellakis et al. 2013; Biesenbender in Chap. 2).

This study defines EU external agenda shaping success as the formal adoption of EU policy measures by non-member states. More precisely, successful agenda shaping refers to agenda-setting, agenda structuring, and agenda exclusion leading to legislative action. Of course, there are alternative ways to conceptualise external agenda shaping or agenda shaping success. External agenda shaping should be observed prior to the adoption of legislation, for example: by looking at preparatory acts, motions or speeches in the relevant bodies. This is usually achieved in detailed case studies or in comparative analyses that have undertaken large data collection efforts (see, e.g. Baumgartner et al. 2009; Jennings et al. 2011; Alexandrova and Timmermans in Chap. 3).[6] The four policy measures under study are briefly introduced in the following. A summary is offered in Table 4.2.

Emergency oil stocks. The requirement to hold emergency oil stocks is the only item of the acquis on oil. Directive 2009/119/EC, accepted by the EnC Ministerial Council in October 2012, obliges the EnC members to hold emergency oil stocks equal to at least 90 days of net imports or 61 days of inland consumption during the

[6] The focus on formal adoption may thus underestimate the size (but not the success as defined here) of EU induced energy policy agendas because having an issue considered by policy makers is a necessary (but not sufficient) condition for policy adoptions whereas consideration by policy makers does not necessarily lead to policy adoption. Certainly, it is also possible that third states adopt national energy legislation conforming to EU rules in response to similar problems without taking account of the EU requirement. If this happens, the present study would overestimate the EU's influence. However, in this context, it is important to note that the legal acts reviewed for this study usually make explicit reference to the EU requirement and can thus be traced back to the EU's influence. All in all, it seems fair to say that the present study provides a rather conservative estimate of the EU's external agenda influence.

Table 4.2 Timeline of four EU energy policies

Holding of emergency oil stocks	Third party access to gas markets	Targets for biofuel content	Targets for energy savings
Directive 68/414/EEC: stockholding for 65 days average daily internal consumption			
Directive 72/425/EEC: stockholding for 90 days average daily internal consumption			
Directive 73/238/EEC: specific measures to mitigate difficulties in oil supply			
Directive 98/93/EC: stockholding for 90 days average daily internal consumption	Directive 98/30/EC: negotiated or regulated terms of access		Directive 93/76/EEC: no targets, but setup of programmes, e.g. on the energy certification of buildings, the billing of heating installations, energy audits
Directive 2006/67/EC: stockholding for 90 days of average daily internal consumption	Directive 2003/55/EC: regulated terms of access; implementation deadline: 2007 (Contracting Parties), 2009 (Moldova), and 2012 (Ukraine)	Directive 2003/30/EC: setup of national indicative targets, reference values of 2 percent by 2005 and 5.75 % by 2010 for all petrol and diesel for transport purposes placed on markets; no implementation deadline, but plans to be submitted by 2007	Directive 2006/32/EC: setup of overall national indicative energy savings target, reference value of 9 % by 2018; implementation deadline: 2011
2008 EnC Ministerial Council decision to include the oil sector and to implement Directive 2006/67/EC			

(continued)

Table 4.2 (continued)

Holding of emergency oil stocks	Third party access to gas markets	Targets for biofuel content	Targets for energy savings
Directive 2009/119/EC: adjustment to IEA rules, stockholding for 90 days of net imports or 61 days of inland consumption	Directive 2009/73/EC: regulated terms of access; implementation deadline: 2015	Directive 2009/28/EC: uniform mandatory national overall targets, share of energy from renewable sources in all forms of transport in 2020 at least 10 % of the final consumption of energy in transport	
2012 EnC Ministerial Council adopts Directive 2009/119/EC, implementation deadline: 2023		2012 EnC Ministerial Council adopts Directive 2009/28/EC, Implementation deadline: 2014	

Sources Buchan (2010), Energy Community Secretariat (2012, 2013), Tosun (2011, 2012), Tosun and Schulze (2013, 2015)

preceding calendar year. The EU rules on emergency oil stocks have a long history that dates back as far as Council Directive 68/414/EEC, which first laid down the obligation to build up and maintain strategic oil stocks. Council Directive 72/425/EEC later raised the obligation for stocks from a 65 days equivalent of the daily internal consumption to a 90 days equivalent. Council Directive 98/93/EC developed and strengthened the existing provisions, but just like the replacing Directive 2006/67/EC, did not change the target for oil stockholding (see Table 4.2 and Tosun 2011, 2012 for an overview). In December 2008, the Ministerial Council decided that the EnC should also implement Directive 2006/67/EC.

Third party access to gas markets. The EU's internal gas market is governed by Directive 2009/73/EC, which repealed Directive 2003/55/EC (which previously repealed Directive 98/30/EC). For the purpose of this study, I focus on one specific provision, i.e. Third Party Access (TPA) to transmission and distribution networks. Even though the internal gas market was already established by Directive 98/30/EC, the focus is on Directive 2003/55/EC because it first established regulated TPA, a provision that remains unchanged by Directive 2009/73/EC.[7] Its implementation was expected by 1 July 2007 for the original Contracting Parties, by 31 December 2009 for Moldova, and by 1 January 2012 for Ukraine. Directive 2003/55/EC provides for the complete opening of national gas markets to competition in order to improve service quality, guarantee fair prices for consumers, establish rules on

[7] In 2007, Regulation (EC) 1775/2005 on Conditions for Access to the Natural Gas Networks (repealed in 2009 by Regulation (EC) 715/2009) was added to the acquis by a Ministerial Council decision. The regulation lays down the details for the regulation of access to the natural gas transmission network.

public service obligations, improve interconnection, and bolster the security of supply. The directive establishes the right of third parties to non-discriminatory access to transmission and distribution systems and to liquefied natural gas facilities. This way, new suppliers and even small ones can enter the market. For this purpose, fair competition conditions must be put in place to prevent dominant positions of traditional operators.

Biofuel contents. Directive 2003/30/EC on the promotion of biofuels is part of the acquis on renewables. According to the directive, conventional transport fuels should be partly substituted with biofuels derived from agricultural crops, notably biodiesel and bioethanol (Di Lucia and Kronsell 2010; Tosun and Schulze 2015). The focus here is on the directive's requirement for setting up national indicative targets for all petrol and diesel for transport purposes placed on markets. In particular, the directive set the reference values at 2 % by 2005 and 5.75 % by 2010. Due to limited implementation success, the EU Commission requested in 2007 that a mandatory minimum target of 10 % for biofuels in the overall consumption of petrol and diesel in transport by 2020 must be set (European Commission 2007, p. 10). This request was incorporated in Directive 2009/28/EC on the promotion of the use of energy from renewable sources setting mandatory national overall targets for the share of energy from renewable sources (not only from biofuels) in all forms of transport at 10 % by 2020. The obligation was taken over for the EnC Contracting Parties in October 2012 by Ministerial Council Decision 2012/04/MC-EnC. The analysis focusses on which EnC members adopted national biofuel targets in line with Directive 2003/30/EC, but without regard to the precise specifications of the targets.

Energy savings. The acquis on energy efficiency consists of three directives dealing with the labelling of energy-related products, the energy performance of buildings, and energy end-use efficiency and savings. The focus here is on the latter (Directive 2006/32/EC), which replaced Council Directive 93/76/EEC and requires, among other things, the adoption of a national indicative energy savings target of 9 % by 2018. The Contracting Parties have to submit National Energy Efficiency Action Plans (NEEAP) containing their targets and the measures taken to achieve the targets in 2007, 2011, and 2017. The present study counts the definition of any indicative target by national authorities as successful transposition, irrespective of the target's exact specification, and therefore any attempt made by third states to approximate the relevant EU rules.

4.5 Patterns of External Agenda Shaping Success

This section reviews whether we can find (descriptive) evidence that the EU has been successful in shaping the EnC members' and observers' energy policy agendas.[8] The focus is on the effects of (pre-)accession conditionality, i.e. the

[8] Norway is excluded as it is the only Western EnC observer and has rather exceptional incentives to accept or reject EU energy policies.

hierarchical mode of external governance. A separate analysis of market and network governance is beyond the exploratory scope if this study.[9] Information on domestic rule adoption and alignment was compiled using the EnC Secretariat's annual implementation reports, various academic and official sources as well as previous studies (Tosun 2012; Tosun and Schulze 2013, 2015). Table 4.3 summarises the patterns of policy adoption across the countries under study.[10]

As has been argued earlier, the credibility of the accession perspective is a decisive factor in the hierarchical mode of external governance (Epstein and Sedelmeier 2008). Moreover, the credibility of conditionality can be expected increase with each step in the accession process (Padgett 2012; Böhmelt and Freyburg 2013; Tosun and Schulze 2015). To illustrate the effects of this mechanism, Table 4.3 also summarises the status of the EnC members and observers in the accession process ranging from the adoption of an association agreement to the conclusion of the accession negotiations.

A number of regularities and variation across countries and across the four policies immediately stand out. To begin with, alignment with EU energy policies can be witnessed over the whole country sample and not only among the EnC member states. But we can also easily see that countries, which are more advanced in the accession process, are more likely to have adopted the four energy policy measures. Thus, accession conditionality seems to be effective. This finding is not trivial if we consider that energy is not a high priority in the accession process of South-Eastern and Eastern Europe.

For example, Croatia has been rather quick in aligning its energy policies with the EU requirements and actually closed the energy chapter of the accession negotiations in 2011 (Montenegro and Turkey have not yet negotiated about energy policy in the accession process). Considering that Croatia has been an accession candidate since 2004 and part of a Stabilisation and Association Agreement (SAA) since 2001, accession conditionality seems to have influenced Croatia's energy policy agenda. This result matches Padgett's (2012) study, who moreover finds that EnC membership had a positive impact on the speed of Croatia's adjustments, especially if compared to the slower progress of Bulgaria and Rumania—countries that adjusted their energy policies, while not being members to the EnC.

FYR Macedonia, which is an EU candidate since 2005, has also adopted all four policies measures under study. So has Albania, which became an official candidate for EU membership in 2014, but had signed an SAA already in 2006. Montenegro and Serbia, which became accession candidates in 2010 and 2012 respectively, have adopted three policies each. Interestingly, Albania, Montenegro and Serbia have all adopted these policies before becoming official accession candidates—quite in

[9] Even though conditionality is likely to be a comprehensive factor for rule transfer, it is also possible that markets and networks supersede the dominant features of conditionality (Schimmelfennig and Sedelmeier 2004, p. 662). Identifying the independent and interactive effects of these mechanisms in EU external energy policy represents an important avenue for future research.

[10] A protocol of the coding decisions and data sources for each country and policy is available from the author.

Table 4.3 EU/EnC status and the adoption of four EU energy policies

Country	Oil stocks	Gas markets	Biofuels	Energy savings	Association agreement	EU application	EU candidate	EU negotiations	EnC member	EnC observer
Croatia	2003	2007	2005	2008	2001	2003	2004–13	2005–13	2006	–
FYR Macedonia	2008	2011	2006	2011	2001	2004	2005	–	2006	–
Albania	2003	2008	2008	2011	2006	2009	2014	–	2006	–
Montenegro	2010	2010	–	2010	2007	2008	2010	2012	2007	–
Serbia	2006	2011	(2009)	2010	2008	2009	2012	–	2006	–
Bosnia-Herzegovina	2013[a]	–	2008[a]	–	2008	–	–	–	2006	–
Kosovo	–	2009	–	2011	–	–	–	–	2006	–
Moldova	–	2009	2007	2011	–	–	–	–	2010	2006–10
Ukraine	2009	2010	(2009)	–	–	–	–	–	2011	2006–11
Turkey	2003	2002	(2012)	2012	1963	1987	1999	2005	–	2006
Armenia	–	2001	–	2007	–	–	–	–	–	2011
Georgia	–	2007	–	–	–	–	–	–	–	2007

Note [a] Targets exist for the Republika Srpska and the Federation of Bosnia and Herzegovina, but no single national target. Parentheses indicate biofuel targets that are below the EU reference contrast to Croatia and FYR Macedonia. This trend could indicate that the EnC facilitates EU rule transfer ahead or even independent of an official candidate status.

Another meaningful observation concerns Moldova and Ukraine. These countries have aligned two (three) policies, while being observers to the EnC and before joining the EnC as full members. Given that EU membership is not a realistic scenario for these countries, this pattern gives another hint that EU external agenda shaping can be successfully exercised through the EnC and its institutions.

Finally, there is the exceptional status of Turkey, which appears to be in an advanced state of energy policy alignment, but refuses to become a full member of the EnC. Turkey can be taken as evidence for the downside of sectoral integration. If the accession prospect lacks credibility, Turkey may see EnC membership as actually decreasing its prospect for full EU membership and a type of 'second class membership'.

Table 4.4 puts successful external agenda shaping in relation to the major frames that are attached to the four policies under study. The different frames attached to each policy were primarily extracted from the respective EU documents (directives). According to Table 4.4, all policy measures claim to contribute to improving the security of supply. For example more efficient gas markets, energy savings and the use of biofuels can all decrease the dependence on energy imports. In fact, the wish to decrease dependency on Russia is one of the most important common denominator of the EnC members.

Yet only one measure—third party access to gas markets—can plausibly be framed in terms of competition or market creation. The setting of mandatory targets for energy savings and the use of biofuels, by contrast, represent interventions into energy markets. Finally, the build-up of emergency oil stocks cannot claim a market creating function either.[11] Energy saving targets and gas markets are moreover expected to contribute to environmental protection, whereas emergency oil stocks cannot claim such a contribution. The issue of biofuel targets is more complicated. While the directive was designed as a contribution to reducing CO_2 emissions and air pollution, biofuels are now also fiercely criticised, for example because of their negative effects on biodiversity and rural development (see, e.g. Levidow 2013).

According to the theoretical argument made above, adding dimensions to issues can broaden the scope of debate and thereby increase the likelihood that an issue will become subject to serious consideration by policy makers. The results presented in Table 4.4 seem to support the argument. Third party access to gas

[11] Certainly, meeting the targets for the use of biofuels should be subject to market rules, i.e. it should be possible for countries to meet their demand by importing biofuels and selling overproduction, which means that there is some market creation. But the setting of targets for renewable energy in fuels cannot be associated with the competition frame as such targets put a new constraint on fuel markets. Similarly, while fair competition among energy service providers should be ensured in the implementation of the energy efficiency directive, the setting of the target itself represents a market intervention. In fact, the regulation was justified by noting that the liberalisation of energy markets had led to efficiency gains and lower costs of energy generation, transformation and distribution, but largely failed to improve efficiency on the demand side (2006/32/EC: (9)).

Table 4.4 The framing of four EU energy policies

	Competition	Security	Environment	Adoptions
Oil stocks	No	Yes	No	8 (66.7)
Gas markets	Yes	Yes	Yes	11 (91.7)
Biofuel targets	No	Yes	(Yes)	5 (41.7)
Energy efficiency	No	Yes	Yes	9 (75.0)

Note Numbers in parentheses are percentages

markets, which is framed in all three dimensions, has been established in every country but one (Bosnia and Herzegovina).

Broadening the scope of debate in the case of the gas market was enabled by a series of events but in particular by the gas disputes between Ukraine and Russia. These events have contributed to increased attention and acceptance of EU gas policies across the country sample. We can thus confirm this volumes' hypothesis that agenda shaping is driven by events, in particular with regard to the security frame. Certainly, many EnC members, for example in the Western Balkans, were directly affected by the threat to be cut off from Russian gas supplies, which has enabled to link the liberalisation (competition) frame to the security frame in such an effective way (Brutschin in Chap. 10). The study can therefore also confirm the hypothesis that establishing links across frames is a powerful strategy for exerting external agenda shaping power.

However, it must be noted that the argument about multiple frames does not exclude the possibility that frames can vary in strength and appeal. For example, it is possible that a single attractive frame is sufficient for leading to policy adoption. The competition frame is certainly one of the most attractive frames in the eyes of the European Commission. Its importance is moreover supported by the inclusion of a number of competition directives in the ECT. Further comparison with other policies that speak to the competition frame are necessary to gain a better understanding of the frame's importance for external agenda shaping.

By contrast, biofuel targets in line with the EU requirements have only been adopted by five countries so far. This may testify to the issue's questionable environmental contribution, which may induce domestic actors like environmental groups to lobby for keeping the issue off the agenda (Tosun and Schulze 2015).

The comparatively low number of adopted requirements to hold emergency oil stocks may not only be due to the low number of supporting frames, but also due to the high costs that are associated with the policy's implementation (Tosun 2011).

4.6 Conclusion

This chapter pursued the objective of examining the capacity of Community institutions to successfully shape the energy policy agendas of third states. For this purpose, the empirical analysis compared the passage of four energy policy measures across the members and observers of the Energy Community (EnC). The results suggest that pre-accession conditionality is an important element of EU external agenda influence. Moreover, there is initial evidence that the EnC facilitates EU rule transfer ahead of or even independent of accession. However, in this context, we must not forget that policy adoption does not imply successful implementation. Generally speaking, the focus on policy adoption is likely to overstate the external influence of the EnC and the EU given that implementation is usually the more costly part of rule transfer and more likely to meet domestic resistance (Schimmelfennig and Sedelmeier 2004).

The study has also shown that a framing perspective can contribute important insight to our understanding of external agenda shaping. In particular, the likelihood of successful external agenda shaping rises for energy policies that can be framed in multiple ways. In this case, the likelihood increases that the policy will encounter a favourable discourse at the national level. Moreover, establishing meaningful linkages across multiple frames can be an important strategy also in external agenda shaping. Finally, events contribute to successful external agenda shaping.

The present study has been exploratory and more detailed analyses will be necessary, in particular to understand the link between external governance and framing strategies. In particular, it could be interesting to see how markets and networks interact with the framing of energy policies. For example, are countries that trade more intensely with the EU more receptive of the competition frame? Which frames are most attractive to the mechanisms of learning and persuasion? Answers to these questions should be of interest to both scholars and practitioners of the European integration process.

Finally, framing strategies should also be studied in relation to domestic factors. Even though the chapter by Brutschin has shown that framing is more important for policy shaping than objective domestic factors, this hypothesis must not be true for external agenda shaping. Moreover, the argument should be also evaluated for other energy policy sectors. Finally, the role of national policy makers and non-state actors should be further explored as they moderate national responses to the EU's external agenda shaping efforts (see, e.g. Grabbe 2001; Subotic 2010; Fagan 2012; Vachudova 2014).

Finally, the third type of agenda shaping, i.e. agenda exclusion (Tallberg 2003), should be studied in greater detail in the context of the EU's external relations. The relevant question is whether the EU's external energy governance can suppress attention to other (pressing) energy-related problems in the non-member states.

References

Bauer, M. W., Knill, C., & Pitschel, D. (2007). Differential Europeanization in Eastern Europe: The impact of diverse EU regulatory governance patterns. *Journal of European Integration, 29* (4), 405–423.

Baumgartner, F. R., & Jones, B. D. (1991). Agenda dynamics and policy subsystems. *The Journal of Politics, 53*(4), 1044–1074.

Baumgartner, F. R., Breunig, C., Green-Pedersen, C., Jones, B. D., Mortensen, P. B., Neytemans, M., Walgraave, S. (2009). Punctuated equilibrium in comparative perspective. *American Journal of Political Science, 53*(3), 602–619.

Birkland, T. A. (2004). "The World Changed Today": Agenda-setting and policy change in the wake of the Sept. 11 terrorist attacks. *Review of Policy Research, 21*(2), 179–200.

Böhmelt, T., & Freyburg, T. (2013). The temporal dimension of the credibility of EU conditionality and candidate states' compliance with the acquis communautaire, 1998–2009. *European Union Politics, 14*(2), 250–272.

Börzel, T. A., & Risse, T. (2012). From Europeanisation to diffusion: introduction. *West European Politics, 35*(1), 1–19.

Bradford, A. (2012). The Brussels effect. *Northwestern University Law Review, 107*(1), 1–68.

Buchan, D. (2010). Energy policy: Sharp challenges and rising ambitions. In H. Wallace, M. A. Pollack & A. R. Young (Eds.), *Policy-making in the European Union* (pp. 357–379). Oxford: Oxford University Press.

Chayes, A., & Chayes, A. H. (1993). On compliance. *International Organization, 47*(2), 175–202.

Correljé, A., & van der Linde, C. (2006). Energy supply security and geopolitics: A European perspective. *Energy Policy, 34*(5), 532–543.

Daviter, F. (2007). Policy framing in the European Union. *Journal of European Public Policy, 14* (4), 654–666.

Di Lucia, L., & Kronsell, A. (2010). The willing, the unwilling and the unable—explaining implementation of the EU biofuels directive. *Journal of European Public Policy, 17*(4), 545–563.

Eberlein, B. (2008). The making of the European energy market: The interplay of governance and government. *Journal of Public Policy, 28*(1), 73–92.

Eikeland, P.O. (2004). *The long and winding road to the internal energy market. Consistencies and inconsistencies in EU policy* (FNI Report No. 8). Lysaker: Fridtjof Nansen Institute.

Eikeland, P. O. (2011). The third internal energy market package: New power relations among member states, EU institutions and non-state actors? *Journal of Common Market Studies, 49* (2), 243–263.

Eising, R. (2002). Policy learning in embedded negotiations: Explaining EU electricity liberalization. *International Organization, 56*(1), 85–120.

Energy Community Secretariat. (2012). *Annual implementation report.* Vienna: Energy Community.

Energy Community Secretariat. (2013). *Annual implementation report.* Vienna: Energy Community.

Epstein, R. A., & Sedelmeier, U. (2008). Beyond conditionality: International institutions in postcommunist Europe after enlargement. *Journal of European Public Policy, 15*(6), 795–805.

European Commission (2006). *Communication from the Commission to the European Council: External energy relations—from principles to action*, (COM(2006) 590 final). Brussels.

European Commission (2007). *Communication from the Commission to the Council and the European Parliament: Renewable energy road map*, (COM(2006) 848 final). Brussels.

European Commission (2011). *Communication from the Commission to the European Parliament, the Council, the European Economic and Social Committee and the Committee of the Regions: On security of energy supply and international cooperation—"The EU energy policy: Engaging with partners beyond our borders"*, (COM(2011) 539 final). Brussels.

Fagan, A. (2012). Building environmental governance in Bosnia-Herzegovina: Europeanisation and transnational assistance in the context of limited statehood. *Environment and Planning C: Government and Policy, 30*(4), 643–657.

Fernandez, R., & Palazuelos, E. (2014). A political economy approach to the European Union gas model: Continuities and changes. *Journal of Common Market Studies, 52*(3), 495–511.

Göler, D., & Kurze, K. (2009). Die EU als transnationaler polity-shaper—Über die Schaffung sektoraler Governance-Strukturen am Beispiel der Energiegemeinschaft. *Österreichische Zeitschrift für Politikwissenschaft (ÖZP), 38*(4), 423–436.

Grabbe, H. (2001). How does Europeanization affect CEE governance? Conditionality, diffusion and diversity. *Journal of European Public Policy, 8*(6), 1013–1031.
Haas, P. M. (1992). Introduction: Epistemic communities and international policy coordination. *International Organization, 46*(1), 1–35.
Helm, D. (2014). The European framework for energy and climate policies. *Energy Policy, 64*, 29–35.
Héritier, A., & Rhodes, M. (Eds.). (2011). *New modes of governance in Europe: Governing in the shadow of hierarchy*. Basingstoke: Palgrave Macmillan.
Jennings, W., Bevan, S., Timmermans, A., Breeman, G., Brouard, S., Chaques-Bonafont, L., et al. (2011). Effects of the core functions of government on the diversity of executive agendas. *Comparative Political Studies, 44*(8), 1001–1030.
Kanellakis, M., Martinopoulos, G., & Zachariadis, T. (2013). European energy policy—A review. *Energy Policy, 62*, 1020–1030.
Knill, C., & Tosun, J. (2009). Hierarchy, networks, or markets: How does the EU shape environmental policy adoptions within and beyond its borders? *Journal of European Public Policy, 16*(6), 873–894.
Knill, C., & Tosun, J. (2012). *Public policy: A new introduction*. Basingstoke: Palgrave Macmillan.
Lavenex, S. (2008). A Governance perspective on the European neighbourhood policy: Integration beyond conditionality? *Journal of European Public Policy, 15*(6), 938–955.
Lavenex, S., & Schimmelfennig, F. (2009). EU rules beyond EU borders: Theorizing external governance in European politics. *Journal of European Public Policy, 16*(6), 791–812.
Lindstrom, N. (2011). Power trips: Europeanization, market-governance, and energy policy in the Western Balkans. *Policy and Society, 30*(3), 197–207.
Mañé-Estrada, A. (2006). European energy security: Towards the creation of the geo-energy space. *Energy Policy, 34*(18), 3773–3786.
Meseguer, C. (2006). Rational learning and bounded learning in the diffusion of policy innovations. *Rationality and Society, 18*(1), 35–66.
Natorski, M., & Herranz Surrallés, A. (2008). Securitizing moves to nowhere? The framing of the European Union's energy policy. *Journal of Contemporary European Research, 4*(2), 71–89.
Noutcheva, G. (2009). Fake, partial and imposed compliance: The limits of the EU's normative power in the Western Balkans. *Journal of European Public Policy, 16*(7), 1065–1084.
Padgett, S. (2011). Energy co-operation in the wider Europe: Institutionalizing interdependence. *Journal of Common Market Studies, 49*(5), 1065–1087.
Padgett, S. (2012). Multilateral institutions, accession conditionality and rule transfer in the European Union: The energy community in south east Europe. *Journal of Public Policy, 32*(3), 261–282.
Perkins, R., & Neumayer, E. (2012). Does the 'California effect' operate across borders? Trading- and investing-up in automobile emission standards. *Journal of European Public Policy, 19*(2), 217–237.
Prange-Gstöhl, H. (2009a). Enlarging the EU's internal energy market: Why would third countries accept EU rule export? *Energy Policy, 37*(12), 5296–5303.
Prange-Gstöhl, H. (2009b). Sektorale Integration in den EU-Binnenmarkt—Zur Nachfrageseite europäischer Energieaußenpolitik. *Österreichische Zeitschrift für Politikwissenschaft (ÖZP), 38*(4), 437–451.
Princen, S. (2011). Agenda-setting strategies in EU policy processes. *Journal of European Public Policy, 18*(7), 927–943.
Renner, S. (2009). The Energy Community of Southeast Europe: A neofunctionalist project of regional integration. *European Integration online Papers (EIoP), 13*(1), 1–21.
Renner, S., & Trauner, F. (2009). Creeping EU membership in South-east Europe: The dynamics of EU rule transfer to the Western Balkans. *Journal of European Integration, 31*(4), 449–465.
Rochefort, D. A., & Cobb, R. W. (1994). *The politics of problem definition: Shaping the policy agenda*. Lawrence: University Press of Kansas.

Schimmelfennig, F., & Scholtz, H. (2008). EU democracy promotion in the European neighbourhood: Political conditionality, economic development and transnational exchange. *European Union Politics, 9*(2), 187–215.

Schimmelfennig, F., & Sedelmeier, U. (2004). Governance by conditionality: EU rule transfer to the candidate countries of Central and Eastern Europe. *Journal of European Public Policy, 11*(4), 661–679.

Schulze, K., & Tosun, J. (2013). External dimensions of European environmental policy: An analysis of environmental treaty ratification by third states. *European Journal of Political Research, 52*(5), 581–607.

Simmons, B. A. (2001). The international politics of harmonization: The case of capital market regulation. *International Organization, 55*(3), 589–620.

Subotic, J. (2010). Explaining difficult states: The problems of europeanization in Serbia. *East European Politics & Societies, 24*(4), 595–616.

Tallberg, J. (2003). The agenda-shaping powers of the EU council presidency. *Journal of European Public Policy, 10*(1), 1–19.

Tosun, J. (2011). When the grace period is over: Assessing the new member states' compliance with EU requirements for oil stockholding. *Energy Policy, 39*(11), 7156–7164.

Tosun, J. (2012). Emergency oil stocks in Southeastern and Eastern Europe: What explains variation in convergence towards the EU model? *Energy Policy, 46*(1), 417–426.

Tosun, J., & Schulze, K. (2013).*Expanding the EU energy acquis: Policy change in the Energy Community.* Paper prepared for the conference Energy transitions: Regulation of energy markets at national, European and international levels. Joensuu: University of Eastern Finland.

Tosun, J., & Schulze, K. (2015). Compliance with EU biofuel targets in South-Eastern and Eastern Europe: Do interest groups matter? *Environment and Planning C: Government and Policy*, forthcoming.

Trauner, F. (2009). From membership conditionality to policy conditionality: EU external governance in South Eastern Europe. *Journal of European Public Policy, 16*(5), 774–790.

Vachudova, M. A. (2014). EU leverage and national interests in the Balkans: The puzzles of enlargement 10 Years on. *Journal of Common Market Studies, 52*(1), 122–138.

Part II
The Commission as Policy Entrepreneur

Chapter 5
Against All Odds: The Liberalisation of the European Natural Gas Market—A Multiple Streams Perspective

Nicole Herweg

Abstract This chapter addresses the questions of why it took uuntil the late 1980s for the liberalisation of the energy markets to enter the institutional agenda and a decade more to be finally adopted. Given the head start energy matters and the idea of a common market had in today's European Union, the long time it took for agenda shaping and policy decision regarding energy liberalisation was surprising. Taking the liberalisation of the natural gas market as an example, the policy process leading to the first out of three gas directives is analysed using a modified multiple streams framework, which covers agenda-setting and decision-making. The analysis reveals that the rise on the institutional agenda resulted from the Commission's success in framing energy matters as competition issues. By documenting its uncompetitive state, a problem window opened. As a competition issue, the Commission had the power to formulate directives unilaterally based on Article 90 of the EEC Treaty instead of negotiating a Council directive. In order to avoid the resulting loss of influence, the member states became willing to negotiate. The Commission coupled the ripe problem and politics stream with the policy stream by adapting policy solutions from the United Kingdom. The negotiations of the resulting draft proposal were lengthy, mainly because of the member states' ongoing resistance against the proposal and their attempts to minimize adjustment costs to European legislation. A spillover effect from the simultaneously negotiated electricity draft finally broke down the legitimacy barrier and led to an agreement on the gas directive.

N. Herweg (✉)
Institute of Political Science, University of Heidelberg, Bergheimer Strasse 58, 69115 Heidelberg, Germany
e-mail: nicole.herweg@ipw.uni-heidelberg.de

J. Tosun et al. (eds.), *Energy Policy Making in the EU*,
Lecture Notes in Energy 28, DOI 10.1007/978-1-4471-6645-0_5

5.1 Introduction: Why the Creation of the Internal Energy Market Is Puzzling

The creation of the Internal Energy Market (IEM) provides a valuable case study to address the questions raised in this volume. Namely, how ideas enter the institutional agenda and how this leads to draft legislation. The timing of the creation of the IEM is puzzling because two predecessor treaties of today's European Union explicitly dealt with energy matters (the Treaties Constituting the European Coal and Steal Community and the European Atomic Energy Community), while the third treaty (the one which established the European Economic Community) had as its intention the launch of a common market.[1] Hence, the obvious assumption is that the next step would have been the creation of an IEM. In fact, the Commission repeatedly had as its aim the development of a common energy policy (Hancher 1990), but this did not lead to an agenda and policy change because it was constantly blocked by member states (Eikeland 2004). Hence until the mid-1980s, European energy policy counted as a major political failure (Matláry 1997) but since then there has been an increase in regulatory activity, which has resulted in three energy packages being passed to date (see Ciambra and Solorio in Chap. 8).

Referring to Kingdon (1984), this chapter focuses on the question of why the time to liberalise the energy markets finally came about. More precisely, it seeks to answer the question of how energy liberalisation rose to the institutional agenda as exemplified by the liberalisation of the natural gas market. Of the three gas directives already adopted (98/30/EC, 2003/55/EC, 2009/73/EC), the policy process leading to the first one will be studied in-depth because it did not just put the subsequent increase in regulatory activity in motion but also encountered the challenge of breaking down the "legitimacy barrier" (Wilson 1979, p. 41). Or as Princen (2011, p. 936) put it, of "claiming authority at the EU-level". Furthermore, the analysis of this policy process promises to deliver insights into successful agenda-setting because the IEM entered the agenda via the low politics route (Princen/Rhinard 2006). The same route that had been used before unsuccessfully to put a common energy policy on the agenda (see Alexandrova and Timmermans in Chap. 3). Hence, this contribution also seeks to answer the question of what changed to make that same route suddenly turn out to be the road to success.

This chapter will go beyond analysing how the institutional agenda was set and how this led to a draft directive concerning common rules for the transmission, distribution, supply and storage of natural gas (including LNG). I also analyse its adoption (see Cox and Dekanozishvili in Chap. 9 for a similar illustration with respect to EU renewable energy policy). The analysis covers this stage of the policy cycle too. Apart from its timing, the fact that the directive was passed at all is puzzling given that almost all member states and the European Parliament opposed

[1] In order to improve the reading flow, this contribution neither distinguishes between the European Commission and its earlier equivalent, nor between the European Union and its forerunner.

the directive but did not veto it. The third question behind this analysis is therefore: How was the first natural gas directive passed despite the resistance of almost all veto players?

The next section introduces the theoretical underpinning and provides information about the scope and set-up of the case study. It is then carried out in Sect. 5.3. Section 5.4 summarises the answers to the questions posed and discusses the insights gained about agenda-setting in the European Union.

5.2 Theoretical Framework

There are various theoretical approaches at hand to study agenda shaping. The three most prominent examples are the models of Cobb et al. (1976), the punctuated equilibrium theory (PET) (Baumgartner and Jones 1993; see also Alexandrova and Timmermans in Chap. 3) and the multiple streams framework (MSF) (Kingdon 1984). The theoretical lens guiding this analysis is the MSF. In its original formulation as introduced by Kingdon (1984), it is limited to explaining agenda-setting in the United States. As the research questions also refer to actual policy formulation and decision-making, this section introduces an extension of the framework which also allows for the analysis of these later policy stages. In contrast to the vast majority of academic research that has applied the MSF to the European context, this contribution fully applies the framework instead of just referring to its individual elements (Ackrill et al. 2013). This section therefore also provides an outline of how the MSF can be applied to the European Union. As a reference point, the original approach is summarised briefly.

5.2.1 Kingdon's Multiple Streams Framework

The MSF departs from the assumption that policy-making follows a rational problem-solving process. Instead, it postulates that it is the combination of compelling problems or political changes, the availability of worked-out alternatives, and the activities of policy entrepreneurs that lead to agenda change.

Analytically, it distinguishes between three largely independent streams which flow through the policy system: (1) the problem stream, which indicates deviations from an ideal state, (2) the politics stream, which refers to electoral, partisan and pressure group factors and (3) the policy stream, which consists of ideas and proposals regarding a particular policy issue. The proposals are developed in policy communities, which are comprised of policy specialists who share a common concern for a specific problem. A change in the problem or politics stream opens a policy window, which is an opportunity for policy entrepreneurs to push their favourite policy towards the institutional agenda or as Kingdon would say the decision agenda.

In order for an agenda change to actually take place, three conditions have to be met: Firstly, the problem, politics, and policy stream are ripe; secondly, a policy window opens due to a change in the problem or politics stream; and finally, at least one policy entrepreneur succeeds in coupling the streams once the window has opened.

5.2.2 European Union Policy-Making and the Multiple Streams Lens

Applying the MSF to European Union policy-making requires Kingdon's framework to be adapted somewhat (Ackrill et al. 2013). The following section introduces the modifications considered for the purposes of this chapter.

As the key concepts of the problem and policy stream can be easily transferred to the European Union, the adjustments concern the politics stream. Mirroring the venues central to the high and low politics route in agenda-setting, the politics stream includes the Commission, the Council of Ministers (referred to as the Council), the European Parliament and the European Council. In line with the original framework, the analysis also covers the activities of interest groups, while it departs from it by omitting the European mood since "the existence of an EU 'public sphere', a pre-condition for having an EU public agenda, is questionable" (Princen and Rhinard 2006, p. 1121).

According to Kingdon, the partisan composition of government and parliament affect which policy perspectives are dominant and hence favour some ideas over others to be coupled with the problem stream. Given the pronounced national orientation in member states' energy policies, this chapter abandons the parties-do-matter-hypothesis but takes into consideration the influx of additional national attitudes that are due to the process of EU enlargement. Furthermore, it focuses on personal turnover in positions with agenda-structuring power. This refers to the start of the terms of office of the Commission President, of Commissioners in the Directorate-Generals involved, of the Council Presidency and of the rapporteur of the responsible Committee: the Committee for Research and Technological Development and Energy (CERT).[2]

Although Kingdon limited the MSF to explain agenda-setting, it is common practice nowadays to expand this approach to explain policy formulation and legitimation too by simply referring policy windows and the coupling process to agenda *and* policy choices (Zahariadis 1992). Although this works in national policy-making settings that are characterised by having only few veto players, it is too imprecise for European policy dynamics. The most obvious challenge is that the

---

[2] Apart from Directorate-General (DG) IV (Competition) and DG XVII (Energy), the IEM touched on the boundaries of other DGs, particularly DG XXI (General Customs Union and Indirect Taxation), DG III (Single Market and Industry) and DG XI (Environment).

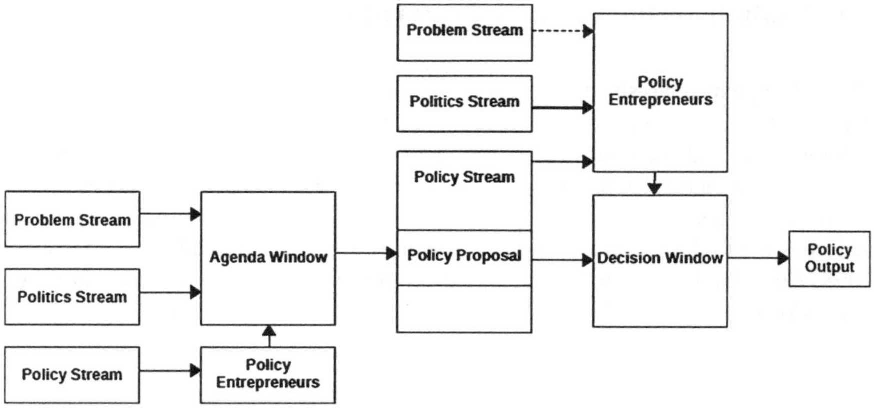

Fig. 5.1 Modified multiple stream framework. Note: The different shapes of the arrows indicate the varying importance of the three streams in the decision window

principle of discontinuity does not apply in the European Union. Consequently, European policy-making processes can easily span different legislative terms. This in turn makes it impossible to refer the same coupling process to agenda-setting and decision-making as the streams rarely remain the same over the whole period under investigation. Therefore, a second coupling process will be introduced (see Fig. 5.1).

The first coupling process refers to the setting of the institutional agenda and is identical to Kingdon's framework. The corresponding policy window is labelled "agenda window". The output of this coupling process is a worked-out proposal that increases the number of alternatives available in the policy stream and opens the "decision window". This second coupling process focuses on policy formulation and legitimation, and it captures the political struggle about the concrete design of the proposal. Which of the ideas comprising the policy stream are seen as suitable for gaining the majority needed for a decision depends on the activities of policy entrepreneurs. The problem stream decreases in importance as soon as the issue has entered the institutional agenda. It will be dealt with irrespectively of the pressure to address it. This does not mean that the problem stream is irrelevant for the decision window because it influences the bargaining dynamics—but not whether bargaining takes place at all. The passing of an act marks the end of this coupling process provided that it was a successful one (see also Herweg 2013).[3]

[3] For an application of the modified MSF, see Zohlnhöfer and Herweg (2014).

5.3 Analysis of the General Agenda-Shaping Process

The subsequent analysis starts with a summary of the state of the streams in the early 1980s. This serves as a reference point for illustrating why only a few policy entrepreneurs had been pushing for the liberalisation of the energy markets and why their coupling activities had no chance of success. The remaining analysis focuses on how the agenda window opened and how policy entrepreneurs' coupling activities led to the introduction of the gas draft in 1992 and finally to its passage in 1998. Empirically, the analysis is based on primary materials, in particular: legislative documents, secondary sources and above all media reports.

5.3.1 State of the Streams in the Early 1980s

As mentioned before, no common energy policy had been established in the course of European integration until the early 1980s. Basically, this was a result of the member states' problem perceptions. According to them, the most important issue in the *problem stream* had been a perceived scarcity of supply. Consequently, the issue of securing supply dominated their agendas (see Eikeland 2004). The perception of scarce supply arose from the belief that finite resources would soon be depleted, which occurred at the same time as forecasts for future high demand (Stern 1992). Apart from this depletion scenario, international focusing events—such as the closure of the Suez Canal in 1956 and 1967 and the two oil crises in the 1970s—fostered the impression that energy security was endangered (see also Alexandrova and Timmermans in Chap. 3 on the role of focusing events for agenda shaping).

As member states preferred to address this problem primarily with national rather than pan-European solutions, the lack of a common energy policy was not perceived as problematic. The *politics stream* was not ripe either. As a result of the focus on finding national solutions, energy issues were historically to a great extent left to the sole responsibility of member states. Regardless of party-political considerations, they had answered almost unanimously to the perceived scarcity of supply by treating energy as a strategic commodity. As such, it had to be dealt with on the national level without exposing it to competition. Consequently, no political initiative for a common European response stemmed from either national or European actors except for the Commission, which proposed the integration of the Community's energy market in 1985 (COM(85) 245 final) but remained unheard.

The *policy stream* was at this time still dominated by the policies almost all member states had pursued in order to secure the supply of energy. Above all, this meant that member states played a substantial part in their respective national economies. This had led to a predominantly state-owned monopolistic energy sector dominated by vertically integrated companies that were bound by long-term and partly anti-competitive contracts. Member states granted these companies exclusive rights in exchange for their fulfilling certain public service obligations. This was far from being compatible with the idea of liberalising natural gas markets. Although not popular, this idea was present in the policy stream as well. The USA, Canada and the United Kingdom (UK) are prominent examples of countries with third party access provisions (TPA), a cornerstone for any liberalisation policy.[4] However, their experiences with TPA did not act as a catalyst for spreading the word about liberalisation but rather served as a reference for opponents of liberalisation (Stern 1992).

To sum up, as long as the security-of-supply frame prevailed, it was unlikely that a change in the problem or politics stream would open an agenda window suitable for pushing through a common energy policy. Furthermore, the policy stream lacked a worked-out alternative in this respect leaving potential policy entrepreneurs empty-handed.

5.3.2 The Single European Act: Setting the Stage for the Agenda Window

As illustrated above, the state of the streams did not support an agenda change. So what changed that made it possible in general to push energy liberalisation onto the agenda? Basically, this was the introduction of the so-called free movement category as included in the Single European Act (SEA). This category refers to the free movement of goods, persons, services and capital by removing all physical, technical and fiscal barriers between member states by 1992.

Although energy was not included in the SEA, it provided the Commission with the opportunity to push for a European energy policy by using the widely accepted free movement category as a means of establishing a new problem perception: Instead of framing energy as an issue of supply security, it could be dealt with as a competition issue (Nylander 2001). In fact, nobody doubted that the energy markets were characterised by the barriers listed above (Palinkas 1989) and that this did not just hinder free trade in this sector but resulted in competitive disadvantages in other energy-intensive sectors. Coincidentally, by the time the SEA was passed, oil prices had begun to fall, which made concerns about the security of supply less urgent (Andersen 1993) and large energy consumers question the great price differentials between member states (Hancher 1990).

Encouraged by these price developments and the broad agreement on the SEA, the Commission started to push for a new problem definition and to draw attention to it. In May 1988, the Commission published its Working Document "The Internal Energy Market", in which it finally investigated "the various existing or potential obstacles to a single energy market" and suggested some main subjects that should

---

[4] Third party access means that pipeline companies either agree or are obliged to carry as much gas as its capacities allow against the payment of a charge for the services the third party has made use of (Stern 1992).

receive attention as a priority (COM(88) 238 final, Article 6). Regarding the natural gas market, the Commission proposed to prioritise the facilitation of the free movement of natural gas whilst referring to the introduction of the common carrier system (Annex to COM(88) 238 final), which would lead to the establishment of common rules for this market sector.[5] Hence, the Commission's Working Document did not just apply the free movement category to the energy sector for the first time but also suggested a further course of action. As a result, the agenda window opened.

Although the problem stream was ripe regarding the liberalisation of energy, the politics and policy streams were not. Hence, policy entrepreneurs faced two major challenges: to promote political support for the blocked IEM and to initiate the development of alternatives because by the late 1980s no European natural gas policy community was engaged in working them out (Matláry 1997). Given the Commission's past attempts to establish a common energy policy, it was not surprising that it was the pivotal policy entrepreneur during the agenda window. The European Council only asked once the Council to push the IEM forward at its Rhodes Meeting in December 1988 but remained silent about it thereafter.[6]

Before illustrating this low politics route a word on the Commission. Owing to institutional ambiguity, it would be misleading to assume that the Commission consistently acted as a coherent actor. Thus, it is essential to prove whether the IEM had been included in the Commission's Working Programme as developed by the Commission President and whether the DGs involved were willing to implement it. Concerning the latter, the focus is on DG Energy and DG Competition being that both count as the most influential DGs regarding the IEM (see Andersen 1993).

With regard to the Commission President, Delors was re-elected in 1989. Hence, the same president, who had been in office when the SEA was passed and had supervised the application of the free movement category to the energy markets, was still in charge. Not surprisingly, he included the IEM in the Commission's Working Programme throughout the entire agenda window in the respective Working Programme. With Cardoso e Cunha replacing Nicolas Mosar as Energy Commissioner in January 1989, this DG was strengthened. While Mosar had left "those ambitious to develop energy policy within the Community somewhat impotent", Cardoso e Cunha was seen as an Energy Commissioner with "a desire for action" and the will to provide "a determined lead" (EC Energy Monthly, 01.01.1989) right from the start of his term of office. Peter Sutherland, Competition Commissioner under Delor´s first term of office, had taken a strong stance for making the IEM real if necessary through competition law (Power Europe 16.03.1989). His successor was Sir Leon Brittan "a liberalisation advocate" (Nylander 2001, p. 306), who had served under Margaret Thatcher in different

---

[5] A common carriage system obliges pipeline companies to carry as much gas as their capacity allows for third parties. If demand is higher than the capacity of the pipeline, capacity has to be offered to all parties on a pro rata basis (Stern 1992).

[6] If the European Council referred to energy, it was only in the context of public procurement and trans-European networks.

cabinet positions and terms in office. Unsurprisingly, he followed Sutherland's track and even opened infringement proceedings against electricity and gas import and export monopolies in all but two member states (Power Europe 28.03.1991).

While the Commission as such agreed on the goal, the completion of the IEM, there were different views on how to achieve it. The vast majority preferred political solutions to implementing the IEM through law, but Sir Leon Brittan favoured using competition rules and formulating directives unilaterally based on Article 90 of the EEC Treaty (Multinational Service 11/1991).[7] Cardoso e Cunha supported this pro-competitive strategy, as can be seen in the fact that he substituted his director of the IEM task force with a director from the DG for Competition after less than a year favouring "a faster, more aggressive approach to the implementation of third party access" (EC Energy Monthly 01.04.1991). On the other hand, he was more cautious regarding the Article 90 approach, particularly in the light of the member states' and his colleagues' resistance (Multinational Service 10/1991). As a consequence, he championed political solutions but did not rule out the Article 90 approach right from the start. Nonetheless, Brittan and Cardoso were close allies and worked together in order to make the IEM a reality (EC Energy Monthly 15.01.1993). With a view to the scope of this chapter, the analysis treats the Commission as a whole where it acted cohesively and highlights the Competition and Energy Commissioner's attempts to couple the streams.

5.3.2.1 The Promotion of Political Support

In order for an act to rise on the institutional agenda, political support is needed. This was a challenging task as member states and the gas industry reacted with fierce opposition to the Working Document (Stern 1998), particularly to the common carrier system. The Commission met this challenge in three steps.

Firstly, for the first time regarding energy policy (EC Energy Monthly 14.02.1992), the Commission brought everyone involved in gas matters together, which gave them the opportunity to voice their position by setting up two Consultative Committees to discuss third party access (TPA) in-depth (COM(89) 334). These committees were established in mid-1990 and chaired by members of the DG for Energy, Competition and the Single Market and Industry. One committee was composed of representatives from member states and the other one consisted of representatives from the gas industry and consumers (International Gas Report 13.06.1991, COM(91) 548 final).

To summarise, both committees failed to hold constructive talks (Stern 1992), and they did not lead to a climate of political support for the Commission's initiative. Nonetheless, it helped the Commission to improve its understanding of the sector, to obtain an overview of possible arguments in favour of and against

---

[7] Article 90(3), today's Article 86(3), entrusts the Commission with the enforcement of competition rules to public undertakings and undertakings that enjoy exclusive rights.

liberalisation (Lyons 1994), as well as all the technical information needed for drafting a proposal (Power Europe, 01.08.1991). Most importantly, the Commission came to understand that a common carrier system was unrealistic, while TPA for large energy consumers was potentially obtainable (EC Energy Monthly, 01.04.1991). Furthermore, the committees contributed to the initiation of a European policy community, as shown by the establishment of Eurogas—the European association of the natural gas industry representing major transmission and distribution companies, or the International Federation of Industrial Energy Consumers (IFIEC), both of which participated in the talks (EC Energy Monthly, 01.07.1991).

Secondly, the Commission followed a dual-track strategy. This consisted of drafting a directive that would introduce common rules for the natural gas market on the one hand and launching infringement proceedings against competition infringements in the gas sector on the other (Platt's Oilgram News 08.04.1991). The Commission thereby underlined its determination to achieve an internal natural gas market.

Thirdly, spearheaded by Leon Brittan, the Commission attempted to change the fallback positions of those involved by threatening to decide on the issue itself. This threat was credible because it was backed by the European Court of Justice (ECJ), which had sanctioned the Commission's use of its powers under Article 90 in the context of liberalising the telecommunications equipment market. Before this ruling, the Commission had announced its intention to use its powers, as specified in Article 90 in the field of energy, should the ECJ confirm its course of action (Journal of Commerce 22.03.1991).

Consequently, in July 1991, two interconnected proposals regarding common rules for the natural gas market were circulated privately to interested parties. In a joint move by the Competition and Energy Commissioner, the Commission circulated one proposal which was signed by Leon Brittan and based on Article 90 and one which was based on Article 100a and signed by the Energy directorate (Stern 1992). The Commission thereby demonstrated its willingness to decide on the liberalisation issue itself if necessary—very much to the discontent of member states, the EP and industries affected by the proposals.

From the point of view of these players, this reduced the fallback positions available to them as they would lose any opportunity to influence the directive′s content. As blocking the proposal became more and more unrealistic, Eurogas changed its strategy and attempted to form an alliance with the EP instead of exclusively lobbying the Commission (International Gas Report, 03.10.1991). Up until then, lobbying had generally taken place in member states and only at this point did it start to be directed at the European level (Nylander 2001).

Against the backdrop of the strong resistance of those involved, Cardoso e Cunha changed his position and excluded the Article 90 approach as a viable option for the Commission. By pushing for a political solution in the form of a Council directive, he left Brittan behind because he still favoured a unilateral decision on the issue (Multinational Service 11/1991). As a consequence, the Commission as a whole decided to drop its Article 90 approach for the time being, but at the same time it did not explicitly exclude a later return to it by stating that the Commission still "reserves the right to make use of all its powers conferred on it by the Treaty as and when appropriate" (COM(91) 548: 9). The knowledge that the Commission could play this card made those involved willing to negotiate a political solution. In this sense, the politics stream had become ripe.

5.3.2.2 The Generation of Ideas

The challenge of drafting a directive without the input of the policy community was less problematic than theory depicts—even given the Commission's limited success in initiating a policy community by setting up consultative committees. The non-existence of a European policy community (at least to all practical extents and purposes) provided the Commission with the freedom to choose ideas as it suited them. In line with Ackrill and Kay (2011), the change in environmental signals, here meaning the application of free movement to the energy markets, provided the Commission with the opportunity to select the policy solution it deemed most suitable.

In this context, a win-win situation for the Commission and the UK emerged. The Commission had always been receptive to lessons drawn from the UK′s experience of liberalisation. In this respect, the Commission was able to profit from Brittan's own experience and contacts with British officials (Nylander 2001). The UK, on the other hand, was keen to minimise possible adjustment costs resulting from changes to regulation and to eliminate economic disadvantages. The latter arose from the possible penetration of UK's domestic liberalised natural gas market by European companies that could draw on an advantageous (national) monopoly position (Europe Energy, 14.06.1991). Hence, the UK provided the Commission with worked-out alternatives derived from their domestic regulations, which was in fact mirrored in many aspects by the Commission's draft directive (Multinational Service 08-09/1991).

Cardoso e Cunha tried to convince member states and the Council of the viability of the draft directive before it was tabled. He, therefore, discussed the proposal with member states by touring capital cities and presenting it in advance to the Energy Council's meeting in late October 1991 (Europe Energy, 31.10.1991; EC Energy Monthly 14.02.1992). According to this new approach, common rules should be introduced in three stages: The first stage referred to price transparency and transit, the corresponding directives for which had already been passed (90/377/EC, 91/296/EEC); the second stage provided for the introduction of common rules; finally, the third stage was planned to expand the common rules according to the experience gained during the second stage of the gradual liberalisation process (COM(91) 548 final). The gas draft was part of the second stage and its main features were: a licensing system for the construction of facilities, unbundling provisions for vertically integrated companies and a TPA system based on eligibility thresholds (Stern 1992).

Taking into account the feedback from Cardoso e Cunha's capitals tour and from the Council, the draft officially submitted on February 21, 1992 differed from the mid-1991 draft in that it proposed a more staggered introduction of TPA based on higher eligibility thresholds than before (EC Energy Monthly, 14.02.1992). As a result of this, a decision window was therefore opened.

5.4 The Decision Windows

The analysis of the decision windows focuses on the bargaining dynamics. Hence, it follows a summary of the activities of those involved and their attempts to gain support for their preferred policy solutions. The negotiating of the draft electricity and gas legislation took place in parallel. In this chapter, the former is only referred to when it is necessary for the explanation of the policy processes concerning the gas directive.

5.4.1 The First Decision Window: A Case of Deadlock

The Energy Council's negotiations of the draft directives during the first decision window were presided over by Portugal (01-06/1992), the UK (07-12/1992), Denmark (01-06/1993) and Belgium (07-12/1993). Given the resistance against the draft directive, its eventual submission could not have been better as both the Portuguese and the British Presidencies were judged as being favourable for moving negotiations forward. Both countries were expected to emphasise the gas draft in the case of Portugal because it originally came from a Portuguese Energy Commissioner (EC Energy Monthly 14.02.1992). In the case of the UK, it strongly supported the Commission's proposal. In fact, both Presidencies placed the internal natural gas market high on their agendas, but both failed to achieve substantial progress owing to strong opposition from member states', above all against the TPA provisions (see also Cox and Dekanozishvili in Chap. 9 for an illustration of attempts by member states to shape European agendas).

The Netherlands, Germany and France particularly opposed the proposal to the point where it was blocked and a redraft was demanded. In May 1992, the issue was debated for the first time and even the Council′s conclusions could not be agreed on. The Portuguese Presidency passed a set of general Presidency conclusions instead (European Energy Report 12.06.1992). Equally daunting were the reactions of the Community's Economic and Social Committee (ESC) and the EP's CERT as they both signalled strong reservations about it (European Report 23.05.1992). The next meeting, under British Presidency in November 1992, did at least end with the Council drawing some conclusions, but its content was disappointing in that it simply asked the Commission to modify the proposal regarding various aspects of the drafts, most importantly the TPA provisions (International Gas Report 11.12.1992). However, under the Presidencies of the Portuguese and British, progress was made regarding the focus of the discussion as it shifted from technical points which questioned the feasibility of energy liberalisation as such to political and philosophical points (EC Energy Monthly 04.12.1992).

Despite earlier announcements (Platt's Oilgram News 04.03.1993), the Danish Presidency did not make the IEM a priority and delayed the Council meeting until June 1993 owing to the Danish referendum on the Maastricht Treaty in May, and its opposition to a directive banning preferential treatment of domestic companies in the licensing of gas and oil (International Gas Report, 11.12.1992). Consequently, no progress was made and the conclusions merely stated that the Commission should take the suggestions expected from the EP into account in modifying its proposals. The Belgian presidency, in turn, made the IEM a high priority as it intended to take the opportunity to force through a rethink of TPA and to submit a new proposal. Therefore, the Council Presidency planned to draw on fellow Belgian CERT rapporteur Claude Desama's report (Europe Energy, 24.06.1993). This did not happen because it took the EP several hearings until November 1993 to discuss the 580 amendments tabled, which Desama managed to reduce to 240 (referring to the proposals for electricity and gas).

The EP vote coincided with the coming into force of the Maastricht Treaty in November 1993, according to which various draft legislation that was pending, among others the draft gas legislation, would henceforth have to be negotiated under the co-decision procedure (COM(93) 570 final). This procedural change resulted in an increase in the EP's influence because the co-decision procedure required the EP's agreement in order to pass draft gas legislation. Although more than a hundred amendments were considered acceptable by the Commission (for instance those stressing the concept of subsidiarity), the majority was not (such as the suggestion to allow distribution companies to keep their supply monopoly) (EC Energy Monthly 08.04.1993, 19.11.1993; Power Europe 03.12.1993).

In order to be considered for the next Energy Council in December 1993, the Commission only had a few weeks to revise it. Three days before the Council was due to meet, the Commission agreed on the amended proposal (COM/93/643FINAL), which incorporated many but not all the points the Council and the EP considered to be key. Owing to the lack of time to study this draft in advance, the Energy Council just took note of it and left further discussions on it for the next Council meeting in May 1994 (European Report 10.12.1993, 15.12.1993).

5.4.2 The Commission's Coupling Activities

During the agenda-setting process, Energy Commissioner Cardoso e Cunha and Competition Commissioner Leon Brittan had acted as policy entrepreneurs, and they continued to do this until the start of the next Commission in January 1993. As both Commissioners did not serve in Delors' third Commission, the following subsection analyses whether their successors filled the remaining gaps and also engaged in coupling the streams. Abel Matutes succeeded Cardoso e Cunha as the Commissioner of the DG for Energy. Compared to his predecessor, Matutes pursued a more cautious strategy and was more willing to compromise. For instance, in light of the EP's increased importance, he gave up the Commission's insistence on compulsory TPA and considered voluntary negotiated TPA instead (EC Energy Monthly, 11.03.1993; Platt's Oilgram News 05.05.1993). Furthermore, he stressed that the Council, the EP and the Commission should cooperate closely based on Desama's report (Power Europe, 09.04.1993), which he described as "excellent". It was far less radical than the Commission's proposal.

While Matutes stressed his interest in reaching a consensus, the new Competition Commissioner Karel van Miert continued to maintain Brittan's threatening position. He carried on with the infringement proceedings dealing with the granting of exclusive import and export rights, which had been initiated in 1991. Encouraged by indications that France and the Netherlands would review their legislation, he announced that the Commission was willing to refrain from further legal action if an agreement on common rules for the internal market in electricity and natural gas could be reached (Power Europe 04.08.1993, EC Energy Monthly 04.08.1993). Otherwise, van Miert stressed "that instead of developing a policy by the normal procedure, elements of energy policy will then be developed via judgements or competition cases in a rather disorderly way (…). Nowhere in the Treaty or anywhere else is there an indication that the energy sector is exempt" (quoted from EC Energy Monthly, 04.08.1993).

As the December Council in 1993 failed to make any progress on that issue, the Commission translated van Miert's rhetoric into action and entered the final stage of the infringement proceedings in mid-June 1994, which meant taking the dispute to the ECJ—much to the disgust of the national governments and utility companies involved as well as the EP. During this time, a ruling of the ECJ (C393/92 Almelo v Ijsselmij) was passed, whereby electricity was to be treated as a good (Power Europe 11.03.1994, Europe Energy 01.07.1994, EC Energy Monthly 26.09.1994). The application of competition rules was permitted by law, which limited member states′ perceived fallback options regarding the ongoing negotiations about common rules.

In sum, both Commissioners were actively engaged in policy entrepreneurship just as their predecessors had done. The means by which they did this differed though. Van Miert pursued the way taken by Brittan and tried to gain political support by changing the cost-benefit ratio owing to the threat from Article 90. Matutes, on the other hand, tried to gain support by settling compromises without resorting to this option, even if that meant watering down the Commission′s initial draft. In light of the stalling negotiations summarised above, the Commission and the Council decided to leave the proposal concerning the natural gas market aside and to concentrate instead on the electricity directive. Hence, contrary to their plans, energy liberalisation was not discussed at the Energy Council meeting in May 1994. The choice of the electricity directive over the gas directive can be accounted for by the fact that the latter was even more controversial. The gas directive was to be rescheduled after substantial progress had been made on electricity liberalisation (European Report 26.11.1994; Financial Times 25.05.1995).

5.4.3 The Natural Gas Draft in a Sort of Hibernation

The subsequent negotiation of the electricity draft took until December 1996, which was when the Council and the EP finally agreed on common rules for this sector and passed the directive (96/92/EC). During this time, the Commission's energy portfolio had faced various changes in commissioners, whereas the competition portfolio remained headed by Karel van Miert. Owing to his election to the EP, Abel Matutes was replaced by Marcelino Oreja in June 1994 until the beginning of the Commission's next term in 1995. In the Santer Commission, Christos Papoutsis took over the energy portfolio. Hence within 2 years, the Energy Commission was faced with its fourth change of commissioner. As all of them required a period of training, this combined—at least—to temporary weaken the energy portfolio. Furthermore, none of Cardoso e Cunha's predecessors followed a hard line as he had done. On the contrary, they all pursued a softer approach by favouring the negotiation of political solutions that were less radical than the Commission's initial liberalisation proposals (Platt's Oilgram News, 2.11.1994) much to the disconcertment of Competition Commissioner van Miert (EC Energy Monthly, 16.12.1994).

Regarding the President of the Commission′s support for the IEM project, Santer backed it right from the start of his term in office and included it in the Commission's Working Programmes. When it became clear that a Common Position concerning the electricity directive was feasible by the next Energy Council in June 1996, Papoutsis started pushing the gas draft back onto the institutional agenda. Out of this initiative stemmed a revised gas directive, which mirrored most of the electricity draft as agreed upon in the Energy Council and largely superseded the latest version of the draft gas legislation (Cameron 2002). With the presentation of this draft at the Council meeting in December 1996, the second decision window was opened.

5.4.4 The Second Decision Window: Spillover from the Electricity Draft

Kingdon (1984) refers to policy windows that open as a result of changes in adjacent policy areas as spillovers. For a spillover to be successful, policy entrepreneurs have to succeed in transferring the winning coalition and in applying successful arguments from the electricity debate to the debate on gas. Indeed, the writing of the compromise draft was facilitated by the experiences those involved had gained during the electricity debate, which was also reflected by a dynamic and positive atmosphere of negotiation (European Report 11.01.1997). But where arguments could not be transferred owing to the inherently given differences between electricity and natural gas, the need for further negotiations became obvious. Furthermore, a change in the problem stream, which had already complicated the agreement on the electricity directive, made it difficult to reach an agreement: The view that energy was a public service challenged the idea of completely deregulating this sector (see Nylander 2001). Closely related to public service issues were questions of how to deal with take-or-pay contracts and emerging markets. In addition to this, the details of the design of TPA provisions and the unbundling of the accounts of vertically integrated gas companies had to be worked out. These issues were addressed between December 1996 and May 1998. During this time, the membership of the Commission and the EP did not change. Desama, who had been the CERT-Rapporteur during the first decision window continued in this position.

The composition of the European and Energy Council had changed slightly in the meantime owing to EU enlargement in 1995 when Austria, Finland and Sweden joined the European Union. The last two countries named strengthened the position of those pushing for exemptions in the opening up of gas markets because their gas markets as such or some of its regions were still limited to the extent of being classified as emerging (EC Energy Monthly 13.12.1996; Energy Economist 01.06.1997). The Council meetings were presided over by Ireland (12/1996), the Netherlands (01-06/1997), Luxembourg (07-12/1997) and the UK (01-16/1998). Contrary to the first decision window, all Council Presidencies made the gas drafts a high priority and were expected to do so by other member states. Despite the efforts of the Council Presidents, negotiations remained difficult. Depending on the issues at stake, the composition of the supporters' and opponents' camps varied.

The extent and design of third party access provisions was one of the most controversial subjects in both decision windows. As France actively opposed the introduction of a liberal TPA solution, its willingness to compromise was important in getting the directive passed. Under the Dutch Presidency, France protracted the negotiations because it was not willing to start negotiations immediately after the presidential elections in June 1997 (Energy Economist 01.06.1997). It is notable that in total, in six member states national elections took place during the two decision windows: In Italy, Ireland, France, Spain and Greece during the first one and in Spain, the UK, France and Ireland during the second one. However, only the French elections in June 1997 were used as an excuse to delay negotiations. This is linked to two facts: Firstly, that France was the only member state which had faced strong domestic opposition against introducing TPA (Financial Times, 31.05.1995). And secondly, the compatibility between the draft directive and the corresponding French policy was very low.

As the negotiations in mid-1997 were at the point of reaching a compromise, it was extremely important for France to enter them well-prepared. But the recent elections had led to a change of government, which did not give the new French representatives enough time to familiarise themselves with the issues at stake. This delay raised concerns from Competition Commissioner van Miert and the then incumbent Luxembourgish Council Presidency. The former pressed for an Energy Council meeting to take place as early as possible and the latter openly considered relinquishing a unanimous vote and opting for a qualified vote in order to reach a common position (European Report, 17.09.1997; Financial Times 08.12.1997).

This was not necessary because all unresolved questions were settled in October 1997, thanks to the willingness of those involved to compromise (European Report 10.12.1997). This common position was finally endorsed at the next Council meeting in February 1998.

The EP discussed some plausible amendments but passed the draft unchanged in late April 1998. Desama was the driving force behind leaving the proposal untouched because he wanted to avoid jeopardising the compromise which had been made, given that the main points made by the EP had already been taken into account as a result of the fact that the electricity draft had been used as a blueprint for the gas draft (Agence Europe 30.04.1998, Cameron 2002). Finally, the Commission recommended to the Council the adoption of the text, which happened in May 1998. The European Council usually takes up those issues that are politically controversial in order to contribute to their final settlement (see Chap. 3 by Alexandrova and Timmermans). But in this case, the European Council remained silent over the gas draft in both decision windows.

To sum up, the most important results of the new directive were as follows:

The minimum degree of market opening was set at 20 % of annual consumption in the year 2000, which would increase to 28 % in 2005 and to 33 % in 2010. This went along with the broadening of the definition of eligible customers starting with customers consuming more than 25 million m^3 of gas annually, which would decrease to 15 million m^3 (2005) and eventually to 5 million m^3 (2010). Customers generating gas-fired power were reconsidered eligible regardless of their level of consumption.

Network access had to be granted via regulated TPA or negotiated TPA, both to be characterised by transparency and non-discrimination. Network access could be refused because of public service obligations, owing to a lack of capacity or in the context of TOP contracts. In the latter case, member states had to notify the Commission about such a refusal, which would have the final say on the issue. Some exemptions were granted to member states, in particular to those that (a) were not connected to another member state′s gas network, (b) had just one main outside supplier or (c) were defined as being an emerging market (98/30/EC; Agence Europe 11.05.1998).

5.5 Conclusion: A New Frame Started the Ball Rolling

So, why had the time to liberalise the energy markets finally come? This policy change was induced by the establishment of a new frame which allowed for a new way of recognising problems (see Cox and Dekanozishvili in Chap. 9). The widespread acceptance of the SEA provided the Commission with the opportunity to apply the free movement category to the energy sector and thereby to demonstrate its uncompetitive state. Consequently, the focus on energy security was challenged to the benefit of competition issues (for further details, see Nylander 2001). In contrast to earlier attempts by the Commission to settle a common energy policy, the new focus entailed it with additional powers, namely its powers under Article 90. Hence, what had changed this time were the fallback options members states perceived as being open to them, which made them willing to enter negotiations. But still, those involved could have made the best of a bad job and blocked the gas directive. A strategy they obviously did pursue during the first decision window. Here, the agreement on the electricity proposal broke down any barriers to legitimacy and demonstrated that liberalising segments of the energy sector was in general possible.

The subsequent negotiations concentrated on the attempts of those involved to convince each other that their own solutions were the best ones, whereby member states tried to minimise the costs involved in implementing European legislation. Whereas the vast majority of theories explaining policy change blank out the agenda-setting process (for an overview about those theories see Tosun 2013), the strengths of the modified MSF thus applied is that it allows to analyse both agenda-setting *and* decision-making. This makes it possible to record differences regarding policy dynamics in a well-structured way.

However, regarding the explanation of agenda change, the MSF does not manage to explain it entirely because one of its necessary conditions is not met, namely that all three streams have to be ripe *before* the agenda window opens. While the problem stream was ripe at that time, the politics and policy stream were not. Future research has to test whether the present case study is an exemption in terms of not complying with this necessary condition or whether it is a peculiarity of the European policy process in general.

Notwithstanding the above, applying the modified MSF would seem to be a promising one as it enables us to shed light on the question of how agenda-structuring impacts decision-making in the European context. This case study suggests that the policy alternatives considered in the coupling process do not necessarily have to be worked out and agreed on by a policy community but can be chosen by decision-makers (see also Ciambra and Solorio in in Chap. 8 and Cox and Dekanozishvili in Chap. 9). However, this goes hand in hand with protracted negotiations as gaining support becomes something to be achieved through action.

Another direction for future research relates to the possibility to combine the MSF with insights stemming from other theories given that it counts as a "synthetic" framework (see also Alexandrova and Timmermans in Chap. 3 for an application of the punctuated equilibrium framework). Synthetic frameworks "bring together much of the research on institutions, networks, socioeconomic process, choices, and ideas" (John 2003, p. 487). Making use of their findings could further strengthen the analytical potential of the MSF (for a theoretical discussion, see Ackrill et al. 2013; Herweg 2013).

References

Ackrill, R., & Kay, A. (2011). Multiple streams in EU policy-making: the case of the 2005 sugar reform. *Journal of European Public Policy, 18*(1), 72–89.

Ackrill, R., Kay, A., & Zahariadis, N. (2013). Ambiguity, multiple streams, and EU policy. *Journal of European Public Policy, 20*(6), 871–887.

Andersen, S. S. (1993). Towards a common EC energy policy. In S.S. Andersen, & K.A. Eliassen (Eds.), *Making policy in Europe. The Europeification of national policy-making* (pp. 133–154). London: Sage Publications.

Baumgartner, F. R., & Jones, B. D. (1993). *Agendas and instability in American politics*. Chicago: University of Chicago Press.

Cameron, P. D. (2002). *Competition in energy markets. Law and regulation in the European Union*. Oxford: Oxford University Press.

Cobb, R. W., Ross, J.-K., & Ross, M. H. (1976). Agenda building as a comparative political process. *American Political Science Review, 70*(1), 126–138.

Eikeland, P. O. (2004). *The long and winding road to the internal energy market*. Lysaker: Consistencies and inconsistencies in EU policy.

Hancher, L. (1990). A single European energy market. Rhetoric or reality? *Energy Law Journal, 11*(2), 217–242.

Herweg, N. (2013). Der Multiple-Streams-Ansatz—ein Ansatz, dessen Zeit gekommen ist? *Zeitschrift für Vergleichende Politikwissenschaft, 7*, 321–345.

John, P. (2003). Is there a life after policy streams, advocacy coalitions, and punctuations. Using evolutionary theory to explain policy change? *Policy Studies Journal, 31*(4), 481–498.

Kingdon, J. W. (1984). *Agendas, alternatives, and public policies*. Boston: Little, Brown.

Lyons, P. K. (1994). *Energy policies of the European Union*. London: EC Inform.

Matláry, J. H. (1997). *Energy policy in the European Union*. London: MacMillan.

Nylander, J. (2001). The construction of a market. A frame analysis of the liberalization of the electricity market in the European Union. *European Societies, 3*(3), 289–314.

Palinkas, P. (1989). The EC on the way to an internal energy market. *Intereconomics, 24*(5), 246–254.

Princen, S. (2011). Agenda-setting strategies in EU policy processes. *Journal of European Public Policy, 18*(7), 927–943.

Princen, S., & Rhinard, M. (2006). Crashing and creeping: Crashing and creeping: Agenda-setting dynamics in the European Union. *Journal of European Public Policy, 13*(7), 1119–1132.

Stern, J. P. (1992). *Third party access in European gas industries. Regulation-driven or market-led?*. London: Royal institute of international affairs.

Stern, J. P. (1998). *Competition and liberalization in European gas markets. A diversity of models*. London, Washington (DC): Royal institute of international affairs.

Tosun, J. (2013). *Environmental policy change in emerging market democracies: Eastern Europe and latin America compared*. Toronto: University of Toronto Press.

Wilson, J. Q. (1979). American politics, then and now. *Commentary, 67*, 39–46.

Zahariadis, N. (1992). To sell or not to sell? Telecommunications policy in Britain and France. *Journal of Public Policy, 12*(4), 355–376.

Zohlnhöfer, R., & Herweg, N. (2014). Paradigmatischer Wandel in der deutschen Arbeitsmarktpolitik: Die Hartz-Gesetze. In F.W. Rüb (Ed.), *Rapide Politikwechsel in der Bundesrepublik. Gründe, Akteure, Dynamiken und Probleme. ZfP-Sonderband 6* (pp. 93–125). Baden-Baden: Nomos.

Chapter 6
Designing Financing Mechanisms for Electricity from Renewable Energy Sources: The Role of the European Commission as an Agenda Shaper

David Jacobs

Abstract This chapter focuses on the agenda-shaping role of the European Commission with respect to support mechanisms for renewable energy sources in an increasingly integrated European electricity market. We analyse the role of the European Commission as an agenda-setter in trying to influence the design of these finance mechanisms over the past two decades. The European Commission at times pursues two contradictory objectives. On the one hand, the European Commission is eager to establish low-carbon electricity system in Europe—with an increasing share of renewables. On the other hand, the European Commission is the guardian of a common European market, trying to establish a level playing field in the European electricity sector for all power generation technologies. We argue that the European Commission has failed with two attempts to harmonise finance mechanisms in the usual co-decision-making process. Consequently, the European Commission is now trying to influence national policy decisions indirectly via state-aid guidelines, which can be implemented without a formal consensus within the European Parliament and EU member states.

6.1 Introduction: The European Commission as an Agenda Shaper for the Creation of a Common Electricity Market and Renewable Energy Support

This chapter deals with the European Commission as an agenda shaper in EU electricity policy. As described in Chap. 1 by Tosun et al., agenda-shaping describes the ability of an actor to influence a certain policy within the political

---

D. Jacobs (✉)
Environmental Policy Research Centre (FFU), Department of Political and Social Sciences, Freie Universität Berlin, Ihnestrasse 22, 14195 Berlin, Germany
e-mail: jacobs@iet-consulting.com; david.jacobs@fu-berlin.de

J. Tosun et al. (eds.), *Energy Policy Making in the EU*,
Lecture Notes in Energy 28, DOI 10.1007/978-1-4471-6645-0_6

decision-making process. The objective of this chapter is to reveal the role of the European Commission in shaping finance mechanisms[1] for electricity from renewable energy sources—both at European level and in EU member states.

We focus on the European Commission since it is the sole supranational agent with formal agenda-setting competences in the EU's institutional setting. In line with Pollack (2003, p. 56), we argue that the agenda-setting power of the European Commission depends on the "voting rules for the adoption of new legislation among legislative principals".[2] Hereby, we distinguish legislative procedures in the European Union which require co-decision-making amongst the Commission, the Parliament and the Council, European Directives, and other publications and legally binding rules that the European Commission can issue and enforce without any formal consensus: Green Papers, White Papers, guidance papers, recommendations, best practice benchmarking and—most importantly—state-aid guidelines for environmental protection and energy.

We operationalize the Commission's agenda-shaping activities by analysing its positions with regards to these different legislative procedures and publications from 1995 to 2013. We argue that the role of the European Commission is somehow ambiguous since it pursues two partially conflicting objectives. On the one hand, the European Commission is eager to establish a low-carbon electricity system in Europe—with an increasing share of renewables. In order to incentivise investment in low-carbon and renewable energy technologies, a high degree of investment security and predictable revenues is needed. On the other hand, the European Commission is the guardian of a common European market, trying to establish a level playing field in the European electricity sector for all power generation technologies (see Chap. 8 by Ciambra and Solorio for an analysis of development of the EU common electricity market).

The design of the liberalised electricity market is centred around short-term electricity trading on spot markets with hourly variations in prices (and revenues). This increases investment risk and capital costs for new power generation plants. In order to understand the role of the European Commission, we need to analyse the debate on financing mechanisms for renewables in the context of the ongoing creation of a common European electricity market.

---

[1] Usually, the term "support instruments" or "support mechanisms" is used in order to describe the discussed payment mechanisms for renewable electricity producers. This terminology is based on the belief that "support" is needed for a number of years before renewable energy sources will be able to compete with other power generation technologies on the liberalised electricity market. However, the author assumes that these types of payment mechanisms might also be necessary in the long-term and that refinancing power plant exclusively via spot market sales is not a viable long-term option. Therefore, the term "finance mechanism" is used.

[2] In addition to the Commission's right of legislative initiative, the voting rules for the adoption of new legislation, Pollack also hypotheses that the formal agenda-setting power of supranational organisations also depends upon "the rules governing the application of amendments" (Pollack 2003, p. 56). However, since no amendments to existing legislation have been implemented for renewable energy finance in the European Union, this is not of relevance for our analysis.

Consequently, this chapter first shortly introduces the reader to electricity market liberalisation in the EU and the Union's energy and climate targets. In this light, different financing mechanisms for renewable energy sources are discussed. In the second part, we analyse the Commission's positions towards the different financing mechanisms for electricity from renewable energy sources that are currently in use. And we trace the various attempts of the European Commission to steer and influence national policy making for renewable energy finance. We conclude by giving a brief outlook on the ongoing conflict between so-called market integration and the need for stable revenues for power producers.

6.2 The Establishment of a Common European Electricity Market and the Strive for a Low-Carbon Electricity System

The liberalisation of European electricity markets started in the 1990s. The Single European Act of 1986 (EU 1986) laid the foundation for the creation of an internal market in the EU, which became effective in 1992 (see Chap. 2 by Biesenbender for the evolving institutional and legal foundations of EU energy policy making). The concept of creating an internal market also applied to the energy sector. Whereas the EU triggered the process of sector restructuring in the mid-1990s, several EU countries—including the UK and several Nordic countries—had established themselves as frontrunners in EU market liberalisation (see Chap. 8 by Ciambra and Solorio). The European institutions, first and foremost the European Commission, pushed for EU market liberalisation because it was believed that price deregulation and privatisation would lead to competition and consequently to declining prices for final consumers (Jamasb and Pollitt 2005; Haas et al. 2006). Directive 96/92/EC concerning common rules for the internal market in electricity (EU 1996) was a first major step towards a common European power market (see Chap. 5 by Herweg for an analysis of the liberalisation of the European gas market). Notwithstanding the lack of direct competences in the energy sector (see Chap. 1 by Tosun et al.; Tosun and Solorio 2011), the European Commission exerted indirect influence because it was now responsible for guaranteeing the functioning of the internal energy market (Matlary 1997; Brand and Witthohn 2002; Hirschl 2008).

The role of the Commission as guarding a level playing field and free trade of electricity in the EU is closely linked to the design of liberalised electricity markets and the European target model. Almost simultaneously to the creation of a common European electricity market, the EU started the transformation process of the European electricity sector in order to reduce carbon emissions. On the one hand, a European carbon market based on a cap-and-trade mechanism was established. On the other hand, policies for an increasing share of renewable energy sources were put in place. First, the Directives 2001/77/EC established an indicative target for electricity produced from renewable energy sources for the year 2010. Second, the

Directive 2009/28/EC set a renewable energy target for the year 2020 (see Chap. 2 by Biesenbender). As indicated by the Commission's Carbon Roadmap, reaching 80 % Green House Gas emission reductions by 2050 would require an almost complete decarbonisation of the European power system (EU Commission 2011). A new 2030 target for renewable energy sources was proposed by the European Commission in early 2014. Most scenarios confirm that the share of renewable energy sources will continue to rise sharply in order to reach this target. The Commission's Green Paper on "A 2030 framework for climate and energy policies" states that high shares of renewable energy sources, energy efficiency and smarter energy infrastructure are "no regrets" options for transforming the EU's energy system (EU Commission 2013a).

Consequently, the European Union—and the European Commission in particular—is following two objectives simultaneously. First, the Commission tries to accomplish the establishment of a common European electricity market. Second, the Commission supports a low-carbon electricity market with high shares of renewable energy. On the one hand, investment in low-carbon technologies and renewable energy sources in particular requires predictable and secure revenues for power producers. On the other hand, a liberalised electricity market is based on short-term trading of electricity on volatile spot markets. In order to understand the ambiguous role of the European Commission as an agenda-setter for renewable electricity financing mechanisms, it is necessary to understand the current market design and the targeted market design for the future—the so-called European target model.

6.2.1 Liberalised Electricity Markets and the European Target Model

Markets are constructed. The basic concepts of liberalised power markets need to be understood in order to comprehend the controversy regarding renewable energy finance mechanisms. The theoretical underpinning of liberalised and competitive electricity market started in the 1970s. One of the crucial innovations of liberalised electricity markets—in contrast to the functioning and regulation of monopolistic electricity systems—was the implementation of marginal cost pricing. Economists such as Alfred E. Kahn developed the concept of marginal cost pricing in the 1970 before it was first implemented—in the airline industry and in US electricity markets—in the early 1980s (Kahn 1970; Joskow 1976; Hirsh 1999). Instead of paying power producers in accordance with their respective levelised cost of energy over the lifetime of a power plant (cost plus regulation), a uniform price per kilowatt-hour is paid to all power producers participating in the market. In a liberalised electricity market, this price is determined via anonymous bids on a spot market. Spot market prices are usually auctioned on an hourly basis, meaning that potential revenues for power producers change hourly (Borenstein 2000;

Joskow 2008). This creates a substantial risk for all power producers that need to refinance their investment via spot market sales of electricity—and this risk generally increases the cost of capital.

Power plants usually operate for a period of 20–30 years and their amortisation period is often equally long. Consequently, investors need to estimate short- and long-term price levels and variations on the spot market. In the case of marginal cost pricing, power plants are dispatched in line with their short-term marginal costs, which correspond to producing one extra kilowatt-hour of electricity in an existing power plant. Their marginal costs are basically the fuel costs and CO_2 costs. The last power plant, which is needed to meet electricity demand, "clears" the market and sets the price for all other power plants. In other words, the market price equals to the marginal generation cost of the marginal power plant. Power generation technologies with no or low fuel costs have relatively low marginal costs. Figure 6.1 shows a typical merit order for electricity spot markets.

When shaping national and European energy policies, the European Commission pursues the establishment of a text book model for liberalised electricity markets. Ultimately, all power producers should be able to refinance their investments via (spot) market sales of electricity and the achievable contribution margins (see Fig. 6.1). Ideally, this market (i.e. the spot market) would be a level playing field for all power producers—with externalities (e.g. carbon emissions and other environmental damages) being internalised via the European Emissions Trading System.

As indicated above, this leads to high investment risk for all power producers and potentially to high costs of capital. In addition, two other factors have to be taken into account in the case of renewable energy sources. First, their relatively high shares of capital expenditures in relation to operation expenditures. Second, the effect of an increasing share of wind and solar photovoltaics (PV) on spot market prices. Power producers need to refinance their capital expenditures (CAPEX) and their operating expenditures (OPEX) via surplus revenues from market sales, the so-called contribution margin. The share of CAPEX and OPEX differs quite considerably from one technology to the next (see Fig. 6.2).

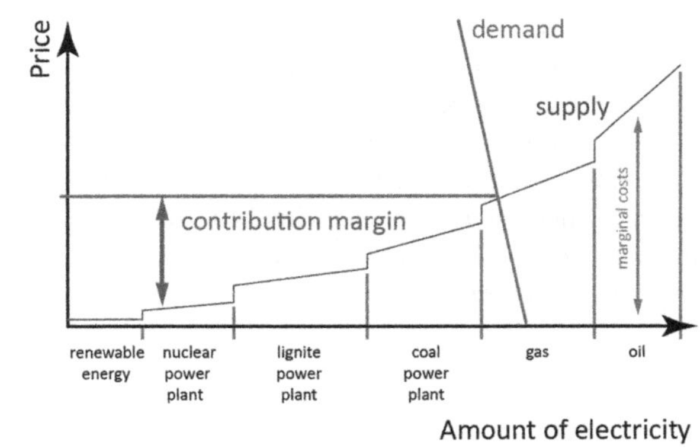

Fig. 6.1 Typical merit order of power plants. *Source* Transdisciplinary panel on energy change (TPEC), IASS Potsdam

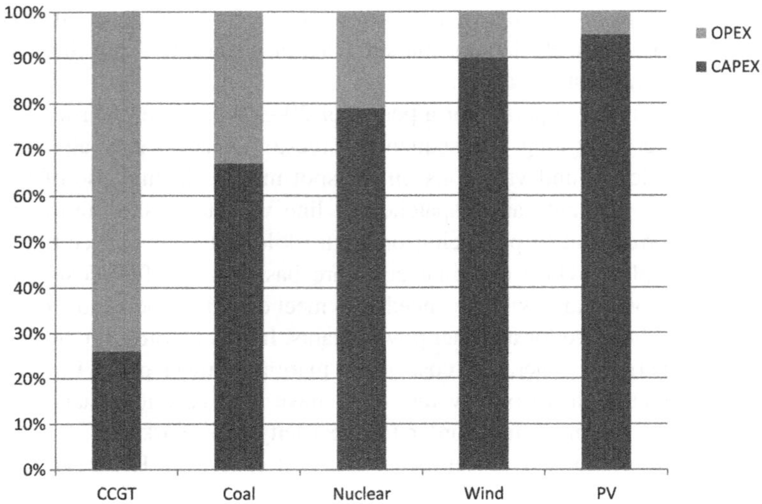

Fig. 6.2 Share of fixed versus variable costs of selected power generation technologies. *Source* Author based on (EIA 2013)

The different share of CAPEX and OPEX leads to different levels of risks associated with investment in different power generation technologies—despite the fact that they are ideally competing on a "level playing field" in a common market. This is one of the aspects frequently overlooked in the debate on a level playing field. By definition, technologies with lower levels of capital cost face lower risk because their investment risk is primarily related to the cost recovery for the fixed capital costs. In other words, short- and long-term price volatilities of the spot market are a bigger risk for wind and PV producers than for gas-fired power producers. To put it simply: an operator of a gas-fired power plant can still decide not to operate the plant if market prices are below the costs for fuel (and CO_2). Therefore, refinancing power plant via spot market sales creates a bias towards technologies with a low share of capital costs (and a high share of fuel costs). However, most low-carbon technologies have a relatively high share of capital expenditures.

In addition, an increasing share of renewable energy sources with very low marginal costs reduces the spot market price. This so-called merit order effect was observed in many countries with a high share of wind and solar PV in the system (Sensfuß et al. 2007; Sáenz de Miera et al. 2008; Ray et al. 2010). To put it in a nutshell, increasing shares of wind and solar PV on the market results in lower spot market prices and thus destroy the basis for refinancing themselves via spot market sales in the future.

6.2.2 *Financing Mechanisms for Renewable Electricity in the European Union in the Context of Electricity Market Liberalisation*

As indicated above, the European Commission is pursuing two partially conflicting objectives. On the one hand, it fosters the transformation of the European electricity sector and tries to enable investments in renewable energy sources and other low-carbon technologies. This requires investment security—especially because these low-carbon technologies are very capital intensive. On the other hand, the Commission wants to establish a common market, which is based on the concept of short-term trading on electricity spot markets. This creates a substantial amount of risk for power producers. In order to understand the ambiguous role of the European Commission as an agenda shaper for renewable electricity financing mechanisms, it is necessary to understand the debate of various financing mechanisms in the light of the ongoing electricity market liberalisation. How far are the different finance mechanisms able to allow for investment security and low capital costs? And how far are they compatible with the European target model for a liberalised market?

A number of different support instruments are applied in EU member states. Nonetheless, the debate within the EU context is primarily focused on Tradable Green Certificate instruments and feed-in tariffs. Recently, auctions have gained increasing importance in the European debate. Other support instruments, fiscal incentives, have played a minor role within the EU policy debate.

6.2.2.1 Quota Obligations

Under a quota obligation, the legislator requires electricity suppliers to provide a certain share of electricity from renewable energy sources. The supplier can either produce electricity itself or buy it from other green electricity producers. In order to increase the flexibility of the system, the supplier is also allowed to make up the required share by trading certificates in many counties, which serve as proof of compliance with legal obligation. Therefore, these mechanisms are called tradable green certificates (TGC) in the EU. The electricity supplier can obtain certificates either by producing renewable electricity or by buying certificates on the national certificate market. If suppliers fall short of reaching the required share, they must pay a penalty. Under this type of support mechanism, renewable electricity producers have two income sources. First, they sell their electricity on the spot market for electricity at the given (hourly) price. Second, they can sell their certificates on the national green certificate market. In theory, the certificate sales compensate for "greenness" of the electricity or the positive attributes of renewable electricity compared with conventionally produced "grey electricity" (Jacobs 2012a, b). This support instrument reflects the functioning of competitive spot market in liberalised power markets. First, the produced power is sold on a spot market—and the price achieved by the renewable electricity producer is the result of supply and demand. Second, the certificates received for each unit of renewable electricity is traded on a (national) trading platform. To a certain extent, this certificate trading platform reflects the functioning of an electricity spot market. In times of high demand, the power producer can achieve higher prices. And in times of low demand, the power producer receives lower prices. However, this support instrument has proven to be ineffective due to the high levels of investment risk resulting from the volatility with both spot market prices and certificate prices (Goldammer et al. 2012). As of 2013, six countries in the EU applied this type of support mechanism. Quota obligations were first implemented in the UK, Italy and Belgium in 2002. Sweden followed in 2003 and Poland in 2004. Romania was the last EU country to implement this support instrument in 2007 (EU Commission 2005; EU Commission 2008a, b, c, d; Resch et al. 2005). In 2011, the UK announced the replacement of the quota mechanism with a feed-in premium mechanism.

6.2.2.2 Feed-in Tariffs

Feed-in tariffs consist of three core design features: a purchase obligation, a pre-defined (fixed) tariff payment level per kilowatt-hour and a long duration of tariff payment. First, the purchase obligation forces the grid operator or utility to buy all renewable electricity—independent of electricity demand. Second, the renewable electricity producer is guaranteed a certain amount of money per unit of electricity produced. Third, this payment is guaranteed over a long period of time (usually 15–20 years), which increases investment security and ideally allows for cost recovery (Mendonça et al. 2009; Jacobs 2012a, b). This support instrument reflects the logic of price regulation under non-competitive markets. Renewable energy producers are exempt from price risk (volatility of spot market price) and volume risk (the risk of not being able to sell the electricity on the market). This finance mechanism delivers a high degree of investment security because power producers are able to predict their revenues over the lifetime of the power plant. Feed-in tariffs and feed-in premiums accounted for the majority of newly installed capacity from wind onshore and photovoltaics (93 % of all wind onshore capacity and nearly 100 % of all photovoltaics capacity installed by the end of 2010 in Europe) (Jacobs 2012a, b; Ragwitz et al. 2012).[3] Besides this high degree of effectiveness, feed-in tariffs have also proven to be efficient since they were able to lower capital cost due to the high level of investment security. The great majority of EU member states use feed-in tariffs for renewable electricity support. As of 2012, feed-in tariffs were established in 24 out of the 27 EU member states. 20 member states use FITs as their main support instrument.

---

[3] By early 2012, this policy mechanism had been implemented at the national level in at least 92 jurisdictions around the world (REN21 2012).

6.2.2.3 Feed-in Premiums

In the case of premium feed-in tariffs, the producer has to sell the renewable electricity on the spot market. As the market price of electricity alone will often not suffice to reach a certain profitability threshold, a reduced feed-in tariff is paid to the producer of renewable electricity. The premium payment usually depends on the technology-specific generation costs. The combination of these two payment components—the electricity market price and the reduced feed-in tariff—should suffice to operate renewable energy power plant profitably (Jacobs 2012a, b). As the premium feed-in tariff consists of both incomes from spot market sales and a "fixed or gliding payment component", it can also be understood as a compromise between the proponents of feed-in tariffs and the proponents of quota-based TGC mechanisms. Premium feed-in tariffs are considered to be more 'market-based' than a fixed feed-in tariff and less problematic in the light of a common European market (EU Commission 2005; Klein et al. 2008). Therefore, the implementation of premium feed-in tariffs have often been considered as a means to overcome resistance to price-based support mechanisms in general (Mendonça et al. 2009). When assessing the risk of premium feed-in tariffs for renewable electricity producers, two design options need to be differentiated. First, a fixed premium payment on top of the revenues from spot market sales. Second, a variable or gliding premium payment, which makes up for the difference between the variable spot market price and a previously determined price that allows power producers to refinance their investment (Couture and Gagnon 2010; Ragwitz et al. 2012). In the case of a fixed premium, the power producer is subject to price risk that is variations on the electricity spot market—in the short-term (hourly, weekly and monthly) and on the long-term (over the period of years that are needed to refinance the initial investment).

6.2.2.4 Auctions

In case of this financing mechanism, the responsible authority is usually auctioning a certain amount of capacity (e.g. 100 MW of wind onshore). Project developers will answer to this call for tender by offering a certain price per kilowatt-hour. Contrary to feed-in tariffs or feed-in premiums, prices are not set administratively but instead the result of competition between different market actors. This is more in line with the underlying idea of competitive markets than administratively set payments levels. In theory, auctioning capacity should guarantee power production at the lowest possible cost (see Rickerson et al. 2010; Becker and Fischer 2013). The risk associated with auctions depends on its design. Policy makers can either auction fixed tariffs, gliding premium payments or fixed premiums on top of the revenues from market sales. In addition, auctions lead to a higher risk during the project development phase because project developers cannot be certain whether their project will be selected or not. Auction mechanisms have been used in a number of EU member states, including the UK (until 1999) and Ireland (until

2005). As of 2010, this support instrument is still applied in Denmark for offshore wind energy. France also made use of this support mechanism from 1996 to 2000. Today, France still uses auctions for large scale solar PV, biomass, wind offshore and in exceptional circumstances for other technologies (Resch et al. 2005; Ragwitz et al. 2006; République Francaise 2010).

6.3 The Commission's Positions Regarding Financing Mechanisms

In this section, we will elaborate on the position of the European Commission regarding different financing mechanisms for renewable energy sources over time. We analyse the Commission's positions with regards to different legislative procedures and publications from 1995 to 2013. This includes White Papers, Green Papers, guidance papers and recommendations, best practise benchmark report, draft Directives and state-aid guidelines.

6.3.1 Early Commission Papers and the Directive 2001/77/EC

Although the first policy initiatives for the support of renewable energy sources were taken in the 1980s, the debate on the best financing instruments for renewable electricity was largely triggered by the liberalisation of European energy markets in the 1990s. First indications of a common European framework for the support of renewable energy sources can be found in the Commission's White Paper of 1995 on an energy policy for the EU. The document stated that "certain forms of energy like renewables may need to be supported initially through specific programmes or subsidies in order for them to find a place on the market". Nonetheless, support for renewable energies should be given in a way that is least harmful for competition. Consequently, "further policy development may need to be considered" and the organisation of national markets should be monitored closely (EU Commission 1995, p. 19).

In the following years, the European Commission and the European Parliament were looking for adequate financing schemes, which would eventually be applied for all European countries in a harmonised framework (Busch 2003). In its 1996 Green Paper *Energy for the Future*, the European Commission criticised the fragmented and rapidly changing nature of national financing mechanisms. The Commission also expressed a clear preference for quota-based support instruments by stressing the need to phase out and replace regulatory policies by "more market oriented measures" making explicit reference to the functioning of quota-based support instruments (EU Commission 1996, p. 34).

Even though the European Parliament does not have formal agenda-setting competences within the EU's institutional framework, it soon expressed its opposing view reflecting the position of many European member states. In a report from 1997, Rapporteur Rothe from the Party of European Socialists called for the establishment of a European feed-in tariff scheme. Even though the term "feed-in tariff" was not explicitly mentioned, the report argued for a purchase obligation of green electricity and a "minimum payment by the utilities… which would at least cover all of the current costs of the producer" (EU Parliament 1997, p. 6). Despite this obvious disagreement on the most adequate financing instrument among the European institutions, the European Commission continued to push for an EU-wide quota-based support instrument and pressured several member states to adopt this type of support instrument by promising a first-mover advantage once this support instrument was introduced Europe-wide (Lauber 2007).

At the same time, the diffusion of feed-in tariff schemes slowed down because many legislators expected a change in the European framework and feared legal insecurity (Busch 2003; Bechberger and Reiche 2007). The European Commission openly criticised the German feed-in regulation, which granted high levels of remuneration for wind energy. And the German feed-in law of 1990 was referred to the European Court (*Preussen Elektra vs. Schlesag*) for its assumed incompatibility with the rules of the internal energy market (Jacobs 2012a, b). The European Commission's 1999 working paper "Electricity from renewable energy sources and the internal electricity market" increased the pressure on feed-in tariff mechanisms. The paper found that, given the shift towards electricity market competition, a move away from a "fixed price tariff approach towards one based on trade and competition is at some stage inevitable" (EU Commission 1999, p. 17). In addition, the paper highlighted the distorting effects of a multitude of national support mechanisms on the functioning of a common European electricity market and criticised the limited competition between different renewable electricity technologies under feed-in tariffs.

In 1999, the energy commissioner, Loyala de Palacio, made one more push for a harmonised European support framework based on a quota obligation (Lauber 2007). However, this political initiative failed following criticism from the European Parliament, industry associations and environmental organisations (Jacobs 2012a, b). In other words, the co-decision-making process—and the opposition from the Parliament and selected European member states such as Spain and German—prevented the European Commission from enforcing their concepts of renewable energy finance mechanisms in a liberalised and common European electricity market. In the following years, Commissioner Palacio tried to take the concerns of member states and industry associations into account and allowed different financing instruments to work in parallel—at least for a certain number of years. After an interim period of 5 years, the European Commission planned to table a proposal for a harmonised support mechanism, which had "to be compatible with the principles of the internal electricity market" (EU Commission 2000, p. 18).

In March 2001, the European Commission had to cope with yet another indirect defeat as the European Court rejected the aforementioned complaint against the

German feed-in tariff mechanisms of 1990. As a consequence, this judgement also undermined the Commission's case against the German feed-in tariff of 2000 and the Commission's intention to make explicit reference to state-aid provisions within the planned directive (Lauber 2007). Finally, the European directive of 2001 accepted heterogeneity of financing instruments—at least for the time being. The European directive fixed indicative renewable electricity targets for the European member states. But—in line with the principle of subsidiarity—national legislators were free to choose any type of financing instrument to achieve these targets. However no later than 2005, the European Commission was expected to table "a well-documented report on experience gained with the application and coexistence of the different mechanisms", which might be "accompanied by a proposal for a Community framework with regard to support schemes" (EU 2001).

6.3.2 The Commission's Assessment Reports for Financing Mechanisms

Under Article 4 of the directive 2001/77/EC, the European Commission was expected to assess the experience gained from the application and coexistence of the different financing mechanisms and possibly make suggestions for a harmonised support mechanism based on their effectiveness, efficiency, simplicity and compatibility with the principles of the internal electricity market. Assessment reports were published in 2005 and 2008.[4] The 2005 assessment of financing instruments was first tabled in December 2005 (EU Commission 2005). The report was compiled by DG TREN—the department of the European Commission responsible for energy matters. The report stated that in most countries the support level had been insufficient to attract investment in renewable electricity generation plants.

Interestingly and contrary to theoretical economic assumptions about the effectiveness and efficiency of support instruments, the report found that feed-in tariffs had been most successful in promoting renewable energy sources. Even though quota-based systems provided significantly higher support levels, they had been less successful in triggering an increase in newly installed capacity. This was especially true in the case of wind energy. Despite the better performance of feed-in tariffs, the European Commission's assessment report did not propose harmonisation based on this financing instrument. It argued that more experience had to be gained from different support schemes and that competition among them "could be seen as healthy at least over a transitional period". In addition, the Commission stated that fixed feed-in tariffs "are difficult to harmonise at EU level [and] may be challenged under internal market principles" (EU Commission 2005, p. 4).

[4] The second assessment report was published in combination with the draft proposal for the Directive 2009/28/EC (see Sect. 4.3).

Interestingly, the assessment report for the first time stresses the difference between feed-in tariffs and "fixed-premium mechanisms", which at that time were implemented in Denmark and Spain. Since a European-wide solution based on certificate trading became less likely in the 2000s, the European Commission showed increasing interest in feed-in premiums because they were at least more market compatible than the widespread fixed feed-in tariff mechanisms.

6.3.3 Directive 2009/28/EC

The preparation for the new directive on renewable energies—the 2001 directive included targets only up to 2010—started as early as 2007. On 10 January 2007, the European Commission presented "an integrated energy and climate change package", the so-called Energy Package. The package consisted of 12 different reports, including a roadmap for renewable energy sources (EU Commission 2007). Among others in this package, the European Commission called for longer term, mandatory renewable energy targets, including the electricity sector, the heating and cooling sector and the transport sector.

Only 2 months later in March 2007, the European heads of states agreed on a binding renewable energy target of 20 % of the total final energy consumption by 2020. The European Commission was asked to prepare a new directive in order to "put in place an integrated policy on energy combining actions at European and member states' level" (EU Council 2007, p. 14)—implicitly suggesting the need for an at least partially harmonised support mechanism.

The first draft of the new European directive for renewable energy sources was tabled after a long delay in January 2008 (EU Commission 2008a, b, c, d). The delay largely arose from the difficulty of allocating the total target of 20 % renewable energy consumption by 2020 among all 27 member states in a fair and transparent way. In contrast to the first directive, the targets were no longer of a voluntary nature, and therefore the allocation of national targets was much more controversial. In order to make the achievement of national targets easier for member states, the European Commission planned to implement certain flexibility mechanisms (Johnston et al. 2008). In 2007 and 2008, the debate centred mostly on the implementation of certificate trading based on guarantees of origin (GOs). This became the hook for the newly emerging harmonisation debate based on a quota-like support mechanism.

Even though the European Commission did not officially speak of the harmonisation of support mechanisms for renewable energies—officials of the Commission argued that they would not prescribe one single support instrument. The long-term effects of Europe-wide certificate trading based on GOs would have been similar to those of implementing a harmonised technology-neutral quota obligation (Ragwitz et al. 2007; Toke 2008; Jacobsson et al. 2009). The implementation of flexibility mechanisms was considered to be necessary since the national targets were not exclusively set according to the renewable energy potential in the different countries. Instead, the national economic strength of a country was also taken into account when national targets were allocated to European member states. Originally, GOs had been implemented for electricity disclosure, that is, proof that a certain unit of electricity was produced via renewable energy sources. Now, GOs were intended to be used for the virtual trade of renewable electricity among EU member states. If a member state was unable to produce a unit of renewable electricity within the country, it could buy a certificate from another member state in order to prove compliance with the national renewable energy target.

An early (leaked) internal draft of the new renewable energy directive included non-restricted GO trading between private actors (renewable electricity producers) and governments. However, this leaked proposal attracted criticism mostly from countries operating with feed-in tariffs as their national support mechanisms would have been undermined by such an approach (Clos and Gabriel 2008). Therefore, the final draft limited the scope of GO trading.

The European Commission was internally divided over the design of GO trading for target achievement. DG Environment emphasised the need for a support mechanism that was compatible with the European emissions trading scheme. A certificate trading scheme for renewable energy support was believed to be more compatible with the emission trading scheme. DG Competition favoured a trading mechanism based on its primary policy objective: the creation of an internal market and market efficiency. Only the DG TREN was opposed to certificate trading because it believed that volatile certificate prices would undermine investment security. Besides, DG TREN acknowledged factors beyond mere macroeconomic analysis, which included the promotion of local economies and public acceptance of renewable electricity support (Nilsson et al. 2009). This conflict within the European Commission also becomes apparent when one compares different documents from the European Commission. While the impact assessment of the new draft directive states that the cheapest option for achieving the 20 % target would be a harmonised TGC scheme (EU Commission 2008a, b, c, d), the report on the assessment of support schemes concludes that harmonisation would be premature (EU Commission 2008a, b, c, d). These assessments of future renewable energy support options differ largely because different DGs have been responsible for drafting the documents. While the assessment report of European support mechanism was carried out by DG TREN, the draft directive and the attached impact assessment were a compromise between all branches within the European Commission (Jacobs 2012a, b).

Eventually, the implementation of GO trade was excluded from the final version of Directive 2009/28/EC due to opposition from the European Parliament and EU member states. The proposal for GO trade was further watered down by an amendment proposed by the European Parliament. According to Rapporteur Turmes from the European Green Party, GOs were to be limited to their original purpose of electricity disclosure and not be used in order to establish an EU-wide certificate trading scheme for target compliance (EU Parliament 2008). The European Parliament suggested different mechanisms for flexible target achievement. At a later stage, the European Council rejected the concept of certificate trading altogether and therefore this element was deleted from the first proposal (Jacobs 2012a, b). Finally, member states were free to select their national financing mechanisms. A second attempt by the European Commission to establish a harmonised European support framework had failed within the co-decision-making process.

6.3.4 DG Energy's Guidance for the Design of Support Schemes

In November 2013, the European Commission issued a set of guidance documents on state intervention in electricity markets. These guidance papers are not of binding in nature for member states. They simply reflect the Commission's views on renewable energy finance mechanisms and other issues, such as generation adequacy. These guidance documents were elaborated primarily by DG Energy (previously called DG TREN).

The "Guidance for the design of renewable support schemes" starts with a justification for public interventions in the EU electricity market via renewable energy support programmes (EU Commission 2013b, p. 3). However, it also stresses the fact that more market exposure is to be imposed on renewable energy producers because energy markets are able to organise "energy production and investment decisions efficiently and cost effectively" (EU Commission 2013b, p. 5). The guidance document gives recommendations for designing six different support mechanisms: auctions (competitive allocation mechanisms), quota obligations, investment support, tax exemptions, feed-in premium and feed-in tariffs.

The European Commission identified a general trend in European finance mechanisms—a move from fixed tariffs to premium feed-in tariffs. However, this can be considered a slightly selective perception of the European reality. Out of the 22 EU member states that have adopted feed-in tariffs (for one or more technologies), only six had adopted premium feed-in tariffs at the end of 2013 and most of these countries had put them in place next to the fixed feed-in tariff payment. The fact that Spain—the first country to implement premium feed-in tariffs back in 1998—had abandoned this financing mechanism in 2013 because of its higher costs in contrast to fixed tariff payment was only mentioned in a footnote.

Nonetheless, the Commission "recommends that feed in tariffs are phased out and support instruments that expose renewable energy producers to market price signals such as feed in premiums are used". The Commission prefers feed-in premiums because it obliges renewable energy producers to find a seller for their electricity (in line with liberalised markets) and the "market signals reach the renewable energy operators through varying degrees of market exposure" (EU Commission 2013b, p. 8). This varying degree of market exposure depends on the design of the feed-in premium. Even though DG Energy is trying to provide a balanced view of the advantages and disadvantages of the different design options, a preference of floating premium over fixed premiums can be read between the lines. According to the DG Energy, a floating premium is more compatible with the European carbon market (because premiums fall when the carbon price goes up and vice versa) and it "allows the investment to take place at a reasonable cost of capital" (EU Commission 2013b, p. 9). On the contrary, a fixed premium could lead to overcompensation and the higher risk might trigger higher capital costs.

6.3.5 Energy State-Aid Guidelines for the Years 2014–2020

Only a few weeks after DG Energy had published its guidelines, DG Competition put forward the draft state-aid guidelines for the years 2014–2020 (EU Commission 2013d). The draft state-aid guidelines were subject to a public consultation process. However, all comments received during this consultation process were of non-binding nature and the European Commission had the final word. The new state-aid guidelines for environmental protection and energy 2014–2020 were published in April 2014 (EU Commission 2014).

The state-aid guidelines indicate in what circumstances a national financing mechanisms might be judged as state-aid. If a support of financing scheme is considered state-aid, the European Commission needs to approve all changes to the financing mechanisms. In this case, the European Commission is directly involved in the design process of financing mechanisms and therefore become an important actor in national policy making. As of 2013, 14 member states had notified their financing mechanisms as state-aid.

The new guidelines set very strict conditions on the design of national support mechanisms in order not to be considered state-aid. This allows the Commission to further expand its influence on national finance mechanisms.

Allowance for aid to renewable energy sources is based on the expectation that renewable energy technologies will become "grid-competitive" in the period between 2020 and 2030, which leads the European Commission to the conclusion that "subsidies and exemptions from balancing responsibilities should be phased out in a degressive way". In order to finance renewable energy sources, so-called "market instruments, such as auctioning or competitive bidding process[es] open to all generators [...] should normally ensure that subsidies are reduced to a minimum in view of their complete phasing out" (EU Commission 2014, p. 31). However, technology-specific auctions can be carried out in exceptional circumstances.

Moreover, remuneration for renewable energy power producers should be "granted as premium in addition to the market price (premium) whereby the generators sell its electricity directly in the market" (EU Commission 2014, p. 34). Fixed feed-in tariffs and selling electricity via a single/central buyer becomes the exception and is only viable for small-scale producers with an installed capacity below 1 MW.[5]

---

[5] Wind energy is exempt up to a size of 6 MW or six generation units.

As indicated in the draft guidelines prepared by DG Competition, the Commission was taking an even more market-oriented stance regarding the recommended design for renewable energy finance mechanisms. Concerning the design of premium feed-in tariffs, DG Competition favoured fixed premium payments over variable or floating premiums. Even though this preference was not stated explicitly, it is revealed by defining feed-in premiums as "a premium paid on top of the market price which exposes renewable energy producers to market prices" (EU Commission 2013d, p. 11).[6] However, the final version of the energy state-aid guidelines is less rigid and consequently also leaves member states the option to support renewable energies via floating premium—thus offering a similar degree of investment security as fixed feed-in tariffs.

6.4 Conclusion: The Future of Renewable Energy Finance and Beyond

In this chapter, we have traced the European debate on financing mechanisms for renewable electricity and the role of the European Commission in shaping these policies. It was shown that the Commission is pursuing two objectives that are sometimes contradicting each other: on the one hand, a common market based on short-term trading on spot markets (and a level playing field for all power generation technologies) and on the other hand, a rapid shift towards low-carbon technologies and an increasing share of renewable energy sources.

In the 1990s, the European Commission was clearly in favour of a European-wide quota-based financing mechanism since this financing instrument was thought to be most in line with the concept of a common European electricity market. However, most member states selected feed-in tariffs because they were able to increase the share of renewables in the most cost-effective way. The initial proposal from the European Commission for a harmonised quota-based mechanism failed in the co-decision process and was rejected by both the European Parliament and the Council.

After a second attempt from the Commission to harmonise support mechanisms had failed due to opposition from the European Parliament and member states at the end of the 2010s, the Commission's interest in alternative finance mechanisms increased. The latest Commission guidelines and draft state-aid rules confirmed the preference for feed-in premiums and auction mechanisms. In fact, the Commission had already shown increasing interest in premium feed-in tariffs as of 2005 because this instrument can be interpreted as compromise between "market integration" and investment security for new power generation capacity.

[6] There is only very limited exposure to market price risk in the case of floating premium payments.

Our analysis revealed that the European Commission is now exerting its influence on national policy making via regulations, which do not require co-decision-making with other European institutions. In this respect, the new state-aid guidelines for environmental protection and energy 2014–2020 are a crucial tool.

Interestingly, the European Commission cannot be viewed as a homogeneous entity. We are also able to depict controversies amongst the different departments of the European Commission—the Directorates General. Whereas the Directorate General responsible for energy (previously DG TREN, now DG Energy) places a stronger emphasis on the need of effective financing mechanisms for renewable energy sources, other Directorates General—first and foremost DG Competition—care more about the creation of a level playing field and so-called market conformity of financing mechanisms. Said succinctly, DG Competition takes the role as the "guardian of a common market" whereas DG Energy understands the needs for stable revenues in order to attract investment in renewable energy sources in Europe. It remains to be seen what type of risk-sharing arrangements are needed in order to further increase the share of renewable energy sources and other low-carbon technologies (Finon and Roques 2013).

Some experts claim that several renewable energy technologies will no longer need support after 2020 if markets are corrected with a sufficiently high price for carbon emissions (Müsgens 2013). This reflects the language used by the European Commission in the new state-aid guidelines. Others claim that finance mechanisms will be needed for much longer, if Europe want to fulfil its climate targets (Verbruggen and Lauber 2009). Especially in markets with high share of fluctuating renewable energy sources, it will be difficult to refinance wind parks and solar PV systems via revenues from energy markets due to the merit order effect (Sensfuß et al. 2008; Leprich et al. 2012).

Interestingly, the difficulty to refinance power generation technologies via volatile spot market sales of electricity goes beyond the domain of renewable energy technology. Nuclear power producers face similar difficulties in refinancing their power plants via short-term trading on spot markets—partly due to their relatively high share of fixed cost and partly due to their long investment cycles (Finon and Roques 2010). Consequently, financing mechanisms which are already in use for renewable energy technologies in Europe are now starting to be implemented in several European member states. The most prominent case is the planned "Contract for differences" scheme in the UK, which works similar to sliding premium feed-in tariffs. The UK regulator has suggested prices of more than 10 €cent/kWh for 35 years plus an indexation to inflation (EDF 2013).

In addition, supplementary markets such as capacity markets are currently being implemented or at least debated in many EU member states in order to guarantee long-term security of supply in liberalised power markets—so-called resource adequacy (EU Commission 2012, 2013c). At the moment, no type of power generation technology seems to be able to refinance itself exclusively via spot market sales of electricity. And the first investment cycle in new power generation capacity after market liberalisation is only starting. Therefore, the confrontation between proponents of high levels of predictable revenues (and investment security) and proponents of text book market liberalisation is likely to continue.

References

Bechberger, M., & Reiche, D. (2007). The spread of renewable energy feed-in tariffs (REFITs) in the EU-25. In L. Mez (Ed.), *Green power markets: Support schemes, case studies and perspectives* (pp. 31–50). Brentwood (UK): Multi-Science Publishing.

Becker, B., & Fischer, D. (2013). Promoting renewable electricity generation in emerging economies. *Energy Policy, 56*, 446–455.

Borenstein, S. (2000). Understanding competitive pricing and market power in wholesale electricity markets. *The Electricity Journal, 13*(6), 49–57.

Brand, E., & Witthohn, A. (2002). Die energiepolitischen handlungsmöglichkeiten der EG. *Energiewirtschaftliche Tagesfragen, 2002*(4), 253–257.

Busch, P. -O. (2003). *Die diffusion von einspeisevergütungen und quotenmodellen: Konkurrenz der Modelle in Europa. FFU-report 03-2003*. Berlin: Environmental Policy Research Center, Freie Universität Berlin.

Clos, J., & Gabriel S. (2008). *Letter to Commissioner Piebalgs on behalf of the International Feed-in Cooperation, 10 January 2008*. Madrid: Ministerio de Industria, Turismo y Comercio.

Couture, T., & Gagnon, Y. (2010). An analysis of feed-in tariff remuneration models: Implications for renewable energy investment. *Energy Policy, 38*(2), 955–965.

EDF. (2013). *Agreement reached on commercial terms for the planned Hinkley Point C nuclear power station, Press release, 21 October 2013*. Paris: Électricité de France.

EIA. (2013). *Levelized cost of new generation resources in the annual energy outlook 2013*. Washington DC: U.S. Energy Information Administration.

EU. (1986). *Single European Act. 25 ILM. 506. European Union*. Brussels: Official Journal of the European Communities.

EU. (2001). *Directive 2001/77/EC of the European Parliament and of the Council of 27 September 2001 on the promotion of electricity produced from renewable energy sources in the internal electricity market. L 283/33. European Union*. Brussels: Official Journal of the European Communities.

EU Commission. (1995). *White paper: An energy policy for the European Union. COM (95) 682 final*. Brussels: European Commission.

EU Commission. (1996). *Energy for the future—renewable sources of energy. Greenpaper for a community strategy. COM (96) 576 final*. Brussels: European Commission.

EU Commission. (1999). *Commission working document, electricity from renewable energy sources and the internal electricity market. SEC(1999) 470 final*. Brussels: European Commission.

EU Commission. (2000). *Amended proposal for a directive of the European Parliament and of the council on the promotion of electricity from renewable energy sources in the internal electricity market, COD 2000/0116. COM/2001/0884 final*. Brussels: European Commission—Official Journal C154E.

EU Commission. (2005). *The support of electricity from renewable energy sources*. Brussels: Commission of the European Communities.

EU Commission. (2007). *Renewable energy roadmap, renewable energies in the 21st century: Building a more sustainable future, communication from the commission to the council and the European Parliament. COM(2006) 848 final*. Brussels: European Commission.

EU Commission. (2008a). *Commission staff working document: Annex to the impact assessment*. Brussels: European Commission.

EU Commission. (2008b). *Impact assessment, document accompanying the package of implementation measures for the EU's objective on climate change and renewable energy for 2020, commission staff working document. SEC(2008) 85*. Brussels: European Commission.

EU Commission. (2008c). *Proposal for a directive of the European Parliament and of the council on the promotion of the use of energy from renewable sources*. Brussels: Commission of the European Communities.

EU Commission. (2008d). *The support of electricity from renewable energy sources, commission staff working document, accompanying document to the proposal for directive of the European Parliament and of the council on the promotion of the use energy from renewable sources*. Brussels: European Commission.

EU Commission. (2011). *A Roadmap for moving to a competitive low carbon economy in 2050 COM(2011) 112 final*. Brussels: European Commission.

EU Commission. (2012). *Consultation paper on generation adequacy, capacity mechanisms and the internal market in electricity*. Brussels: European Commission.

EU Commission. (2013a). *A 2030 framework for climate and energy policies. COM(2013) 169 final*. Brussels: European Commission.

EU Commission. (2013b). *European Commission guidance for the design of renewables support schemes—commission staff working document. Accompanying the document communication from the commission. Delivering the internal market in electricity and making the most of public intervention (SWD(2013) 439 final)*. Brussels: European Commission.

EU Commission. (2013c). *Generation adequacy in the internal electricity market—guidance on public interventions SWD(2013) 438 final*. Brussels: European Commission.

EU Commission. (2013d). *Paper of the services of DG Competition containing draft guidelines on environmental and energy aid for 2014–2020, December 2013. DG Competition*. Brussels: European Commission.

EU Commission. (2014*). Guidelines on state aid for environmental protection and energy 2014–2020, communication from the commission, C(2014) 2322*. Brussels: European Commission.

EU Council. (2007). *Presidency conclusion, 8/9 March 2007. 7224/07*. Brussels: European Council.

EU Parliament. (1997). *Report on the communication from the commission on energy for the future: Renewable sources of energy—green paper for a community strategy (COM(96)0576—C4-0623/96), Committee on Research, Technological Development and Energy, Rapporteur: Mrs. Mechtild Rothe. A4-0168/97*. Brussels: European Parliament.

EU Parliament. (2008). *Draft European parliament legislative resolution on the proposal for a directive of the European Parliament and of the council on the promotion of the use of energy from renewable sources (COM(2008)0019—C6-0046/2008—2008/0016(COD)), Committee on Industry, Research and Energy, Rapporteur: Claude Turmes, 2008/0016(COD)*. Brussels: European Parliament.

Finon, D., & Roques, F. (2010). Contractual and financing arrangements for new nuclear investment in liberalized markets: Which efficient combination? In F. Lévêque, J.-M. Glachant, & J. Barquínet (Eds.), *Security of energy supply in Europe—natural gas, nuclear and hydrogen*. Cheltenham: Edward Elgar Publishing.

Finon, D., & Roques, F. (2013). European electricity market reforms: The visible hand of public coordination. *Economics of Energy and Environmental Policy, 2*(2), 107–124.

Goldammer, K., Hakkarainen, P., Jacobs, D., & Volkert, D. (2012). *Stellungnahme der plattform energiewende zur diskussion, erneuerbare energien wie fördern? Quotenmodelle vs. EEG*. Potsdam: Institute for Advanced Sustainability Studies.

Haas, R., Glachant, J.-M., Keseric, N., & Perez, Y. (2006). Competition in the continental European electricity market: Despair or work in progress? In F. P. Sioshani & W. Pfaffenberger (Eds.), *Electricity market reform: An international perspective* (pp. 265–315). Oxford: Elsevier.

Hirschl, B. (2008). *Erneuerbare energie-politik, eine multi-level policy-analyse mit fokus aufden deutschen strommarkt*. Wiesbaden: VS Research.

Hirsh, R. F. (1999). *Power loss: The origins of deregulation and restructuring in the American electric utility system*. Boston: MIT Press.

Jacobs, D. (2012a). *Policy convergence in the European Union: The case of feed-in tariffs in Germany, Spain and France*. Farnham: Ashgate Publishing.

Jacobs, D. (2012b). *Renewable Energy policy convergence in the EU—The evolution of feed-in tariffs in Germany, Spain and France*. Farnham: Ashgate Publishing.

Jacobsson, S., Bergek, A., Finon, D., Lauber, V., Mitchell, C., Toke, D., & Verbruggen, A. (2009). EU renewable energy support policy: Faith or facts? *Energy Policy, 37*(6), 2143–2146.

Jamasb, T., & Pollitt, M. (2005). *Electricity market reform in the European Union: A review of progress toward liberalization and integration*. Cambridge: University of Cambridge, Center for Energy and Environmental Policy Research.

Johnston, A., Neuhoff, K., Fouquet, D., Ragwitz, M., & Resch, G. (2008). The proposed New EU renewables directive: Interpretation, problems and prospects. *European Energy and Environmental Law Review, 17*(3), 126–145.

Joskow, P. L. (1976). Contributions to the theory of marginal cost pricing. *The Bell Journal of Economics, 7*(1), 197–206.

Joskow, P.L. (2008). Lessons learned from electricity market liberalization. *The Energy Journal,* 0 (special issue), 9–42.

Kahn, A. E. (1970). *The economics of regulation: Principles and institutions*. Cambridge: MIT Press.

Klein, A., Merkel, E., Pluger, B., Held, A., & Ragwitz, M. (2008). *Evaluation for different feed-in tariff design options: Best practice paper of the International Feed-in Tariff Cooperation*. Karlsruhe and Laxenburg: Fraunhofer Institut für Systemtechnik und Innovationsforschung and Vienna University of Technology Energy Economics Group.

Lauber, V. (2007). The politics of European Union policy on support schemes for electricity from renewable energy sources. In L. Mez (Ed.), *Green power markets—support schemes, case studies, and perspectives* (pp. 9–29). Brentwood: Multi-Science Publishing.

Leprich, U., Hauser, E., Grashof, K., Grote, L., Luxenburger, M., Sabatier, M., & Zipp, A. (2012). *Kompassstudie marktdesign—leitideen für ein design eines stromsystems mit hohem anteil fluktuierender erneuerbarer energien*. Saarbrücken: IZES gGmbH—Institut für ZukunftsEnergieSysteme.

Matlary, H. (1997). *Energy policy in the European Union*. Basingstoke: Macmillan.

Mendonça, M., Jacobs, D., & Sovacool, B. (2009). *Powering the green economy: The feed-in tariff handbook*. London: Earthscan.

Müsgens, F. (2013). Equilibrium prices and investment in electricity systems with CO_2-emission trading and high shares of renewable energies. Cottbus: University of Technology Cottbus.

Nilsson, M., Nilsson, L. J., & Ericsson, K. (2009). The rise and fall of GO trading in European renewable energy policy: The role of advocacy and policy framing. *Energy Policy, 37*(11), 4454–4462.

Pollack, M. A. (2003). *The engines of European integration: Delegation, agency and agenda setting in the EU*. Oxford: Oxford University Press.

Ragwitz, M., Held, A., Resch, G., Faber, T., Huber, C., & Haas, R. (2006). *Monitoring and evaluation of policy instruments to support renewable electricity in EU Member States*. Karlsruhe: Frauenhofer Institute Systems and Innovation Research.

Ragwitz, M., Resch, G., & Schleich, J. (2007). *Increased auctioning in the EU ETS and trade of guarantees of origin for renewables: A comparison of the impact on power sector producer rents, working paper sustainability and innovation, S 8/2007*. Karlsruhe: Fraunhofer Insititute for Systems and Innovation Research.

Ragwitz, M., Winkler, J., Klessmann, J., Gephart, M., & Resch, G. (2012). *Recent developments of feed-in systems in the EU—a research paper for the International Feed-in Cooperation*. Berlin: Ministry for the Environment, Nature Conservation and Nuclear Safety (BMU).

Ray, S., Munksgaard, J., Morthorst, P. E., & Sinner, A.-F. (2010). *Wind energy and electricity prices: Exploring the merit order effect*. Brussels: European Wind Energy Association.

REN21. (2012). *Renewables 2012—global status report*. Paris: Renewable Energy Policy Network for the 21st Century.

République Francaise. (2010). *National action plan for the promotion of renewable energies*. Paris: Ministère de l'Écologie, de l'Énergie, du Développment durable et de la Mer.

Resch, G., Lopez-Polo, M.-A., Auer, H., & Hass, R. (2005). *Electricity from renewable energy sources in EU-15 countries—a review of promotion strategies*. Vienna: Energy Economics Group.

Rickerson, W., Flynn, H., Hanley, C., Jacobs, D. & Solano-Peralta, M. (2010). Fiscal and non-fiscal incentives for adopting renewable energy: Feed-in tariffs in latin america and the caribbean. Washington, DC.

Sáenz de Miera, G., Del Río González, P., & Vizcaíno, I. (2008). Analysing the impact of renewable electricity support schemes on power prices: The case of wind electricity in Spain. *Energy Policy, 36*(9), 3345–3359.

Sensfuß, F., Ragwitz, M., & Genoese, M. (2007). *Analysis of the price effect of renewable electricity generation on spot market prices*. Karlsruhe: Fraunhofer Institut System- und Innovationsforschung.

Sensfuß, F., Ragwitz, M., & Genoese, M. (2008). The merit-order effect: A detailed analysis of the price effect of renewable electricity generation on spot market prices in Germany. *Energy Policy, 36*(8), 3086–3094.

Toke, D. (2008). The EU renewables directive—what is the fuss about trading? *Energy Policy, 36* (8), 3001–3008.

Tosun, J., & Solorio, I. (2011). Exploring the energy-environment relationship in the EU: Perspectives and challenges for theorizing and empirical analysis. In J. Tosun & I. Solorio (Eds.), *Energy and Environment in Europe: Assessing a Complex Relationship? European Integration online Papers (EIoP),* (Special Mini-Issue 1, Vol. 15, Article 7).

Verbruggen, A., & Lauber, V. (2009). Basic concepts for designing renewable electricity support aiming at a full-scale transition by 2050. *Energy Policy, 37*(12), 5732–5743.

Chapter 7
The EU Energy Poverty and Vulnerability Agenda: An Emergent Domain of Transnational Action

Stefan Bouzarovski and S. Petrova

Abstract This chapter explores the organisational and political complexities surrounding the adoption of energy poverty agendas and policies at the EU decision-making level. Theoretically, it is based on the literature on policy mobilities. Empirically, it engages in a triangulation of data from the secondary literature and interviews in various EU institutions. The analysis shows that agenda-shaping in the EU poverty domain has been mainly driven from above and has been highly contingent on attempts to 'define' and 'identify' the problem. There is little evidence to suggest that particular events or dynamics have provided a central impetus for European action in this domain. Only in recent years have energy poverty concerns started to enter mainstream EU policy agendas, principally as a result of the Commission's efforts surrounding the implementation of the Third Energy Package.

7.1 Introduction: Addressing Energy Poverty at the European Scale

In decision-maker and academic circles alike, the concept of 'EU energy policy' is generally associated with measures to address residential and industrial consumption practices or transnational security issue.[1] There is little recognition or knowledge of

[1] The research leading to this chapter has received funding from the European Research Council under the European Union's Seventh Framework Programme (FP7/2007–2013)/ERC, Grant Agreement Number 313478.

S. Bouzarovski (✉) · S. Petrova
SEED, University of Manchester, Arthur Lewis Building, Oxford Road, Manchester M202SQ, UK
e-mail: stefan.bouzarovski@manchester.ac.uk

S. Petrova
e-mail: saska.petrova@manchester.ac.uk

S. Bouzarovski
Department of Economic Geography, University of Gdańsk, Bazynskiego 4, 80-952 Gdańsk, Gdańsk, Poland

J. Tosun et al. (eds.), *Energy Policy Making in the EU*,
Lecture Notes in Energy 28, DOI 10.1007/978-1-4471-6645-0_7

the fact that the EU is becoming increasingly involved in a new strategic effort situated at the nexus among household fuel use, affordability and residential energy efficiency. This process is mainly associated with the intensifying drive to formulate and implement pan-European policies aimed at preventing and ameliorating energy (or fuel) poverty—a condition where a household is unable to access energy services in the home to a socially and materially acceptable level (Bouzarovski et al. 2012).

The relative invisibility of EU energy poverty policies can be attributed to the fact that debates around the social and housing dimensions of energy use have traditionally received little attention at the national scale within most member states. The UK and Ireland represent a notable exception; the condition of 'fuel poverty' received early political recognition in these two countries, albeit with considerable political difficulty (Boardman 2010). The last 5 years have seen an increasing acknowledgment of the European energy poverty problem by decision-makers across the continent. This trend has been motivated, in part, by growing public concerns over the affordability of energy: an issue that reached major proportions in the case of Bulgaria leading to the downfall of the country's government in 2012.

The rising recognition of energy poverty has been accompanied by the emergence of a number of new regulatory documents, policy proposals and high level discussions on the topic. But the emergence of a new polity with respect to the understanding of energy poverty as a genuinely pan-European problem has not been associated with a commensurate amount of academic attention. There is limited appreciation of the systemic processes that lie behind the political acceptance of energy poverty at the European scale, especially in terms of the power actors, interests and relations that have driven the increasing prominence of this issue within EU regulation and debates.

This situation has transpired despite the fact that the constituent dynamics of some of the political developments and institutional structures associated with adjacent programmatic sectors are well known (for example, there is a sizeable body of research of the underlying principles and implementation challenges associated with EU policy in the environmental policy and security domains—see McCormick 2001). It is also necessary to understand how the various emergent components of EU policy on the subject are being influenced, shaped and accepted by member states themselves.

Updating the results of an earlier study (Bouzarovski et al. 2012), this chapter explores the organisational and political complexities surrounding the adoption of energy poverty agendas and policies at the EU decision-making level. Theoretical insights from the policy mobilities literature (see Peck 2011; McCann and Ward 2012) have been employed towards an empirical exploration of the actors, interests and power relations' discourses implicated in the entrance and proliferation of energy poverty concerns into the EU political agenda. Our dependent variable is the process of agenda-shaping within the EU's emergent energy poverty policy. This has been examined with the aid of a triangulation of data from the secondary literature and interviews in various EU institutions; 15 such interviews were undertaken during 2011 and 2012—their results are presented summarily in the chapter as the surveyed individuals asked that their identities are kept confidential.

In our empirical explorations, we draw upon the emergent body of work on the nature of agenda-setting processes at the EU level. As such, energy poverty policies at the European scale can be seen as part of the broader policy effort in the EU energy poverty domain, which is often being seen as 'driven by events' and subject to 'soft' governance mechanisms (Tosun et al. in Chap. 1; Tosun and Solorio 2011).

Authors working in this vein have also argued that 'despite the centrality of climate change concerns in the rhetoric of the European Commission, an effective integration of environmental goals into energy policy is difficult to achieve' (Tosun and Solorio 2011, p. 1; but see Ciambra and Solorio in Chap. 8 or Cox and Dekanozishvili in Chap. 9 for cases in which the European energy agenda was linked with the climate change agenda). Their findings are inspired by the broader literature on agenda-setting, where it is contended that the definition and identification of a problem plays a key role in consequential policy stages. The process can take place in both a bottom-up and top-down manner while involving multiple international actors (Cobb and Elder 1983). In the text that follows, we explore the extent to which some of these claims hold true in the case of European energy poverty.

The analysis of the evidence that we have gathered is presented in three sections: in the first, we examine the broader regulatory framework relevant to the intersection between energy affordability, energy efficiency and social welfare. The second discusses the origins of direct EU energy poverty policies as they relate to initial efforts to create an agenda in this domain. The third section scrutinises the more recent role and activities of various organisations in this domain to provide an account of the emergent political discourses aimed at encapsulating the driving forces of, and mitigating strategies for, energy poverty in Europe. The conclusion evaluates the success of policies to date while highlighting the pathways that have allowed for action aimed at addressing the domestic energy deprivation of European households to become 'mobile'. We also speculate on the likely future development of EU activities in this sphere.

7.2 Energy Poverty: Key Underpinnings

Before proceeding to discuss the evolution of EU policies in the energy poverty domain, it is worth briefly exploring the wider theoretical and practical issues associated with the conceptual intersection among energy, poverty and housing. As was noted above, this is an area which has often remained invisible to politicians and scientists alike—indeed, a government minister in the UK infamously claimed that 'people do not talk of "clothes poverty" or "food poverty", and I do not think that it is useful to talk of "fuel poverty" either' (Campbell 1993, p. 58). When seen in this context, it is easy to see why and how the early establishment of a clear 'fuel poverty' definition in the British academic and decision-making polity was so groundbreaking. Indeed, it was the UK where the first comprehensive state policies to address fuel poverty were created—in addition to the emergence of integrated scientific debates about the driving forces and consequences of living in homes with inadequate energy services. The initially established interpretation of fuel poverty in the UK, where this condition is principally seen as the inability to purchase affordable warmth, remained in place for more than 20 years resistant to outside criticism. Until a few months ago, fuel poverty in the UK was described as a situation in which a household needs to spend more than 10 % of its total income (before housing costs) on all fuel used to heat its homes to an acceptable level (Bouzarovski 2014).

Two aspects of this definition have been particularly controversial in the scientific and policy-making community: First, 'needing to spend' refers not to actual expenditure but to a hypothetical level that is closely related, inter alia, with the thermal energy efficiency of the dwelling (ibid); Second, 'acceptable level' is taken to mean that the home is heated in line with the standards recommended by the World Health Organization (WHO)—18 °C for bedrooms and 20–21 °C for living rooms (ibid). The UK now uses a definition of fuel poverty based on the findings of a recent government-sponsored review undertaken by Professor John Hills at the London School of Economics.

The background work for report involved multiple stages of consultation with experts, non-governmental organisations and think tanks involved in the topic. Having concluded that the existing UK definition has resulted in a situation whereby fuel poverty statistics are too sensitive to movements in gas and electricity bills as well as "the precise assumptions made for what are seen as adequate temperatures for people to live at, and the incomes reported to a survey that is mainly not focused on income measurement, the report suggested that the government adopt a new indicator about the extent of fuel poverty, which would consider households poor if (i) their 'required fuel costs' are above the median level for the entire population; and (ii) spending that amount would leave them 'with a residual income below the official poverty line" (Hills 2012).

In essence, controversies around the definition of fuel poverty in the UK reflect a broader unease among academics and policy makers alike with respect to the methods and approaches for measuring the incidence and character of inadequate energy services in the home. This has traditionally been an extremely challenging task in light of the specific nature of the problem, which is:

- difficult to detect, due to being private and confined to the domestic domain by its very nature;
- highly variable over time and space, since an individual may fall in and out of fuel poverty at many stages during the life course, and the extent of domestic energy deprivation experienced by one household may be very different to that of its neighbours;
- sensitive to cultural and social context, since expectations and perceptions of energy services in the home are highly subjective.

Statisticians, researchers and decision-makers have used three types of methods to observe and measure fuel poverty. Some of them have employed direct surveys to examine the level of energy services (space heating or cooling, lighting, refrigeration and so on) and subsequently comparing the obtained values to a given standard. In most cases, they have relied on analyses of the extent to which patterns of household energy expenditure across the population vary in relation to preset absolute and relative lines.

A distinct strand of work has focused on obtaining the subjective impressions of households about the level of energy service obtained in the home. It should be pointed out that the first approach has not been used on a large scale within the EU due to the technical impracticalities and ethical issues associated with it (Bouzarovski 2014). Adding to this are the difficulties of defining adequate energy service standards in part because of cultural specificities: As was pointed out above, it is known that a home normally considered well-lit and warm in one geographical context may not be seen as such in another (ibid). But national statistical agencies across the EU do gather expenditure data via household budget surveys that, when combined with census data and information compiled through other research studies, have allowed experts to identify the depth of fuel poverty. Other than a limited number of countries and international organisations (such as the World Bank), this method of energy poverty data collection has not found much policy application.

At the same time, EU debates on questions of domestic energy deprivation have largely been influenced by self-reported data relevant to energy poverty collected principally through/in Eurostat's Statistics on Income and Living Conditions survey (or SILC, preceded between 1994 and 2001 by the European Community Household Panel—ECHP) as well as national statistical agencies. SILC and ECHP 'consensual' indicator about the share of population that feel 'unable to keep the home adequately warm' has provided the only directly relevant and internationally comparative tool for judging the extent of energy poverty at the EU scale.

These surveys have often been cited in—and provided the motivation for—international action on the issue due to collecting various objective data about dwelling quality and the material conditions of households, which allows for self-reported views of thermal comfort to be cross-referenced against other built environment and economic strain indicators. However, experts working in the field have often questioned the quality of these sources, while emphasising that they do not contain enough relevant information to make informed policy decisions.

EU action on the energy poverty front has been further complicated by the multiple meanings of the concept of 'fuel poverty', since numerous related concepts have been used to describe this condition in other settings. This includes, inter alia, notions of 'energy precariousness', 'energy deprivation' and narrower terms that refer to some of the symptoms of this condition, such as: 'cold homes', 'energy non-payment' or 'energy disconnection'. The existence of a distinct body of research on 'energy poverty' in the developing world also needs to be noted here: Such work has mainly been focused on investigating and ameliorating the consequences of inadequate access to 'modern' energy services as a result of the lack of adequate energy infrastructure. In recent years, various scholars have started to use an 'energy vulnerability' framework to emphasise the technically and temporally precarious nature of access to energy services per se. Insights from the 'capabilities' approach and relative poverty have also been added to the equation.

7.3 European Policies to Address the Energy-Housing Poverty Nexus: Setting the Context

Despite the scarcity of academic research on the extent and depth of European energy poverty, there is now a sufficient body of evidence to suggest that this predicament is widespread across the continent. It is likely to affect millions of households. The lack of adequate energy services in the home is particularly pronounced in Southern and Eastern European states due to their overall higher rates of general income poverty and energy inefficient dwellings. Nations situated on the 'Atlantic Rim'—Ireland, the UK, France and Belgium—are also seen as vulnerable to above average rates of domestic energy deprivation (Bouzarovski 2014).

However, many European governments have traditionally refused to recognise the existence of an energy poverty problem in their territory let alone the whole of the EU. This means that energy poverty is rarely framed as a European issue—a situation that is further exacerbated by the fact that the alleviation of more general income poverty and social exclusion is primarily a responsibility of the EU's member states. Yet the rootedness of this predicament in broader housing, social welfare and infrastructural systems means that member state-level efforts to address it have often been indirectly affected by EU legislation in related spheres. For example, considering that the inadequate energy efficiency of the housing and appliance stock is one of the main driving forces of energy poverty, it can be said that European policy in the energy sector has played an important ancillary role in addressing domestic energy deprivation. This is particularly true in the case of:

- Directive 2010/31/EU on the Energy Performance of Buildings (a recast of the Directive 2002/91/EC), which addresses housing conditions through better energy efficiency of buildings—thus helping address some of the causal factors of energy poverty. Each member state is obliged to develop its own methodology to implement the goals of this Directive;
- Directive 2010/30/EU on the labelling and standard product information of the consumption of energy and other resources by energy-related products—inefficient appliances are a key contributor to energy poverty;
- Directive 2006/32/EC on energy end-use efficiency and energy services, repealing Council Directive 93/76/EEC;
- Directives for labelling various household appliances (94/2/EC, 95/12/EC, 95/13/EC, 96/60/EC, 97/17/EC, 98/11/EC, 2001/40/EC and 2002/31/EC),
- Directives 2003/54/EC and 2003/55/EC, which provide for the right of consumers to have a contract with their energy provider, the right to receive transparent information on prices, and the right to be given adequate notice if contractual conditions are changed. These have been crucial in addressing the position of vulnerable consumers vis-à-vis utility companies (it is often the case that energy poor households pay, on average, higher energy prices than the rest of the population);

- Directive 2005/29/EC, which outlaws unfair commercial practices, also including the energy sector.

Also significant in this context is the European Commission's communication titled 'Energy 2020—A strategy for competitive, sustainable and secure energy'. It defines the bloc's energy priorities until 2020 and sets the actions to be taken in order to tackle the multiple challenges of saving energy, achieving a market with competitive prices and secure supplies, boosting technological leadership and effectively negotiating with the EU's international partners. While issues surrounding intra-EU energy cooperation are left open, policy proposals within the document include a number of energy poverty-relevant topics:

- The management of internal energy markets, such as the strengthening of regulation to increase competition, consumer protection and increase of security of supply;
- Infrastructure, such as gas pipelines and interconnectors between national electricity and gas networks, simplified procedures for permissions and financing, as well as.
- Energy efficiency, which could include strengthening ecodesign regulation, financing, and revisions of the Energy service and CHP directives.

A degree of spillover into the domain of energy poverty can also be found in relation to EU policies to reduce regional, economic or social inequalities. The 2000 Lisbon summit in particular provided an important political push towards poverty amelioration. At this gathering, a decision was made for member states to coordinate their policies for combating poverty and social exclusion on the basis of the 'open method of co-ordination'—a determination which has resulted in the adoption of an increased number of legal and policy instruments by relevant European bodies. The EU's commitment in this context has been reflected, for example: by the launch of the 'European Year Against Poverty and Social Exclusion' in January 2010. Also of relevance is the Commission's Communication titled 'Europe 2020—A Strategy for Smart, Sustainable and Inclusive Growth', which is strongly focused on social cohesion and fighting poverty through, inter alia, measures in the energy sector (mainly energy efficiency and renewable energy sources). The key element—and one of the seven flagships—of 'Europe 2020' is the 'Platform Against Poverty and Social Exclusion', which has helped promote a set of innovative approaches for addressing poverty and social exclusion in member states and candidate countries. The Platform is aimed at creating a joint commitment among the Member States, EU Institutions and the stakeholders to fight poverty and social exclusion.

It should also be pointed out that the European energy poverty sphere has also been influenced by the activities of the Council of Europe (CoE) in the domain of housing policy. They are comprehensively reflected in a CoE report on this issue (Council of Europe 2008) drafted by the Group of specialists on housing policies for social cohesion. The report aims to aid the improvement of housing access among vulnerable social groups in Europe. It has resulted in a set of specific guidelines, which stipulate the key prerequisites for an effective housing policy in this domain while listing a range of potential policy tools. Such efforts have been further assisted by the increasing role of the European Court of Human Rights and case law under the Revised European Social Charter with its associated collective complaints mechanism. As stated by the above mentioned CoE report,

> it is the Revised European Social Charter which gave a special emphasis to the housing problems of vulnerable social groups, which were reinforced by the CoE's Revised Strategy for Social Cohesion (Council of Europe 2008).

Nevertheless, none of these frameworks have made explicit mention of energy poverty. While they have helped address the driving forces of the condition via their specific sectoral policies, the lack of an integrated EU perspective has constantly undermined member state-level efforts to tackle domestic energy deprivation via an ambitious and comprehensive approach.

7.4 Initial Efforts to Establish an Energy Poverty Policy: 'The Third Energy Package'

The notion of 'energy poverty' finally entered the vocabulary of the EU in 2009 after years of lobbying and advocacy work by a number of international organisations, academics and political groups. The institutional framework for this development was provided by the process of drafting the Third Energy Package. Political action within the European Parliament led to the integration of energy poverty concerns within the Directives 2009/72/EC and 2009/73/EC of the European Parliament and of the Council, 'concerning common rules for the internal market in electricity and natural gas supply'. The compromise text of the directives recognised the existence of a 'growing' energy poverty problem in Europe, requiring member states 'who are affected and which have not yet done so' to ensure the necessary energy supply for vulnerable customers, and 'aiming at decreasing the number of people' suffering from this situation. National governments were subsequently asked to formulate 'appropriate measures' to address energy poverty, including the development of national energy action plans. It was noted that:

> In doing so, an integrated approach such as in the framework of social policy, could be used and measures could include social policies or energy efficiency improvements for housing. At the very least, this Directive should allow national policies in favour of vulnerable customers (European Parliament 2009).

The increasing prominence of energy poverty within the EU political sphere during this period was reflected in the Opinion on 'Energy poverty in the context of liberalisation and the economic crisis' issued by the European Economic and Social Committee (EESC) on the 14th of July 2010. Having concluded that 'energy poverty affects the energy sector' while also impacting 'health, consumer affairs and housing', the Committee suggested that 'the EU adopt a common general definition of energy poverty that can then be adapted by each Member State'. It furthermore proposed that 'existing statistics should be harmonised so that the most rigorous assessment possible can be made of the energy poverty situation in Europe'. While emphasising that 'the number of families affected by energy poverty in Europe could increase', the Committee insisted that 'it would make sense to set up a European Energy Poverty Monitoring Centre, which could fit within an existing body such as the Agency for the Cooperation of Energy Regulators'.

Article 2.7 of the Committee's conclusions pointed out that 'energy poverty is caused by a combination of three factors: low income, inadequate building quality and high energy prices'. During an informal meeting of EU energy ministers on the 6th of September 2010, the European Commission agreed to produce a report presenting a definition of vulnerable energy customers. According to a subsequent news item:

> The meeting, convened by Paul Magnette, Belgian climate and energy minister, saw a rare debate on energy poverty … "This was the first time in 10 years that the issue of consumers was directly addressed by energy ministers", said Magnette … Energy poverty is an everyday problem for over 50 million Europeans who are estimated to be unable to pay their energy bills and maintain comfortable living standards, Magnette said … The idea is not to harmonise social policy, which is for the most part a national competence, Magnette told journalists after the two-day meeting. But he said the EU must acknowledge the problem and see whether there is a need to propose a new piece of legislation or change existing measures (Euractiv 2010).

The Commission's report, published at the end of November 2010, listed existing and future EU energy policies which are likely to affect the manner in which consumers' interests are taken into account in energy policy. It emphasised the importance of mechanisms such as energy ombudsmen, complaint boards and consumer protection authorities in dealing "efficiently with complaints and facilitate out-of-court dispute settlements" (European Commission 2010). It also encouraged "Member States to adopt appropriate long-term policy solutions, and not only temporary relief' so as to 'replace direct subsidies for high energy bills with a support for improving the energy quality of the dwellings" (ibid). While pointing out that "energy efficiency measures should be an integral part of welfare policies", the report also underscored that:

> There is no consensus on what actually constitutes energy poverty … One possible way to quantify the number or proportion of households struggling to settle their energy bills is to try to count the households that spend more than a predefined threshold share of their overall consumption expenditure on energy products. An alternative method could focus on those households that have (or have had in recent times) payment difficulties or are in arrears with energy bill payments. Given the diverse situations of energy consumers in different parts of the EU, the Commission does not consider it appropriate at this stage to propose a European definition of energy poverty or of vulnerable customers (ibid).

The findings of the report were to be followed up at a subsequent Energy Council meeting, when the Commission Report would be scrutinised. However, as pointed out by CECODHAS Housing Europe—the European Federation of Public, Cooperative and Social Housing:

> While the Informal Energy Council in September was dedicated to the most vulnerable energy consumers as well as the phenomenon of energy poverty, the formal Energy Council of December 3rd has adopted conclusions on "an Energy Policy for Consumers" which does not fully recognise the complexity and accurateness of the phenomenon of energy poverty (CECODHAS Housing Europe 2010).

Thus, despite an ambitious departure, initial efforts to establish a pan-European energy poverty policy were unsuccessful. The reasons for this are unclear. However, there is evidence to suggest that one of the decisive roles was played by background lobbying from the governments of several powerful member states (such as Germany), who did not have an explicit national-level energy poverty approach. For such states, the pan-European recognition of a 'new' type of deprivation could have caused significant political difficulties due to the need to recognise a distinct new group of vulnerable people in the face of energy price increases and sector restructuring commitments brought about by the low-carbon energy transition (see also Ciambra and Solorio in Chap. 8 and Cox and Dekanozishvili in Chap. 9) on the ability of national policy entrepreneurs to shape the EU energy agenda.

7.5 Developments After the 2010 Energy Council: The European Economic and Social Committee Takes the Lead

In contrast to the Energy Council and Commission's reluctance to tackle energy poverty—even when the issue was explicitly put on the political agenda, the European Parliament took a more decisive approach (see also Chap. 12 by Tosun). On the 15th of December 2010, it adopted a resolution on the Revision of the Energy Efficiency Action Plan, which states that the Parliament:

> … believes it is essential that the homes of energy poor households are improved to the highest possible energy efficiency standards and without raising the daily costs for the energy poor; Stresses that this will often require substantial investment in homes but will on the same time generate a lot of non-energy benefits, e.g. by reduced mortality, improved general wellbeing, lower levels of indebtedness and reducing healthcare costs by reducing indoor pollution and thermal stress (European Parliament 2010).

More significantly, the European Economic and Social Committee (EESC) continued to maintain a vocal political debate on the subject while regularly issuing opinions that called for the Union's institutions to take a more decisive stance on the issue. In a way, the EESC set the agenda and maintained the focus of political debates on the topic, despite having little executive or legislative influence. In October 2012, the EESC co-organised a conference together with the European Local Inclusion and Social Action Network, which was accompanied by news reports that "no country in the EU had been spared rising energy prices" (EESC 2012). Cases such as that of Latvia—where energy costs had recently increased by

27 in 2011—were cited, in addition to the predicted rise of German energy prices by up to 15 %, and the fact that 42 % of French households were reported to have 'cut back on heating their homes to save on energy bills'. The EESC's president Staffan Nilsson was quoted as emphasising the need for:

> determined action at EU level to combat energy poverty: the EU could not ignore a problem that affected up to 125 million Europeans … Mr. Nilsson reiterated that adopting an EU-wide definition of the phenomenon should be the first step in recognising and mapping the issue. This had to be flexible and not a rigid, one-size-fits-all definition … Rather than opt for a top-down definition of fuel poverty, the authorities should be given the latitude to offer tailor-made solutions (EESC 2012).

These claims reflect the broader tone of the EESC's opinions on this and other matters of EU energy policy. One can observe a consistent line of argument in favour of a comprehensive strategy, involving multiple stakeholders and taking into account the need for simultaneous action in several different sectors. In line with this determination, the EESC's trans-sectoral 'Study group for co-ordinate European measures to prevent and combat energy poverty' organised a hearing on energy poverty issues at the beginning of July 2013. It hosted members of numerous government bodies, commercial organisations and advocacy groups, including: representatives of Eurelectric's Retail Customers Unit, Euro gas (an association representing the European gas wholesale, retail and distribution sectors), Consumer Futures (a UK consumer representation group), the French Red Cross, the European Anti Poverty Network (an advocacy network of groups and individuals working against poverty) and CECODHAS Housing Europe. Presentations at the hearing highlighted the highly divergent views that some of these organisations hold on issues of domestic energy deprivation: from the rather narrow specific and direct understandings elaborated by representatives of the commercial sector to the humanitarian concerns asserted by many socially oriented international non-governmental organisations.

Overall, the hearing marked a steep change from the level of previous debates on the subject, since it brought forth specific ideas about the detection, measurement and monitoring of energy poverty at the European scale—as well as the need for acknowledging and addressing the reality of the problem via joint action. The proposal for establishing an EU energy poverty observatory was elaborated in further detail, accompanied by the idea to create an 'European energy security and solidarity pact'.

It is not true to say that other EU bodies with greater policy-making influence have not been involved in calls to act on this issue. In January 2013 for example, the European Parliament's Committee on Industry, Research and Energy adopted a motion for a resolution on the 'Energy Roadmap 2050'—a communication produced by the European Commission in 2011, which stated that "vulnerable consumers are best protected from energy poverty through a full implementation by Member States of the existing EU energy legislation and use of innovative energy efficiency solutions" while emphasising that "the social aspects of energy pricing should be reflected in the energy policy of Member States' since 'energy poverty is one of the sources of poverty in Europe" (European Commission 2011). In this document, the Parliament:

> … welcomes the inclusion of the social dimension in the Energy Roadmap 2050; considers that, in this respect, special attention should be given to energy poverty and employment; insists, with regard to energy poverty, that energy should be affordable for all, and calls on the Commission and the Member States, and on local authorities and competent social bodies, to work together on tailored solutions to counter such issues as electricity and heat poverty, with a special emphasis on low income, vulnerable households that are most affected by higher energy prices (European Parliament 2013).

Having emphasised that energy efficiency and savings are'one of the most effective ways to reduce energy bills', the motion also called for the promotion and development of such measures in addition to the stimulation of "demand- and supply-side actions and creating awareness campaigns" (ibid) towards the enhancement of behaviour change. A review of 'national measures such as taxation, public procurement and heat pricing' was also suggested, especially in the contexts where they are hindering energy efficiency investment or the "optimisation of heat production and use" (ibid). The motion also asked member states to "report on a regular basis on actions taken to protect households from rising energy bills and energy poverty" while emphasising the need for a "highly skilled workforce ready to play its part in the energy transition" (ibid). Appeals for a broader and more inclusive dialogue in relation to the social aspects of the Energy Roadmap were also made.

It is worth pointing out that the motion was one of the first EU-level documents to explicitly connect social welfare issues and decarbonisation. The need for developing a strategy sensitive to the situation of more vulnerable member states was underlined in order to prevent a massive increase in energy poverty. In an incorrect transposition of the UK definition, energy poverty was designated as a situation in which over 10 % of a household's budget is actually spent on energy (as opposed to needing to spend 10 % on energy—see Boardman 2010). The decision to highlight the wider structural dimensions of domestic energy deprivation reflects the tone of several recent public discussions on related issues in the European Parliament. In late 2012, Polish MEP Wojciech Olejniczak called for extra measures to protect rural areas, which he felt were the most threatened by energy poverty. Speaking at a parliamentary debate on EU energy policy towards rural regions, he said that:

> The EU needs to review rural energy as part of overall energy policy … The focus of EU energy policy should not be only on large infrastructure projects, but should include decentralised energy and regional and local levels (The Parliament 2012).

However, the Energy Roadmap is not the only EC activity in the energy poverty domain. Following the Fourth Citizens Energy Forum (CEF) in London—an annual gathering of energy regulators which features representatives of, inter alia, national energy regulators, industry bodies and consumer associations—the EC established the Vulnerable Consumer Working Group (VCWG): A collaborative effort between two Commission services (the Directorate General for Energy and the Directorate

General for Health and Consumers) aimed at working together closely with the CEF in supporting the implementation of the Third Energy Package. The institutional setup of this body has allowed for the EC to work closely with consumer associations (such as BEUC—the European Consumer Organisation), public bodies/ institutions (the Council of European Energy Regulators, Ministries, Ombudsmen), industry (Eurogas, Eureletric) and academia in influencing the European agenda on issues such as consumer protection and energy poverty.

Its discussions have offered the opportunity for many of these actors to present their views about the EC's and MS's adoption of EU energy legislation in the domain of consumer vulnerability to energy price increases and market liberalisation. As such, they have helped affirm the centrality of the notion of 'vulnerability'—both as an explanatory concept and a policy framework—in the process of transforming the European energy market.

Just like the EESC, the VCWG's work has generated path-breaking policy discourses and agendas in the European energy poverty domain. Its focus on the notion of vulnerability has moved the debate on the subject beyond the static notion of 'poverty' onto more complex understandings of the inherently dynamic driving forces of deprivation. It has also allowed for an emphasis on processes happening at the scale of individual households—as opposed to commercial and industrial consumers—even though the Third Energy Package can technically be extended to encompass all demand-related activities. The Group has also opened up a broad-based discussion about the need to identify and target households that require assistance with respect to meeting their energy needs.

Despite the limitations on its mandate posed by the provisions of the Third Energy Package, which says that any direct financial measures to benefit vulnerable consumers must not undermine the completion of the free internal market, or endanger competition, there has been an insistence that companies should provide inclusive, distinct and appropriate forms of support. The VCWG has also reviewed indirect methods of assistance while providing and promoting examples of good practice. It has often emphasised the importance of energy efficiency measures as a principal method for addressing the lack of adequate space heating or cooling, as well as issues with the consumer appliance stock. The outcomes of the Group's work in the vulnerability domain have been reflected in, inter alia, the provisions made by the EC's Internal Energy Market Communication released in autumn 2012.

To a certain extent, the action of EU organisations in the energy poverty domain has been influenced by international non-governmental organisations working in this field. Particularly, notable have been the activities of advocacy groups such as the International Network for Sustainable Energy (INFORSE) and the International Union of Tenants and the European Federation of Public Service Unions; this is in addition to the high-profile work of the European local inclusion and social action network (ELISAN), the European Anti Poverty Network (EAPN) and the aforementioned CECODHAS Housing Europe. A good illustration of the prominence of the energy poverty agenda in the work of these organisations is provided by the Resolution on Energy Strategy for Europe 2011–2020 adopted by the Executive

Committee of the European Trade Union Confederation (ETUC) in late 2010. It states that:

> … National Energy Actions Plans should focus more on measures to reduce "energy poverty", [a] concept that must get a common European definition. The effectiveness of these measures could be increased through a better coordination with the National Action Plans for social inclusion and social protection (ETUC 2010).

Industry-funded lobby groups such as the World Coal Association have also voiced concerns over the rise of energy poverty. Their arguments have mostly been articulated in opposition to decarbonisation-driven energy price increases. It is also worth noting the work of the Central and Eastern Europe Bank watch Network, Southeastern Europe Change Net and the World Wildlife Fund in the Balkans. Such organisations have urged EU funds to urge international development banks to invest in energy efficiency as a method of alleviating energy poverty. Also of significance is the growing number of EU-supported projects aimed at generating practical and scientific knowledge on the topic.

In recent years, such initiatives have included FinSH (Financial and Support Instruments for fuel Poverty in Social Housing—2007–2010) Energy Ambassadors (Campaign to fight against fuel poverty and raise awareness on energy efficiency and energy savings—2009–2011), EC-LINC (Energy Check for Low Income Households—2011–2014) and ACHIEVE (Actions in low income households to improve energy efficiency through visits and energy diagnosis—2011–2014). Although such work has mainly been practitioner-led and -orientated—due to being funded by the Intelligent Energy Europe programme, which has a specific remit in this regard, it should be pointed out that the EVALUATE project (Energy Vulnerability and Urban Transitions in Europe, 2013–2018) has a principally scientific remit and is supported by the European Research Council.

7.6 Conclusions: A Precarious Future

The EU has become increasingly committed to tackling energy poverty through direct and indirect regulation. Many uncertainties remain unresolved in its attempts to address the complex needs of vulnerable groups. The rise of income inequality as a result of the economic recession has increased the demand for new policies in this domain—partly as a result of the pronounced existence of energy poverty-related problems in Southern and Eastern European states. In addition to the indirect energy poverty-relevant regulation arising as a direct consequence of EU-level actions in the housing, energy and—to a lesser extent social domains—a key impetus for more direct government policy in this sphere has been provided by the mechanisms stemming from the Third Energy Package.

In this context, it is worth noting the significant—and relatively fast—development of a distinctive EU agenda on energy poverty accompanied by a range of ground-breaking steps in terms of defining the normative procedures through which the condition is to be recognised and addressed. In this process, it is possible to observe a process of policy mobility between the national scale—where most energy poverty conceptual frameworks and policies were initially developed—and that of the EU, which serves as a forum for integrating and recombining such registers only to return them back to member states for implementation. Thus, many components of EU energy policy act as "immutable mobiles" (Latour 1997), which demonstrate the importance of a social-constructivist understanding of policy mobilities-and-mutations, sensitive to the constitutive roles of spatiotemporal context (Peck 2011, p. 773).

In response to some of the starting positions that we aimed to investigate in this contribution, it can be said that agenda-shaping in the EU poverty domain has been mainly driven from above and has been highly contingent on attempts to 'define' and 'identify' the problem. There is little evidence to suggest that particular events or dynamics—such as the enlargement of the EU or the protests in Bulgaria (but see Brutschin in Chap. 10)—have provided a central impetus for European action in this domain. As such, the link between them and other EU energy policies is weak because they have been driven by institutions such as the EESC, which has traditionally sat outside this policy domain. Only in recent years have energy poverty concerns started to enter mainstream EU policy agendas, principally as a result of the Commission's efforts surrounding the implementation of the Third Energy Package.

Overall, current energy poverty policies in the EU context vary drastically from country to country while lacking intersectoral coordination in terms of energy (affordability and accessibility), social welfare and housing policies (Bouzarovski 2014). The need for the creation of policy initiatives that will specifically tackle energy poverty as a multidimensional and cross-sectoral phenomenon is therefore likely to become a key site of political action in the years to come. This may entail, inter alia, the development of specific EU regulation to fight energy poverty—as well as the incorporation of energy poverty indicators in monitoring and evaluation mechanisms at the EU and national level. Another distinct possibility is the explicit integration of the energy-poverty-housing nexus in cohesion policy: A step that is of particular importance for new and forthcoming member states, where the rise of domestic energy deprivation is largely predicated upon access to adequate housing and networked infrastructure.

References

Boardman, B. (2010). *Fixing fuel poverty: Challenges and solutions*. London: Earthscan.

Bouzarovski, S. (2014). Energy poverty in the European Union: Landscapes of vulnerability. *Wiley Interdisciplinary Reviews: Energy and Environment, 3*(3), 276–289.

Bouzarovski, S., Petrova, S., & Sarlamanov, S. (2012). Energy poverty policies in the EU: A critical perspective. *Energy Policy, 49*, 76–82.

Campbell, R. (1993). Fuel poverty and government response. *Social Policy and Administration, 27*, 58–70.

Cobb, R. W., & Elder, C. D. (1983). *Participation in American politics: The dynamics of agenda-building*. Baltimore: The Johns Hopkins University Press.
Council of Europe. (2008). *Housing policy and vulnerable social groups*. Strasbourg: Council of Europe.
Dijol, J. (2010). *Energy poverty: No mention at the Energy Council*. Brussels: CECODHAS Housing Europe.
EESC. (2012). *EESC president argues for urgent EU action to eradicate energy poverty*. Brussels: European Economic and Social Committee.
ETUC. (2010). *Resolution on energy strategy for Europe 2011–2020*. Brussels: European Trade Union Confederation.
EurActiv. (2010). *EU to define vulnerable energy customers*. Brussels: Euractiv.
European Commission. (2010). *An energy policy for consumers, commission staff working paper*. Brussels: European Commission.
European Commission. (2011). *Communication from the commission to the European Parliament, the council, the European social and economic committee and the committee for the regions. Energy roadmap 2050*. Brussels: European Commission.
European Parliament. (2009). *Directive 2009/72/EC of the European Parliament and of the council of 13 July 2009 concerning common rules for the internal market in electricity and repealing Directive 2003/54/EC*. Brussels: Official Journal of the European Union.
European Parliament. (2010). *Report on the revision of the energy efficiency action plan—A7-0331/2010*. Brussels: European Parliament.
European Parliament. (2013). *Report on the energy roadmap 2050, a future with energy*. Brussels: European Parliament.
Hills, J. (2012). *Getting the measure of fuel poverty: Final report of the fuel poverty review*. London: School of Economics and Political Science—Centre for Analysis of Social Exclusion.
Latour, B. (1997). *Science in action: How to follow scientists and engineers through society*. Cambridge: Harvard University Press.
McCormick, J. (2001). *Environmental policy in the European Union*. Basingstoke: Palgrave.
McCann, E., & Ward, K. (2012). Policy assemblages, mobilities and mutations: Toward a multidisciplinary conversation. *Political Studies Review, 10*, 325–332.
Peck, J. (2011). Geographies of policy: From transfer-diffusion to mobility-mutation. *Progress in Human Geography, 35*, 773–797.
The Parliament. (2012). *MEPs call for action to combat energy poverty. MEPs call for action to combat energy poverty*. Brussels: The Parliament Magazine.
Tosun, J., & Solorio, I. (2011). Exploring the energy-environment relationship in the EU: Perspectives and challenges for theorizing and empirical analysis. *European Integration Online Papers, 15*, 1–15.

Part III
Influential Member States

Chapter 8
The Liberalisation of the Internal Energy Market: Is the EU Dancing at a British Tempo?

Andrea Ciambra and Israel Solorio

Abstract This chapter aims to highlight relevant turning points with the convergence or divergence of the United Kingdom's and the EU's policy discourse on the liberalisation of an integrated energy market have affected the formation of a European energy policy agenda. It adopts Tallberg's (2003) three-tiered agenda-building model to analyse three phases in which the United Kingdom has been a key player in shaping the internal energy market agenda: the 1970s, with an agenda exclusion strategy pursued as long EU interests did not match British preferences on market liberalisation; the 1980s–1990s, with an explicit uploading of Britain-to-EU agenda-setting strategy promoting energy market liberalisation according to successful domestic experiences; the 2000s, with an agenda-structuring approach that attempted to assert Britain's leadership in climate-change action. The chapter ultimately argues that the goals, regulatory instruments and market-driven vision uploaded from the United Kingdom to the EU is the grounds for the current paradigm for energy policy making in the EU. The transformation towards sustainability goals and the ability of one actor to alter policy balances through narrative and discourse set out a valuable precedent for more cross-policy research in EU agenda-setting studies.

A. Ciambra (✉)
Institut de Dret i Tecnologia, Universitat Autònoma de Barcelona, Campus UAB–Edifici B, 08193 Bellaterra (Barcelona), Spain
e-mail: andrea.ciambra@uab.cat

I. Solorio
Environmental Policy Research Centre, Freie Universität Berlin, Ihnestr 22, 14195 Berlin, Germany
e-mail: isolorio@zedat.fu-berlin.de

J. Tosun et al. (eds.), *Energy Policy Making in the EU*,
Lecture Notes in Energy 28, DOI 10.1007/978-1-4471-6645-0_8

8.1 Introduction: A Focus on the British Tempo

The liberalisation of the internal energy market has been on the to-do list of European Union (EU) institutions for more than 20 years, which saw the European Commission (1988, 1994) issue a number of policy recommendations, communications and guidelines to construct a consistent energy market. Since then, three legislative packages on electricity and natural gas infrastructure have entered into force (see Herweg in Chap. 5 and Brutschin in Chap. 10 for an analysis of the liberalisation of the European gas market). Several cross-border initiatives and bodies have been established, a number of documents on technological development and integration of Europe's energy network have been issued, and consistent programmes to expand this *acquis* to newly accessed Member States—as well as to export it outside EU borders (see and Solorio and Morata 2012)—have been developed. Several attempts to use the creation of an EU internal energy market as a catalyst for a coherent and common EU energy policy were frustrated by irresolute Treaty innovations both in the Single European Act (SEA) of 1987 and in the Maastricht Treaty that established the EU and marked the inception of the internal market in 1992, which ruled energy policy out of the scope of integration. In spite of these obstacles, the EU has nonetheless developed a formal competence in this policy area (see Biesenbender in Chap. 2). Consequently, for the last two decades the Commission has been frequently granted the political 'merit' of benefitting from closely related policy actions to achieve energy policy goals on the way to strengthening the EU's energy security, liberalising its energy markets (Buchan 2009) and promoting the 'greening' of EU energy policy—especially since the early 2000s (Solorio et al. 2013). These achievements notwithstanding, today "the EU is not on track to" allow consumers to "start reaping the full benefits of the internal energy market" (European Commission 2012, p. 2).

The pace of this strenuous transformation, moreover, has not always been under the control of Berlaymont's officials, and it was not inspired *only* by the Commission's long-term vision of an interconnected, efficient and full-fledged internal market. Quite on the contrary, we argue that this process has evolved at what can be defined a *British tempo*.

This chapter will highlight relevant turning points at which Britain's and the EU's policy discourse on energy and the liberalisation of an integrated energy market have either diverged or converged to affect the European energy policy agenda. We argue that the United Kingdom has been a key player in shaping the internal energy market agenda at three different stages: (1) in the 1970s by making use of an *agenda exclusion* strategy at any time in which energy market development did not match British interests, (2) in the 1980s–1990s through an *agenda-setting* strategy that promoted the liberalisation of energy markets by 'uploading' the British system to the EU level and (3) mostly during the 2000s through an *agenda-structuring* approach that attempted to assert the British leadership in climate-change action (see Cox and Dekanozishvili in Chap. 9 for an assessment of Germany's subsequent strategy to promote climate-change action by shaping the European agenda on renewable energy).

Section 8.2 frames the research puzzle within the book's analytical framework and emphasises the role that political discourse plays in the problem-definition and agenda-setting phases of EU policy-making. Section 8.3 suggests a discourse-based methodology to identify significant turning points in the evolution of agenda-setting dynamics. Section 8.4 re-reads the history of the liberalisation process of the EU internal energy market as a series of re-framing attempts by competing sets of interests, for example: the attempt of the United Kingdom to lead the energy market agenda-shaping process by *uploading* to the EU the criteria and guidelines of its domestic regulation and the attempt of the Commission to harness several windows of opportunity to establish a fully integrated EU-wide energy market. Section 8.5 analyses the relationship between heterogeneous oscillations in the discursive *tempo* of EU energy policy (e.g. *upload* vs. *download* agenda-setting attempts, competing sets of interests and variations in EU level or domestic political balances) and the impact on the EU energy liberalisation agenda.

8.2 The Theoretical Framework: Policy Agenda and Final Outcomes

This chapter aims to retrace the processes and dynamics that made energy market liberalisation in Europe a contested priority in its public policy agenda. In order to do so, it relies on agenda-setting studies in the European context and underscores two key dimensions in the creation of a policy agenda: the ability of certain actors to define problems (i.e. *frame* them) in a way which is more consistent with their own interests and the ability of certain actors to carry out policy negotiations in venues that grant them higher chances to obtain favourable outcomes, also known as venue shopping.

"Venue shopping" techniques can play a fundamental role in analysing the Commission's activity in EU energy policy (Baumgartner and Jones 1991, p. 1050). After all, it is the actor "who determines what politics is about" and who controls the decision-making process" because the definition of the alternatives is the choice of conflicts, and the choice of conflicts allocates power" (Schattschneider 1957, p. 937). The way a problem is defined or 'framed' by interested policy actors willing to advance a solution for it can become a powerful political weapon in the right hand. The problem-definition and issue-framing phases thus become crucial to define power balances, hierarchies and consensus-building capacities throughout any policy-making process. We agree with Princen (2011, p. 929) that "mobilisation of interest is what agenda-setting is about". Accordingly, this section approaches energy market agenda-setting at the EU level as: First, a matter of how policy actors have explicitly defined the issue in their public stance and discursive activity. And second, as a matter of how a specific actor (i.e. the British government) has managed to focus all negotiations and policy pressures on a specific institutional venue (i.e. the Council of the EU).

Problem-definition and issue-framing were already central in Kingdon's (1984) classic work on agenda-setting, whose distinction between *problem stream* and *policy stream* set a standard for theoretical elaboration on this topic (see Herweg in Chap. 5). Economic and social indicators, past failures and successes and concrete feedback from the recipients of policies can advise policy actors about what problems and issues should be addressed in order to take the reins of the policy-making process. Similarly, whenever actors spot an opportunity to provide an effective and timely solution, they will have an incentive to address issues that "float by", so "they can attach their solutions" to those problems they had purposely tailored and defined in the first place (Kingdon 1984, p. 165). More recent works have reflected on the adaptability of these analytical premises to a very peculiar case of policy-making, namely the EU's (Baumgartner and Mahoney 2008; Héritier 1997; Princen 2009, 2011). At the end of the 1990s, semi-quantitative and game-theoretical models spread quickly, mostly thanks to the success of rational-choice institutionalism (Pollack 1997), aiming to explain EU decision-making outcomes through indexes and statistical repetitions, which somewhat tried to craft probabilistic models that may help analysts to *reliably predict* the most likely outcomes of legislative negotiations at the EU level (see for instance Garrett and Tsebelis 1999 and Tsebelis 2002).

We build on this basic literature to draw a key conclusion about agenda-setting in the EU, i.e. that "controlling the agenda is about controlling participation" (Princen 2011, p. 929). There are events, conditions and unpredictable situations that may bring about a rupture and alter the often volatile consensus balances of a given community. There are actors who can act as re- or pro-active "policy entrepreneurs" (Kingdon 1984) and harness favourable conditions to move the agenda focus towards their preferred sets of interests. There are actors who can prevent change or at least resist such pressures act as "veto players" (Tsebelis 2002). Accordingly, we agree with Tallberg (2003, p. 4) that the focus on issue-definition alone can be dangerously misleading for agenda-setting studies insofar as these reductively "equate influence over the EU agenda with the launch of new political initiatives".

In this regard, Tallberg's (2003, p. 5) three-tiered model of "agenda-shaping" acknowledges several things: the "conceptual umbrella" including the ability to introduce new issues in the policy debate (agenda-setting), highlight or make one issue already in the agenda more visible or compelling (agenda structuring) and veto specific items off the agenda (agenda exclusion). First, that agenda-setting as a theoretical framework is flexible enough to include non-positive or non-proactive behaviours such as vetoes, contestation and exclusive coalition building (see Bouzarovski and Petrova in Chap. 7 for an illustration of thwarted agenda-setting processes in EU energy poverty policy). Second, that a number of actors in a number of institutional settings (e.g. member states facing their own constituencies rather than other governments within the Council, or the Commission when advancing a legislative proposal rather than lobbying the Committee of Permanent Representatives) can use a number of tools and opportunities to affect policy making.

The liberalisation of the EU energy market has been a contested process. EU-wide goals and vision have struggled for visibility and resources against long-settled national interests, and national regulatory models have struggled to become the blueprint for a European experiment. The broad and comprehensive conceptualisation of agenda shaping developed by Tallberg suits the objective of this chapter to study how diverging upward and downward pressures have affected the liberalisation process allowing the narration of diverse actors in several institutional venues to set the *tempo* of a fledgling EU energy policy.

8.3 Measuring Discursive Change in Agenda-Setting Processes

Most studies in the policy-framing and agenda-setting literature raise questions of an empirical and methodological nature. Even under the hypothesis that agenda-setting dynamics—i.e. who and how decides that an issue is worth being discussed and acted upon, where and by what means?—*do affect* the final outcomes of the policy process. How does this happen? What makes an agenda-setting effort more effective than another? There must be something about the actors' posture, the language they use and the way they interact with others that tells whether or not they have contributed to, hindered or even ignored how the agenda has been made. These questions touch on the long-standing debate about the possibility for policy analysts to positively infer from the language, the discourse, the narratives and the meaning used by policy actors and the contested "theoretical assumption that words matter" and "are never neutral" (Duranti 1997, p. 5).

Methodologically speaking the issues of *how* and *how much* non-material and non-tangible factors—like language, meaning, discourse, and the ideas that underpin and provoke them—matter are still fiercely open to debate (Baumgartner 2013; Béland and Cox 2010; Blyth 2002, 2010; Chwieroth 2007; Cox and Béland 2013). The political narrative about the construction of the EU internal energy market through market liberalisation and infrastructural integration shows a recurring pattern. It is an issue that has historically been put forward by the Commission as a fundamental *tessera* in the mosaic of Europe's energy policy (see Biesenbender in Chap. 2), i.e. a measure which might lead to a lesser energy dependence on foreign supply and more sustainable consumption.

This narrative was particularly important in order to wear out the Member States' hostility to any liberalisation policies for the EU energy market during the 1990s. As long as the security-of-supply frame prevailed during the first four decades of European integration, Member States saw market liberalisation and the opening of new opportunities to tackle transversal EU-wide issues as a potential interference in the complex relationship with national energy companies and meddling in their complete control on domestic energy policy, especially abroad (see Tosun 2011, p. 7157; Herweg in Chap. 5). The discursive change advocated by the Commission had an impact not only on the process of market liberalisation but also on governance 'layering' within the EU and the division of labour as the integration process moved on.

8.3.1 Characteristics of the EU Internal Energy Market

The liberalisation of the EU internal energy market is a crucial case study of agenda-setting process for two diverse and yet related reasons. First, the discourse on market liberalisation and its policy consequences have set the tone and pace of EU energy policy as a whole. As we illustrate in this chapter, the Commission's emphasis on market creation during the 1970 and early 1980s was essentially a reaction to the powerful member states' (such as Britain or France) realistic or threatened veto on any measures directly affecting their 'sovereign' ability to administrate national energy resources. In a few years' time, the market liberalisation agenda favoured the Commission's goal of gaining a foothold in Europe's energy issues (see Biesenbender in Chap. 2). And in recent years, the internal energy market has become the main arena in which the EU has laid out its strategy to face energy and environmental challenges such as climate change and the construction of a sustainable low-carbon integrated energy market.

Second, as far as the actors involved in this process are concerned, the liberalisation of the internal energy market mirrors the role played by the United Kingdom as an agenda shaper throughout the creation process of an embryonic EU energy policy, which was *exactly at the same time* the Commission strengthened its ability as a policy entrepreneur. This case allows the analyst to verify whether a couple of crucial expectations in agenda-setting studies are indeed tenable: whether policy entrepreneurship is a sufficient condition to achieve a high agenda status, and whether non-active behaviours (e.g. vetoing) can allow an actor to affect the agenda despite the lack of active entrepreneurship or policy initiative.

8.3.2 Process-Tracing Technique and Data

This chapter develops a process-tracing exercise about the Commission's agenda in order to show how it has been influenced by Britain's position (within the Council) at three different stages: (a) 1970s and early 1980s, a time characterised by global energy market instability and the Commission's attempt to lead a coordinated European reaction, (b) late 1980s and early 1990s, a period marked by the emergence of a coherent liberalisation agenda, and (c) late 1990s and the mid-2000s, a period characterised by a constant correlation between energy and environmental priorities in the EU as well as internationally. In this process-tracing exercise, narrative data—mostly primary official sources from press releases, speeches, official statements and public notes, as well as secondary sources from established literature whenever strictly necessary—will be analysed to identify *discursive vehicles* that mirror the evolution of language and policy discourse in the agenda-setting negotiations over the liberalisation of the EU internal energy market. All relevant language elements and speech acts that comply with two very basic criteria fall in this category. First, their ability to qualify as discourse, i.e. as part of the (Hajer 2005, p. 300).

> Ensemble of ideas, concepts, and categories through which meaning is given to social and physical phenomena, and which is produced and reproduced through an identifiable set of practices.

Second, the possibility to determine in an unequivocal way the source of the discursive vehicle, so that the ideas underpinning it, the vision embodied in it and the policy preferences conveyed by it can be clearly attributed to a specific policy actor. The degree of 'deviation' from an actor's expected or standard preferences and positioning can work as an indicator to 'measure' to what extent its agenda-setting priorities or interests have been affected.

8.4 Who Decided the Meaning of Energy Liberalisation?

The aim of this section is to re-read the history of the liberalisation of the EU's internal energy market in order to pinpoint those exogenous events, punctual actions or irreversible decisions that elicit alterations of the balances between diverging positions and conflicting goals so significant as to shift the agenda-setting power from one player to another. The following sub-sections identify three crucial stages at different times in the integration process: the 1970s as an early stage of agenda exclusion; the 1980–1990 decades as the setting for Britain's first-move to re-frame the energy policy discourse; the 2000s as the breeding ground for the emergence of the 'climate-energy' and sustainability agendas.

8.4.1 The 1970s: Britain and Agenda Exclusion, Defending Sovereignty?

Energy has historically been a delicate issue in the relationship between the United Kingdom and the rest of continental Europe, ever since Britain refused to lead the project of a united Western Europe in the post-World War II years and be part of the European Coal and Steel Community (ECSC) because of substantial sovereignty concerns (Kitzinger 1960, p. 20). Being an "island of coal floating in a sea of oil and gas" made this relationship even more complicated (McGowan 2011a, p. 189). Energy policy was never a significant obstacle during the negotiation process of the United Kingdom's accession to the European Economic Community (EEC), at least until the 1973–1974 oil crisis inevitably urged energy issues into the EEC agenda and exacerbated the latent political competition between Britain and its European partners.

In 1972, the Commission launched the communication *Necessary progress in community energy policy* arguing: "it should be clearly realised that the role of the public authorities on the Community energy market needs to be strengthened, albeit without endangering the unity of the market" (European Commission 1972, p. 6). Indeed, the Commission's plea generated positive responses during the European Summit meetings of October 1972 in Paris (Spaak 1973, p. 35). The process, however, was hampered when the "Commission also approached the Council with proposal for oil sharing" (Lucas 1977, p. 59), an attempt which proved to be a deal-breaker in the Council. Shortly after joining the EEC in January 1973, Britain had already grown a significant interest to jealously defend its North Sea oil and gas reserves. In 1974, the British Secretary of Energy argued that the United Kingdom had "little to gain from any likely Community Policy" suggesting that the country could be self-supporting on energy matters (Department of Energy 1974, p. 1). The strength of being one of Europe's main producers of oil and gas transformed the United Kingdom into a key veto player, especially when the Commission decided to route towards less dependence on external energy supplies (Simonet 1974). When protecting the North Sea oil and gas reserves, British representatives were instructed to "have in mind the Government's overall intention to renegotiate the terms of entry to EEC" (Department of Energy 1974, p. 3).

Against this national backdrop, the United Kingdom's energy policy vis-à-vis Europe's appeared to pursue a few crucial objectives: (a) preserving the advantages derived from its domestic energy endowment; (b) continuing support for Transatlantic cooperation on the subject; (c) cooperating in developing appropriate European policies that were to be administered nationally under any circumstances unless the devolution of any powers to the Commission may lead to actual domestic benefits (Department of Energy 1974, p. 2). The British government pre-emptively shut several key strategic doors, which avoided cooperation on sensitive energy policy matters such as: the management and exploitation of North Sea energy sources. As for the integration and consistency of the European energy market, no specific position was taken by the United Kingdom. Britain made clear, however, that the position of national companies like British Petroleum was not to be weakened by the establishment of Community-wide policies (Department of Energy 1974, p. 2). Partly as an outcome of this de facto British veto, the Community objectives were downgraded to (a) "the setting of a Community target for a reduction in the consumption of primary forms of energy" and (b) "the maintaining of intra-Community trade in crude oil and petroleum products" (European Commission 1975, p. 1).

In an attempt to meet Britain's demands, the Commission specified that "these two proposals do not constitute in themselves a means of distributing available supplies" (European Commission 1975, p. 1). The Commission's energy policy goals put further emphasis on market concerns. The key objective was "to ensure the unity of the Community market by facilitating use of supplies" (European

Commission 1975, p. 1). In this regard, the United Kingdom not only succeeded in scrapping the creation of a European Energy Agency off the Community agenda (McGowan 2011, p. 198), avoiding the creation of a 'single-voice' venue for international energy affairs (Lucas 1977, p. 66) and resisting the idea of putting North Sea reserves at the service of the Community. But it also made a big step towards easier access to a broader market for the thriving British energy companies. National energy policies, affecting the overall relationship with the EEC, were designed to create the best conditions to meet the governmental objectives on the use of the North Sea reserves (Cabinet Office 1978). In the aftermath of the oil crisis, the United Kingdom used its power as a lever to intervene selectively and 'negatively' (i.e. as a veto player) in the elaboration of the EEC agenda. In a context in which the Commission still lacked any resources and formal power in this policy field and France agreed to undermine "the scope of a collective response by the Community" (McGowan 2011, p. 197), the United Kingdom effectively managed to phase out any sensible advance in energy policy from the formal agenda.

8.4.2 Late 1980s and Early 1990s: Britain as a First-Mover Agenda Setter

The Commission began being more cautious and pragmatic in its strategic planning. In the *New Community Energy Objectives* communication (European Commission 1985, p. 2), the Commission invited the "Council to adopt both horizontal and sectoral objectives" in external relations as well as in the integration of the Community's energy market, energy security and environmental protection policies. Promoting this new market-driven approach (Padgett 1992, p. 56), the Commission itself recognised that "it is arguable that not enough attention has been paid in the past to the advantages that would result from a more integrated common market in energy" (European Commission 1985, p. 16). With the adoption of the Single European Act (SEA) in December 1985, the internal market became a "focal point" of Community intervention (Padgett 1992, p. 57). The Delors Commission, formed by "a number of liberally minded Commissioners" (McGowan 2011, p. 199), brought about the idea that completing the internal market could boost European integration while asserting once and for all the Commission's role as a policy entrepreneur in the European arena. Delors "made the White paper (*on the internal market*) the Commission's priority in the first months of his presidency" (Drake 2000, p. 1966, emphasis added). Interestingly though, "partly as a reflection of the past energy policy failures, the Commission did not include energy in the initial agenda for the Single European Market" (McGowan 1989, p. 550).

The SEA and the Single Market Programme laid the groundwork for the development of a Community energy policy through two policy highways: liberalisation and competition (Tosun and Solorio 2011, p. 4). Building upon successful experiences in other policy fields, the Commission launched the internal energy market (IEM) working paper in 1988 arguing that the "legal instruments available to the Community for the attainment of the internal energy market are no different from those which allow the realisation of Europe without frontiers" (European Commission 1988, p. 7). Besides the institutional innovations of the SEA, what had changed in Europe so that the Commission could dare carrying out such a bold initiative in the energy field? Economically, oil prices had decreased significantly as much as demand–supply balances in the global energy markets had stabilised. Politically, the *wind* had somehow changed among several key member states, which realised that the plans of the Commission could probably lead to beneficial domestic effects. The end of the 1970s and then the 1980 brought about "dramatic changes" in Britain's general economic policy that progressively affected the energy sector too (Matláry 1997, p. 29). Between 1980 and 1990, the British energy industry went through deep changes in structure, which was characterised mostly by the privatisation of many sub-sectors: the oil industry was privatised between 1982 and 1987, the natural gas industry in 1986, non-nuclear-generated electricity in 1990 and 1991, the coal industry in 1995, and finally nuclear power in 1996.

The United Kingdom became a *first-mover* in promoting the transformation of the energy sector Europe-wide following the growing 'liberal wave' that affected the global economy as a whole (Padgett 2003). By framing a new EU energy policy discourse through market-oriented proposals, the Commission won the support of the United Kingdom as an important ally. In order to strengthen its credibility, the Delors Commission involved two savvy British politicians. Lord Cockfield "authored the 1985 White Paper making 300 recommendations on how the single market could be brought into being" (Johnsons 2012, p. 3). At the same time, "Commissioner Sir Leon Brittan actively sought to apply general community law for enforcing member states to dismantle national monopolistic energy structures" (Eikeland 2004, p. 11; see also Herweg in Chap. 5 and Brutschin in Chap. 10).

The Commission managed to build a somewhat *impossible alliance* to commence the liberalisation of EU energy markets. During the 1990s, the liberalisation of energy became the flagship of all European policy efforts in this field. The British experience in energy market liberalisation. Once an insurmountable obstacle to the Community's energy agenda, it became an actual "best practice" (McGowan 2011, p. 199). Britain was acting not only as a promoter-by-example but also as an active supporter of the Commission's proposals in the Council. Schmidt (1996) gives a quite detailed explanation of the bargaining process within the Council during the negotiation of the first energy liberalisation package. In general terms, the British reaction towards the internal energy market was positive, actively supporting liberalisation measures at the EU level that resonated with the ones already enacted domestically. Britain remained hostile to "any proposal that involves planning and increased bureaucracy in Brussels" (Matláry 1997, p. 86). While it is true that the liberalisation process in the 1990s resulted in a kind of internal energy market "à la carte" (Jabko 2006, p. 97)—given all national restraints to any model implying adaptation costs, it should be remarked that the United Kingdom was a determinant player in the general conception of the IEM and in a number of particular situations.

As for the electricity sector, the "strong emphasis on open access to interconnection/transmission networks at non-discriminatory tariffs" and the requirement of "the supervision of interconnection/transmission network access by regulatory authorities independent of market players" were key triggers of the market-building process (Humphreys and Padgett 2006, p. 386). In this specific regard, another veto came from a similarly powerful actor in this field, France, the largest electricity exporter in the Community at the time. It was "unimaginable" to proceed without its consent (Schmidt 1996, p. 21) to such an extent that the Commission had to make substantial concessions: third-party access to the network. By attempting to affect long-established interests of monopolistic and public-controlled utilities, the creation of the IEM met the resistance of many national governments that saw the renovation of their domestic markets as an unpleasant prospect.

The effects of this confrontation became most visible when, at the beginning of the 2000s, the Commission negotiated an upgrade of the energy package. It tried to overcome some member states' foot-dragging by involving a "broad range of stakeholders in a bottom-up process to identify and seek consensus on the harmonisation of cross-border transmission system issues" (Eikeland 2008, pp. 12–13). Eventually by 2011, after a complex policy process giving birth to two additional liberalisation packages (Buchan 2009, pp. 20–27), the internal energy market resembled the British model more than ever before. As Ipek and Williams (2010, p. 22) argue, "the UK led on liberalisation of energy markets in Europe as early as the 1980s to facilitate competition and ensure efficiency in Britain's gas and electricity markets". Ultimately, the British strategy got marginally closer to the EU's but defended its national interests proportionally.

8.4.3 Late 1990s and 2000s: Structuring the Low-Carbon and Sustainability Agenda

While the establishment of the IEM was the first concrete success in the attempts of the Commission to increase its shares in EU energy policy making, the growing concern and potential of a European environmental policy framework opened another significant policy highway to further 'europeanise' energy policy (Solorio 2011; Tosun and Solorio 2011). The first Commission proposals on the way to 'greening' EU energy policy were welcomed reluctantly by the United Kingdom. This policy opportunity sprawled across Europe at a time when Britain was generally identified as a laggard in environmental affairs (Rayner and Jordan 2011, p. 98). It had firmly rejected several proposals: a carbon tax, arguing that the United Kingdom could be able to meet its CO_2 emissions cut objectives even without any such instruments (McGowan 2011, p. 2013). After the carbon tax debacle, the future of the EU climate change and environmental policy was cast into doubt (Andersen 2000).

It was the election of a new Labour government led by Tony Blair, who was to remain in power from 1997 to 2007, that brought about a new agreement between the Commission and the United Kingdom to put forward a consistent EU climate policy through a low-carbon and sustainability-driven market (Rayner and Jordan 2011, p. 99). In 1998, the Commission launched *Partnership for Integration: a strategy for integrating environment into EU policies* (European Commission 1998), building on the premise that the "implementation of Treaty objectives requires, therefore, [...] an approach to Community policy making based on the recognition that all policies must contribute to sustainable development" (European Commission 1998, p. 5). The United Kingdom used its 1998 Council Presidency to ride a 'green wave' aiming to shape a more sustainable internal energy market. The inception of the so-called 'Cardiff Process' was a first concrete step towards environmental policy integration and "sustainable development as the new paradigm that was supposed to guide all policy-makers" (Lenschow 2002, p. 3). This new consensus, based on Britain's political traditions and procedural approaches, eased the transition from strategy to practice, which brought about advances such as the directive on renewable electricity, biofuels or the establishment of the EU emissions trading system (for the discussion of the role of Eastern enlargement, see Brutschin in Chap. 10).

The process was not always smooth. The United Kingdom acted as a *first-mover* bearing in mind the opportunity to lower adaptation costs (Rayner and Jordan 2011, p. 102) but performed unsatisfactorily on renewable energy policies (see Cox and Dekanozishvili in Chap. 9 for an analysis of the German influence on the EU's renewable energy agenda). In an attempt to retake hold of the reins of the energy and climate-change agendas in Europe, Britain emphasised those specific policy instruments that could be easily uploaded from the British context up to the European level (Rayner and Jordan 2011, p. 105). The new British Council Presidency of 2005 linked the development of the IEM with the fight against climate change and took the lead on an issue that would redefine energy policy in the EU (Morata and Solorio 2012, p. 8). The Blair government approached its presidency term with a definite agenda on climate change in mind to be translated at the European level. Blair chose the Hampton Court European Council summit in September 2005 as the stage to present a plan for the creation of a common EU energy policy—a move that many observers interpreted as a 'U-turn' of Britain's traditional position on these matters (Euroactiv 2005).

Despite the lack of concrete results from the Hampton Court discussion, the summit laid the groundwork for further EU action in the energy field and a shift in the order of policy priorities. Discursively, climate change had by then captured the limelight of the EU's energy policy narrative. As stated in the background paper Dieter Helm prepared for the British presidency, "climate change was recognised in the EU back in the 1980s, but the constraints have only begun to bite in this decade" (Helm 2005, p. 5).

This new agenda was consistent with a long-term *vision* of energy policy that the Commission had held for decades. The Blair administration moved in as an *agenda-structurer* "reviving interest in energy policy" and picking out climate change to win the reluctance of most (national) policy laggards across the EU. In 2006, the Commission began pushing the energy debate forward with the paramount goal of laying down the foundations of a new global energy policy (European Commission 2006, 2007). Noticeably, climate change figures as the new 'long-term' priority guiding the 'green' dimension and more generally Europe's environmental commitment. This new approach was confirmed when the Commission launched its proposal for the new European Energy Policy, which specified that "meeting the EU's commitment to act now on greenhouse gases should be at the centre of the new European Energy Policy" (European Commission 2007). In 2007, *An Energy Policy for Europe* and the Strategic Energy Technology plan, *Towards a low carbon future*, set the pace of further policy initiative on the part of the Commission, which lead to a number of achievements in the field—the definition of the so-called '20-20-20' goals on carbon emissions cut, renewable sources and energy savings (see also Biesenbender in Chap. 2); the development of carbon capture and storage (CCS) technologies (see Fuchs in Chap. 11); and a long-term energy efficiency strategy that eventually led to a new directive entered into force in December 2012.

Overall, the 'greening' of EU energy policy had a strong British character. While the Commission had been a persistent supporter of this policy frame for decades, it was the British government and in particular the Blair administration that played a fundamental role in framing the climate-change agenda and opening an unprecedented window of opportunity to expand the 'portfolio' of energy policy-making options available to EU institutions. Under the 'climate-energy' umbrella, new legislation on renewable energy sources was approved, an updated model for carbon emissions trading schemes was designed, and most notably the *third energy legislative package* was approved. It repealed existing legislation on the EU's electricity and gas internal markets and entering into force in 2009. The overall result is not only that the IEM has become the fundamental arena where the EU energy policy is developed, but also that the climate/environmental objectives are conditioned by the market rules.

8.5 Conclusion: A Discursive Route to Agenda-Building Consensus?

This discursive study on the liberalisation of the internal energy market aimed to show the diverse roles played by the United Kingdom in its complex agenda-shaping intervention on EU energy policy. The fundamental conclusion that can be drawn from this analysis is that while the Commission acted as a persistent policy entrepreneur, energy market liberalisation and the construction of a broader EU energy policy could hardly enter the EU policy agenda without Britain's strong discursive leadership. When faced with either the opportunity to preserve its domestic interests or lead the process of steady integration of EU energy markets, the United Kingdom has gone through all stages of agenda shaping (Tallberg 2003) and determined the degree of mutual 'contamination' between national and EU-level energy policy narratives and priorities accordingly (see Table 8.1).

The first stage spans across the 1970s and early 1980s in the context of a global oil crisis, instability of international energy markets and an embryonic participation of the Community in the energy issues (provided the peculiarity of the Euratom framework and the slow exhaustion of the European Coal and Steel Community). Despite pressing concerns about the security of energy supply in the Community, Britain adopted a rigid position to defend national sovereign control over its North Sea oil and gas reserves. With a de facto veto power, the United Kingdom limited the room for manoeuvre of the Commission and watered down the emerging narrative on a Community-wide crisis response and energy policy development. The

Table 8.1 Evolution of agenda-shaping processes in EU energy market liberalisation

	1970s–early 1980s	Late 1980s–mid-1990s	Mid-1990s–2000s
EU energy policy development	Embryonic community participation	Designing of the internal energy market	Promoting sustainable energy market strategies
British role in the agenda-setting process	Agenda exclusion	Agenda-setting	Agenda structuring
Attempt to "upload" British energy policy model	Uploading limitations to preserve domestic interests	Uploading as a "first-mover" on liberalisation strategies	Uploading through council presidency prerogatives
British position and interaction	Rejection of any community involvement in north sea reserves	First-mover of energy liberalisation. Strong supporter of commission's liberalising proposals	1998 Council presidency to focus "greener" energy policy. Market-driven environmental policies. 2005 presidency to promote low-carbon policy discourse
Commissions' position and action	Watering cooperation proposals down. Focus on reduction of energy consumption and increase of internal energy trade	Backing the British agenda on liberalisation to increase its own involvement in the EU arena. Reliance on British politicians' upload narrative	Using cardiff process and hampton court summit as consensus-building opportunities for EU-wide energy policy

Source Own elaboration

British insistence on *agenda exclusion* curbed the potential of the Commission's entrepreneurship as well as the acknowledgment of rational energy consumption and stronger internal energy integration and trade as key opportunities to address security-of-supply issues.

The evolution of the international and European energy context triggered a significant change in the British position on the negotiation of a Community energy policy. This second stage—spanning across the second half of the 1980s and the early 1990s—saw the UK act as a *first-mover* in the liberalisation of the EU energy market. This radical change in the British perception of EU energy policy and the market opportunities connected to it instilled new momentum to the liberalisation agenda and rewarded the Commission's entrepreneurship on this subject. Theoretically, the analysis of this agenda-setting phase in the construction of the energy market contests the long-standing assumption that policy entrepreneurship alone generally allows an actor to successfully set the agenda in a way that is resonant with its own interests. The impact of the British U-turn on energy liberalisation shows that, in spite of exceptionally good or proactive entrepreneurship, the institutional constraints and rules of a rigid policy-making environment such as the EU *require* national consensus and intergovernmental momentum to significantly affect agenda-setting processes.

Finally, the third stage spans across the late 1990s and mid-2000s and sees the emergence of the sustainability and climate-change priorities in EU energy policy narratives. By tactically controlling this process, Britain responded to the growing relevance of EU environmental policy strategies and the possibility that the Commission developed a regulatory approach trespassing into heavier supranational competences. Britain's defensive approach avoided greater adaptation costs by uploading the domestic *modus operandi* on environmental policy and structuring the agenda around this core issue. It did so by harnessing the tools and opportunities of the Council Presidency in two different occasions: in 1998, investing on the institutionalisation of the a 'greener' energy policy by building consensus around the Cardiff process; in 2005, by uploading to the EU level the low-carbon objectives and market-oriented solutions to climate-change challenges using this new paradigm as a lever to initiate the restructuration of the internal energy market. The traditional discursive policy entrepreneur, the Commission abided by the agenda-setting power of the United Kingdom but at the same time, maximised its policy returns insofar as it used British interests to promote its own agenda.

Ultimately, this chapter has shed light on the agenda-shaping process that led to a more liberalised and sustainable EU internal energy market. The process has been dominated by the interplay between two key actors, the United Kingdom and the Commission: an agenda shaper that made full use of the powerful toolkit (acquiescence, veto, and entrepreneurship) at its disposal vis-à-vis a policy entrepreneur with unchallenged discursive resources and visibility and frustrated agenda-setting abilities curbed by legislative and institutional constraints.

For EU energy policy to play the Commission's tune, it has to go at a *British tempo*. The governance structure of the EU does not exclude other actors from taking action in this direction in the future (see also Cox and Dekanozishvili in

Chap. 9). The ongoing challenge in shaping the agenda and the debate on the creation of a common electricity market for renewable energy illustrates the complex interplay between the Commission and involved member states (see Jacobs in Chap. 6). One of the conclusions that can be drawn is that the narrative and discursive changes which affected EU energy policy throughout the last 40 years can be either catalysed or hindered by a number of events, decisions and political dynamics. These are ultimately hardly predictable and depend on institutional and political constraints from the local, national and European levels. In other words, the current narrative of a sustainability-driven energy policy in Europe is the result of combined interest pulls and pressures that defended Britain's national preferences and the Commission's ambition to affect EU policy-making in as many fields as possible. The establishment of this narrative is a sort of historical precedent that may serve as a blueprint for discursive policy action by other actors in different contexts or policy fields—be they other interested and sufficiently power Member States or other European institutions, such as the European Parliament.

In institutionalist terms, the British tempo that has let energy policy evolve since the 1970s is a political constraint that all actors will have to take into consideration. The goals, the regulatory instruments and the market-driven vision uploaded from the United Kingdom to the EU have become the current paradigm for energy policy-making in the EU and it has already adapted to the fledgling and comprehensive vision of sustainability and climate-change action. In order to affect this path-dependent balance and swerve EU energy policy towards another set of shared interests and common goals, the construction of a new consensus will likely require significant political and discursive investments in a rapidlychanging global context and with a sensitive impact on the daily lives of EU citizens.

Acknowledgments Israel Solorio is grateful to the Secretaría de Ciencia, Tecnología e Innovación of the Mexico City Government for the postdoctoral grant to carry out the research at the Environmental Policy Research Centre of the Freie Universität Berlin, which resulted in this contribution.

References

Andersen, S. (2000). *EU Energy Policy: Interest Interaction and Supranational Authority*. In Arena Working Paper No. 05/00. Oslo: Centre for European Studies, Universitetet i Oslo.

Baumgartner, F.R. (2013). Ideas and Policy Change. *Governance, 26*(2), 239–258.

Baumgartner, F.R., & Jones, B.D. (1991). Agenda Dynamics and Policy Subsystems. *Journal of Politics, 53*(4), 1044–1074.

Baumgartner, F.R., & Mahoney, C. (2008). The two faces of framing. Individual-level framing and collective issue definition in the EU. *European Union Politics*, *9*(3), 435−449.

Béland, D., & Cox, R.H. (2010). *Ideas and politics in social science research*. Oxford: Oxford University Press.

Blyth, M. (2002). *Great transformations: Economic ideas and institutional change in the twentieth century*. Cambridge: Cambridge University Press.

Buchan, D. (2009). *Energy and climate change: Europe at the crossroads*. Oxford: Oxford University Press.

Cabinet Office of the United Kingdom (1978). *Benefits of north sea oil. Note by the secretary of the cabinet. CP (78)16,* 6 February 1978.

Chwieroth, J.M. (2007). Testing and measuring the role of ideas: The case of neoliberalism in the international monetary fund. *International Studies Quarterly, 51*(1), 5–30.

Cox, R.H., & Béland, D. (2013). Valence, Policy Ideas, and the Rise of Sustainability. *Governance, 26*(2), 307–328.

Department of Energy of the United Kingdom (1974). *EEC energy policy. Note by the secretary of state for energy*. 7 May 1974.

Drake, H. (2000). *Jacques delors: Perspectives on a European leader*. New York: Routledge.

Duranti, A. (1997). *Linguistic anthropology*. Cambridge: Cambridge University Press.

Eikeland, P. (2004). *The long and winding road to the Internal Energy Market. Consistencies and Inconsistencies in the EU Energy Policy.* FNI Report, No. 8/2004. Oslo: Fridtjof Nansen Institute.

Eikeland, P. (2008). *EU internal energy market policy: new dynamics in the brussels policy game?*. FNI Report, No. 14/2008. Oslo: Fridtjof Nansen Institute.

EurActiv (2005). *Blair calls for stronger EU energy policy co-operation*. Brussels: EurActiv.

European Commission. (1972). *Necessary progress in community energy policy. Ref. COM (72) 1200.* Brussels: European Commission.

European Commission. (1976). *Implementation of the energy policy guidelines drawn by the European council at its meeting in Rome on 2 December 1975. COM (76) 20.* Brussels: European Commission.

European Commission. (1985). *New Community energy objectives. COM (85) 245 final.*Brussels: European Commission

European Commission. (1988). *The internal energy market. commission working document. Ref. COM (88) 238 final.* Brussels: European Commission.

European Commission. (1994). *Green paper for a European energy policy. Ref. COM (94) 659 final.* Brussels: European Commission.

European Commission. (1998). *Partnership for integration: A strategy for integrating environment into EU policies. COM (1998) 333 final.* Brussels: European Commission.

European Commission. (2006). *A European strategy for sustainable, competitive and secure energy. Ref. COM (2006) 105 final.* Brussels: European Commission.

European Commission. (2007). *An energy policy for Europe. Ref. COM (2007) 1 final.* Brussels: European Commission.

European Commission. (2012).*Making the internal market work. COM (2012) 663 final.* Brussels: European Commission.

Garrett, G., & Tsebelis, G. (1999). Why Resist the Temptation to Apply Power Indices to the EU? *Journal of Theoretical Politics, 11*(3), 291–308.

Hajer, M. (2005). Coalitions, practices, and meaning in environmental politics: from acid rain to BSE. In D. Howarth & J. Torfing (Eds.), *Discourse theory in European politics. Identity, policy and governance*. Basingstoke: Palgrave Macmillan.

Helm, D. (2005). *European energy policy: Securing supplies and meeting the challenge of climate change*. background paper prepared for the United Kingdom Presidency of the EU, Oxford.

Héritier, A. (1997). Policy-making by subterfuge: interest accommodation, innovation and substitute democratic legitimation in Europe - perspectives from distinctive policy areas. *Journal of European Public Policy, 4*(2), 171–189.

Humphreys, P., & Padgett, S. (2006). Globalization, the EU, and domestic governance in telecoms and electricity. *Governance, 19*(3), 383–406.

Jabko, N. (2006).*Playing the market: A Political Strategy for Uniting Europe* (pp. 1985–2005). Ithaca:Cornell University Press
Hoerber, T. (2013). *The origins of energy and environmental policy in Europe: The beginnings of a European environmental conscience*. London: Routledge.
Johnson, J. (2012). *Britain must defend the single market*. London: Centre for European Reform.
Kingdon, J. (1984). *Agendas, alternatives, and public policies*. New York: Longman.
Kitzinger, U.W. (1960). The six and the seven. *International Organization, 14*(1), 20–36.
Lenschow, A. (2002). Greening the EU: An Introduction. In A. Lenschow (Ed.), *Environmental policy integration: Greening sectoral policies in Europe*. London: Earthscan.
Lucas, N.J.D. (1977). *Energy and the European Communities*. London: Europa Publications.
Matláry, J. (1997). *Energy policy in the EU*. Basingstoke: Palgrave Macmillan.
McGowan, F. (1989). The single energy market and energy policy: Conflicting agendas? *Energy Policy, 17*(6), 547–553.
McGowan, F. (2011). The UK and EU energy policy: From awkward partner to active protagonist? In V. Birchfield & J. Duffield (Eds.), *Toward a common EU energy policy. Problems, progress, and prospects*. New York: Palgrave Macmillan.
Padgett, S. (1992). The single European energy market: The politics of realization. *Journal of Common Market Studies, 30*(1), 53–75.
Padgett, S. (2003). Between synthesis and emulation: EU policy transfer in the power sector. *Journal of European Public Policy, 10*(2), 227–245.
Pollack, M. A. (1997). Delegation, agency, and agenda setting in the European Community. *International Organization, 51*(1), 99–134.
Princen, S. (2009). *Agenda-Setting in the EU*. Basingstoke: Palgrave Macmillan.
Princen, S. (2011). Agenda-setting strategies in EU policy processes. *Journal of European Public Policy, 18*(7), 927–943.
Rayner, T., & Jordan, A. (2011). The United Kingdom: A paradoxical leader? In R.K.W. Wurzel & J. Conelly (Eds.), *The EU as a leader in international climate change politics*. New York: Routledge.
Schattschneider, E.E. (1957). Intensity, visibility, direction and scope. *The American Political Science Review, 51*(4), 933–942.
Schmidt, S.K. (1996). Sterile debates and dubious generalisations: European integration tested by telecommunications and electricity. *Journal of Public Policy, 16*(3), 233–271.
Simonet, H. (1974). *Presentation by Mr. Simonet, Vice-President of the Commission, of the documents of energy policy adopted by the Commission*. Brussels: European Commission.
Solorio, I., Bechberger, M., & Popartan, L. (2013). The European Energy Policy and its 'Green Dimension': Discursive hegemony and policy variations in the greening of energy policy. In P. Barnes & T. Hoeber (Eds.), *Sustainable development and governance in Europe—the evolution of discourse*. London: Routledge.
Solorio, I., & Morata, F. (2012). Introduction: The re-evolution of energy policy in Europe. In F. Morata & I. Solorio (Eds.), *European energy policy: An environmental approach*. Cheltenham: Edward Elgar.
Solorio, I. (2011). Bridging the Gap between Environmental Policy Integration and the EU's Energy Policy: Mapping out the 'Green Europeanisation' of Energy Governance. *Journal of Contemporary European Research, 7*(3), 396–415.
Spaak, F. (1973). An energy policy for the European Community. *Energy Policy, 1*(1), 35–37.
Tallberg, J. (2003). The agenda-shaping powers of the EU Council Presidency. *Journal of European Public Policy, 10*(1), 1–19.
Tosun, J. (2011). When the grace period is over: assessing the new member states' compliance with EU requirements for oil stockholding. *Energy Policy, 39*(11), 7156–7164.

Tosun, J., & Solorio, I. (2011). Exploring the energy-environment relationship in the EU: perspectives and challenges for theorizing and empirical analysis. In J. Tosun & I. Solorio (Eds.), *Energy and Environment in Europe: Assessing a Complex Relationship. European Integration online Papers*, Special Mini-Issue No. 1, 15(7).

Tsebelis, G. (2002). *Veto Players: How Political Institutions Work.* Princeton: Princeton University Press.

Chapter 9
German Efforts to Shape European Renewable Energy Policy

Robert Henry Cox and Mariam Dekanozishvili

Abstract This chapter demonstrates how Germany strove to shape the European Union's (EU) emerging policies on renewable energy. We argue that German decision-makers were motivated by three factors. First, they were influenced by a broad consensus in their own country about the desirability of renewable energy and believed the solutions that worked for Germany would also work for the entire EU. Second, Germany sought to protect the regulatory innovations it had developed by promoting those same regulations at the European level. Third, by establishing a European system that resembled its own, German decision-makers sought to give its own entrepreneurs in the renewable sector a competitive edge in the broader European market. We demonstrate this argument with a process tracing of the development of the 2009 Directive on Renewable Energy Sources (RES).

9.1 Introduction

Germany is a leader in the production of renewable energy and the development of renewable energy technologies. Consequently, when the EU began to develop a renewable energy policy for itself, Germany strove to shape the European agenda. This chapter shows how and why Germany took on this leadership role at the European level (see Ciambra and Solorio in Chap. 8 for an analysis of the British influence on the EU's energy agenda). In terms of why, we argue that German officials saw the challenges facing Europe as similar to the ones they faced in their

R.H. Cox (✉)
Walker Institute for International and Area Studies, University of South Carolina,
817 Henderson Street, 251 Gambrell Hall, Columbia, SC 29208, USA
e-mail: rhcox@sc.edu

M. Dekanozishvili
Department of Politics and Geography, Coastal Carolina University,
125 Chanticleer Drive West, Office 344, Conway, SC 29526, USA
e-mail: mdekanozi@coastal.edu

J. Tosun et al. (eds.), *Energy Policy Making in the EU*,
Lecture Notes in Energy 28, DOI 10.1007/978-1-4471-6645-0_9

own country. They felt that the solutions they had successfully developed could just as successfully be deployed as responses across the EU. In addition, its earlier initiatives in promoting renewable energy had made Germany a world leader and it sought to preserve this leadership position.

Germany's leadership in renewable energy has two dimensions. On the one hand, to promote renewable technologies, Germany adopted a number of regulatory innovations designed to protect and promote infant industries in the renewable sector. On the other hand, as these industries developed, they became leaders in technological innovation. German officials believed that by shaping the European agenda they would preserve both of these leadership roles. By encouraging the EU to adopt its regulatory innovations, Germany could create a European regime very much like its own. When it came time to comply with the new European system, the costs of compliance for Germany would be lower than the costs for other European countries. Furthermore, creating similar regulatory regimes across Europe would also give a competitive advantage to German producers of renewable technologies. Because these companies had already learned to operate under the German regulatory regime, a similar European regime would allow them to move faster in the wider European market for renewable energy.

In addition to these strategic concerns, German officials exploited a tactical window of opportunity to push their agenda. During the first half of 2007, Germany held the 6-month rotating Presidency of the EU. This provided a unique opportunity to advance the development of renewable energy, and German officials made good use of this opportunity. We show how this agenda shaping had profound influence on the EU's Directive on Renewable Energy Sources (RES) adopted in 2009.

9.2 The Logic of German Agenda Shaping

Agenda shaping describes the ability of political actors to influence the salience of certain items or issues, introduce new issues on the agenda (agenda setting), put emphasis on some issues (agenda structuring) and ultimately influence the outcome of the policy decision. Whether those groups are key individuals who occupy important positions of power or well organised and influential groups, the emphasis is on the actions of those actors—their abilities to garner resources, gain access to key decision-makers, advance or block a discussion, mobilise supporters, etc. (see Tosun et al. in Chap. 1 for an assessment of the institutional and legal foundations of EU energy policy over time).

Much of the research on agenda shaping emphasises the strategic calculations made by policy makers who strive to control the agenda because doing so allows them to steer the final outcome in a favourable direction (Baumgartner and Jones 2009; Tallberg 2003). Some research on agenda setting focuses on the role of ideas in the process, they suggest that ideas are used by agenda setters to frame debates, to simplify complex relationships and to build linkages with other policy actors who share similar ideas (Liefferink and Andersen 1998). As this chapter shows, successful agenda shaping involves a combination of strategic interests and good ideas. What makes agenda shapers successful is not only their innate skills in pursuing their interests but also the broader context of normative frames, discourses and ideas that can provide a fertile ground for their policy preferences. Thus, to successfully promote their interests, policy makers need ideas. And to make their ideas compelling, they need to build upon or amplify broader societal values. Successful agenda shapers integrate their understandings of what is right and proper with what is strategically desirable.

The logic of German efforts to shape European policies on renewable energy is like a pattern that Ruggie (1982; see also Abdelal and Ruggie 2009) showed American officials following as they rebuilt the world economy after the Second World War. Ruggie called this new regime "embedded liberalism", and he identified its main characteristics as a desire for free trade, currency stability and domestic capital controls. American officials were driven by two objectives. On the one hand, the American domestic economy was familiar and widely supported. It produced economic growth as well as a strong degree of social legitimacy. This led Americans to think of theirs as a normatively desirable model for other countries. In addition, building a global economy along American standards would give American multinational firms a competitive advantage in global markets. Because they already knew the regulatory environment of the American systems, American firms would enjoy lower learning costs in global markets if they confronted a regulatory system they had already learned to negotiate. Thus, a combination of normative ideas and pragmatic economic interests combined to create a preference in the minds of American officials.

Though the EU is smaller than the global economy, its institutional framework affords its member states a similar chance to shape transnational affairs in accordance with its domestic interests. Many of the larger states in the EU often seek to project their own domestic understandings of policy problems onto the European policy agenda (Kohler-Koch and Rittberger 2006). This has certainly been the case for Germany and the specific case of renewable energy but also more generally with regard to environmental protection (see, e.g. Knill and Lenschow 2001; Knill and Tosun 2011) and policies related to risk and uncertainty (see, e.g. Löfstedt 2004; Tosun 2013). As renewable energy became an important topic in the European policy discussions, German leaders endeavoured to make the emerging European policy regime resemble the German one. Germany as a forerunner in renewable energy, with a well-developed regulatory framework ahead of others in the EU, sought to prepare the ground for other member states to follow. Germany's effort to shape the European agenda was driven by a combination of both 'norm entrepreneurship' based on the logic of appropriateness and rational strategising based on logic of consequences (March and Olsen 1998). These efforts have not been without resistance (see Jacobs in Chap. 6 for an illustration of the Commission's resistance against the German feed-in law of 1990).

Norm entrepreneurship centred on a rising concern about climate change, and an ambition to be a global promoter of the "right norm". In addition, German officials understood climate change to be a transnational issue that cannot be solved by unilateral measures. Moreover, these officials also believed that German norms, principles and solutions were right and appropriate for a common European response to climate change. In that respect, the concept of ecological modernisation (*Ökologische Modernisierung*) was widely accepted as a norm among policy makers in Germany. The idea is that stringent environmental measures can help to modernise the economy because ecological modernisation demands the development of new technologies and industrial practices. An additional benefit is that these technologies can be exported to other markets.

Ecological modernisation also embraced other principles that have been widely accepted in Germany. Climate protection was another norm that German officials felt was equally appropriate for the EU. The norm appeared equally acceptable for the risk-averse German society in which the precautionary principle was already well ingrained. In addition, climate protection can be envisaged as one of those post-materialistic values, which according to Inglehart (1985) gets embraced by affluent liberal democracies, such as Germany (see Ciambra and Solorio in Chap. 8). So, the concept of ecological modernisation became widely accepted as a macro political norm in Germany, especially after a Social Democratic Party (SPD) and Green Party coalition came to government in 1998 (Jänicke 2011). Economic growth and environmental protection were increasingly regarded as parallel achievable goals and the Best Available Technology (BAT) principle became the guiding principle for Germany's eco-industrial policy (ökologische Industriepolitik), which featured in Germany's pragmatic considerations and underlined German "norm entrepreneurship" to support renewable energy at the EU level (but see Fuchs in Chap. 11 for an opposite assessment).

A second, well-recognised motivation for member states to strive to control the development of an EU policy, is to expand the market for their own industry. As Héritier et al. (1996) state, high-regulating states may have an interest in expanding technology markets for their own industry. Because Germany had a well-developed regulatory framework nationally based on feed-in tariff (FIT) system that encouraged industry to develop renewable energy technologies, German introduction of ambitious energy/climate targets into EU legislation would create additional demand for such technology and provide excellent opportunity for Germany's export-oriented industry. Renewable energy represents a shift to knowledge-based high tech and is in line with Germany's post-industrial transition. Ambitious CO_2 targets have been a driving force for innovation and technology diffusion and regarded necessary for retaining Germany's technological leadership in innovation and for supporting Germany's export-oriented renewables industry. In that regard, the EU's goals for reducing carbon dioxide levels and binding renewable energy targets were considered important to create even higher European demand for renewable technology.

A third motivation for member states to control the EU agenda is to guide the EU to adopt regulations that are similar to those already in place at home. This process of "uploading" one's domestic regime allows member states to minimise the costs of implementing EU policies (Börzel 2002, p. 194; see Ciambra and Solorio Chap. 8). As member states have distinct institutions, they compete at the EU level for policies that conform to their own interests and approaches (Héritier et al. 1996). EU policy making opens opportunities to upload national standards, measures and solutions to the European level to ensure that no administrative and implementation costs are incurred when it comes time to comply with the new European rules (Knill and Lenschow 2001). German leadership was inspired by the desire to export its own national standards and/or preferred national problem-solving philosophies to reduce regulatory adjustment costs. Germany actively pursued gatekeeping to avoid the adoption of undesirable policies and measures at the EU level that would have been economically or politically costly to comply with. 'Uploading' is an effective strategy to maximise the benefits and minimise the costs of European policies and reduces the need for legal and administrative adaptation in subsequent 'downloading'. The more a European policy fits the domestic context, the lower the adaptation costs in the implementation process (see Börzel 2002).

A fourth rationale for German efforts to influence the EU agenda was to strengthen its leadership role in global climate change negotiations. Helping to create a unified European position would enable Germany to shape transnational affairs in accordance with its domestic interests and accepted norms—and to project European understanding of policy problems onto the global level. Due to its economic strength and booming climate mitigation technologies, Germany has become a "trend-setter" in international climate change politics (Jänicke 2008) and overachieved Kyoto targets by reducing its greenhouse gas emissions by 21.3 %. Coupled with its leadership in renewable technology exports, ambitious and unified EU targets would give Germany a stronger position to become a "trend-setter" in international climate politics and exert more influence on other players (e.g. US and China) in upcoming climate change negotiations. As the Kyoto commitment period approached and reaching a post-Kyoto agreement featured increasingly on the global agenda, feelings of urgency began to surface. By fostering a more unified European position that also reflected German domestic concerns, Germany sought to strengthen its global influence.

Finally, another reason German officials push issues at the European level is to enhance their legitimacy at home by pushing popular issues on the EU agenda or by using the EU as a scapegoat against domestic obstacles. Entrepreneurs may effectively use international institutional features to strengthen their arguments in domestic debates (Finnemore and Sikkink 1998, p. 893). Vertical venue shopping is a way to circumvent domestic backlashes against ambitious climate policy measures. Vertical venue shopping from the member state to the EU level is a classic way in which issues reach the EU agenda (Princen 2011).

Uploading may enable national governments to address problems which preoccupy their constituencies but can no longer be dealt with effectively at the domestic level due to inter-ministerial wrangling and turf battles between different state agencies or interest groups. Thus, the EU served as a venue not only to diffuse German standards and regulations at the EU level to embed others but also to reinforce and legitimate solutions that were subject to dispute domestically.

To summarise our argument, German motives for promoting renewable energy at the EU level were based on mutually reinforcing logic of appropriateness and logic of consequences, in other words: on a self-interested norm entrepreneurship due to an intimate connection between norms and rationality (Finnemore and Sikkink 1998). Promoting renewable energy was precisely the case in which Germany pursued environmental as well as economic rationales. All norm promoters at the international level need some kind of organisational platform through which to channel influence. The rotating EU Council Presidency provided such a platform for Germany's agenda-shaping efforts, as we demonstrate in the following section.

9.3 Germany's Agenda-Shaping Efforts: Renewable Energy Sources Directive of 2009

The EU renewable energy policy is governed by the 2009 European Commission (2009), which was adopted as a part of the EU's so-called climate-energy package. The Renewable Energy (RES) directive outlines the policy framework for increasing the share of renewable energy in the energy consumption of the EU to 20 % by 2020. The Commission suggested this target in the Renewable Energy Roadmap (COM 2006a, p. 848 final). The European Council meeting held in the spring of 2007 endorsed the target (Council of EU 2007). Several months later in January 2008, the Commission presented the proposal for a new directive. After 11 months of negotiations, the final agreement on the directive was reached in December 2008.

The most important and innovative element of the directive was the binding nature of the 20 % target. This new legislation replaced the previous directive 2001/77/EC (the RES-E directive), which entailed a goal to achieve 21 % of the EU's electricity from renewable energy sources by 2010. It set out individual differentiated targets for each EU member state. However, they were of indicative non-binding nature. Only few member states (Germany, Denmark and Hungary) met their specific targets before 2007, and the EU was still short of the 21 % target (COM 2006b, p. 849 final).

Though most countries failed to meet their targets, Germany had already overfulfilled its target by 2007. Germany's Renewable Energy Sources Act (EEG), which was modified in 2004, set ambitious targets to increase the percentage of renewable energy sources in Germany's power supply to at least 12.5 % by 2010 and to at least 20 % by 2020 (EEG 2004). Because of their own ambitious achievements, German officials felt they should push the EU to be more ambitious as well. "It was necessary to address RES and CO_2 obligations at the EU level to have a strong and unified voice in the upcoming climate change negotiations of the post-Kyoto regime. Chancellor Merkel decided to put RES binding targets on the EU agenda and push forward the 20/20/20 initiative. Holding the Council Presidency in the first half of 2007 provided an important institutional platform for Germany to push the binding RES target" (Interview 2013a: Representative of German Federal Ministry of Economics and Technology).

9.4 German Presidency and Binding Targets for Renewable Energy

9.4.1 German Presidency and Its Priorities

Germany made EU energy policy a top priority and a special focus during its EU presidency in 2007. Climate change has been one of the pronounced priorities of the German EU Presidency, which tied in nicely with Germany's simultaneous presidency of the G8 leaders in 2007 (Barysch 2007). The timing of Germany's rotation on the Council Presidency in the first half of 2007 also coincided with a fortuitous institutional reform. Germany was the first member state to preside over the newly instituted Trio Presidency that was introduced to ensure more continuity for political initiatives. The Trio Presidency consisted of three countries which developed a common programme for their 18 months serving successive rotations as Council President.

Thus, when Germany assumed the first trimester of its Presidency with Portugal and Slovenia, it established an agenda that lasted for 18 months. Moreover, the timing of the rotating Council Presidency seemed to leave Germany a peerless leader in Europe as Britain's powerful leader, Tony Blair, was leaving office and France was scheduled to hold presidential elections in the Spring of 2007 (Barysch 2007). So, Germany assumed the Council Presidency at a time when British agenda-shaping initiatives were already diminishing (see Chap. 8 by Ciambra and Solorio for an in-depth illustration of these processes). The timing of the Council Presidency, hence, provided a leadership opportunity for Germany, or in agenda-setting parlance the opening of a policy window through politics stream (Kingdon 1984).

The work programme of the German Presidency was derived from three key elements of the Lisbon Agenda, a broad programme to foster economic revival that had been promoted by the Commission. According to the Programme of the Council Presidency:

> A sustainable Europe which creates jobs and prosperity needs an active environmental policy. Faced with dynamic growth in important newly industrialised countries, global challenges such as climate protection and resource scarcity require "green" innovations. To this end, we need an ecological policy for innovation and industry at the European level, which systematically promotes environmental technologies such as energy- and resource-efficient processes and products, or renewable energies. In this way, we can also achieve the highest possible level of environmental protection, sustainable economic development, competitiveness and not least of employment (German Presidency Programme 2007).

Germany framed the impetus for the energy/climate policy in the context of the Lisbon Strategy and strove to translate the broad goals into specific measures to expand the share of renewable energies.

The European initiative was an extension of an ambitious domestic strategy (IEA 2007, p. 72). Germany's parallel attempt to push RES targets in the framework of EU Energy-Climate package demonstrates an 'uploading' to the EU of a preferred solution that later would be 'downloaded' domestically at no or minimal cost and, at the same time, strengthen German-led EU leadership in upcoming climate change talks. The member states are known to pursue different Europeanisation strategies: strategies for 'uploading' their most preferred policy designs to the European level (Börzel 2002, p. 194; see also Alexandrova and Timmermans in Chap. 3). 'Pace-setting' is one of such strategies member states pursue to push their preferred policies at the European level. When the strategy is successful, a pacesetter's preferred policies and solutions are exported to the European level and subsequently adopted by other member states. However, pacesetting presupposes established domestic policies as well as the capacity to push them through the European negotiation process while often times facing a fierce opposition from other member states (Börzel 2002, p. 199).

The Council Presidency presented Germany with such a pacesetting opportunity. Germany's success in pushing the RES binding targets on the EU agenda rested on defining the problem and framing the issues in a way that ensured receptiveness at the EU level. Although, a binding 20 % target met resistance from France and the UK initially, Germany succeeded in convincing Member States that enough flexibility would be introduced to achieve their targets.

9.4.2 German Presidency: Issue Framing

Germany, as a member state holding the Presidency, sought to satisfy national preferences within the confines of its formally delegated role, and the particular interests which concerned the German government influenced its behaviour. As more than just a strategic actor, Germany also displayed policy entrepreneurship during its EU Council Presidency. A policy entrepreneur can take an active role in agenda shaping through issue framing by emphasising some issues and de-emphasising others (agenda structuring) (Tallberg 2003). Successful entrepreneurship requires the right tactics, right frames and strategy to ensure issue receptiveness. The European Council Presidency offers many resources for agenda setting. "The EU member state holding the Presidency possesses a position and an arsenal of means, both formally anchored and developed through informal institutional practices, that enable forms of agenda-shaping" (Tallberg 2003, p. 5; see Alexandrova and Timmermans in Chap. 3 for a discussion of the role of policy entrepreneurs in agenda-shaping processes).

Any agenda-setting strategy entails framing the problem in the early stage in the development of an issue. Some attributes of a problem may be highlighted as they lend themselves to a particular solution, while other attributes of the problem are downplayed (Rochefort and Cobb 1994, p. 4; see also Finnemore and Sikkink 1998). Germany took an active part in framing perceptions of the problem at the EU level in a way that would be in line with its own environmental standard-setting philosophy: a broadly accepted norm of ecological vulnerability and concern over climate change. 'Green growth and jobs' became a keyword that would be appealing for Germans as well as other Europeans concerned with unemployment. Promoting the renewable industry in Germany had a very positive employment impact. The number of employees in RES sector reached 2,50,000 in 2007 (Federal Ministry for the Environment, Nature Conservation and Nuclear Safety 2010). Germany wanted to upload the same solution at the EU level, which also resonated well with the EU's Lisbon Agenda. Germany strove to create the most competitive and dynamic knowledge-driven economy.

In addition to "green growth and jobs", Germany also stressed the importance of renewable energy for Europe's energy security and for strengthening Europe's resilience in the event of external shocks. Important focusing events helped to reveal problems that policy makers need to tackle. The dispute between Russia and Ukraine in 2006 served as a focusing event and brought attention to the EU's energy vulnerability owing to its heavy reliance on Russian natural gas. Germany vaunted employment and energy security as an added value of RES in addition to its contribution to hitting Europe's overarching 20 % emission reduction goal (Buchan 2009). The "security of supply" in the aftermath of the first Russian-Ukrainian cut-off seemed to be an appealing frame (see Natorski and Surralles 2008).

Entrepreneurs develop frames that can address the ideological and national proclivities of policy-makers and ensure political receptiveness. They can do it by using big words that are likely to arouse interest at high political levels, alerting a broader range of interests to the issue (Princen and Rhinard 2006) or by tying in with stated policy priorities and commitments. Both climate change and security of supply frames that Germany employed were politically appealing due to their "issue proximity", or the degree to which they affect the personal interest of a broad public. Germany had good reason to expect that framing the need for binding renewable energy targets as a problem of climate change would ensure a favourable reception (see Ciambra and Solorio in Chap. 8). This is because climate change enjoyed ideational consensus in Germany, was experiencing rising EU-wide awareness and the discourse had become the EU's trademark in the international arena. In this context, it was not in the interest of any European leader to go against any proposal to address climate change. Indeed, after the political agreement on the 20-20-20 targets at the EU spring summit 2007, the German Chancellor Merkel was hailed in the German press as the "Climate Chancellor" (Dehmer 2007).

The upcoming Copenhagen Summit provided a propitious moment for Germany's policy entrepreneurship at the EU level. Timing provides strategic opportunity to 'venue shop'. As Princen (2007, p. 12) points out, "a key feature of the focus on venues is that it enables one to look for moments of 'issue internationalisation', i.e. where national collective action problems can become international (Community) ones". The concurrent rise of attention in the Commission to the issue of climate change provided the German Presidency with an important resource in its push to place binding targets for renewable energy on the EU agenda. Linking an issue to established policies is a practical way of claiming authority at the EU level, both legally and politically (see Herweg in Chap. 5 for an illustration of *problem definition* and issue linkage in agenda shaping for the European gas directive). From the legal perspective, issue linkage is important to show that an issue over which the EU has no or little authority falls under another issue area over which it does have authority. Then, it follows almost automatically that the EU is entitled to deal with it. This is particularly important in the EU energy domain, which lacks legal basis and has traditionally been under the national competence. Germany employed issue-linkage strategy when it presented RES policies as a contribution to the EU's Lisbon Agenda—a top priority of Jose′ Manuel Barroso's Commission endorsed by the European Council.

Not only did it set the agenda, Germany also pushed its agenda. Germany played an important and active role in persuading member states to adopt binding targets. After the publication of the RES Road Map in January 2007, the German Presidency called for a new framework directive for renewable energy that would include specific national targets. Member States did not agree on the nature of the target, i.e. whether they should be binding or indicative. The revised version of the Council conclusions emphasised the need to take into account "national circumstances, potentials and starting points" (Council of the EU 2007). Nonetheless, Energy Council ministers agreed on the 20 % target, differentiated national overall targets and left it to Member States to decide on national sectoral targets. It was left to the European Council to decide on the nature of the target. The European Council of March 2007 finally adopted binding targets for renewable energy and marked the triumph of Germany's agenda-shaping efforts.

9.4.3 The Window of Opportunity for a Renewable Energy Initiative

Circumstances can also be an important factor in an agenda-setting strategy by creating "windows of opportunity" (Kingdon 1984). These windows are points in time when circumstances favour policy action. However, they require that a savvy entrepreneur recognises the window and steps through it. German entrepreneurs had been interested in promoting renewable energy at the EU level long before they assumed the Presidency and then fully exploited the window when it opened in 2007. German efforts to shape the EU's agenda started back in 2004 well before its EU Presidency. The German Federal Ministry of the Environment (BMU) organised the "European Conference for Renewable Energy—Intelligent Policy Options" in cooperation with the Commission and the renewable industry (Conference Conclusions 2004). As we have seen, Germany's policy entrepreneurship played an important role in achieving political agreement on a binding EU-wide RES target. However, the context within which the process unfolded also precipitated the opening of policy window in problem and politics stream and created a political momentum that contributed to the political receptiveness of the policy initiative.

First, the Lisbon Strategy, an effort to promote high tech job growth, was proving to be a failure by 2004. This was a serious concern for President of the Commission Manuel Barroso, who was one of the most prominent proponents of the Lisbon Agenda (Barroso 2005). Consequently, the Commission felt an urgency to grab on an issue of high salience. Climate change provided the chance to link a popular issue with a re-framed Lisbon Agenda. In light of the Stern Review in Britain and Intergovernmental Panel on Climate Change Report, both of which offered pessimistic assessments of the severity of the damage being done by climate change, these linkages proved very powerful. The Commission also knew that Germany would support ambitious binding targets for reducing greenhouse gas emissions as well as expansion of renewable energy (Interview 2013a, Representative from the Federal Ministry of Economics and Technology). There seemed to be a perfect alignment between the Commission's Road Map and the German Presidency's agenda.

Second, the Russian-Ukrainian gas crisis of 2006 was a focusing event that heightened the security of supply and energy dependency concerns and revealed the real need for diversification. It was a wake-up call for the policy makers in the EU. In Kingdon's terms, the crisis opened the problem stream (Kingdon 1984). The window of opportunity was there and it was up to the policy entrepreneurs to seize the opportunity. German presidency together with MEPs, the Commission and RES industry did it indeed.

9.5 Shaping the Policy Instruments of the 2009 RES Directive

In addition to establishing targets for the EU's renewable energy policy, Germany also desired to influence the type of policy instruments the EU developed to meet those targets. But on this point, important differences surfaced between the positions of Germany and the Commission. Germany's support for ambitious renewable energy targets had been conditional on being able to keep its feed-in-tariff (FIT), which has been viewed a successful policy instrument for promoting the development of renewables in Germany (Duffield and Westphal 2011). The Commission, on the other hand, backed by a number of other member states wanted a quota system for encouraging renewable energy. German officials believed it would have been economically as well as politically and administratively costly to implement the new obligatory quota system advocated by the Commission. Moreover, adoption of this policy instrument at the EU level would jeopardise the future of FIT in Germany due to the growing opposition to the FIT from some interest groups (Interview 2013b, Representative of the Federal Ministry for Environment; see Jacobs in Chap. 6). German activism in the negotiation of RES 2009 directive is perhaps the best example of fighting hard to put its own stamp on the details.

After the political agreement had been reached by the heads of state to establish a 20 % target for the production of renewable energy, the Commission had the task of translating the political compromise into a legislative proposal. The question of support mechanisms became a key issue. The debate over the policy instruments and support schemes was not completely new though. There were two opposing camps. On the one side stood those who supported an EU-wide tradable renewable electricity certificate (TREC). This mechanism would allow some countries to meet their renewable targets by purchasing from other countries electricity generated by renewable sources.

It was believed that this system would encourage harmonisation of the European electricity market (Wettestad et al. 2012). Proponents of the TREC system included the Commission (especially DG internal market and DG competition) in coalition with the traditional electricity industry. In their view, different national support schemes would result in distortions of trade and competition. Faced with opposition from the group of FIT supporters, the proponents of the tradable green certificates somewhat modified their position. The focus on the tradable certificate shifted to allow for flexibility so that member states could achieve obligatory targets. Yet, the basic model behind this policy instrument was that it was a market-based instrument that would allow 'flexibility' in a harmonised European energy market (European Commission 2008).

On the otherside, Germany led the opposing camp, which advocated a feed-in-tariff as the policy instrument. The FIT did not depend on a harmonised electricity market and could be individually adopted by any country. The pro-FIT coalition included the Spanish government and renewable energy associations (e.g. BWE, European Renewable Energy Federation (EREF), members of the European Parliament and international environmental NGOs (Lauber and Schenner 2011)). The arguments presented by the pro-FIT camp during the discussions and negotiations preceding the 2001 RES-E Directive and later 2009 RES Directive were very much in line with Germany's concerns and its self-interested "norm entrepreneurship" efforts.

Initially, the pro-FIT camp led by Germany framed the issue of support mechanism in terms of climate change and energy security concerns and argued for the FIT's effectiveness in providing RES producers with a stronger position against conventional electricity producers in creating new jobs and new SME-based export industry (Hirschl 2008, pp. 347–348). But FIT supporters never bothered to present the FIT as a market-based instrument nor did they emphasise the compatibility of FIT with market liberalisation—unsurprisingly so because Germany was fiercely against the EU's liberalisation package and a laggard in liberalisation of its electricity market (see Herweg in Chap. 5). Instead, the pro-FIT coalition shifted the focus towards the issue of subsidiarity and questioned the EU's competence to impose an EU-wide support scheme.

The 'subsidiarity' frame proved successful as it appealed to many governments that wanted to retain national support schemes. The result was that the Commission failed in its attempt to push through its favoured TREC. The 2001 RES-E Directive did not require member states to recognise the purchase of a guarantee of origin from other member states or the corresponding purchase of electricity as a contribution to the fulfilment of a national quota obligation (Directive 2001/77/EC).

The debate between the two coalitions reemerged in 2008 after the Commission presented its original proposal for the Directive of 2009. Germany, albeit no longer holding the EU presidency, took an active effort to shape the EU agenda in line with German concerns and impeded the adoption of policy measures proposed by the Commission. A major concern of the German government in relation to tradable certificates was that a creation of single market for these would allow companies from other member states to enter and be treated as domestic German producers and profit from existing extensive feed-in-tariffs in Germany, especially in the photovoltaic sector.

On the other hand, German wind power operators would leave Germany for other places, where they would enjoy more preferential support schemes. This would be detrimental to the local ownership of renewable production and would make target fulfilment more expensive. "We did not want such a shopping around as we would have lost grips on cost or quantity control" (Interview 2013a, the Representative from the Federal Ministry of Economy). Cost-control related concerns and worries about target fulfilment and threats to FIT led to sharp criticism of the Commission's proposal by German negotiators. The government's position was also supported by the renewable industry which relied on the FIT for long-term planning and investment security (Interview 2013b, Representative from the Federal Ministry of Environment).

9.5.1 Framing the Policy Instruments

Germany was at the forefront of the coalition opposing the Commission's tradable certificates. Its efforts in this regard involved the creative framing of issues to present its preferences as the most sensible ones. Germany influenced the EU agenda by emphasising the issue of subsidiarity and the need for flexibility to maintain well-functioning national support schemes. In January 2008, Germany and Spain (backed by Latvia and Slovenia) wrote to the Commissioner for Energy Andris Piebalgs arguing that the proposal for tradable certificates posed a direct threat to the FIT support systems and would not be acceptable for them (Toke, 2008, p. 3003). Germany, Spain and Poland, later joined by the UK, put forward an alternative proposal, which acknowledged and emphasised the need for flexibility and shifted attention from the Commission's 'internal market' frame to the question of whether a RES support scheme should be controlled at the Community or national level. They spoke henceforth of "non-trading flexibility" (Toke 2008).

Similar to the framing strategy used during the negotiations of 2001 RES-E Directive, Germany and its allies re-framed the issue as one of subsidiarity. They insisted that the promotion of renewable energy was not only about pursuing renewable investments anywhere in the EU at lowest costs, but it was also about local or national benefits renewable energy provided to employment and to stimulating technological progress. The German experience fit well with the argument that a FIT system favoured local ownership of renewable energy, while the 'market-based' system favoured control and ownership of renewable energy by the main electricity supply corporations (Lauber and Schenner 2011). Germany's re-framing shifted the discussion away from the question of which support scheme was the most appropriate towards the question of which level of control was most appropriate. Germany made it clear that abandoning harmonisation of support schemes at the EU level and adopting flexibility in target compliance was a precondition for a compromise between the two opposing camps.

Another important element in the framing process was that supporters of the FIT system presented the issue in terms of losses. The German Ministry for the Environment argued that a mandatory EU-wide certificate trading scheme would incur additional costs of €4 billion per year in Germany by 2020 and €100 billion per year by 2020 for the EU as a whole (Schöpe 2007). In addition, the scheme would endanger technological diversity, undermine the position of small and medium sized enterprises vis-à-vis corporate electricity incumbents due to insecurity of investment, and run the risk of the population disallowing the excessive concentration of renewable energy deployment in the best locations (EREC 2007). Because people generally value losses more than gains, Germany strove to portray its opponents as the advocates of solutions that would impose losses (Zahariadis 2003).

At the same time, the German-led opposition linked the superiority of the FIT system with its efficiency, innovation potential and the ability to build up Europe's industrial leadership. The FIT system would afford confidence to investors by fixing prices it offered a fully predictable revenue stream. Moreover, by adapting different support levels to the specific needs of different technologies, it would encourage competition and innovation within each technology (EREC 2007). As a result of successful efforts of the German-led coalition, the German-Polish-UK proposal became the basis for the renewable energy trading system agreed in December 2008. Some voluntary "flexible mechanisms" were established, including allowance of "statistical transfers" of renewably generated electricity between countries and joint support schemes and joint projects. But the mandatory introduction of a trading system, as initially proposed by the Commission, was not included in the Directive (see Jacobs in Chap. 6; Wettestad et al. 2012).

9.5.2 The Window of Opportunity

Although Germany's skillful framing of the issue and successful efforts to mobilise supporters has had a great influence on the final content of the RES 2009 directive, we should not underestimate the context in which the process took place and how it turned out to open a favourable window for Germany's preferred solutions. As the security of supply concerns had been on the rise and occupied the minds of EU policy makers, the preoccupation with the internal market took a back seat. This shift weakened the position of those supporting the Commission's original proposal for tradable certificates. As the overarching EU agenda swayed away from internal market efficiency to issues of security, competitiveness and innovation (see Biesenbender in Chap. 2), it played further into the hands of those advocating against harmonisation (Toke 2008).

Time pressure created by the French Presidency's determination to obtain an agreement by the end of 2008 was an important factor as well—especially in light of upcoming elections for the European Parliament. Germany and the European Parliament were among the two actors most fiercely opposed to the trading scheme and took advantage of another time pressure. The Commission at the time was eager to adopt the directive with ambitious binding targets so that the EU could play a leadership role in upcoming international climate talks (Interview 2013c, Representative from the Commission). Thus, when Germany pushed the binding renewable energy targets on the EU agenda, the desire of all parties to reach a quick decision allowed Germany to push its advantage and forestall the adoption of the mandatory trading system.

Based on the above examination of Germany's agenda-shaping efforts, we propose that the German success was determined by three interrelated factors: institutional opportunities, successful issue framing, and seizing windows of opportunity (see also Herweg in Chap. 5 and Ciambra and Solorio in Chap. 8). The Council Presidency enjoys a 'problem formulation prerogative', which allows it to frame and define concerns that deserve collective attention (see Alexandrova and Timmermans in Chap. 3). The Presidency can call attention to an issue by including it in the programme and act as a gatekeeper in relation to external and unexpected events, by allowing some to be subject to collective deliberation, while excluding others (Svensson 2000, p. 24).

9.6 Conclusion: German Solutions for European Problems

The EU provides an easy platform for countries that are global trendsetters to amplify their activities and broadcast them more widely. As we demonstrated in this chapter, Germany sought to shape the EU agenda on renewable energy because it thought the problems that Germany had successfully tackled were the same ones facing all of Europe, and the solutions it had successfully employed at home could as easily solve the problems facing Europe. This orientation is a common motivation for countries that seek to shape the actions of international organisations. It was a demonstration in "norm entrepreneurship" taking norms that were well-regarded at home and imprinting them at the European level. For Germany, using policy instruments to promote renewable energy was desirable not simply on economic grounds but also because it improves the world we live in. As a result, Germany framed the EU objective in lines similar to its domestic notion of "environmental modernisation," whereby renewable energy policy is as much about shifting industrial capacity to the needs of the twenty-first century as it is about pursuing worthy environmental projects.

Yet for good ideas to be successful, it helps if they are also reinforced by compelling interests that enhance the motivation to support them. In the case of Germany, shaping the EU's policy on renewable energy offered two compelling motivations derived from self-interest. The first was a motivation the government had to reduce its costs of complying with European demands and directives. Because Germany had already taken initial steps to establish a regulatory regime supportive of innovation in the renewable sector, it sought to resist changing that regime. By uploading its regulatory regime to the European level, Germans could reduce the effort they would later have to expend to comply with European demands.

In addition, because German entrepreneurs had already learned successfully to negotiate the German regulatory system, a wider European market modelled on the German system would give them a distinct advantage over competitors from other European countries. We suggested that this strategy is similar to the "embedded liberalism" pursued by American architects of the global economy after World War II.

But good strategies also need savvy political skills. The art of agenda shaping in this case lay in Germany's successful efforts to frame the issues in a favourable light, identify and exploit institutional venues to push its agenda and exploit windows of opportunity that opened when new circumstances created a favourable terrain. We showed that both in the development of the EU's framework for renewable energy. And in the creation of the 2009 directive that outlined the instruments for achieving policy goals, Germany consistently pushed its advantage and seized on opportunities when they appeared. In the face of efforts to create a uniform scheme for supporting renewable energy, Germany protected its own feed-in tariff by using the EU's own principle of subsidiarity as a framing device. The result was a decision that showed Germany again as a leader in global efforts to promote renewable energy and demonstrated the appeal of German solutions for global problems.

References

Abdelal, R., & Ruggie, J. G. (2009). The principles of embedded liberalism: Social legitimacy and global capitalism. In D. Moss & J. Cisternino (Eds.), *New perspectives on regulation* (pp. 151–162). Cambridge: Tobin Project.

Barroso, J. M. (2005). *Working together for growth and jobs: A new start for the Lisbon strategy.* Conference of Presidents, European Parliament, Speech 05/67. Brussels.

Barysch, K. (2007). *What to expect from the German Presidency, centre for European Reform.* Briefing Note, London, UK.

Baumgartner, F. R., & Jones, B. D. (2009). *Agendas and instability in American politics*. Chicago: University of Chicago Press.

Börzel, T. A. (2002). Member state responses to Europeanization. *Journal of Common Market Studies, 40*(2), 193–214.

Buchan, D. (2009). *Energy and Climate Change: Europe at the Crossroads*. Oxford: Oxford University Press.

Council of the EU (2007) Brussels European Council. March 8,9. *Presidency Conclusions*7224/1/07 REV 1.

Dehmer, D. (2007). Die Klimakanzlerin. *Der Tagesspiegel.*

Duffield, J. S., & Westphal, K. (2011). Germany and EU energy policy: Conflicted champion of integration? In V. L. Birchfield and J. S. Duffield (Eds.), *Toward a common European Union energy policy* (pp. 169–186). New. York: Palgrave Macmillan.

EC. (2001). Directive 2001/77/EC of the European Parliament and of the Council of 27 September 2001 on the promotion of electricity produced from renewable energy sources in the internal electricity market. *OJ L* 283, 33-40. October 27, 2001.

EREC. (2007). *Renewable energy technology road map up to 2020*. EREC, Brussels.

European Commission. (2006a). Renewable energy road map: Renewable energies in the 21st century: Building a more sustainable future. COM (2006) 848 Final. Brussels.

European Commission. (2006b). Communication from the commission to the council and the European Parliament, green paper follow-up action report on progress in renewable electricity. COM (2006) 849 final. Brussels.

European Commission. (2008). Proposal for a directive of the European parliament and of the council on the promotion of the use of energy from renewable sources. COM (2008) 19 final, Brussels.

European Commission. (2009). Directive 2009/28/EC of the European Parliament and of the Council of 23 April 2009 on the promotion of the use of energy from renewable sources and amending and subsequently repealing Directives 2001/77/EC and 2003/30/EC, Brussels.

Federal Ministry for the Environment, Nature Conservation and Nuclear Safety. (2010). *Renewable energy sources act: Key features, developments and perspectives.* Berlin.

Finnemore, M., & Sikkink, K. (1998). International norm dynamics and political change. *International Organization, 52*(4), 887–917.

Héritier, A., Knill, C., & Mingers, S. (1996). *Ringing the changes in Europe. Regulatory competition and the transformation of the state*. Berlin: De Gruyter.

Hirschl, B. (2008). *Erneuerbare Energiepolitik im Mehrebenensystem.* Wiesbaden: VS Research.

International Energy Agency (IEA). (2007) Energy policies of IEA countries: Germany 2007 Review OECD.

Inglehart, R. (1985). New perspectives on value change. *Comparative Political Studies, 17*(4), 485–532.

Interview. (2013a). Representative from the German federal ministry of economics and technology (BMWi). June 3, Berlin, Germany.

Interview. (2013b). Representative from the German federal ministry for environment, nature conservation and nuclear safety (BMU). June 5, Berlin, Germany .

Interview. (2013c). Representative from the European commission DG-Energy. June 23, Brussels.

Jänicke, M. (2011). German climate change policy: Political and economic leadership. In R. K. W. Wurzel & J. Connelly (Eds.), *The European Union as a leader in international climate change politics* (pp. 129–146). UACES Contemporary European Studies: Routledge.

Johannesburg Renewable Energy Coalition. (2004). *European Conference for Renewable Energy —Intelligent Policy Options*. Berlin. 19–21, January 2004. *Conference Conclusions and Recommendations to Renewables.*

Kingdon, J. (1984). *Agendas, alternatives, and public policies*. Boston: Little, Brown.

Knill, C., & Lenschow, A. (2001). Adjusting to EU environmental policy: change and persistence of domestic administrations. In M. G. Cowles, J. Caporaso & T. Risse (Eds.), *Transforming Europe: Europeanization and domestic change* (pp. 116–136). Ithaca: Cornell University Press.

Knill, C., & Tosun, J. (2011). Environmental policy. In H. Heinelt & M. Knodt (Eds.), *Policies within the EU multi-level system* (pp. 171–188). Baden-Baden: Nomos.

Kohler-Koch, B., & Rittberger, B. (2006). The 'governance turn' in EU studies. *Journal of Common Market Studies, 44*(1), 27–49.

Lauber, V., & Schenner, E. (2011). The struggle over support schemes for renewable electricity in the European Union: A discursive-institutionalis analysis. *Environmental Politics, 20*(4), 508–527.

Liefferink, D., & Andersen, M. S. (1998). Strategies of the "green" member states in EU environmental policy-making. *Journal of European Public Policy, 5*(2), 254–270.

Löfstedt, R. (2004). The swing of the regulatory pendulum in Europe: From precautionary principle to (regulatory) impact analysis. *Journal of Risk and Uncertainty, 28*(3), 237–260.

March, J. G., & Olsen, J. P. (1998). The institutional dynamics of international political orders. *International Organization, 52*(4), 943–969.

Natorski, M., & Surrallés, H. A. (2008). Securitizing moves to nowhere? The framing of the European Union energy policy. *Journal of Contemporary European Research, 4*(2), 71–89.

Presidency of the Council of the European Union. (2007). Europe—Succeeding Together, Presidency Program. January 1 to June 30 2007. Federal Government of Germany, Brussels.

Princen, S. (2007). Agenda-setting in the European Union: A theoretical exploration and agenda for research. *Journal of European Public Policy, 14*(1), 21–38.

Princen, S. (2011). Agenda-setting strategies in EU policy processes. *Journal of European Public Policy, 18*(7), 927–943.

Princen, S., & Rhinard, M. (2006). Crashing and creeping: Agenda-setting dynamics in the European Union. *Journal of European Public Policy, 13*(7), 1119–1132.

Rochefort, D. A., & Cobb, R. W. (1994). Problem definition: An emerging perspective. In D. A. Rochefort & R. W. Cobb (Eds.), *The politics of problem definition: Shaping the policy agenda* (pp. 1–31). Lawrence: University Press of Kansas.

Ruggie, J. G. (1982). International regimes, transaction, and change: Embedded liberalism in the postwar economic order. *International Organization, 36*(2), 379–415.

Schöpe, M. (2007). Meeting the EU 20 % RE objective by 2020: MS efforts and compensation schemes. Presentation given at the 5th Amsterdam Forum. October 2, 2007.

Svensson, A. (2000). In the service of the European Union. The role of the presidency in negotiating the Amsterdam Treaty 1995–1997. Ph.D. dissertation, Uppsala University.

Tallberg, J. (2003). The agenda-shaping powers of the EU Council Presidency. *Journal of European Public Policy, 10*(1), 1–19.

The Renewable Energy Sources Act. (2004). Germany: Bundestag.

Toke, D. (2008). The EU renewables directive: What is the fuss about trading? *Energy Policy, 36* (8), 3001–3008.

Tosun, J. (2013). How the EU handles uncertain risks: Understanding the role of the precautionary principle. *Journal of European Public Policy, 20*(10), 1517–1528.

Wettestad, J., Eikeland, P. O., & Nilsson, M. (2012). EU climate and energy policy: A hesitant supranational turn. *Global Environmental Politics, 12*(2), 67–86.

Zahariadis, N. (2003). Coupling, complexity, and the future of European integration. *Review of Policy Research, 20*(2), 285–310.

Part IV
Framing and Reframing

Chapter 10
Shaping the EU's Energy Policy Agenda: The Role of Eastern European Countries

Elina Brutschin

Abstract This chapter traces the role of eastern European countries during the negotiations of the third gas directive and their role in bringing on the decision agenda the so-called "Gazprom clause". It is argued that the enlargement did not significantly change the interest heterogeneity on the liberalisation issues and that the main explanatory power for successful decision agenda thus lies in the framing strategies that were utilised before the negotiations. Followed by a number of events, such as building of the Nord Stream pipeline and Ukrainian gas crisis of 2006, many member states used the momentum to reframe the debate as a foreign policy issue rather than as a competition policy issue. This served as a basis for the securitisation of the European energy policies and successful mobilisation of other participants in the policy process, which resulted in the inclusion of the "Gazprom clause" in the final version of the third gas directive.

10.1 Introduction: The Role of Eastern European Countries in Gas Market Dynamics

From the implementation perspective, the liberalisation of the European gas market has been a disappointment. The EU policies have not led to the breaking up of the oligopolistic structures within the gas chain; some observers even argue that certain reforms have caused a consolidation of power of the dominant companies (Fernandez and Palazuelos 2014). Nonetheless, it is surprising that given the rigid structures of the gas market and the powerful interests within, any changes, no matter how small they are, were possible at all. The first directive 1998/30/EC (see Herweg in Chap. 5 for an analysis of the first directive), the second directive 2003/55/EC (see Eberlein 2008 for the second energy package) and the third directive 2009/72/EC (see Eikeland 2011

E. Brutschin (✉)
International Relations Department, Webster University Vienna,
Praterstr. 23a, 1020 Vienna, Austria
e-mail: elina.brutschin@webster.ac.at

J. Tosun et al. (eds.), *Energy Policy Making in the EU*,
Lecture Notes in Energy 28, DOI 10.1007/978-1-4471-6645-0_10

for an in-depth analysis of electricity and gas directives) were passed against the opposition of some of the most powerful member states.

The three above-mentioned directives, which were part of the broader energy packages, indicate that the legislative process was incremental and long: 17 years have passed since the initial proposal tabled by the Commission (European Commission 1992) until the adoption of the third directive. This gives ground to various agenda-setting and decision-making dynamics that were certainly influenced by internal (enlargements, changes in the decision-making rules, poor implementation) as well as external (instabilities on the market) changes. There is not so much analyses concentrating on the agenda-setting within the gas market liberalisation (with the exception of Herweg in Chap. 5) but many scholars agree that the political entrepreneurship of the Commission was one of the key explanatory factors for the agenda-setting and policy-making dynamics of the energy packages (Brutschin 2013; Eberlein 2008; Eikeland 2011; Eising 2002; Pollak and Slominski 2011). Additionally, it is argued that the United Kingdom, as one of the main proponents of liberalisation, was successful in shaping the agenda-setting of the European energy policies (see Ciambra and Solorio in Chap. 8).

Surprisingly, the role of the changing number of actors involved—one of the most important explanatory factors of agenda-setting dynamics (Schattschneider 1960)—is rarely addressed in much detail. It can be suspected that the eastern European enlargement of 2004, which added ten new member states including Poland as a significant energy producer and consumer, was a possible "game changer". For instance, Geden and Fischer (2008) argue that many eastern European countries might favour liberalisation of the European energy markets hoping to decrease their dependence on Russian gas. Geden and Fischer thus further suspect that there could be certain package deals between western and eastern European countries: eastern European countries making concessions in the environmental sector and western European countries in the energy sector (Geden and Fischer 2008, p. 48). However, it could also be argued that the role of the eastern European countries goes hand in hand with the implementation of the existing energy acquis and that many eastern European countries will thus oppose liberalisation of the energy market because it is costly. Even though some scholars have argued that the implementation of liberalisation across eastern countries might be problematic (Gaman 2010); a systematic analysis shows that generally the eastern countries display a high degree of compliance in the energy sector (Tosun 2011). The previous debate shows that the role of the eastern European countries for the liberalisation of the gas market is an interesting and under-represented research arena and that a systematic empirical analysis that goes beyond speculations is still missing. This leads us to the following questions: What was the role of the eastern European countries in the agenda-setting dynamics and which agenda-setting strategies did they employ?

To answer these questions, we proceed as follows. In the second section of this chapter, we discuss the possible effects of the changing number of actors by linking interest-based and framing approaches. Subsequently, we present methods utilised to measure member states preferences and framing strategies. And finally, we analyse the agenda-setting dynamics during the third gas directive with the emphasis on the role of the eastern European states. The political crisis in Ukraine in 2014 and the subsequent call of the Polish Prime Minister, Donald Tusk, to create an Energy Union (Tusk 2014) underlines the main finding of this chapter: that eastern European countries can be an important driving force behind the European energy policies.

10.1.1 Why a Focus on the Third Gas Directive?

To trace the possible effects of the changing number of participants, it is necessary to specify the dependent variable to show that there was variation on the dependent variable and more importantly to explain why the third gas directive that was negotiated after the enlargement is particularly interesting.

Within the agenda-setting approaches, there are varying definitions of agenda (see Tosun et al. in Chap. 1). In this chapter, we concentrate on the decision agenda within the broader scope of institutional agendas: defined here as issues that are included in the initial legislative proposal of the Commission [compare (Princen 2010)]. Successful decision agenda subsumes issues that were included in the initial proposal and later in the final version of a legislative act. In order to (1) show the variation across issues discussed throughout the liberalisation process and (2) to trace the successful decision agenda during the third gas directive, we have developed Table 10.1.

For a systematic comparison, we had to limit the scope of issues, which we have derived from the broader liberalisation instruments introduced by the Commission even before the negotiations over the first gas directive have started. The European Commission's definition of liberalisation can be summarised as breaking up of national monopolies in energy production, transmission and distribution (European Commission 1988). The instruments of achieving this goal are generally associated with "sector restructuring, introduction of competition in wholesale generation and retail supply, effective regulation of transmission and distribution networks, establishing an independent regulator, and privatisation" (Jamasb and Pollitt 2005, p. 2). Based on this definition, we observe the evolution of the liberalisation efforts and thus of the dynamics of agenda-setting and policy making by looking at the specifics across five issues: (1) Third Party Access (TPA) to transmission and distribution networks, (2) Form of Unbundling in transmission and distribution, (3) Form of Dispute Resolution, (4) Deadlines for transposition and (5) Regulations for external participants. A systematic comparison of how these issues were presented in the initial legislative proposal and what was in the end adopted might serve as a rough indicator to detect successful agenda-setting. This can later be used as a basis to trace the actors who framed the successful issues and the strategies of these actors. A number of important observations arise from the comparison based in Table 10.1. Certainly, one of the key turning points in the liberalisation process was

Table 10.1 Evolution of the EU gas market liberalisation

		First gas directive (98/30/EC)[a]	Second gas directive (2003/55/EC)[b]	Third gas directive[c] (2009/72/EC)
Third party access	COM proposal	Commercial principles (Article 3)	Regulated by a national authority (Article 14)	Not changed (Article 18)
	Final act	Negotiated (Article 15) or Regulated access (Article 16)	Member states shall ensure the regulation (Article 18)	Regulated (Article 32)
Unbundling	COM proposal	Complete (ownership unbundling) (Article 21)	Separate in its legal form, organisation and decision-making (Article 10)	Ownership unbundling (Article 7) or independent system operator (Article 9)
	Final act	Separated accounts (Article 13)	Specification about the separation in its legal form and a clause that ownership unbundling is not an obligation (Article 9)	Ownership unbundling (Article 9, 14, 26) or Independent system operator (Article 13,17)
Dispute resolution	COM proposal	General dispute resolution mechanisms (Article 25)	National regulatory authority (Article 22)	National regulatory authority and european level coordination through an agency (Article 24a-24f)
	Final act	Competent authority (Article 21)	Competent bodies with the function of regulatory authorities (Article 25)	National regulatory authorities and european level coordination (Article 35-40)
Third countries	COM proposal			Operators shall not be controlled by a person or persons from third countries (Article 7a)
	Final act			Certification in relation to third countries (Article 11)
Deadlines	COM proposal	31 December 1992	100 % by 1 January 2005 (Article 18)	18 months (Article 2)
	Final act	20 % by 2000 28 % by 2003 33 % by 2018	100 % by 1 July 2007 (Article 33)	By March 2011 Article 11 by March 2013

Source own elaboration from the official documents (similar elaboration for gas and electricity markets Buchan 2010)

[a] The initial proposal is presented in European Commission (1992) and the final act in European Commission (1998)

[b] The initial proposal is presented in European Commission (2001) and the final act in European Commission (2003)

[c] The initial proposal is presented in European Commission (2007) and the final act in European Commission (2009)

the first directive (as pointed by Herweg in Chap. 4). If we think of the directives in terms of the degree of change (Hall 1993), then the first directive was a "third order" change (the most significant change) because it marked an establishment of new policy goals. It thus conditioned the subsequent directives regarding the main instruments of liberalisation. However, it also displays a very light form of liberalisation with no significant pressure to break up the monopolies in the distribution and transmission. Table 10.1 also makes it clear that across the three directives, the first directive presents the biggest mismatch between the initial proposal and the final act. This of course is mainly the result of the directive being the first and that in subsequent negotiations the Commission has probably learned to exclude the issues that were not able to find broader political support. Additionally, the mismatch between the initial proposal and the final act makes the tracing of successful decision agenda much more difficult.

The second directive then represents a calibration of the existing policy instruments, thus the "first degree" change (the smallest change). The adjustment and stricter regulation of the third party access and the form of unbundling in transmission and distribution networks were necessary because of the growing discontent with the lack of reciprocity and the growing "merger culture" of French and German companies. Significant impulses for a new directive were provided by the pro-liberalisation coalition led by the UK and supported by the European Parliament (Brutschin 2013; see Ciambra and Solorio in Chap. 8). Stricter regulation instruments were not included due to prevailing strong opposition from Germany, in particularly regarding the regulatory oversight (Pariente-David and Swanson 2003) and from France because of strong domestic resistance to unbundling (Brutschin 2013).

The third directive could be interpreted as "second degree" change since it not only adjusted existing policy instruments but also added some new ones. The biggest prominence was the new regulation of access for the third countries or the so-called "(Anti-) Gazprom clause", which protects the European gas market from third countries and requires consultations with the Commission regarding any acquisitions from third countries. Additionally, new approaches to regional cooperation and solidarity were included in the directive as well. The calibration of the existing policy instruments went beyond general expectations (Eikeland 2011). Not only was there finally a clause on ownership unbundling (even though it was relativized by permitting the so-called independent transmission operator and independent system operator) the third directive also significantly upgraded the powers of the national regulators. Given these significant changes and the inclusion of new issues in the third directive, which were negotiated after the eastern European enlargement in 2004 and in 2007, the third gas directive represents an interesting case study to trace the possible effects of the changing number of participants and the role of the eastern European countries.

10.1.2 Identifying Successful Decision Agenda

Table 10.1 can also be used to trace the successful decision agenda from the third gas directive: the issues that were included in the initial proposal as well as in the final legislative act. Generally, it seems that there was still significant calibration within the issues from the first and second gas directive. The third party access was further regulated even though it was not on the initial proposal of the Commission. The main bone of contention throughout the whole liberalisation process, the issue of transmission and distribution unbundling, was further negotiated and the initial proposal was significantly weakened. In turn, the powers of the national regulatory authorities and the coordination mechanisms were much more specific and upgraded in the final act as compared to the initial proposal.

The regulation of access to transmission as well as distribution networks from third countries was a completely new issue that could not be traced in the first or second directive. This clause clearly represents a case of successful decision agenda as it is included in the initial proposal and in the final directive. Additionally, this so-called "Gazprom" clause or "Anti-Gazprom clause"—an important mechanism to coordinate common energy policy—was apparently heavily lobbied for by Poland (Eikeland 2008). This leads again to the question whether the significant change observed during the third gas directive and the Gazprom clause can be explained through the changing number of the participants and the eastern European enlargement. If this is the case, then what are the exact mechanism behind it?

10.2 Theoretical Framework: Economic Interests or Framing?

Essentially, the main mechanism that will allow actors to push the policy into their preferred direction is the polysemic nature of liberalisation that allows many different interpretations. The concept of liberalisation offers multiple framing directions. Framing (definition of a problem) that will mobilise significant number of participants within a policy process is considered to be one of the main strategies for a successful agenda-setting (Princen 2011). However, in order to show that framing or a new definition of a problem was one of the main explanatory factors, it is necessary to show that a pure shift in the economic interests is not a better explanation.

Especially given the enlargement, one could argue that new member states have strengthened the pro-liberalisation coalition and this is why we could observe changes and new agendas. At the same time, if we follow the logic of the veto player theory (Tsebelis 2002), which deduces that an increasing number of veto players will increase policy stability by reducing the winset—the political space that includes points that can change status quo (SQ) and by increasing the core—the political space that includes points that cannot change the SQ, we would expect that an increasing number of actors might lead to a decreasing number of successful agendas. If it however can be shown that the winset was not significantly changed through the enlargements, then we can suspect that framing strategies deliver better explanations for observed change. In order to show whether the winset was changed, we need to find a way to assess member states interests. This is addressed in the following section.

10.3 Methods and Sources

In Chap. 8, Andrea Ciambra and Israel Solorio discuss the methodological concerns within agenda-setting studies that arise when scholars attempt to infer from language. This is especially problematic when we want to infer actors' interests regarding certain issues or later when the framing strategies and their success are analysed. I thus suggest first utilising an alternative measurement of actors' interests based on the so-called material interests (Brutschin 2013) and then to apply process-tracing techniques to analyse the framing strategies.

10.3.1 Positions Based on Material Interests

Scholars have utilised expert interviews (Benoit and Laver 2007), hand coding content analysis (Veen 2011), roll calls (Hagemann 2007) or opinion surveys (Hug and König 2002) to measure interests, preferences and positions of actors on certain issues. More recently, researchers started also to rely on quantitative text analyses and scaling of interest group positions from their position papers (Klüver 2009). Unfortunately, none of these techniques could be applied to gas market liberalisation because there are no systematic sources of information.

Nonetheless, general interests could also be inferred based on the so-called material interests. The main assumption of material interest based studies is that certain variables that are specific for each actor can significantly shape the actor's positions on a certain issue. The interests are then inferred based on the assumption that actors will not be in favour of an issue that is too costly for them. This approach thus operates within the Rational Choice framework.

The applications of material variables can be found in research on environmental policies. So for instance, Sprinz and Vaahtoranta (1994) could show that preferences of states in international environmental negotiations are largely shaped by the countries' ecological vulnerability and abatement costs. In a more recent study, looking at the US debates on climate change Fisher (2006) could trace that senators from coal dependent states were more likely to oppose the Climate Stewardship Act of 2003. Both examples suggest that certain material conditions can largely determine the starting negotiation positions or even explain why actors change their positions. Gas market, given its relative stable market structures, lends itself to this sort of analyses. Before we can proceed with the analysis, it is necessary to determine, which dimensions to include in the inference of material interests.

Starting from the basic assumption that material variables should reflect the costs of possible policy changes, the first dimension of a high importance is the share of gas as a source of energy for the economy of a country. This can serve as a proxy to assess the salience of the issue. It is plausible to assume that countries which heavily rely on natural gas as a source of energy will be much more interested in the developments of the gas markets (The Netherlands, UK, Austria) than the countries that barely include gas in their energy mix (Cyprus, Greece, Portugal). This, however, does not allow predictions regarding the possible position towards the direction of change. Here an additional dimension that can reflect additional costs of change is needed. Therefore, the market concentration could be taken as the main indicator to assess the possible costs of completely liberalising the market. By assuming that the further away from the complete liberalisation a member state is, the more costly it will be to change the market; it can be argued that member states that have a highly concentrated market will oppose liberalisation, while member states that have a liberalised market will support liberalisation to share the benefits.

Decisive for the assessment of possible material interests is the combination of the discussed dimensions. It can further be deduced that if the domestic market of a member state is not very concentrated and the consumption is very low, a member state will probably support the liberalisation but not to the same degree as states with the higher level of consumption. In a similar manner, the member states that have high concentration but low consumption should also oppose liberalisation but not to the same degree as the member states that have high levels of consumption. It was decided to use simple average to distinguish between low and high levels across both dimensions. Table 10.2 summarises the expectations based on the level of consumption and the level of concentration.

The data was then collected through Eurostat, the official source of the European statistics. The data for gas market concentration was not available and therefore the data for the concentration of the electricity market was used as it can be assumed that for a given member state, there will be minimal differences between the electricity and gas market concentration. We will look at the year 2007, the year when the proposal for the third gas directive was initiated.

Table 10.2 Deriving material interests

	High concentration (above average)	Low concentration (below average)
High consumption (above average)	Strongly opposing	Strongly supporting
Low consumption (below average)	Mildly opposing	Mildly supporting

10.3.2 Framing Strategies

To collect narrative data for the tracing of the framing strategies and key developments, I will rely on official documents, secondary literature and media analysis. In the context of the European gas market liberalisation, it is not probable that one news resource consistently reports on the developments of the sector and actors' positions towards liberalisation. It is therefore suggested to cover a larger sample of media. For this purposes the databank LexisNexis[1] is one of the best available options as it combines a large pool of international news. The databank was searched for the combinations of words "gas directive" and "Gazprom clause". The period under consideration was then restricted to the years 2006–2010.

10.4 Analysis of Preferences and Framing Strategies

In the following section, we will elaborate what could be expected based on the market structures and then subsequently describe the framing patterns that have emerged prior and during the negotiations.

10.4.1 Positions Based on the Initial Market Situation

The first rough overview as presented in Fig. 10.1 suggests that almost 10 years after the first gas directive (1998), there was still a great variety across the gas market structures (assuming that concentration of the electricity market is a good proxy for the gas market) within the European Union in 2007. There were states, which had already relatively low market concentration, such as the United Kingdom, Poland and Finland but also states, which had a high market concentration such as Cyprus, Estonia and Greece. This finding additionally highlights that given a relatively low level of harmonisation, the negotiations over the third gas directive were not necessary easier as compared to the previous directives; in fact, poor implementation was one of the main reasons to start negotiations over a new directive.

As it was previously argued, it is necessary to show how the changing number of participants has affected the possible winset and core based on the possible positions towards liberalisation. If it can be shown that eastern European enlargement did not significantly change the winset, we can expect that the framing strategies of certain new and old member states were responsible for the successful decision agenda that was traced in Sect. 10.1.

---

[1] Accessed through Institute of Advanced Studies: http://www.lexisnexis.com/hottopics/lnacademic/. Last access: April 2014.

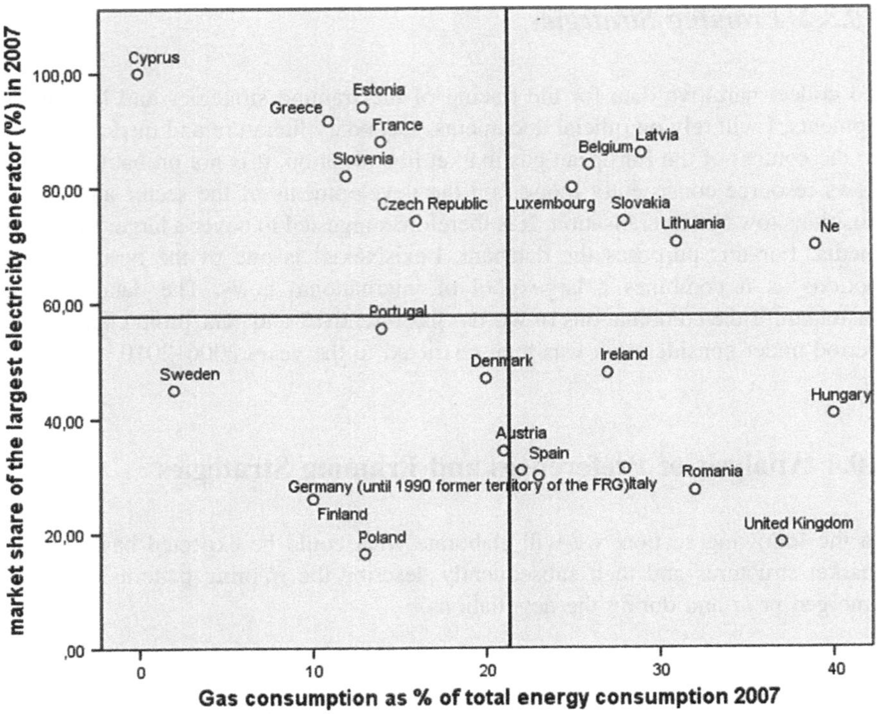

Fig. 10.1 Gas market structures in the new and old member states (Data for Bulgaria was not available.)

Table 10.3 then summarises what interests could be derived based on the theoretical expectations discussed in Sect. 10.3.1. There are some new member states, who—given their high market concentration and saliency of gas in their energy mix—might strongly oppose the liberalisation. However, there are also new member states in particular Hungary, Romania and Poland that might be interested in supporting liberalisation. Even though at first sight it might seem that the enlargement might have strengthened the anti-liberalisation coalition; if we calculate the voting shares within the new member states, the possible opposing coalition (strongly and mildly opposing states) makes up for 52 votes and the possible pro-liberalisation coalition (strongly and mildly supporting states) 53 votes.[2] It can thus be preliminary concluded that the eastern enlargement has not significantly changed the possible interest heterogeneity within the negotiation space on gas market liberalisation (i.e. the winset has not decreased). More importantly, this theoretical exercise suggests that the UK (see Chap. 8 by Ciambra and Solorio for more details on its leading role in the pro-liberalisation coalition) has gained another powerful

[2] Voting calculator access through: http://www.consilium.europa.eu/council/voting-system-at-the-council?tab=Voting-calculator. Last access: October 2014.

Table 10.3 Material interests new versus old member states

	High concentration (above average)	Low concentration (below average)
High consumption (above average)	Strongly opposing	Strongly supporting
Old member states	Belgium, Luxemburg, The Netherlands	Ireland, United Kingdom, Spain, Italy
New member states	Bulgaria, Latvia, Lithuania, Slovakia	Hungary, Romania
Low consumption (below average)	Mildly opposing	Mildly supporting
Old member states	France, Greece	Austria, Denmark, Finland, Germany, Portugal, Spain, Sweden
New member states	Czech Republic, (Cyprus), Estonia, Slovenia	Poland

ally (Poland) within the Council of the EU. As will be shown later, Poland is not only an important energy player but is a powerful coalition builder within the eastern European countries.

The results of this analysis obviously depend a great degree on the assumption that this allows a correct inference of member states positions towards gas market liberalisation. It is thus interesting to compare whether this was translated into coherent behaviour or whether similar positions were expressed by the member states in public debates. Unfortunately, a systematic comparison is not possible: the documents provided by the Council of the EU do not relate positions of specific member states and media often discuss only some of the biggest member states. However, we can test the plausibility of this analysis by relating it to member states positions discussed in the secondary literature or media.

A major confirmation can be found in the conclusion that the UK represents a member state that is strongly supporting liberalisation (see Ciambra and Solorio in Chap. 8). That Germany is put in the category of the mildly supporting countries and France into mildly opposing countries is the first striking anomaly, whereas many studies have argued that Germany and France have been constantly blocking the liberalisation process (Eikeland 2011; Geden and Fischer 2008). Nonetheless, in-depth analyses of German and French stances on the energy market liberalisation conclude that Germany and France rather than having a strict opposing position have followed the domestic election cycle (Schumann 2005) and agreed to many controversial issues after the national elections (Brutschin 2013). Ironically, they were also among the major winners of the first liberalisation waves as German and French companies could increase their influence at the European level through mergers and acquisitions, especially in eastern Europe (Codognet et al. 2002; Dempsey 2006). It can therefore be suspected that strong opposition voiced in the media was part of bargaining tactics rather then sincere preferences.

Additionally, another explanatory factor for the deviations between material interests and rhetoric might be that traditionally some of the member states have built coalitions with other member states across different energy issues. And some countries support certain coalitions rhetorically even if an issue does not correspond to their behaviour. So for instance, Austria has supported the coalition led by France, which includes Germany, Bulgaria, Greece, Luxemburg, Latvia and Slovakia, who introduced a weaker form of unbundling during the negotiations over the third gas market (Iago 2008a) even though Austria had "a leading role in the opening up of its gas market" (Council of the EU 2006a). In a similar vein, Austria has also supported Germany when the later was opposing the Commission and EU Parliament's proposal on the Agency for Cooperation of Energy Regulators (Iago 2008b).

Generally, Table 10.3 provides a good overview of the possible tendencies within the European gas market. The main goal of this exercise is not to measure the exact positions in negotiation but rather to show that the increasing number of participants through the eastern enlargement did not significantly change the existing dynamics. The overview nonetheless highlights that some eastern European countries, especially Poland, Hungary, and Romania have the potential to play a pivotal role in the liberalisation negotiations. Based on the structure of their gas markets they might be interested in speedy liberalisation.

10.4.2 Turning Points and Framing

This section traces the origins of the successful decision agenda that was identified in Sect. 10.1.2. In Sect. 10.4.1, it was argued that there were no significant changes to the existing distribution of member states' interests therefore the framing strategies of the main actors should be analysed in more detail as they might offer better explanations for the successful decision agenda. Since the chapter strives to highlight the role of the eastern European countries, the analysis concentrates on the Council of the European Union where member states directly negotiate with each other. Even though the European Parliament is an important venue that probably also significantly influenced the decision agenda (Eikeland 2011), an in-depth analysis of the Parliament would go beyond the scope of this chapter and therefore it is left to future research.

Through the official Council documents, we can trace certain turning points and the main points of contention. However, the opinions and arguments of specific member states are not disclosed and when tracing the framing strategies we have to rely on the reports from the secondary literature and media. First issue that was targeted by the Council was the issue of unbundling, which was the main concern of one of the first meetings of the energy Council in February 2008 (Council of EU 2008a). The debate regarding the Gazprom clause was then intensified during the energy Council in spring 2008 where the concerns over the legal implications were discussed (Council of EU 2008b). Given the scope of the policy process, we therefore concentrate on the years before the Commission's proposal was tabled (2005, 2006) until the final agreement was reached (2009).

The engagement of eastern European countries in the liberalisation of the energy market within the framework of the third gas directive can be better understood at the backdrop of a number of events, which enabled subsequent securitisation: (1) the agreement to build Nordstream between Germany and Russia through the Baltic Sea in 2005 (BBC 2005) that was denoted by Polish minister of national defence as a "geopolitical disaster" (Sikorski et al. 2007), (2) Gazprom's negotiations to significantly increase gas prices in the eastern European neighbourhood in a quid pro quo manner (Dempsey 2005; Parker and Ostrovsky 2005) and culminating in (3) the disputes between Russia and Ukraine over the gas price in January 2006 and 2009, which exposed Poland's and other countries' vulnerabilities to Russian gas (Jeziorski 2006). Consequently, in many member states directly or indirectly affected by these events, the energy issue was redefined as an element of national security (Geden et al. 2006, p. 21).

Straight after the enlargement (2004) many eastern European countries considered Gazprom's activities and allegedly purely economically motivated disruptions of oil and gas supplies in the eastern neighbourhood with a great suspicion (Larsson 2006, p. 172ff). This was enhanced after the Nord Stream deal was signed. The project Nord Stream, an offshore pipeline which was initiated to connect Russia to Germany without having to deal with transit countries, was one of the first tests of the European energy unity after the enlargement. It instantly led to vivid debates and pointing fingers at Germany, not only from eastern states such as Poland, Estonia, Latvia and Lithuania but also from Finland and Sweden. These states quickly built a coalition arguing that the project did not make any sense economically and that it would have detrimental effects on the European energy security (Whist 2008, p. 7ff).

The culmination of the eastern European fears was the gas shortage in Ukraine in January 2006 (Stern 2006). Straight after the crisis a number of initiatives followed. Poland was prominently acting through the media and other institutional venues. Already on January 4, 2006, Poland together with Hungary, the Czech Republic and Austria presented a joint position on how to diversify energy supplies in Central and Eastern Europe (Jeziorski 2006). At the end of January 2006, Poland, the Czech Republic, Slovakia, Austria, Hungary, Slovenia, Croatia and Romania discussed coordinated strategies to reduce their dependence on Russian gas (Geden et al. 2006, p. 20). In March 2006, Poland even took the initiative to propose a "European Energy Security Treaty" to the Council of the EU (Council of the EU 2006b). The main goal of the Treaty would be to "require a country's commitment to cooperate in bringing assistance to a Party affected by restrictions in energy supplies, and to build and develop the necessary organisational and technical infrastructure designed to permit such cooperation". Through this, the treaty would "invoke the political solidarity linking the Euro-Atlantic community" (Council of the EU 2006b, p. 4). Functioning integrated market would be the first step on the way to such a community. Also Lithuania, albeit in a troubled relationship with

Poland, was joining the securitization debate and supporting initiatives for a common energy policy in order for Europe not to become Russia's "energy hostage" (BBC 2006). It can thus be concluded that Poland and other eastern European countries had the outmost interest in the further liberalisation and integration of the gas market.

It was easy to convince other states that a new initiative at the European level was necessary. Even if a state was not directly affected by the disruption (for example the UK), there was a growing debate on how the possible shortage or any future possible disruptions from the Russian side might affect the European gas prices (Greenwood 2006). The securitization debate then was picked up by the Commission when the energy commissioner at the time, Andris Piebalgs, has called for a more cohesive energy security policy (Benoit and Laitner 2006). One of the concrete actions was the decision to create the Gas Coordination group in November 2006, which should ensure fast coordination during a major supply disruption (European Commission 2006).

Even though the Polish proposal was not successful and the "European Energy Security Treaty" was not created, the results of the Polish agenda-setting attempts are clearly reflected within the third gas directive (2009/73/EC). For instance, paragraph 55 of the gas directive paraphrases some of the core ideas presented by Poland through the "European Energy Security Treaty": "in order to contribute to security of supply whilst maintaining the spirit of solidarity between Member States, notably in the event of an energy supply crisis, it is important to provide a framework for regional cooperation in a spirit of solidarity" (European Commission 2009). Additionally, as mentioned in the introduction, the Polish delegation put the so-called Gazprom clause regulating the access of third countries on the decision agenda (Eikeland 2008). However, the success of this item is relative. As can be seen from the overview in Table 10.1, the initial proposal suggested to categorically exclude the control of transmission and distribution operators by a person or persons from third countries. However in the final directive, the certification process under the auspices of the national regulators was introduced, offering more leeway to member states. It can be suspected that the weaker clause was negotiated under the significant pressure from Germany (European Observer 2008) and Italy (Iago 2009a), which have strong ties with Gazprom through different pipeline projects. Even though, the "Gazprom Clause" was not as strict as intended it has led to a significant discontent from the Russian side (Iago 2008c).

Apart from Poland, the Czech Republic has also played an active role, especially during its presidency (first half of 2009) and the final negotiations. The Czech Republic has experienced Russian power not only through the crisis with Ukraine but also directly in 2008, when Russia decreased its oil deliveries by 50 %, allegedly due to technical problems. For Czech politicians, it was clearly retaliation for the negotiations with the US over the anti-missile shield. Therefore, the Czech Republic made a political agreement on the third energy package one of the highest priorities during its presidency (Iago 2009b).

The fast action and the broadening coalitions show that within the new member states it was not difficult to build a strong coalition united by the common threat of dependency on Russian gas. The main framing strategy was to securitise energy policies and to define them as an important part of foreign policy. It was similarly observed by other scholars that the new member states were building upon the framing strategy of the UK on interpreting the liberalisation of the gas market in the light of the security concerns (Geden et al. 2006). However, in the case of the eastern European countries the security concerns went beyond the rhetoric: there were some serious concerns about the security of the European gas supply chain accompanied by a number of events supporting the securitization rhetoric.

Thus even though eastern European countries were not successful in building common energy policy and energy security community (Natorski and Herranz Surrallés 2008), many elements that were brought up through the securitization of the energy market found their way into the final directive and present examples of successful decision agenda.

10.5 Conclusion: The Role of the Eastern European Coalition

The analysis within this chapter strives to link the interest-based explanations with the role of the framing strategies in order to explain successful decision agenda. It was shown that the addition of new member states did not significantly change the possible pro-liberalisation coalition as there were some member states who were opposing liberalisation and some states who were in favour of liberalisation. The interest-based approach thus cannot fully explain the agenda dynamics. Therefore, we have also traced the role of the framing strategies.

The eastern European countries led by Poland initiated the securitisation of the energy policy at the backdrop of high dependency on Russia and successfully inserted some new policy instruments (Gazprom clause and regional solidarity) in the initial proposal of the directive, which were (albeit in altered version) included in the final version of the directive.

This analysis thus suggests that the eastern European countries indeed played an important role in the decision agenda of the gas market liberalisation and thus are one of the main explanatory factors for the significant policy changes. The energy security at the European level remains one of the strategic issues within the cooperation of the so-called Visegrad group: Poland, Hungary and the Czech and Slovak Republics (Visegrad Group 2014). As a reaction to the crisis in Crimea (Ukraine), Poland is again calling for a EU Energy Union (EurActiv 2014) and it will be interesting to observe whether this time the securitisation will be more successful than during the 2006 crisis.

Building upon the findings elaborated by Nicole Herweg (see Chap. 4), which showed that decisive for the agenda-setting and decision-making during the first gas directive was its framing as a competition issue, we could trace that liberalisation of the gas market during the negotiations over the third gas directive was reframed as a foreign policy issue. Relating the liberalisation to the energy security debate by the new member states, who were directly affected by the events that were perceived as credible threats, allowed this shift. This in turn confirms the findings by Alexandrova and Timmermans who showed in Chap. 3 that the venue of high politics is highly attentive to security issues.

There are some other alternative explanations for the successful decision agenda. For instance, the role of the European Parliament was not directly addressed in this chapter even though some scholars (Eikeland 2011) and media suggest that the strict stances of the European Parliament on unbundling were decisive for the deeper reforms within the energy sector. This was certainly an important factor but unbundling was a policy instrument initiated already during the first gas directive and it is not clear, given that the European Parliament was not able to put through full ownership unbundling of distribution and transmission networks, whether any significant progress was achieved. The eastern European countries however proposed some of new instruments and have overcome the resistance from the member states such as Germany, Italy and France. Nonetheless, a systematic analysis of agenda-setting through the European Parliament within energy sector remains an interesting topic for future research.

References

BBC. (2005). Russia and Germany sign gas deal. *BBC.*

BBC. (2006). Lithuania's Adamkus warns EU against being Russia's hostage over energy. *BBC Monitoring Former Soviet Union.*

Benoit, B., & Laitner, S. (2006). Eu energy chief vows action to avoid future supply disruption. *Financial Times.*

Benoit, K., & Laver, M. (2007). Estimating party policy positions: Comparing expert surveys and hand-coded content analysis. *Electoral Studies, 26*(1), 90–107.

Brutschin, E. (2013). *Dynamics in EU policy-making: The liberalization of the European gas market.* Ph.D. Thesis, University Konstanz.

Buchan, D. (2010). Energy policy. Sharp challenges and rising ambitions. In H. Wallace, M. A. Pollack & A. R. Young (Eds.), *Policy Making in the European Union* (pp. 358–379). New York: Oxford University Press.

Codognet, M.-K., Glachant, J.-M., Leveque, F., & Plagnet, M.-A. (2002). Mergers and acquisitions in the European eectricity sector: Cases and patterns. *CERNA.*

Council of EU (2006a). *Study on unbundling of electricity and gas transmission and distribution system operators—Annex Country Overview.*

Council of EU (2006b). *Proposal for a European Energy Security Treaty—presentation by Polish Delegation.*

Council of EU (2008a). *Notes from the Presidency to the Delegations* (File 6324/08). Brussels, February 18, 2008

Council of EU (2008b). Contribution of the Legal Service (File 9891/08). Brussels, May 26, 2008

Dempsey, J. (2005). Russia seeks pipeline control. *The International Herald Tribune.*

Dempsey, J. (2006). German Utilities Amass Empires in eastern EU. *The International Herald Tribune.*

European Commission (1988). *The Internal Energy Market. Commission Working Document* (1988).

European Commission (1992). *Proposal for a Council Directive concerning common rules for the internal market in natural gas.* (COM(91) 548 final). Brussels.

European Commission (1998). Directive 98/30/EC of the European Parliament and of the Council of 22 June 1998 concerning common rules for the internal market in natural gas.

European Commission (2001). Proposal for a directive of the european parliament and of the council amending Directives 96/92/EC and 98/30/EC concerning common rules for the internal market in electricity and natural gas. COM(2001) 125 final.

European Commission (2003). Directive 2003/55/EC of the European Parliament and of the Council of 26 June 2003 concerning common rules for the internal market in natural gas and repealing Directive 98/30/EC.

European Commission (2006). *Commission decision of 7 November 2006 establishing the composition of the Gas Coordination Group.*

European Commission (2007). Proposal for a Directive of the european parliament and of the council amending directive 2003/55/EC concerning common rules for the internal market in natural gas.

European Commission (2009). Directive 2009/72/EC of the European Parliament and of the Council of 13 July 2009 concerning common rules for the internal market in electricity and repealing Directive 2003/54/EC (2009).

European Observer (2008). EU weakens "Gazprom Clause" on foreign energy investors. *EU Observer.*

Eberlein, B. (2008). The making of the European energy market: The interplay of Governance and Government. *Journal of Public Policy, 28*(1), 73–92.

Eikeland, P. O. (2008). *EU Internal Energy Market Policy: Fridtjof Nansens Institutt*

Eikeland, P. O. (2011). The third internal energy market package: New power relations among member states, EU institutions and non-state actors? *Journal of Common Market Studies, 49*, 243–263.

Eising, R. (2002). Policy learning in embedded negotiations: Explaining EU electricity liberalization. *International Organization, 56*(01), 85–120.

EurActiv. (2014). Poland Calls for EU Energy Union. *EurActiv.*

Fernandez, R., & Palazuelos, E. (2014). A political economy approach to the european union gas model: Continuities and changes. *JCMS. Journal of Common Market Studies, 52*(3), 495–511.

Fisher, D.R. (2006). Bringing the Material Back In: Understanding the U.S. Position on Climate Change. *Sociological Forum, 21*(3), 467–494.

Gaman, I. M. (2010). La Libéralisation des Marchés de L'Ectricité et du Gaz Naturel au Niveau Européen—Enjeux et Défis Actuel. *Romanian Journal of European Affairs, 10*(2), 30–51.

Geden, O., & Fischer, S. (2008). *Die Energie- und Klimapolitik der Europäischen Union.* Saarbrücken: Nomos.

Geden, O., Marcelis, C., & Maurer, A. (2006). Perspectives for the European Union's External Energy Policy: Discourses, Ideas and Interests in Germany, the UK, Poland and France. *SWP Working Paper.*

Greenwood, C. (2006). Ukraine Gas Crisis Could hit Britain. *Birmingham Post.*

Hagemann, S. (2007). Applying ideal point estimation methods to the council of ministers. *European Union Politics, 8*(2), 279–296.

Hall, P. A. (1993). Policy paradigms, social learning, and the state: The case of economic policymaking in britain. *Comparative Politics, 25*(3), 275–296.

Hug, S., & König, T. (2002). In view of ratification: Governmental preferences and domestic constraints at the amsterdam intergovernmental conference. *International Organization, 56* (02), 447–476.

Iago, D.a. (2008a). Energy markets: IMCO opts for third way on ownership unbundling. *Europolitics Energy.*

Iago, D.a. (2008b). Energy Council: Broad agreement on liberalization to face difficult future. *Europolitics Energy.*

Iago, D.a. (2008c). EU-Russia permanent partnership council: Talks sign off ninth progress report. *Europolitics: New Neighbours.*

Iago, D.a. (2009a). Security of Gas supply: Commission proposes new rules on supply crisis. *Europolitics Energy.*

Iago, D.a. (2009b). Czech Presidency: Energy Security Dominates the Agenda. *Europolitics Energy.*

Jamasb, T., & Pollitt, M. (2005). Electricity market reform in the european union: Review of Progress toward Liberalization & Integration. *The Energy Journal, Special Issue: Eruopean Electricity Liberalisation,* 11–43

Jeziorski, M. (2006). Gas Pains, *The Warsaw Voice Online.*

Klüver, H. (2009). Measuring interest group influence using quantitative text analysis. *European Union Politics, 10*(4), 535–549.

Larsson, R. (2006). Russia's Energy Policy: Security dimensions and russia's reliability as an energy supplier: Swedish Defense Research Agency.

Natorski, M., & Herranz Surrallés, A. (2008). Securitizing Moves To Nowhere? The Framing of the European Union's Energy Policy. *Journal of Contemporary European Research, 4*(2), 71–89.

Pariente-David, S., & Swanson, C.-A. (2003). Multi-Utilities; A Blessed Union? *Power Economics.*

Parker, G., & Ostrovsky, A. (2005). *Baltic states face Gazprom 'threat' to euro entry hopes.* Moscow: Financial Times.

Pollak, J., & Slominski, P. (2011). Liberalizing the EU's Energy Market: Hard and Soft Power Combined. In G. Falkner (Ed.), *The EU's decision traps: Comparing policies* (pp. 92–110). Oxford: Oxford University Press.

Princen, S. (2010). Agenda-Setting. In E. Versluis, M. van Keulen, & P. Stephenson (Eds.), *Analyzing the European Union Policy Process* (pp. 107–131). Palgrave Macmillan: Houndmills, Basingstoke, New York.

Princen, S. (2011). Agenda-setting strategies in EU policy processes. *Journal of European Public Policy, 18*(7), 927–943.

Schattschneider, E. E. (1960). *The semisovereign people: a realist's view of democracy in America.* New York: Holt, Rinehart and Winston.

Schumann, D. (2005). *Interessenvermittlung im Europäischen Mehrebenensystem.* Wiesbaden: Deutscher Universitäts-Verlag.

Sikorski, R., & Olex-Szczytowski, M. (2007). *Rostowski, J.* Financial Times: Russian gas pipeline would be geopolitical disaster for EU.

Sprinz, D., & Vaahtoranta, T. (1994). The Interest-Based explanation of international environmental policy. *International Organization, 48*(1), 77–105.

Stern, J. (2006). *The Russian-Ukrainian gas crisis of January 2006.* Oxford Institute for Energy Studies.

Tosun, J. (2011). When the grace period is over: assessing the new member states' compliance with EU requirements for oil stockholding. *Energy Policy, 39*(11), 7156–7134.

Tsebelis, G. (2002). *Veto players. how political institutions work.* Princeton: Princeton University Press.

Tusk, D. (2014). A united Europe can end Russia's energy stranglehold. *Financial Times.*

Veen, T. (2011). Positions and salience in European Union Politics: Estimation and validation of a new dataset. *European Union Politics, 12*(2), 267–288.

Visegrad Group (2014). *Official Statements.*

Whist, B.S. (2008). *Nord Stream: Not Just a Pipeline.* Fridtjof Nansen Institute.

Chapter 11
Building the Agenda for Carbon Dioxide Capture and Storage: Limits of EU-Activism

Gerhard Fuchs

Abstract This chapter analyses the agenda-setting processes for the Carbon Dioxide Capture and Storage (CCS) technology by referring to the theory of strategic action fields. CCS is a technology aiming to reduce CO_2 emissions from power plants using fossil fuels, especially coal. The origins of the CCS debate can be traced back to sustainability-oriented Norwegian policy and was catapulted on the European Union's (EU) agenda around 2005. A sudden wave of hectic activity followed within the EU. However, the technology is presently largely off the official EU agenda again. The reasons are changing conditions in the environment of the field and failed framing processes.

11.1 Introduction: Agenda-Setting and the Potential of CCS

There is widespread consensus among international organisations such as the International Energy Agency (IEA) and official policy statements by both national governments and the supranational executive of the European Union (EU) that energy systems need to be transformed. However, actual transition is proceeding very slowly (see Verbong and Loorbach 2012; Geels 2013). The global energy system faces a variety of challenges, which require adaptation. While large energy infrastructures are a precondition for economic development, the dominant ways of generating electricity from fossil fuels (coal, oil, gas) have also been made responsible for the human-induced part of climate change. Climate change mitigation in theory requires global decarbonisation (Unruh 2000), but the cost of achieving reductions in emissions is high (Barrett 2009) and global negotiations about commonly agreed aims and measures are stalling. A sustainable energy

G. Fuchs (✉)
Institute for Social Sciences, Sowi VI, University of Stuttgart, Seidenstr. 36/II, 70174 Stuttgart, Germany
e-mail: gerhard.fuchs@sowi.uni-stuttgart.de

J. Tosun et al. (eds.), *Energy Policy Making in the EU*,
Lecture Notes in Energy 28, DOI 10.1007/978-1-4471-6645-0_11

transition arguably requires, either direct regulation or price instruments (Fischer and Newell 2008; Unruh 2002) and/or favourable frameworks for the development of alternative energy resources (e.g. renewables). From this, it follows that the process of energy transitions are fundamentally political. The EU has committed itself to reduce CO_2 emissions by 60–80 % until 2050 (see Jacobs in Chap. 6). This aim poses a real economic challenge especially with regard to the future usage of coal as a resource. More potent and novel technologies are required. The most important candidate in this regard is the Carbon Capture and Storage (CCS) technology. In general, the technological part of a solution to the challenges of climate change could be twofold: (a) Alternative ways of generating energy can be developed and implemented; (b) the use of fossil fuels can be made more climate-friendly. These are then the two options: either develop and use new technologies for energy generation or make existing procedures and facilities work in a more socially desirable way. The CCS technology is an example of the latter option, which is aiming at making conventional power plants work more climate-friendly and issue less emissions. CCS would signify the creation of a new technological path, which faces many hurdles. For example, inter-organisational research and development networks, suitable regulatory frameworks and a new cognitive frame will be important. Arguably, if CCS can realise its potential to reduce CO_2 emissions in the EU by over 50 % by 2050 as claimed by experts (Stangeland 2007), this would help a lot in achieving the envisaged overall reduction targets.

The chapter explains how CCS has entered the EU agenda by analysing the pioneering efforts in Norway. Moreover, the case of Germany is used to exemplify the agenda-setting impact of the EU. It is mainly based on information drawn from qualitative interviews.[1] The agenda-setting processes in the three cases under investigation happened very differently. CCS in Norway has enjoyed stronger political support than in most other countries. Early CCS initiatives were motivated by the challenge of reconciling relatively ambitious climate policy targets with growing emissions from Norway's off-shore oil and gas operations, whose expertise and project opportunities formed the basis for these initiatives. The early start of the CCS debate established a broad coalition of supporters including recruitment of much of the environmental sector (government agencies and some NGOs). Unlike in other EU states, the beginnings of the CCS debate were not directly linked to electricity generation because of Norway's heavy reliance on hydraulic power, which might have eased the way for CCS in Norway. Only later attempts to add gas-fired generators to Norway's previously emissions-free power supply created conflict in which CCS became politically relevant, leading to ministerial demission and government crisis. These dynamics accelerated the agenda-setting process on CCS in the EU, which in turn influenced the member states' policy agendas. CCS

---

[1] The data sources are expert statements solicited in the course of the project "Die Bedeutung des Standortes Deutschland für den Kraftwerksbau vor dem Hintergrund einer zunehmenden Internationalisierung von Innovationsprozessen" funded by the Volkswagen Foundation, (cp. Weimer-Jehle et al. 2009) during 2007–2009, document analysis and 12 additional expert interviews conducted in 2010–2012.

entered the EU agenda building on the knowledge produced elsewhere (including Norway), industry lobbying and the situational prominence of the energy security issue after the year 2000.

However in Germany, the agenda was defined and driven forward by actors interested in keeping coal alive. Opposition mainly came from two sides. Opponents at the national level argued that CCS would just prolong the lifetime of an undesirable fossil trajectory. The second part of the protest originated mainly at the local level and places destined for the storage of the captured carbon dioxide. These protesters joined forces with the national opposition. The coalition thus comprised local opponents and concept opponents fighting against the established parties and building new coalitions. This coalition building process was moreover driven by the EU requirement to develop a specific CCS-related regulatory framework. Without this requirement, the process might have worked out quite differently.

In sum, Norway was a driving force in establishing an EU agenda for CCS while Germany became active only after the parameters were set by the European Commission. The cases for this study were thus selected on the basis of the following reasoning: Technological progress made it possible for Norway to use CCS, which induced the EU actors to discuss the possibility of CCS and to eventually make it compulsory for member states. The EU's promotion of CCS is surprising to the extent that there are some uncertain risks with CCS and usually the existence of the precautionary principle would have raised the expectation that EU policy makers are more careful in the adoption of this technology (see, e.g. Tosun 2013). Finally, the implementation of CCS has been controversial in Germany, a country that is usually regarded as a frontrunner in EU environmental policy (Jacobs in Chap. 6 and Cox and Dekanozishvili in Chap. 9). This latter aspect makes the politics of CCS adoption worth studying.

The analysis of agenda shaping processes is guided by the two following questions: How did the CCS agenda arise? How did the CCS agenda stabilise? The chapter is structured as follows. It first briefly outlines the technological background of CCS. Then, Sect. 11.3 introduces the theory of strategic action fields. Sections 11.4 through 11.6 present the case studies of Norway, the EU and Germany. Section 11.7 discusses the empirical findings in light of the theory and indicates avenues for future research.

11.2 The Promise of CCS—Now and Then

Coal actually presents a serious challenge for climate change oriented policies in the field of electricity generation both in the EU and worldwide. Many countries still rely strongly on coal for the generation of electricity. In the EU, this is especially true for Poland (90 %) and Germany (44 %). The traditional reliance on coal has been strengthened over the last years due to decreasing prices, which make its use economically more valuable. In 2012, EU-countries were burning coal at the fastest pace since 2006 and surging imports especially from US producers cut prices by

26 % in 1 year. This increase is an indirect effect of the so-called "shale gas revolution" in the US, which led to increasing US coal exports and decreasing coal prices from 130$/tonne in March 2011 to 85$/tonne in May 2012 (IEA 2013).

The expansion of coal-fired power generation is likely to continue. Germany's E.ON and RWE, the biggest utilities in Europe's largest power market, are planning to shut down unprofitable gas-fired plants even after the German government's *Energiewende*-decision promoting gas to replace nuclear energy.[2] Europe's higher coal use also frustrates the European Commission's policies to penalise carbon emissions. Coal-fired power plants are a major reason why the Energy Sector Carbon Intensity Index, i.e. the amount of CO_2 emitted for each unit of energy supplied, has remained essentially static and has changed by less than 1 % since 1990 (IEA 2013). Therefore, it comes as no surprise that the IEA argues that the continued coal expansion "presents a major threat to a low-carbon future" (IEA 2013). Arguably, the development and implementation of CCS could provide a solution for this problem because it would enable coal (and gas) burning without CO_2 emissions.

Current CCS capacity captures worldwide only 6 million tonnes (Mt) of CO_2 per year. There are provisions to contract CCS capacity for a further 13 Mt CO_2 in 2013 and more distant plans, which would bring the total to 90 Mt CO_2. But this would still capture less than 1 % of electricity sector CO_2-emissions in 2012 (IEA 2013, p. 56). The IEA-director expressed serious concerns: "I am particularly worried about the lack of progress in developing policies to drive CCS deployment. Without CCS, the world will have to abandon its reliance on fossil fuels much sooner and that will come at a cost" (IEA 2013, p. 5).

Quite surprisingly, in spite of this consent among experts and no diverging arguments from official national or EU-politicians, CCS progress is very slow (see Ricci et al. 2014). Norway and Germany are among the technology leaders in CCS development (cp. Weimer-Jehle et al. 2009). The German industrial area of Schwarze Pumpe, about 4 km (2.5 miles) south of the city of Spremberg, became home to the world's first CCS coal plant. Norway on the other hand does not only feature the oldest commercially viable CCS installations but also the world's foremost research centre on CCS (the CO_2 Technology Centre at Mongstad).

What are the main technological features of CCS? CCS aims to capture CO_2 at the major point source emitters: fossil fuel-fired power stations, production units for oil, gas, chemicals, steel and cement. It is thus a technology whose importance goes beyond the electricity generating sector but given the amount of CO_2 emitted in electricity generation it is the most promising field of application. CCS in the way it is being implemented in Europe at the moment involves three basic steps: (1) capture of CO_2, (2) transport to a suitable disposal site and (3) long-term storage. There are different technologies involved in these three steps and also

[2] Shortly after the Fukushima catastrophe, the German federal government in 2011 decided to shut down 8 of the 17 German nuclear power plants immediately with the rest following until 2022. This decision is usually referred to as the "Energiewende"-decision.

different types of shareholders. Installing CCS equipment increases first of all the production costs of equipment owners. Therefore, without government regulation, it is unlikely that respective equipment will be deployed voluntarily. Moreover, only if CCS installations will be deployed in considerable numbers will the costs for them significantly decrease (see also chapter Jacobs in Chap. 6 for an illustration of the different types of costs associated to the provision of electricity from different renewable energy sources). Another aspect concerns the transport of the captured CO_2. This will usually be done by pipelines. Finally, a storage site has to be identified in which the CO_2 is stored until it can be further used. Potentially, the CO_2 needs to be stored indefinitely.

11.3 Agenda-Setting and the Theory of Strategic Action Fields

This chapter pursues two purposes. One, it focuses on processes of energy transition and sheds light on how a system characterised by a strong degree of path dependence can be redirected or how a new path might be created. The other purpose is to assess which analytical framework is best suited to analyse agenda-setting processes with regard to CCS regulation. The majority of analyses on energy systems are stability oriented. They place institutions and structures in the centre of their analysis and use the influence of different structures and institutions as an explanation for the behaviour of individual or corporate actors. The question of change is very difficult to answer within such a framework. Change implies a variation in structures and institutions. Is there an analytical option that helps us better understand these processes of change? This question seems particularly interesting when analysing how CCS made it to the agenda of EU policy makers.

I argue that the theory of strategic action fields might help us understand this phenomenon. It is usually attained by behind-the-scenes action to convince multiple actors and groups that a particular agenda is in their interests. When the groups meet, the agenda as well as the terms of discussion are usually set and the identity and interests of actors are framed. This ensures that actors have to come to understand their interests within certain bounds, thus closing off many other courses of possible action (Fligstein and McAdam 2012, p. 51).

Agenda-setting and its direction crucially depends on previous coalition building and strategic positioning of actors. It has been repeatedly argued that in times of dramatic changes or cases of path creation new ways of organising "cultural frames" or "logics of action" come into existence. These are wielded by skilled social actors, sometimes called "institutional entrepreneurs", who come to innovate, propagate and organise strategic action fields (Fligstein and McAdam 2012, p. 4).

In the process of getting action, institutional developments take place. Using the terminology of transition theory, we can assume that initially "niches" come into existence resulting from the activities of actors dissatisfied with the status quo.

More or less isolated attempts to develop new social practices can be observed. Certain mechanisms seem to be necessary to work for a niche to be able to effectively challenge the incumbent actors and the practices that reproduce the status quo. One of these issues is that processes of coalition building take place in order to broaden the support base for the new practices. Usually niche developments are advanced by actors sharing a more or less stringent set of values and convictions. In order to become mainstream, other people and groups with different convictions have to be co-opted.

The Theory of Strategic Action Fields as developed by Fligstein and McAdam (2012), with respect to new emerging fields, is interested in asking and answering the following questions: (1) Who were the key actors that vied for control of the emerging field? (2) What alternative conceptions of the strategic action field did these key actors represent? (3) What resources—material, political, ideological—did each of the main combatants bring to the founding struggle? (4) Who prevailed in this struggle and why? (5) What role, if any, did external actors—especially state actors—play in the outcome of the founding episode? (6) What were the principal terms of the settlement eventuated at the close of the episode? (7) What, if any, internal governance units were established at this time to help routinize and safeguard the settlement? While this theoretical approach does not allow for explaining agenda building per se, it is useful for anticipating the consequences of agenda building in the sense whether new policies will be adopted.

Fligstein and McAdam (2012, p. 188) put up the proposition that "Unorganized social spaces become organized through a crescive social process akin to a social movement. This means that such orders can coalesce very quickly to produce an incumbent-challenger structure. Strategic action fields are stable when they have role structures and rules governing action that are based on either hierarchical incumbent-challenger structures or political coalitions."

I consider the field of CCS in the 1980s as "unorganized social space". In the early years, there were no fixed roles and positions, no clear future for technology development. Conventional electricity generation was dominated by established actors and technologies. Insofar, CCS emerged as a new field but also came into existence *next to an established field* (see proposition three: New strategic action fields are likely to emerge near existing strategic action fields, ibid. p. 189). Proposition five claims that strategic action fields are generally destabilised by *external shock* originating from other strategic action fields, invasion by other groups of organisations, actions of the state or large scale crises such as wars or depressions (see Cox and Dekanozishvili in Chap. 9). Changes in external *political coalitions* or changes in external hierarchies can destabilise the basis of a strategic action field (ibid.).

As it will be demonstrated for the case of Norway, the precondition for CCS trials to go ahead was a change in the composition of the Government, which provided an opportunity for actors to organise. The important elements of destabilisation for the CCS initiatives came from changing frame conditions. In spite of the fact that CCS was championed by industrial and civil society actors, the role of the state remained paramount. This is in line with proposition six: "States will be the focus of much action during episodes of contention, as both causes of crises and sites of contention to resolve the conflict" (ibid.). Proposition eight finally claims that "New frames and forms of action within a field will generally originate in invader or challenger groups. Skilled actors will attempt to use these new frames and/or forms of action to build a new political coalition based on interest or fashion a new set of cultural understandings that reorganises the interests and identities of field members" (ibid.).

An organisational field may cut across the boundaries of a single industry and also include additional actors such as regulatory and government agencies or capital providers, be they private or public. With regard to the focal level of analysis and its upper and lower boundary levels, there is ample evidence that they are strongly interrelated. Recurrent activities on the corporate level are also oriented towards the organisational field.

For a new field like CCS to emerge, the actors involved in the negotiation of the initial settlement must achieve a degree of consensus on three issues: (a) They must arrive at a general shared understanding of what is going on in the field, what is at stake, (b) a set of relatively fixed actors in the field whose roles and comparative status/power are consensually defined by others in the strategic action field will be present and (c) a set of shared understandings about the nature of the rules that will govern interaction in the field can be recognised.

It can be said that skilled actors are oriented towards dealing with an external event by framing agendas, buildings coalitions, eventually leading in positive cases to innovative actions supported by state actions. The following section analyses the agenda-setting processes for the three cases by tracing the emergence of coalitions between actors supporting or opposing CCS and by assessing the role of external events.

11.4 Norway: The Frontrunner in Applying a New Technology

For generating electricity, Norway uses nearly exclusively water power. The significant domestic oil and gas reserves are mainly exported. Thus, the discussion on CCS in Norway was advanced by actors, which did not have a significant role in the domestic electricity providing system. Leading actors for the development of the technology and a respective agenda had been the oil company Statoil, research institutes like The Foundation for Scientific and Industrial Research (SINTEF) and the Technical University of Trondheim. Already in the 1980s, the idea of capturing and storing CO_2 had been put forth. The concept of CCS in Norway originated between 1986 und 1988, when researchers from the Norwegian research institution SINTEF suggested the capture and storage of CO_2 in a study conducted for Norway's largest oil company Statoil. At the same time, Brundtland chaired the *World Commission on Environment and Development* of the United Nations.

Under her chairmanship, a comprehensive report on sustainable development was published. In 1991, Brundtland introduced for Norway a CO_2 tax for fossil fuels and fossil fuel using sectors. This tax helped increase efforts in the 1990s to push forward plans for the capturing of CO_2 in the oil and gas fields.

Initially, this happened as pure research efforts but also in the form of projects testing whether the procedure was commercially viable. The interest of the oil- and gas industry is derived from two activities linked with the CCS technology: the so-called EOR (Enhanced Oil Recovery) and the EGR (Enhanced Gas Recovery). By both methods, CO_2 is injected into off-shore oil and gas fields in order to improve the efficiency of exploitation. This framing of the technology quickly brought other actors into the playing field and the actor network. Norway's biggest industrial plant constructing company Kvaerner and international oil companies contributed to the research efforts. The driving force in Norway thus has been the oil- and gas industry, which started R&D activities as well as partnerships with scientific institutes. Its prime interest was the injection and storage of CO_2 in the nearly empty oil and gas fields. On the other hand, it was the strong political impetus engineered by the government and the introduction of the carbon tax for off-shore petroleum activities, which triggered Statoil to investigate options for cost-effective CO_2 handling at their off-shore Sleipner West gas field. These actors succeeded in building a strong coalition framing their activities as being both ecologically as well as economically sound. Starting in 1996, Statoil began with the first commercial use in the gas field Sleipner West in the North Sea.

From 1997 onward, research activities for CCS also received public support money from the KLIMATEK programme sponsored by the Norwegian government. After Kvaerner had been successful with starting its first pilot installation of a CO_2 capturer, Norway's second biggest technology company, Aker, also invested in R&D for CO_2 capturing. Tjernshaugen summarises: "The CO_2 tax in its time became a key driver in promoting CCS technology in Norway" (Tjernshaugen 2011, p. 213). This tax was opposed by industry in general but supported by the environmental movement.

But growing electricity demand could not be matched by domestic water power alone. Environmental concerns were discouraging the building of new water dams. At this point, the Norwegian energy provider Naturkraft got a license to construct two new gas-fired power plants. In 1998, Norway's second largest oil company, NorskHydro, launched its Hydrokraft project. This included the development of a pre-combustion capture technology with an integrated reformer combined cycle for a proposed 1,200 MW power plant. Larsen and Ruud (2005) explain that the Hydrokraft project fits in the fierce political discussion about the two concessions received by power company Naturkraft—a consortium of Statoil, Norsk Hydro and Statkraft—to build gas-fired power plants.

The debate was originally about whether or not to build these combined cycle plants. But after several influential environmental NGOs—including Bellona and Nature and Youth—introduced the concept of CCS in the public domain, it changed rapidly to whether to build these plants with or without CCS (Tjernshaugen 2008). Influenced by the 'Joint action against gas-fired power plants', which is considered as the broadest environmental movement campaign of the decade, the Norwegian pollution control authority (SFT) refused to issue the full emission permits required by Naturkraft to develop gas power in Norway (Tjernshaugen and Lee 2004). This implied that the only way to comply was to build a CCS facility as an integral part of the power plant. However, this implication caused a strong parliamentary opposition. This was especially so after Norsk Hydro's decision in 1999 to put the Hydrokraft project temporarily on hold because of technical and financial difficulties. This political crisis resulted in the resignation of the minority government led by Bondevik in March 2000.

CCS seemed to be the only option if attempts to decrease energy consumption were not successful and if the government wanted to stick to the political aim (in the meantime also laid down in the Kyoto Protocol) to reduce CO_2 emissions. In this second phase, the CCS agenda changed and the framing also needed adjustment. Now, electricity generation was of concern and the conflict between economic and environmental considerations arouse again albeit with different actors being in the forefront of the debate. Since the private R&D activities, the Norwegian policies as well as the geological storage potentials made ever bigger research efforts possible, which were now supported by the EU (in spite of the fact that Norway is not a member of the EU), CCS gained solid support among the Norwegian public and most of the active NGOs. The initial debate on whether to build new gas-fired power plants turned into a debate about the pro and cons of CCS technology (cp. van Alphen et al. 2009, p. 49), which was easily won by the supporters of CCS coming from different camps.

For the European Commission, the Norwegian developments were important because they demonstrated that CCS was a politically and socially acceptable technology. Furthermore, with the Norwegian developments underway, industrial and civil society actors had formed strongly in favour of CCS. Norwegian actors were instrumental in helping to draft the first EU statements, running lobbying efforts on the EU level and still today Norwegian actors are dominating the CCS support coalition at the EU level.

In 2011, the government's position was guided by the idea that no new concessions for gas-fired power plants would be granted if the CCS technology is not used. Norway eventually funded not only activities within Norway but also European projects to further develop CCS technology. In principle, the CCS commitment remained alive, but it had become far more fragile. The lagging global CCS technology development made obvious that the costs for CCS development and deployment had to be covered mainly by the Norwegian government and its affiliated industry with little chances for technology export. The situation in 2013 looks more open than ever. Nevertheless, one finds the largest research facilities dealing with CCS (CO_2 Technology Centre Mongstad) and considerable state funding (coupled with the fact that the energy actors like Statoil are also more or less public actors) in Norway. The substantial financial government support for CCS worried the competition directorate of the European Commission. But given the fact that CCS enthusiasm in Europe soon began to ebb, no actions followed.

In conclusion, it can be said that CCS in Norway was driven forward by a growing and broad coalition of actors coming from politics, industry and civil society forming a strong support coalition. The development of the technology did not lead to a disruptive change but was inclusive, oriented towards existing actor coalitions and broadening them in a largely consensual manner. In the Norwegian CCS case the field structures were not fundamentally transformed. A broad coalition of industrial and civil society actors supporting the CCS technology was established. Overall, the field showed a high degree of adaptive capacity and was able to push technology development forward. Norway has been successful in building an innovation system around the CCS technology (van Alphen et al. 2009).

11.5 The European Union: The Promoter of the New Technology

As was discussed in other chapters of this volume, the EU struggled to develop a consistent energy policy (see, e.g. Tosun et al. in Chap. 1 and Biesenbender in Chap. 2). This might look surprising at first sight because the predecessor organisations of the EU were highly engaged in energy issues: EURATOM and the European Coal and Steel Community. Even if the EU is and was formulating far-reaching goals, we can still observe highly divergent energy policies in member states. As in other areas, the EU concentrated its more recent efforts on competition law. But even more so than in other policy fields, liberalisation has not led to the creation of powerful common institutions or a "true" common market. In 1988, the European Commission presented a Communication advocating the establishment of an Internal Energy Market (European Commission 1988). In 1996, an important decision was made concerning the opening of European energy markets, which aimed at establishing common rules for transmission, distribution, supply and storage and implied a system of third-party access in the gas sector (see, e.g. Herweg in Chap. 5 and Brutschin in Chap. 10). In Germany, liberalisation took place as a reaction to this EU activism and had the imminent effect that a quasi-oligopoly was created in the electricity provider market. Four utilities emerged in the process which (based on EU rulings) had to give up on their cross-country networking business which was transferred to.

CCS does not fit easily into this picture. It has little to do with creating a common market. CCS-related policies concentrate on the support of a specific technology for which there was (and is) no market (see also Jacobs in Chap. 6). The European Commission was supporting CCS experiments in Norway and elsewhere, but it did not consider it an important item on its energy agenda (see also Bouzarovski und Petrova in Chap. 7 for an analysis of a similarly neglected issue on the European energy agenda). "Interestingly, the EU's CCS policy appears to have emerged without the kind of heavyweight support from prominent industries or member states or sustained Commission support evident in other areas of climate policy" (Boasson and Wettestad 2013, p. 105).

CCS was brought to the table rather suddenly, making use of knowledge produced by a tightly knit epistemic community (industry, science), continuous research efforts, industry lobbying (Emission Fossil Fuel power Plants; ZEP) and the situational prominence of the energy security issue after the year 2000 (European Commission 2000). The CCS process is very unusual because it does not fit into the standard picture of EU agenda-setting. It has to be seen in the extraordinary environment where international climate negotiations seemed to falter, the incumbent actors of the old fossil regime heavily opposed restrictions on their activities and the decision of President Bush to play the CCS card as a justification for his refusal to do something about CO_2 emissions. CCS seemed to be a solution, which would enable to reduce emissions on the one hand without having to fight the opposition of industry on the other (see also Markusson et al. 2012).

DG research initiated the European Technology Platform for ZEP. The Norwegian NGO, Bellona, was given the role as a secretariat of the ZEP and used this position to encourage ZEP to launch proposals for EU policy. It was supported by the UK interests, who looked towards China and the possibilities to include China into any kind of climate-related negotiations.[3] ZEP played an important role in preparing EU initiatives. Neither the Parliament nor the member states were usually involved. CCS policy was developed in a special process with only one parliamentary reading and the European council as the key decision maker, not the Environmental council or the Parliament.

CCS first appeared as a plausible technology option in the Commission's White Paper from 2005, "Winning the battle against climate change" (European Commission 2005). Furthermore, the Commission's Green Paper on Energy in March 2006 listed CCS as a tool for combatting climate change while still securing future energy supply (European Commission 2006). This has to be seen in the context of the sudden halt to exports of natural gas to Ukraine by Russia. Following this focusing event, the agenda was dominated by a discussion on energy dependence from Russia. The Green paper's introduction of CCS alongside measures to increase energy efficiency and the production of renewables. This revealed the Commission's developing views on CCS: it could contribute to achieving both energy and climate security. In addition, CCS was interpreted as a symbol for the technological capabilities of the EU. The idea that Europe will not be able to meet its long-term greenhouse gas reduction targets without deploying CCS was officially recognised by the EU heads of state in March 2006 (see Praetorius and Von Stechow 2009, p. 147). German Chancellor Angela Merkel engineered a unanimous backing for the Commission's comprehensive Climate and Energy Package by all 27 heads of state in 2007 (see also Cox and Dekanozishvili in Chap. 9 on the role of Germany in linking the European energy and climate change policy agendas).

[3] The biggest proportion of CCS-related Community documents is related to discussions with China.

The "Merkel miracle" or rather the Communique from the European Council meeting on 8–9 March 2007 engaged with CCS on three levels. First, it asked the Commission to establish a legal framework for CCS to allow CO_2 to be safely stored deep underground. Second, it endorsed the Commission's suggestion to draw up a policy to stimulate construction and operation by 2015 of up to 12 demonstration plants (European Commission 2013). Third, it called for a Strategic Energy Technology plan for Europe and asked the Commission to prepare a road map for developing European industrial initiatives for key low-carbon emitting technologies, which placed CCS top of a list of six. The fact that CCS was ranked highest by the global technological community provided this option with a significant amount of legitimacy in the field. It acknowledged (clean) coal as part of the solution to climate change and energy security. Utilities also embraced coal: "Interest in new coal plants has been sparked by relatively low coal prices over the last 5 years, making them more profitable than gas plants. However, the strongest driver for new coal is the desire by companies to maintain a portfolio of generating capacity that includes a range of fuels, to hedge against markets, security of supply or policy risk" (Lockwood 2008, p. 6). Two years later a comprehensive legal framework for the geological storage of CO_2 was introduced and two major funding schemes to support a demonstration programme of up to 12 large scale CSS projects were introduced.

In its paper "Sustainable power generation from fossil duels: aiming for near-zero emissions from coal after 2010" (European Commission 2007), the Commission outlined the numerous hurdles facing the implementation of CCS, but also its potential to ensure continued access to fossil fuel energy—while reducing CO_2 emissions. In 2007, the European Council announced that it aims to support up to 12 large-scale demonstration projects by 2015 setting aside approximately a subsidy of one billion Euro subsidy (European Commission 2013), which was later further increased. The promise of CCS also provided legitimation for the White Paper's endorsement of future coal. Utilities joined the support coalition but were not keen to deploy the technology voluntarily and looked for government support and handouts. Most of the corporate activity on CCS has "been focused on basic scientific research and lobbying governments for subsidies and support rather than investments needed to deploy the technology on a commercial scale" (Bowen 2011, p. 2256). From the early 1990s up to the 7th Framework programme (ending 2013), the EU budget for R&D for CCS has increased from 35 million to approximately 369 million. A particularly important development has been the establishment of the European Technology Platform for zero emission fossil fuel power plants initiated by the Directorate General for Research, Technology and Development of the European Commission in spring 2005. It included various branches of industry (utilities, oil and gas, equipment suppliers), science and research communities and environmental NGOs. The European Commission finances half of the costs of the ZEP Secretariat, the other half being met by industrial members. The 26 members were recently increased to 39. The ZEP set the year 2020 as a target for the commercial implementation of CCS. This means projects need to be up and running by 2015 at the latest. By 2008, the CCS agenda seemed to be firmly established and driven forward by a coalition of politicians, economic actors and some (mainly Norwegian) NGOs. Their common point was to have CCS ready as a technology if it should be required to implement it for security or environmental reasons. The utilities supported the idea because it offered the chance to continue running fossil fuel power plants. It was unclear, who was supposed to pay for the development and installation of the technology. Already by 2010, firms began pulling out of their commitments to develop CCS and member countries, notably Germany had difficulties issuing a regulatory framework beneficial to the aims of the European Commission. The reason for the firms to move out was that the expected heavy fines for emitting CO_2 did not materialise. Thus, there was no economic rationale for developing CCS. Additionally, climate change was not any longer a topic of ultimate importance for European governments. The effects of the financial crisis, economic growth and unemployment became far more important. It is unlikely that the European Commission will be able to spend its money earmarked for CCS projects. CCS is still mentioned in the Commission's Energy Roadmap 2050 (European Commission 2011), but it fails to mention any instruments that would enable CCS actually to happen.

CCS as an important issue on the EU agenda has disappeared from most of the official Commission statements of the years 2012 and 2013. The CCS support coalition in 2013 urged the EU to take up the issue again. "The window of opportunity has not yet closed for the EU to maintain its global technology leadership in CCS, but the time to act is now" (5 March 2013; http://bellona.org/news/ccs/2013-03-ccs-leadership-coalition-welcomes-the-ccs-communication). CCS gets some passing references, but it is not any longer treated as a priority issue. The first round of the EU's funding programme failed to deliver financial support for any CCS project in the EU.

11.6 CCS in Germany: A Reluctant Adopter of EU Policy

CCS was brought onto the German policy agenda because of EU policy making, but the country has been reluctant to embrace this new technology. There are some reasons that can be given for that. First of all, coal (absent in Norway) still plays an important role for electricity generation in Germany. 25.7 % of the energy generated in Germany has brown coal as its source; an additional 18.5 % is derived from hard coal (AG Energiebilanzen 2013). The brown coal used is nearly exclusively coming from domestic sources and is at the same time the only competitive domestic fossil material used for electricity generation. After a period of stagnation, coal-fired power plants are again expanding in the German market, i.e. most planned construction projects are coal-fired power plants (cp. Pahle 2010). In its role as buyers of power plant technologies, the German utilities have a substantial interest in technological innovation that would allow them to continue running the coal-fired plants and build new ones. This refers to a further improvement of technology already in use to increase efficiency, but it also elicited an interest in CCS, which could lower CO_2 emissions significantly.

In the early 2000s, politicians, industry and research shared the conviction that the pressure to reduce emissions would continue and this belief was further strengthened by the fact that the German Government committed the country to an ambitious climate policy (40 % CO_2 reduction target by 2050 announced by the Federal Government). CCS seemed to be a suitable solution to continue running coal-fired power plants and reduce emissions at the same time. The importance of coal is also highlighted by the fact that Germany is considered to be a worldwide leader in the development of technologies relevant for the running of coal-fired power plants (Weimer-Jehle et al. 2009). If CCS becomes a technological development with a worldwide appeal (especially in countries like China and India), German industry and research needed to jump on the bandwagon. Innovation activities in the area of coal-fired power plants and CCS in Germany are recent and were executed by a limited number of predominantly big actors. These were multinational companies like Siemens, Alstom and Hitachi Power Europe, which as dominant constructors of power plants build technically highly developed components like turbines, boilers and generators. Innovations are driven forward in clusters of research networks in non-university research institutes (e.g. Research Centre Jülich), big university institutes, the R&D departments of the producer companies and the R&D departments of the customers, usually the four big energy providers RWE, E.ON, Vattenfall and EnBW are represented (cp. Rogge and Hoffmann 2009, p. 7)—sometimes all of them at the same time.

Driving actors in the development of CCS and the spread of its idea in Germany were the firms constructing power plants, the domestic brown coal industry and the big energy providers, which operate the majority of the German coal-fired power plants. Additionally, the companies were confronted with rising pressures towards their coal-fired power plants. In 2003, the Council of the EU and the European Parliament decided to implement emission trading, which came into force in 2005. As a response, Utilities companies started various research and development programmes for the reduction of CO_2 emissions. The focus was put on CCS. E.ON, RWE and EnBW began pilot projects as well as research programmes in 2005/2006. Vattenfall already started its first project in 1998 and intensified their engagement from 2003 on. This accounts for different methods of CCS and different projects often done with various cooperation partners.

The support coalition included the government, which was both concerned about CO_2 reduction aims and the competitiveness of the domestic industry. It was a coalition consisting of the incumbent actors in the field. These were the same actors that already in the past had worked in a cooperative manner to set the agenda and establish a stable field. The interest of these actors was sparked by the developments on the international level (expert consensus on CCS) and the more immediate plans of the European Commission. Thus, Germany was a latecomer in CCS research and development. The framing of the CCS agenda centred more on the industrial policy aspects and the necessity to follow technological trends. It was much more defensive than the positive frame in Norway and the EU. Given the importance of the equipment manufacturing firms from an industrial policy point of view, early R&D activities were supported by the Federal Government and started mainly after the aforementioned EU decisions had been made. The way forward for CCS seemed to be open and necessary.

The leading actor in this respect was and still is the Ministry of Economic Affairs. Within the so-called COORETEC initiative for the promotion of research and development of future-oriented power plants with fossil fuels, research projects and pilot installations for the capturing of CO_2 were supported. At the site *Schwarze Pumpe* in Brandenburg, a big and traditional brown coal extracting area, the first ever trial installation for a CO_2-poor brown coal-fired power plant based on the Oxyfuel procedure was built. The pilot installation started to work in 2008 and was run by the energy provider Vattenfall. The aim was to test and further develop the technology in order to make it commercially viable. In a parallel effort, Vattenfall also developed a 300 MW-demonstration project, which was supposed to start operation in the years to come.

It was planned to be again situated in Brandenburg, this time at Jänschwalde. In contrast to the Norwegian situation, the driving forces for the development of CCS clearly came from the incumbent actors of the field. Innovation activities followed an established incremental course typical for this type of field, based on the interests of the incumbent actors and their networks. It soon became clear, however, that the third step in the CCS development process (looking for suitable sites to store the captured CO_2) would run into difficulties. No established mechanisms were available and the approval of actors became necessary, which hitherto had not played any role in the calculations of the coalition driving forward CCS. Pilot installations could run without much difficulties because they were relying on established rules not specifically tailored to the technology CCS. The EU's decision required the implementation of specific national comprehensive regulations on CCS. This meant that before getting money from the European Commission new regulations had to be fixed and at any rate the Commission had set a deadline until which member states would have to formulate respective regulations. The EU required a solution to the CO_2-storage problem included in the regulations. There had to be a way to deal with the question what sites will eventually be able to be selected for CO_2 storage and what the procedures for selecting them are. This instigated a heated public debate initiated by local interests close to the potential storage sites, which demanded to have a veto over siting decisions. The commercial exploitation of CCS in the end had to cope with severe acceptance problems, which threatened the success of the whole endeavour. Massive resistance against the exploration of possible storage sites became organised. Various citizen initiatives came into existence, which gradually gained the support of environmental organisations and from other associations, like the "Farmers'Association" and the Association of Water Power Companies (Schulz et al. 2010).

After massive protests, the regional (state) governments became reluctant in their support of the Federal Government's plans to push CCS. Especially, the resistance of the state government of Schleswig-Holstein made it impossible to pass a federal law on CCS (http://www.schleswig-hostein.de/MELUR/DE/Service/Presse/PI/2013/0113/MELUR_130129_CCS_Gesetzentwurf.html). As a consequence, the energy provider RWE stopped its plans for building a demonstration power plant using the CCS technology in Hürth (North Rhine-Westphalia). Even before this decision, RWE had failed in its attempt to gain EU support for the project. The EU gave as a justification for its decision the public opposition against the search for storage sites in Germany.

The only existing legal approval for the exploration of potential commercial CO_2 sites, two sites in the state of Brandenburg, were based on state regulations, given the absence of federal rules. The permission was granted with the expectation that a new federal law would soon be passed, which would then grant legitimacy to the state's actions. Since the federal law did not materialise, the state government announced that the exploration permit can only be considered as temporarily valid. After long negotiations, a new federal law was finally passed, which put the responsibility for accepting the technology in the hands of regional governments that did not have any interest in supporting CCS. Lobbying by the incumbent actors for a different solution was hardly visible. This was due to the changing field environment: neither the worldwide spread of CCS materialised nor the expected attempts to charge CO_2 emissions. There is now neither a national nor a world market for the technology and in addition no political will for regulatory actions. It is no wonder that presently (2014) Germany is increasing its CO_2 emissions and burning more coal than before. As such, the technology implementation process looks doomed and no suitable agenda that would promote its legitimacy.

Similar to the situation in Norway, the technology development process was advanced by established industrial actors, based on political decisions favouring the technology. Unlike Norway however, CCS did not succeed in building a solid support coalition reaching beyond the established field actors. Decision-making took place in closed circles until the necessity arose to go public for establishing a new regulatory framework and in the following search for storage sites. Local protests against CCS storage sites became quickly organised, national NGOs became active in the opposition against CCS and soon there was a vibrant nationwide discussion. CCS had moved from the institutional to the systemic agenda (see Tosun et al. in Chap. 1). CCS became a topic in Germany only once decisions on the European level were taken. It might sound strange that the German government was very instrumental in bringing forward European decisions and an EU framework for CCS implementation but utterly failed in the German adaptation of these regulations. The EU was asking for a dedicated regulatory CCS framework that at the end did not only stop already existing trials but also foreclosed any developments in the immediate future. The field CCS in Germany at the moment can thus be best described as an unorganised social space. Actors are unsure what to do and how to proceed. The agenda-setting process as initiated by the EU has not been sustainable on the member state level as the German example shows.

Table 11.1 Summary of results

	CCS/Norway	CCS/Germany	CCS/EU
External event	Brundtland report/ oil and gas industry business options	CO_2 reduction targets, potential world market developments	Energy security, saving coal
Support coalition	Government, NGOs, industry	Government, incumbent industry actors	Commission, national governments, expert epistemic community
"Innovative" actions	Tax, funding of research	Funding of research and demonstration projects	Funding of research and demonstration projects, regulatory framework
Role of government	Regulatory activism	Arbiter	Enabler
Field development	Proactive adaptation	Unorganised social space	Unorganised social space
Technology development	Preconditions available	Stopped	Delayed

11.7 Conclusion

This chapter traced agenda-setting processes for the CCS technology in Norway, Germany and on the EU level. The emphasis on the one hand was on analysing how technological developments and agenda-setting processes are embedded in specific national, European and sectoral contexts. On the other hand, I have put emphasis on a process perspective. The process perspective is informed by the theory of strategic action fields (Fligstein and McAdam 2012). I started with the expectation that a change in the framing of policies has to find its expression in a change within the dominant actor constellation. Changes in actor constellations are the product of a period of contention. Actors from society, industry or the state attempt to change the existing field consensus and thus the position of the incumbent actors. Incumbent actors will try to defend their position and damage the position of the challengers. The outcome of such a process cannot be easily predicted. It depends on the ability of the actors to frame the situation in a light that is beneficial to their strategy, to organise around this frame and develop (innovative) instruments to push forward their aims even against resistance (see also Herweg in Chap. 5, Butschin in Chap. 10 and Tosun in Chap. 12 for a similar conclusion on the role of framing in agenda-setting processes) (Table 11.1).

In Norway, the CCS development was driven forward by a broad coalition of actors, which came primarily from outside the electricity generating sector. Successful co-optation strategies brought together a coalition of actors from neighbouring fields, the general public and the incumbent actors. After 2005, a window of opportunity was opening for CCS. But emerging attributions of opportunity or threat do not in and of themselves guarantee innovative collective action.

These developments helped shape the European agenda. As a consequence, the European Commission sought to foster CCS in member states by framing it as a means to achieve both energy security and climate change mitigation.

The CCS technology in Germany was supposed to be executed "from above" with the help of the established actors and networks consisting of energy providers, research institutes, hardware producers and political actors. They tried to push through a technological option against growing public opposition. The eventual failure to commercialise CCS is signified by the successful attempts of the opponents of CCS to organise and a lacking capacity of the established actors to co-opt them (like in Norway).

The empirical examples shed light on agenda-setting processes in situations of high scientific and technological uncertainty. Placing the topic of CCS on the policy agendas of the EU was easily done by linking it to the issue of climate change and by pointing to the Norwegian experiences. It has proven much more difficult to maintain the discussion and to link it with a debate on concrete political strategies and decisions in the absence of any best practices to rely on. These processes have led to a disruption between the agenda-setting and decision-making stages. The future development of the policy agendas on CCS is likely to depend on technological progress and future pressure (i.e. climate change pressures).

References

AG Energiebilanzen. (2013). Bilanzen 1990–2012. http://www.ag-energiebilanzen.de/7-0-Bilanzen-1990-2012.html

Barrett, S. (2009). The coming global climate-technology revolution. *Journal of Economic Perspectives, 23*(2), 53–75.

Boasson, E. L., & Wettestad, J. (2013). *EU climate policy. Industry, policy interaction and external environment*. Farnham: Ashgate.

Bowen, F. (2011). Carbon capture and storage as a corporate technology strategy challenge. *Energy Policy, 39*(5), 2256–2264.

European Commission. (1988). *The greenhouse effect and the community*. COM (88) 656, 16 November.

European Commission. (2000). *Green paper: Towards a European strategy for the security of energy supply*. COM (2000) 769 final, 29 November.

European Commission. (2005). *Communication from the commission to the council and the European parliament. Winning the battle against global climate change*. COM (2005) 35, 9 February.

European Commission. (2006). *Communication from the commission to the council and the European parliament. Sustainable power generation from fossil fuels: Aiming for near-zero emissions from coal after 2020*. COM (2006) 843 final.

European Commission. (2007). *Commission staff working document. Accompanying document to the communication from the commission to the council and the European parliament. Sustainable power generation from fossil fuels: Aiming for near-zero emissions from coal after 2020. Impact Assessment*. SEC (2006) 1722, 10 January 2007.

European Commission. (2011). *Communication from the commission to the European parliament, the council, the European economic and social committee and the committee of the regions. Energy roadmap 2050*. COM (2011) 885 final, 15 December.

European Commission. (2013). *Communication from the commission to the European parliament, the council, the European economic and social committee and the committee of the regions on the future of carbon capture and storage in Europe*. COM (2013) 180 final, 27 March.

Fischer, C., & Newell, R. G. (2008). Environmental and technology policies for climate mitigation. *Journal of Environmental Economics and Management, 55*(2), 142–162.

Fligstein, N., & McAdam, D. (2012). *A theory of fields*. Oxford: Oxford University Press.

Geels, F. (2013). *Politics and power in low-carbon electricity transitions: A multi-level analysis of green niche-innovations and resilient regimes*. Ms prepared for Theory, Culture & Society.

International Energy Agency. (2013). *Tracking clean energy progress 2013*. Paris: International Energy Agency.

Larsen, O. M., & Ruud, A. (2005). *Coherence of environmental and innovation policies. A green innovation policy in Norway*. ProSus Report 05/04. Oslo: University of Oslo, ProSus.

Lockwood, M. (2008). *After the coal rush: Assessing the policy options for coal-fired power generation*. London: Institute for Public Policy Research.

Pahle, M. (2010). Germany's dash for coal: Exploring drivers and factors. *Energy Policy, 38*, 3431–3442.

Praetorius, B., & von Stechow, C. (2009). Electricity gap versus climate change: electricity politics and the potential role of CCS in Germany. In J. Meadowcroft & O. Langhelle (Eds.), *Caching the carbon: The politics and policy of carbon capture and storage* (pp. 125–157). Cheltenham: Edward Elgar.

Ricci, E., Bosetti, V., Baker, E., & Jenni K. (2014). From expert elicitations to integrated assessment: Future prospects of carbon capture technologies. Nota Di Lavoro 44.2014. Milan: Fondazione Eni Enrico Mattei.

Rogge, K., & Hoffmann, V. (2009). *The impact of the EU ETS on the sectoral innovation system for power generation technologies—findings for Germany*. Paper submitted to DIME workshop on "environmental innovation, industrial dynamics and entrepreneurship", 10–12 May 2009, Utrecht, Netherlands.

Schulz, M., Scheer, D., & Wassermann, S. (2010). Neue Technik, alte Pfade? Zur Akzeptanz der CO_2- Speicherung in Deutschland. *GAIA, 19*(4), 287–296.

Stangeland, A. (2007). A model for the CO_2 capture potential. *International Journal of Greenhouse Gas Control, 1*, 418–429.

Tjernshaugen, A. (2008). Political commitment to CO_2 capture and storage: Evidence from government RD&D budgets. *Mitigation and Adaptation Strategies for Global Change, 13*(1), 1–21.

Tjernshaugen, A. (2011). The growth of political support for CO_2 capture and storage in Norway. *Environmental Politics, 20*(2), 227–245.

Tjernshaugen, A., & Lee, H. (2004). *Shaming and framing: Norwegian nongovernmental organizations in the climate change negotiations*. CICERO Working Paper 2004:09, Oslo.

Tosun, J. (2013). How the EU handles uncertain risks: Understanding the role of the precautionary principle. *Journal of European Public Policy, 20*(10), 1517–1528.

Markussen, N. et al. (2012) A socio-technical framework for assessing the viability of carbon capture and storage technology. *Technological Forecasting and Social Change, 79*(5), 903–918.

Unruh, G. C. (2000). Understanding carbon lock-in. *Energy Policy, 28*(12), 817–830.

Unruh, G. C. (2002). Escaping carbon lock-in. *Energy Policy, 30*(4), 317–325.

van Alphen, C., van Ruijven, J., Kasa, S., Hekkert, M., & Turkenburg, W. (2009). The performance of the Norwegian carbon dioxide, capture and storage innovation system. *Energy Policy, 37*, 43–55.

Verbong, G. P. J., & Loorbach, D. (2012). *Governing the energy transition: Reality, illusion or necessity*? New York: Routledge.

Weimer-Jehle, W., Wassermann, S., & Fuchs, G. (2009). *Erstellung von Energie- und Innovationsszenarien mit der Cross-Impact-Bilanzanalyse: Internationalisierung von Innovationstrategien im Bereich der Kohlekraftwerkstechnologie*. Ms. 11. Symposium Energieinnovation Graz/Austria.

Chapter 12
Regulating Hydraulic Fracturing: The Effects of Issue Redefinition

Jale Tosun

Abstract The possibility of extracting shale gas using hydraulic fracturing on a large scale has invoked a public and political debate about the creation of an appropriate regulatory regime for such activities at the European level. The issues of shale gas extraction and the use of hydraulic fracturing were brought onto the EU policy agenda by the European Council. The policy image created by the European Council was a positive one, which linked shale gas production with the security of energy supply. The resulting policy process developed around a different policy image that highlighted the uncertain risks related to hydraulic fracturing in regard to human health and the environment. This redefinition of the policy image was primarily the result of the European Parliament's involvement in the policy process as well as the expansion of the political conflict over this issue. While the potential risks of hydraulic fracturing dominated the policy process, the overall outcome of the policy process was a mild reform of the existing legal basis. From this, it follows that issue redefinition certainly resulted in changes in the dynamics of the policy process but had limited effects on the outcome of this process.

12.1 Introduction: Agenda-Setting Via the High-Politics Route

Hydraulic fracturing—better known as fracking—is a process of drilling and injecting a mix of chemicals, sand and water into the ground at a high pressure in order to release natural gas inside rock formations (Rahm 2011; Davis 2012). It is an established and tested technology that has been used in small-scale conventional hydrocarbon extraction for three decades in several European countries including Denmark, Germany, Poland, Spain, Sweden, and the United Kingdom (European Parliament

J. Tosun (✉)
Institute of Political Science, Heidelberg University, Bergheimer Strasse 58, 69115 Heidelberg, Germany
e-mail: jale.tosun@ipw.uni-heidelberg.de

J. Tosun et al. (eds.), *Energy Policy Making in the EU*,
Lecture Notes in Energy 28, DOI 10.1007/978-1-4471-6645-0_12

2012a, p. 15). Recently, fracking methods have become more advanced and are now complemented by the technique of horizontal drilling, which encompasses the drilling of vertical wells with horizontal extensions. The combination of fracking with the technology of horizontal drilling increases the volume of shale gas extracted, thereby making it commercially viable (McGowan 2014, p. 44). The difference between conventional natural gas and shale gas stems from the deposits in which they are trapped. Shale gas is natural gas located in deep-shale deposits, which are sedimentary rocks with low permeability. Conventional gas is natural gas that has migrated to pools in permeable rocks (Joskow 2013).

In 2012, the major producers of shale gas were the United States and Canada with a share of shale gas in total natural gas production of 39 and 15 %, respectively.[1] Over the last decade, the expansion of natural gas production due to the use of fracking technology led to a sharp decrease in gas prices in the United States (Johnson and Boersma 2013, p. 390). This shale gas revolution resulted in an increased substitution of coal by natural gas, which affects not only the energy market in the United States but also beyond. In fact, the surplus coal produced in the United States has been exported to Europe where it has displaced more expensive natural gas as a feedstock for power generation, thereby increasing the EU's overall coal consumption (Aalto and Korkmaz-Temel 2014, p. 767).

The prospect of producing cheap gas has prompted other countries' interest in the production of shale gas by using fracking, including Europe—especially as gas consumption has continuously grown in Europe, turning international gas trading into an important component of Europe's energy security (see Herweg in Chap. 5, Ciambra and Solorio in Chap. 8 and Brutschin in Chap. 10). Natural gas imported from non-EU countries accounts for almost half of the Union's gas supply, with gas mostly coming in via pipelines from Russia, Algeria and Azerbaijan. The natural gas supply is backed up by imports of liquefied natural gas from Algeria, Qatar, Nigeria, Trinidad and Egypt (Weijermars et al. 2011, p. 403). What is important to note is that the development of European unconventional gas resources could, in principle, reduce the EU's growing dependency on imports (see Weijermars et al. 2011, p. 404).

This potential of shale gas has not gone unnoticed by European energy producers and policy makers. In March 2010, about twenty energy firms applied for shale gas research and exploration permits with the French government (Weile 2014, p. 12). Shortly after granting the permits, a group consisting of non-governmental organisations (NGOs), local politicians and members of the Greens/European Green Alliance group in the European Parliament as well as citizens protested against this decision.[2] The fracking opponents managed to produce a petition of more than 100,000 signatures, which was forwarded to the French

[1] Information retrieved from http://www.eia.gov/todayinenergy/detail.cfm?id=13491 (accessed on 26 April 2014).

[2] The following website is dedicated to the controversy surrounding shale gas and fracking in France and illustrates the web search of the term "shale gas" until May 2012: http://controverses.sciences-po.fr/climateblogs/shalegas/timeline/ (accessed on 5 July 2014).

parliament. The petition together with the prospect of the elections for the Senate to be held in September 2011—which is primarily chosen by municipal officials—prompted the French government to take action (Weile 2014, p. 12). As an immediate reaction the government instituted a moratorium and cancelled the exploration permits that were already granted for projects using fracking. In addition, they banned the exploration and exploitation of hydrocarbons by means of hydraulic fracturing (for an overview, see, e.g. Cournil 2013).

The extraction of shale gas and the use of fracking technology entered the EU's policy agenda at more or less the same time as the controversy taking place in France on 4 February 2011 when the European Council made the following statement:

> In order to further enhance its security of supply, Europe's potential for sustainable extraction and use of conventional and unconventional (shale gas and oil shale) fossil fuel resources should be assessed.

This statement could, in principle, have led to a policy process finishing with the adoption of legislation facilitating the use of fracking for the production of shale gas. Yet the actual policy process went into a different direction during which some actors advocated the adoption of a restrictive regulatory approach because of the public health and the environmental concerns associated with this activity (see, e.g. McKenzie et al. 2012; Johnson and Boersma 2013; McGowan 2014; Schirrmeister 2014). In fact, not only France but also Bulgaria instituted a ban on the use of fracking technology, and some actors have vocally expressed demands for an EU-wide ban of these activities. However, at the same time Poland is considered as one of the most promising areas endowed with shale gas in Europe and the Polish government is eager to take advantage of this resource endowment (Uliasz-Misiak et al. 2014, p. 69). Thus, the member states' stances on shale gas extraction and the use of fracking technology are quite diverse. The picture is complemented by a European Commission that at least initially appeared reluctant to propose new rules and a European Parliament that was eager to keep the issue on the policy agenda but failed to push through its preference for stricter regulation (see Bouzarovski and Petrova in Chap. 7).

This chapter aims to illuminate the political debate concerning fracking after it was brought onto the policy agenda by the European Council, that is, via the high-politics route (see Princen and Rhinard 2006; Alexandrova and Timmermans in Chap. 3). The main research interest lies not in the agenda-setting dynamics but the subsequent policy process. The focus on the policy process is motivated by the existence of a legal principle for dealing with situations in which the relationship between activities and their potential hazard cannot be established, which are situations related to uncertain risks: the precautionary principle (Tosun 2013a, b). Considering that the use of fracking technology is associated with a number of uncertain risks, it should be instructive to see to what extent this principle has been used to shape the policy process and its outcome. As a matter of fact, one of the main findings is that the precautionary principle was not invoked in a systematic fashion by the proponents of stricter regulation. Furthermore, the chapter shows that agenda-setting via the high-politics route does not necessarily lead to substantial policy change. In light of the growing legal competencies of the EU in the field of energy policy (see, e.g. Tosun and Solorio 2011; Tosun et al. in Chap. 1; Biesenbender in Chap. 2), this finding in particular yields important insights for policy making in the EU's multilevel polity.

What are the characteristics of the policy process concerning the issue of shale gas extraction by using fracking technology? And what role has the precautionary principle played in it? These are the research questions that guide this chapter. The next section introduces concepts of attention, actors and images as the main components of policy agenda-setting theory and the theoretical underpinning of this study. Section 12.3 introduces the precautionary principle and explains how it can affect EU policy making. Section 12.4 then outlines the characteristics of the policy process. Section 12.5 discusses the policy process in light of the policy agenda-setting theory. Section 12.6 summarises the key findings and presents some concluding remarks.

12.2 Attention, Actors and Images

Studies of agenda-setting typically concentrate on one of the two following perspectives. The first one is the question about how exactly a certain issue enters the decision-making agenda. This literature strand primarily addresses the extent to which mass media (co-)determine the political agenda (see, e.g. Walgrave et al. 2008; van Aelst and Walgrave 2011). The second perspective concentrates on the effects of the various forms of agenda shaping for the policy process that follows the placement of an issue on the agenda (see, e.g. Engeli et al. 2012a; Tosun 2013a). This study follows the second perspective and derives expectations about the policy process based on three elements: attention, actors and images. These elements are derived from Engeli et al. (2012b, pp. 9–10), who build on the work of Schattschneider (1960) and Baumgartner and Jones (1993).[3]

The main assumption of the model is that the policy process is determined by the underlying political conflicts over a given issue. In this context, the first factor that needs to be taken into account is the level of both public and political attention given to certain issues. The higher the level of attention—or politicisation—given to an issue, the more controversial is the policy process that follows initial agenda-setting.

[3] For the sake of completeness, it should be noted that Engeli et al. (2012b) introduce another element—that is, institutional venues—, which, however, for the case at hand is deemed irrelevant.

Attention is closely connected to the number and types of actors that are involved in the conflict definition of an issue. Usually, issues of low attention are characterised by the participation of a limited group of actors in the policy process, and politicised issues are characterised by the involvement of more actors. Different types of actors typically have different preferences regarding the outcome of the policy process, which leads to controversial politics.

The third element refers to the image of the issue concerned. The public policy literature usually addresses the image of issues under the heading of problem definition (see, e.g. Knill and Tosun 2012, pp. 98–106). One of the frequently used concepts of problem definition is provided by Stone (1989, p. 282). Accordingly, problem definition refers to a causal story which identifies harm, describes what causes the harm, assigns blame to those causing it and claims that the government is responsible for stopping the activity in question. Put simply, issue images are about a certain perspective from which issues are seen and about the exclusion of alternative views (Engeli et al. 2012b, p. 9). The process by which these images are generated is known as framing (Knill and Tosun 2012, p. 102).

While it is plausible that these three elements define conflict around particular issues, the theoretical model put forward by Engeli et al. (2012b) does not clarify the relationship among them. The definition of the issue image can be the result of new actors entering the stage. This latter perspective is adopted by Princen (2011), who argues that strategies of gaining attention involve directing issues towards the 'right' venue in order to mobilise (potential) supporters and framing the issue in the 'appropriate' way in order to arouse interest in it. The very image of an issue can lead to the involvement of a broader group of actors. In a similar vein, higher attention can result in the expansion of the actor constellation, as can the emergence of new actors raise the level of politicisation. The problem that causality can go in both ways for each pair of factors and their combination cannot be resolved here. Fortunately, however, this flaw does not threaten the validity of the theoretical argument to be made.

This study contends that the issue of shale gas production by using fracking was redefined by the involvement of the European Parliament in the policy process. While the European Council linked shale gas production with the issue of securing energy supply, the European Parliament managed to bring about a political debate that focused more narrowly on the issue of fracking and the risks associated with it (Bomberg 2013). At the same time, it argues that issue redefinition mostly affected the policy process but had a limited impact only on the outcome of this process (see Bouzarovski and Petrova in Chap. 7). The reason for this is that the actors supporting stricter regulation lacked internal cohesion regarding their preferences for the design of the new EU policy measure addressing fracking, which weakened their position in the policy process. As a consequence, the actors' preferences need to be better integrated in agenda-shaping theory in order to provide for a more complete explanation of the consequences of agenda shaping for the policy process and its outcome.

12.3 The Precautionary Principle as a Basis for Regulatory Action

The precautionary principle provides an opportunity for policy makers to propose and adopt policies before an uncertain risk materialises and even in the absence of scientific evidence. By legitimising anticipatory policy intervention, the precautionary principle seeks to circumvent unwarranted harm from absent or belated responses to uncertainty and risk (Eckley and Selin 2004, p. 79). It is an abstract legal principle that is implemented through policy making (see, e.g. Fisher et al. 2006; Van Asselt and Vos 2008; Aven and Renn 2010; Zander 2010; Tosun 2013b); it can therefore produce a whole range of different policy responses (Tosun 2013a).

The EU formally adopted the precautionary principle with the Maastricht Treaty (see, e.g. O'Riordan and Jordan 1995; Löfstedt 2004; De Sadeleer 2006; Zander 2010). It is laid out in Article 191(2) of the Treaty on the Functioning of the EU as a provision for taking action in the field of environmental protection. Thanks to case law (Löfstedt 2004; Alemanno 2007), the scope of application has been extended to any situation

> where scientific evidence is insufficient, inconclusive or uncertain and there are indications through preliminary objective scientific evaluation that there are reasonable grounds for concern that the potentially dangerous effects on the environment, human, animal or plant health may be inconsistent with the chosen level of protection (European Commission 2000, pp. 9–10).

The application of the precautionary principle shall be (1) proportional to the chosen level of protection, (2) non-discriminatory, (3) consistent with comparable measures already in place, (4) based on a cost-benefit analysis of action and non-action, (5) subject to review when new scientific data becomes available and (6) facilitate the production the scientific evidence necessary for a more comprehensive risk assessment (European Commission 2000, p. 3). The EU institutions apply the precautionary principle when they propose policies and decide on the correct implementation of EU law by the member states with regard to uncertain risks. In a complementary vein, the member states can make recourse to the precautionary principle when adopting national policies that deviate from EU rules (Zander 2010: 2; see also Tosun 2013a, b).

The precautionary principle can be used to modify the EU's legal framework that is applicable to hydraulic fracturing since there is uncertainty about potential health and environmental impacts. Furthermore, the European Commission (2012a p. 2) explicitly recognises the following:

> EU action is justified, because impacts can be not only local and regional but also have cross-cutting, transboundary environmental implications: impacts to surface and groundwaters, as well as to air quality do not respect national borders so that impacts in one country can give rise to, or worsen pollution problems in other countries.

Fracking is associated with the contamination of groundwater supplies, resulting from the migration of chemicals used for the shale gas extraction. Moreover, energy companies typically do not disclose the chemical ingredients used in hydraulic fracturing as they regard them as trade secrets (Davis 2012, p. 180). This makes it challenging to assess the degree to which the fluids used for hydraulic fracturing contain toxic compounds. It is also problematic that large amounts of water must be withdrawn from underground aquifers in order to utilise this technology. The list of problems is complemented by other potential environmental hazards related to fugitive methane emissions, anthropogenic seismicity, noise pollution and land use (Johnson and Boersma 2013, pp. 391–393). In fact, the public debate on fracking in some member states has almost exclusively focused on the uncertainty about potential hazards related to this activity. In the case of Germany, Schirrmeister (2014, p. 6) shows that opponents of this technology were eager to depict it as "something new that needs further evaluation of its potential chances and risks".

In light of the general uncertainty surrounding fracking, proponents of new measures to adapt European law to the specificities of unconventional fossil fuel projects could have referred to the precautionary principle. In this way, they would have had a legal basis for proposing stricter regulation (see Zander 2010, p. 2). Therefore, the expectation put forward here is that the proponents of stricter regulation redefined the issues of shale gas extraction and fracking in such a way that they were characterised by risk and uncertainty in a view to justify regulatory action on the basis of the precautionary principle (see Tosun 2013b). From this perspective, issue redefinition in the case at hand should not only yield consequences for agenda shaping but also for the policy process since the precautionary principle legitimises anticipatory regulatory action. Put differently, redefining an issue to be able to invoke the precautionary principle represents a most-likely case of influencing the policy outcome by means of issue redefinition. Consequently, if issue redefinition does not affect the policy outcome in this specific case, it seems unlikely that it will do so in other cases.

12.4 Characteristics and Outcome of the Policy Process

While the issue of shale gas production was first placed on the EU policy agenda in February 2011 by the European Council, the European Commission was vital in stabilising the agenda by means of the *Energy Roadmap 2050*. In this document, the European Commission (2011, p. 12) recognises the potential of shale gas and other unconventional gas sources and argues that—together with internal market integration (see Herweg in Chap. 5, Ciambra and Solorio in Chap. 8 and Brutschin in Chap. 10)—the use of these sources "could relax concerns on gas import dependency".

During the preparation of the *Energy Roadmap 2050*—which started in March 2011—the European Commission commissioned a legal assessment of the EU environmental regulatory framework applying to shale gas practices. On 27 January 2012, the Energy Commissioner, Guenther Oettinger presented the study prepared by the law firm Philippe & Partners entitled *Unconventional Gas in Europe*. Based on a sample of four member states (France, Germany, Poland and Sweden), the study concluded that there are no significant gaps in coverage in the existing EU legislative framework, at least for regulating the current level of shale gas activities (Philippe & Partners 2011, p. 102). Based on this conclusion, Guenther Oettinger stated that there would be no need to change EU legislation (McGowan 2014, p. 52).

Yet it must be emphasised that the interpretation of the study's conclusions was not as straightforward as claimed by Guenther Oettinger. The European Parliament group of the Greens/European Green Alliance (2012) pointed out in an open letter to the Energy Commissioner that the study itself qualified its own findings . In fact, the study concludes that there "is no reason for complacency, since this assessment explicitly refers to the current level of experience and scale of operations as can be expected during the exploration phase" (Philippe & Partners 2011, p. 102). The authors further emphasise that shale gas production on a larger scale will require further investigations about the

> appropriateness of the regulatory framework(s) – both on EU as well as on Member State and/or regional level", and may entail "some adjustments to legislation [...] in order to improve its appropriateness and practicability with a view of regulating shale gas activities" (Philippe & Partners 2011, p. 102).

The study prepared for the European Commission was already part of requests it had received to clarify the EU legal framework that is applicable to hydraulic fracturing and to conclude whether that legal framework is appropriate (European Commission 2012a, p. 1). The European Parliament's Committee for Environment, Public Health and Food Safety had adopted its own initiative report, which called on the European Commission to introduce an EU-wide risk management framework. This call was based on a study by Lechtenböhmer et al. (2011), which highlighted a number of potential drawbacks of the EU's environmental legal framework applicable to hydraulic fracturing (European Commission 2012a, p. 1). One of the drawbacks identified was that there was a too high threshold for environmental impact assessments to be carried out on hydraulic fracturing activities. This indicates that the European Parliament was as important as the European Commission for stabilising the policy agenda concerning shale gas production by using fracking.

As a reaction to the open letter signed by nine members of the Greens/European Green Alliance group and because of the interest of market players and broader public concern (European Commission 2012a), the European Commission decided to gather more information in order to determine whether or not the level of environment and human health protection provided by the applicable EU regulatory framework is appropriate. It commissioned three additional studies, which should address the potential impacts of EU shale gas developments on the EU's energy market, on climate change and on the environment. Of these, the third study that specifically assessed the environmental risks raised a number of questions regarding the adequacy of the EU regulatory framework (European Commission 2012a, p. 1).

From the press release published on the occasion of the presentation of the three studies, one can infer that the European Commission (2012b) pursued two goals by commissioning the studies. First, by stressing that the studies would inform ongoing work examining the need for a risk management framework for shale gas developments in Europe, the European Commission could signal its commitment to evidence-based policy making.[4] Second, the European Commission used the presentation of the studies to launch a public consultation process with the member states and the stakeholders. In this way, the European Commission could demonstrate its willingness to broaden the set of actors involved in the policy process and to practice 'inclusive governance' (Bomberg 2014).

In November 2012, the European Parliament's Committee on Industry, Research and Energy and the Committee on Energy and Environment, Public Health and Food Safety both adopted resolutions according to which a "robust regulatory regime" would be needed for all shale gas activities, including fracking (European Parliament 2012b). Resolutions are not legally binding, but they suggest a political desire to act in a given policy area. While the European Parliament generally accepted each member states' right to exploit energy resources, the resolutions emphasised the need for creating a regulatory level playing field in line with the EU safety and environmental protection legislative framework. While the resolution adopted by the Committee on Industry, Research and Energy is generally more supportive to shale gas development than the resolution of the Committee on Energy and Environment, Public Health and Food Safety (McGowan 2014, p. 52), it still calls on the European Commission to take the necessary steps to prevent harm to the public and the environment.

All in all, by the adoption of the two resolutions the European Parliament supported the European Commission's strategy of increasing the scientific knowledge base regarding shale gas extraction and hydraulic fracturing. However, what the majority of the European Parliament could not agree on was an amendment urging the member states not to authorise any new fracking operations in the EU; it was rejected by 391 votes to 262, with 37 abstentions (European Parliament 2012b). This suggests that the European Parliament's position as a whole was not as clear as one might have expected recalling how actively it had called for action (see McGowan 2014).

When the European Parliament adopted the resolutions, the European Commission was right in the middle of organising the public consultation process, which took place from 20 December 2012 until 23 March 2013. This process involved the member states and third countries through a technical working group on the environmental aspects of shale gas production. In parallel, the hydrocarbons industry, industry associations, NGOs and the general public were consulted via an Internet-based public consultation (European Commission 2012a, p. 5). 22,875 respondents participated in the Internet-based consultation. Responses came from 22,122 individual respondents and 753 institutional respondents (covering 696 organisations). More than 90 % of citizen responses came from five EU countries:

[4] For an empirical assessment of how the European Commission uses scientific expertise, see Rimkutė and Haverland (2014).

Poland, France, Romania, Spain and Germany. The institutional respondents covered 696 organisations, mostly companies (33 % of all institutions) and NGOs (32 %). The majority of respondents (more than 50 %) from many EU countries believed that unconventional fossil fuels should not be developed in Europe at all.[5] Respondents from Poland are the most favourable ones to unconventional fossil fuels, with more than 59 % of respondents believing that unconventional fossil fuels should be developed in Europe anyway. A majority of respondents (more than 50 %) in most EU countries (all except for Poland, Romania and Slovenia) stated that the current framework is not appropriate to address the identified challenges and risks (BIO Intelligence Service 2013).

In the next stage, the European Commission organised an open stakeholder meeting on 7 June 2013 in Brussels to present the results of the online consultation. The discussion covered, inter alia, the need for overall planning and site selection, operational aspects and community impacts of shale gas exploration and exploitation. In particular, questions related to the disclosure of chemicals, strategic planning, baseline monitoring, geological conditions, well integrity and health issues were touched upon.[6]

Then, in September 2013 the European Commission published another study prepared by Milieu Ltd. (2013) on the regulatory provisions governing key aspects of unconventional gas development in Bulgaria, Denmark, Germany, Lithuania, Poland, Romania, Spain and the United Kingdom. The study revealed that there are

> a number of potential regulatory gaps and legal uncertainties, but also areas where the current legislation may be deemed sufficient to cover the specific impacts of unconventional gas exploration and exploitation (Milieu Ltd. 2013, p. 7).

The study showed that the member states rely mainly on the general mining, hydrocarbons and environmental legislation and its related permitting procedure transposing the EU legislation to regulate such activities and very few of them were found to have adopted specific requirements (Milieu Ltd. 2013, p. 77). Thus, with this study the previous assessment of the European Commission based on the study prepared by Philippe & Partners (2011) stating that the member states possessed appropriate regulatory frameworks finally became rejected.

On 9 October 2013, the European Parliament tightly voted in favour of an amendment to Directive 2011/92/EU of the European Parliament and the Council of 13 December 2011 on the assessment of the effects of certain public and private projects on the environment, known as the environmental impact assessment directive (for an overview, see Ederli 2014). This directive defines certain criteria, including the information that must be submitted to national authorities for a project to be assessed for approval. The amendment required environmental impact

---

[5] Austria, Belgium, Bulgaria, Cyprus, Czech Republic, Denmark, Estonia, Finland, France, Germany, Greece, Ireland, Italy, Latvia, Luxembourg, Malta, the Netherlands, Romania, Slovak Republic, Spain, Sweden, and the United Kingdom.

[6] Information retrieved from http://ec.europa.eu/environment/integration/energy/uff_event_7june2013_en.htm (accessed on 26 April 2014).

assessments to be performed for all shale gas and other unconventional drilling activities, thereby removing the discretion that member states previously had as to whether or not to require a full environmental impact assessment as part of the permitting process for certain projects. With 332 votes to 311 and 14 abstentions, the Member of European Parliament (MEP), Andrea Zanoni (Alliance of Liberals and Democrats for Europe) was granted the mandate to negotiate a first-reading agreement with the EU ministers (European Parliament 2013). The initiative of the European Parliament was supported by the Committee of Regions (2013).

Altogether, the European Commission was confronted with demands for tightening the regulatory framework for fracking activities by the European Parliament and environmental NGOs, who participated in the public consultation process as well as the Committee of Regions. As concerns the European Council, at its meeting on 22 May 2013, it repeated the importance of the goal of securing the energy supply. In the conclusions of the European Council meeting, shale gas production is not mentioned explicitly, but it is stated that "guidelines set by the European Council in February 2011 remain valid and must continue to be implemented […]".

The European Commission responded to the call for EU action by adopting a Recommendation on 22 January 2014, which invites the member states to follow minimum principles when applying or adapting their legislation applicable to hydrocarbons exploration or production using high volume hydraulic fracturing. Member states are also invited to inform the European Commission annually about measures taken. The Recommendation includes a review clause to assess the effectiveness of this approach. The Recommendation was accompanied by a Communication outlining the potential new opportunities and challenges stemming from shale gas extraction in Europe, as well as an Impact Assessment that examined the socio-economic and environmental impacts of various policy options.[7] While with this approach and the documents published, the European Commission keeps open the possibility to propose further legal clarification in the future, the adoption of a legally non-binding Recommendation in order to respond to the various calls is a remarkably mild reform, especially considering the pains the European Commission had taken to engage in a broad fact-finding and consultation mission. In fact, the European Commission (2012a, p. 2) stated that different legal approaches in the member states would increase the risk of deficiencies in transboundary environmental protection as well as undermine the functioning of the internal market due to unlevel playing fields.

What was the outcome of the European Parliament's initiative? To recall, the European Parliament demanded in its two resolutions adopted in November 2012 that the emergence of shale gas production required "robust regulatory regimes" (European Parliament 2012b). On 12 March 2014, the European Parliament adopted its first reading position to the revised environmental impact assessment

[7] Following Reh et al. (2013) EU policy makers tend to choose this informal arena when redistributive and salient acts are concerned.

directive with 528 votes to 135 and 15 abstentions. While introducing tougher rules on exposing the environmental impact of oil and conventional gas exploration, the requirement of mandatory environmental impact assessments for the extraction and exploration of shale gas was removed from the text. This was the outcome of the trilogue talks—that is, informal negotiations—in which the European Parliament had entered with the Council of Ministers and the European Commission in autumn 2013.[8] These informal negotiations typically take place before the European Parliament issues its formal opinion and before the Council of Ministers adopts its common position (Reh et al. 2013, p. 1119). In this context, Häge and Kaeding (2007) argue that the European Parliament usually has an advantage in such negotiations relative to the Council of Ministers thereby having higher impact on the content of legislation. Yet, the case at hand challenges this argument. Since agreement was reached in the trilogue talks, the approval of the European Parliament's position went smoothly on 14 April 2014 in the Council of Ministers.

Table 12.1 gives an overview of how cohesively the MEPs from the individual member states voted. Perfect cohesion by all MEPs can only be observed in those cases when a vote in favour of the proposal was cast (Bulgaria, Croatia, Hungary, Lithuania, Malta, Poland, Slovenia, and Slovakia). This empirical picture is remarkable since not all MEPs from one member state belong to the same factions, indicating that national considerations might have played a role in the voting decisions (see, e.g. Mühlböck 2012 for a more general discussion). Then, there are the MEPs from Austria and Ireland who mostly voted against the proposal . In this context, the voting of the Irish MEPs is particularly interesting since seven of them voted against the majority of their parliamentary groups (for an overview, see Ederli 2014).

To provide the complete picture, Table 12.2 presents the voting by parliamentary groups. The table shows that cohesion was very high among the members of the European Conservatives and Reformists, the European People's Party and the Greens–European Free Alliance. However, also four MEPs of the latter group voted against the majority vote in the group and therefore for the proposal: two of them come from the United Kingdom, one from Belgium and one from Denmark.

All in all, in light of the findings of the studies commissioned both by the European Commission and the European Parliament, the actual outcome of the policy process is surprisingly moderate. Even though the policy process involved a large number of actors, it must be stated that it was controversial only in the very early phase when the European Commission decided to "play down the role that shale gas might play in European market" (McGowan 2014, p. 52).

However, in the course of the policy process, the positions of the European Commission and the European Parliament converged and so there was reason to expect that more ambitious legislation would be brought on the way. The European

[8] Information retrieved from http://ec.europa.eu/environment/integration/energy/unconventional_en.htm (accessed on 26 April 2014).

Table 12.1 Voting in the European Parliament by member state

Member state	For	Against	Abstention	Total present	Cohesion
Austria	8	10	1	19	28.95
Belgium	15	3	1	19	68.42
Bulgaria	17	0	0	17	100
Croatia	12	0	0	12	100
Cyprus	4	2	0	6	50
Czech Republic	17	0	2	19	84.21
Denmark	7	1	0	8	81.25
Estonia	5	1	0	6	75
Finland	7	3	1	11	45.45
France	36	22	4	62	37.1
Germany	67	26	0	93	58.06
Greece	13	3	1	17	64.71
Hungary	20	0	0	20	100
Ireland	3	9	0	12	62.5
Italy	55	1	1	57	94.74
Latvia	8	1	0	9	83.33
Lithuania	10	0	0	10	100
Luxembourg	5	1	0	6	75
Malta	4	0	0	4	100
Netherlands	14	10	0	24	37.5
Poland	42	0	0	42	100
Portugal	17	5	0	22	65.91
Romania	24	1	3	28	78.57
Slovakia	12	0	0	12	100
Slovenia	7	0	0	7	100
Spain	35	17	0	52	50.96
Sweden	14	5	0	19	60.53
United Kingdom	50	14	1	65	65.38

Notes Own elaboration based on data provided by www.votewatch.eu

Parliament's agreement to the modified proposal for the revision of the environmental impact directive can be explained by the need to coordinate its legislative activity with the European Council. In the European Council, there is no member state really pushing for tighter regulatory standards at the EU level (see Jacobs in Chap. 6, Ciambra and Solorio in Chap. 8 and Cox and Dekanozishvili in Chap. 9) —not even France. At the same time, shale gas production is foreseen in some EU countries including Poland and the United Kingdom (see Bomberg 2013). It appears that the member states do not push for stricter EU-wide rules when it is not clear at this point what the true commercial potential of shale gas production is.

Table 12.2 Voting in the European Parliament by group

Group	For	Against	Abstention	Present	Cohesion
Alliance of liberals and democrats for europe (ALDE)	69	7	1	77	84.42
European conservatives and reformists (ECR)	44	0	2	46	93.48
Europe of freedom and democracy (EFD)	16	8	2	26	42.31
European people's party (EPP)	222	10	3	235	91.7
The Greens–European free alliance (Greens–EFA)	4	51	0	55	89.09
European United Left–Nordic Green Left (GUE-NGL)	6	27	0	33	72.73
Non-inscrits (NI)	14	11	6	31	17.74
Progressive alliance of socialists and democrats (S&D)	153	21	1	175	81.14

Notes Own elaboration based on data provided by www.votewatch.eu

12.5 Linking the Policy Process to Theory

Section 12.2 introduced the concepts of attention, actors and images, which are now applied to explaining the policy process subsequent to agenda-setting. The issue of shale gas extraction by using hydraulic fracturing has initially received attention by the European Council, which then called upon the European Commission to assess the legal and practical feasibility of shale gas extraction. The political attention level was enhanced and sustained by the European Parliament, which managed to redefine the issue as one that entailed risks to human health and the environment (Bomberg 2013). Without the European Parliament's involvement, the attention the European Commission paid particularly at the beginning of the policy process may have subsided. From this perspective, the European Parliament as an actor that succeeded in redefining shale gas extraction from an issue of securing energy supply to one connected to risks helped to increase and maintain the political and public attention with this topic is well in line with the model put forward by Engeli et al. (2012b). As a result, the plausibility of the theoretical reasoning of that model can be confirmed.

However, the model suggests that in such constellations the policy process should also become more controversial (see, e.g. Chap. 11 by Fuchs for an example). This cannot be confirmed for the case at hand. Only at the very early stage, there was a division between the view of the European Commission and that of the European Parliament. Once noticing the degree of public concern and realising the negative impact of an unclear regulatory situation for the market players, the European Commission engaged in gathering information to check the appropriateness of the EU's relevant legal framework. These efforts were accompanied by the European Parliament's continued calls for tougher regulation. In light of the various steps the European Commission has taken steps to better understand the potential negative effects of fracking, it is rather surprising that it eventually only adopted voluntary measures that aim at inducing the member states to define some minimum criteria. Even more surprising is the mild revision of the environmental impact assessment directive which the MEPs adopted.

The responses of both actors appear even less ambitious when considering that the EU offers a legal basis for adopting stricter regulatory standards in a situation marked by uncertain risks: the precautionary principle. In its resolution, the Committee on the Environment, Public Health and Food Safety (European Parliament 2012a, p. 6) makes recourse to the precautionary principle by stating that

> it is essential that the precautionary and the polluter pays principles are applied to any future decisions about the development of fossil fuel resources in Europe, taking into account potential impacts from all stages of the exploration and exploitation process.

Nonetheless, the actors—especially the MEPs—made only sporadic reference to this principle and also abstained from using it to demand regulatory actions. As a result, the principle did not result in the proposing and adoption of stricter regulation. This finding has important implications for both the literature on agenda-setting and research on the use of the precautionary principle. Concerning agenda-setting, this study clearly shows that high levels of attention do not necessarily lead to major policy change. For this to happen, the proponents of policy change need to have a coherent view of how the modified policy arrangements should look like, which is a condition in line with the veto player approach (Tsebelis 2002). In regards to the precautionary principle, this study again supports the view that the precautionary principle can only lead to stricter regulatory standards if there is a sufficiently cohesive group of proponents as with any other policy measure (Tosun 2013b). If this is not the case, the precautionary principle will only play a marginal role in policy making. Put differently, this study shows that the precautionary principle does not automatically lead to the adoption of stricter regulatory standards.

Based on the findings presented, the model by Engeli et al. (2012b) could be seminally developed further by including considerations about the internal coherence in the individual actor groups' preferences. The analysis has shown that MEPs from some member states did not support the call for stricter regulation. Consequently, the power of the European Parliament vis-à-vis the other EU institutions in the policy process was diminished. Of course, considerations about preference coherence are not essential for explaining the agenda-setting process per se, but they are helpful for making more precise predictions about the outcomes of the policy process.

12.6 Conclusion

The issue of shale gas extraction by using hydraulic fracturing has entered the EU policy agenda at the European Council meeting in February 2011. Technological progress opening up the possibility to extract unconventional fossil fuels in order to diversify EU energy supply and positive economic effects of shale gas production in the United States were preconditions for agenda-setting (European Commission 2012a, p. 1). In response to the European Council's (2011) statement to explore "Europe's potential for sustainable extraction and use of conventional and unconventional (shale gas and oil shale) fossil fuel", the European Commission started to take action and so did the European Parliament.

The strategies of the two actors were obviously very different—at least at the very beginning of the policy process. The European Commission was eager to downplay the potentially harmful effects of fracking, whereas the European Parliament managed to redefine this issue as an uncertain risk and made recourse to the precautionary principle, albeit to a limited degree (see also Bomberg 2014). Interestingly, despite the different goals, both actors relied on expert opinions and used commissioned reports to justify their most preferred courses of action.

All in all, the policy process was characterised by high attention levels, the involvement of different groups of actors at different levels of government and the need to reconcile the variety of—not very well defined—preferences expressed in regard to the regulation of hydraulic fracturing. Despite the high attention levels, the policy process was only controversial at the very beginning of the policy process. The European Commission soon realised that it had to react to public concerns. This culminated in efforts taken by both the European Commission and the European Parliament to assess whether or not the level of environment and human health protection provided by the applicable EU regulatory framework is appropriate. The European Commission even launched a public consultation process to involve more actors. Despite the accordance of the studies conducted on behalf of these two institutions, they both came up with mild proposals. Thus, in terms of the overall outcome of the policy process, the rules have been very moderately tightened by the adoption of a Recommendation by the European Commission in January 2014 that invites the member states to follow minimum principles and requirement of mandatory environmental impact assessments for oil and conventional gas exploration, which does not explicitly refer to shale gas production.

While the European Commission has from the very beginning been rather hesitant to tighten the relevant EU regulatory framework, the European Parliament's behaviour is rather surprising considering its constant calls for stricter regulation. This finding can be explained by the substantial opposition within the European Parliament to a more ambitious reform. In fact, the voting of the MEPs shows that national considerations were important (see, e.g. Ederli 2014). In this context, the voting of the Irish MEPs displays some signs of a nationally rather than ideologically determined preferences. Future research is invited to address this issue. Thus, given the incoherence in the policy preferences of the European Parliament, it becomes clear why the outcome has been such a modest one, especially since the European Parliament had to reach agreement with the Council.

This study provides numerous insights that especially relate to the case of hydraulic fracturing in the context of shale gas projects but also help to improve our understanding of policy processes subsequent to agenda-setting. Most importantly, this chapter has shown that agenda-setting via the high-politics route does not necessarily lead to major policy reform. So even though the high-politics route of agenda-setting is important, it is difficult to determine the consequences for the policy process. This is how this chapter relates to the analyses presented in Chap. 2 by Biesenbender and Chap. 3 by Alexandrova and Timmermans. Then, it ties into the study presented by Fuchs in Chap. 11 by underlining that the precautionary principle has played a marginal role in this particular policy process, which corresponds to the author's analysis of the adoption of the CCS technology at the EU level. In the past, the precautionary principle has been used to justify rather strict regulatory decisions (Tosun 2013a, b), and critics such as Sunstein (2005) have even argued that it might stimulate 'policy over-reactions' (see Maor 2014). In this context, other academic observers have pointed out that the use of the precautionary principle depends on the respective preferences of the actors (see, e.g. Caduff and Bernauer 2006). This latter view can be confirmed on the basis of this study.

In closing, it is important to point out the increasing attention paid to the security of energy supply in the EU. While current EU energy policy mostly reflects the commitment to mitigating climate change, it is conceivable that in the future priority is given to questions about the security of supply. In fact, the Russia–Ukraine crisis of 2014 has widely been regarded as a reminder that the security of energy supply is not guaranteed (see Brutschin in Chap. 10). Consequently, it is possible that the issue of shale gas production might be redefined one more time in the near future in order to bring it back to the original image created by the European Council.

Acknowledgments The research leading to this chapter has received funding from the project entitled "Agenda Setting in European Energy Policy: Actors, Preferences and Strategies" funded by the Fritz Thyssen Foundation (Grant Number: Az. 10.13.2.141).

References

Alemanno, A. (2007). *The shaping of the precautionary principle by European Courts: From scientific uncertainty to legal certainty*. Bocconi legal studies research paper.

Aalto, P., & Korkmaz Temel, D. (2014). European energy security: Natural gas and the integration process. *Journal of Common Market Studies, 52*(4), 758–774.

Aven, T., & Renn, O. (2010). *Risk management and governance*. Heidelberg: Springer.

Baumgartner, F. R., & Jones, B. D. (1993). *Agendas and instability in American politics*. Chicago: University of Chicago Press.

BIO Intelligence Service. (2013). *Analysis and presentation of the results of the public consultation unconventional fossil fuels (e.g. shale gas) in Europe*. Final report prepared for European Commission DG environment. Brussels: European Commission.

Bomberg, E. (2013). *The comparative politics of fracking: Networks and framing in the US and Europe*. APSA 2013 Annual meeting paper, American political science association 2013 annual meeting. http://ssrn.com/abstract=2301196.

Bomberg, E. (2014). Shale governance in the European Union: Principles and practice. *Issues in Energy and Environmental Policy, 15*. http://closup.umich.edu.

Caduff, L., & Bernauer, T. (2006). Managing risk and regulation in European food safety governance. *Review of Policy Research, 23*(1), 153–168.

Committee of the Regions. (2013). Fracking: Local and regional authorities call for compulsory environmental impact assessments. Press Release CoR/13/93.en.

Cournil, C. (2013). Adoption of legislation on shale gas in france: Hesitation and/or progress? *European Energy and Environmental Law Review, 22*(4), 141–151.

Davis, C. (2012). The politics of "fracking": Regulating natural gas drilling practices in Colorado and Texas. *Review of Policy Research, 29*(2), 177–191.

De Sadeleer, N. (2006). The precautionary principle in EC health and environmental law. *European Law Journal, 12*(2), 139–172.

Eckley, N., & Selin, H. (2004). All talk, little action: Precaution and its effects on European chemicals regulation. *Journal of European Public Policy, 11*(1), 78–105.

Ederli, L. (2014). *Die Novellierung der europäischen Umweltverträglichkeitsprüfungs-Richtlinie [The reform of the European environmental impact assessment directive].* Heidelberg (Unpublished Manuscript).

Engeli, I., Green-Pedersen, C., & Larsen, L. T. (Eds.). (2012a). *Morality politics in Western Europe*. Basingstoke: Palgrave Macmillan.

Engeli, I., Green-Pedersen, C., & Larsen, L. T. (2012b). Theoretical perspectives on morality politics. In I. Engeli, C. Green-Pedersen & L. T. Larsen (Eds.), *Morality politics in Western Europe* (pp. 5–26). Basingstoke: Palgrave Macmillan.

European Commission. (2000). *Communication from the commission on the precautionary principle*. Brussels, 2 February 2000. Commission of the European Communities. COM(2000) 1.

European Commission. (2011). *A Roadmap for moving to a competitive low carbon economy in 2050*. Ref. COM (2011) 112 final. Brussels, 8 March 2011.

European Commission. (2012a). *Roadmap: Environmental assessment framework to enable a safe and secure unconventional hydrocarbon (e.g. shale gas) extraction*. Brussels: European Commission.

European Commission (2012b). *Midday express of 2012-09-07 news from the European Commission's midday briefing*.

European Council. (2011). *Conclusions of the Presidency*. EUCO 2/11. Brussels: European Council.

European Parliament. (2012a). *European Parliament resolution of 21 November 2012 on the environmental impacts of shale gas and shale oil extraction activities*. 2011/2308(INI). Strasbourg: European Parliament.

European Parliament. (2012b). *Shale gas: Member states need robust rules on fracking, say MEPs*. Press release energy 21 November 2012.

European Parliament. (2013). *Shale gas: New fracking projects must pass environmental test*. Press release environment 9 October 2013.

Fisher, E., Jones, J., & von Schomberg, R. (Eds.). (2006). *Implementing the precautionary principle: Perspectives and prospects*. Cheltenham: Edward Elgar.

Greens/European Green (2012). Open letter. http://www.greens-efa.eu/fileadmin/dam/Images/Topics/Energy_and_transport/Letter%20to%20Commissioner%20Oettinger.pdf. Accessed 26 April 2014.

Häge, F. M., & Kaeding, M. (2007). Reconsidering the European Parliament's legislative influence: Formal vs. informal procedures. *Journal of European Integration, 29*(3), 341–361.

Johnson, C., & Boersma, T. (2013). Energy (in) security in Poland the case of shale gas. *Energy Policy, 53*(1), 389–399.

Joskow, P. L. (2013). Natural gas: From shortages to abundance in the United States. *The American Economic Review, 103*(3), 338–343.

Knill, C., & Tosun, J. (2012). *Public policy: A new introduction*. Basingstoke: Palgrave Macmillan.

Lechtenböhmer, S., Altmann, M., Capito, S., Matra, Z., Weindrorf, W., & Zittel, W. (2011). *Impacts of shale gas and shale oil extraction on the environment and on human health*. Brussels: European Parliament.

Löfstedt, R. (2004). The swing of the regulatory pendulum in Europe: From precautionary principle to (regulatory) impact analysis. *Journal of Risk and Uncertainty, 28*(3), 237–260.

Maor, M. (2014). Policy bubbles: Policy overreaction and positive feedback. *Governance, 27*(3), 469–487.

Milieu Ltd. (2013). *Regulatory provisions governing key aspects of unconventional gas extraction in selected member states—final report*. Brussels: Milieu Ltd.

McGowan, F. (2014). Regulating innovation: European responses to shale gas development. *Environmental Politics, 23*(1), 41–58.

McKenzie, L. M., Witter, R. Z., Newman, L. S., & Adgate, J. L. (2012). Human health risk assessment of air emissions from development of unconventional natural gas resources. *Science of the Total Environment, 424*(1), 79–87.

Mühlböck, M. (2012). National versus European: Party control over members of the European Parliament. *West European Politics, 35*(3), 607–631.

O'Riordan, T., & Jordan, A. (1995). The precautionary principle in contemporary environmental politics. *Environmental Values, 4*(3), 191–212.

Philippe & Partners. (2011). *Final report on unconventional gas in Europe*.

Princen, S. (2011). Agenda-setting strategies in EU policy processes. *Journal of European Public Policy, 18*(7), 927–943.

Princen, S., & Rhinard, M. (2006). Crashing and creeping: Agenda-setting dynamics in the European Union. *Journal of European Public Policy, 13*(7), 1119–1132.

Rahm, D. (2011). Regulating hydraulic fracturing in shale gas plays: The case of Texas. *Energy Policy, 39*(5), 2974–2981.

Reh, C., Héritier, A., Bressanelli, E., & Koop, C. (2013). The informal politics of legislation explaining secluded decision making in the European Union. *Comparative Political Studies, 46*(9), 1112–1142.

Rimkutė, D., & Haverland, M. (2014). How does the European Commission use scientific expertise—results from a survey of scientific members of the commission's expert committees. *Comparative European Politics,*. doi:10.1057/cep.2013.32.

Schattschneider, E. E. (1960). *The semisovereign people: A realist's view of democracy in America*. New York: Holt, Rinehart, and Winston.

Schirrmeister, M. (2014). Controversial futures—discourse analysis on utilizing the "fracking" technology in Germany. *European Journal of Futures Research, 2*(1), 1–9.

Stone, D. A. (1989). Causal stories and the formation of policy agendas. *Political Science Quarterly, 104*(2), 281–300.

Sunstein, C. (2005). *Laws of fear: Beyond the precautionary principle*. Cambridge: Cambridge University Press.

Tosun, J. (2013a). *Risk regulation in Europe: Assessing the application of the precautionary principle*. New York: Springer.

Tosun, J. (2013b). How the EU handles uncertain risks: Understanding the role of the precautionary principle. *Journal of European Public Policy, 20*(10), 1517–1528.

Tosun, J., & Solorio, I. (2011). Exploring the energy-environment relationship in the EU: Perspectives and challenges for theorizing and empirical analysis. In J. Tosun & I. Solorio (eds.) *Energy and environment in Europe: Assessing a complex relationship* (Vol. 15, Issue 7). European Integration online Papers, Special Mini-Issue No 1.

Tsebelis, G. (2002). *Veto players: How political institutions work*. Princeton: Princeton University Press.

Uliasz-Misiak, B., Przybycin, A., & Winid, B. (2014). Shale and tight gas in Poland—legal and environmental issues. *Energy Policy, 65*(1), 68–77.

Van Aelst, P., & Walgrave, S. (2011). Minimal or massive? The political agenda-setting power of the mass media according to different methods. *The International Journal of Press/Politics, 16*(3), 295–313.

Van Asselt, M. B. A., & Vos, E. (2008). Wrestling with uncertain risks: EU regulation of gmos and the uncertainty paradox. *Journal of Risk Research, 11*(1/2), 281–300.

Walgrave, S., Soroka, S., & Nuytemans, M. (2008). The mass media's political agenda-setting power a longitudinal analysis of media, parliament, and government in Belgium (1993 to 2000). *Comparative Political Studies, 41*(6), 814–836.

Weile, R. (2014). Beyond the fracking ban in France. *Journal of European Management & Public Affairs Studies, 1*(2), 11–16.

Weijermars, R., Drijkoningen, G., Heimovaara, T. J., Rudolph, E. S. J., Weltje, G. J., & Wolf, K. H. A. A. (2011). Unconventional gas research initiative for clean energy transition in Europe. *Journal of Natural Gas Science and Engineering, 3*(2), 402–412.

Zander, J. (2010). *The application of the precautionary principle in practice comparative dimensions*. Cambridge: Cambridge University Press.

Part V
Conclusion

Chapter 13
Building the EU's Energy Policy Agenda: Insights Gained

Jale Tosun, Sophie Biesenbender and Kai Schulze

Abstract This chapter summarises the main findings of this volume. Based on the individual contributions, we first illustrate the characteristics and dynamics of EU energy policy. Next, we engage in a structured overview of the theoretical and empirical insights provided into agenda building throughout this book. Finally, we point to promising avenues and directions for future research and present some concluding remarks.

13.1 Introduction: Patterns of EU Energy Policy

Despite being the first area of cooperation among European states, it took a long time for EU energy policy to develop into a discrete policy field (see Tosun et al. in Chap. 1). In particular in the last few years, energy issues have been increasingly placed on the EU's political agenda (see Alexandrova and Timmermans in Chap. 3), which at most times has indeed resulted in the adoption of new energy policies (see Biesenbender in Chap. 2). Today, EU energy policy consists of measures relating to the economic, environmental, security and social aspects of energy. Furthermore,

J. Tosun (✉)
Institute of Political Science, Heidelberg University, Bergheimer Strasse 58, 69115 Heidelberg, Germany
e-mail: jale.tosun@ipw.uni-heidelberg.de

S. Biesenbender
Institute for Research Information and Quality Assurance, Schützenstraße 6a, 10117 Berlin, Germany
e-mail: biesenbender@forschungsinfo.de

K. Schulze
Faculty of Economics and Social Sciences, University of Potsdam, August-Bebel-Str. 89, 14482 Potsdam, Germany
e-mail: kai.schulze@uni-potsdam.de

J. Tosun et al. (eds.), *Energy Policy Making in the EU*,
Lecture Notes in Energy 28, DOI 10.1007/978-1-4471-6645-0_13

the EU is eager about ‘exporting’ its energy policies to non-member states, in particular via the Energy Community (see Schulze in Chap. 4).

The *economic dimension* of energy policy is examined in detail by Nicole Herweg (Chap. 5), Andrea Ciambra and Israel Solorio (Chap. 8) and Elina Brutschin (Chap. 10). All three contributions shed light on how various facets of energy market liberalisation ended up on the EU’s political agenda. The *environmental dimension* of EU energy policy is addressed by the contributions of David Jacobs (Chap. 6) and Robert H. Cox and Mariam Dekanozishvili (Chap. 9), which deal with the promotion of renewable energy. These two chapters complement each other very well since one concentrates on the role of the Commission (Chap. 6) and the other draws attention to the importance of influential member states such as in the present case Germany (Chap. 9). Chapter 11 by Gerhard Fuchs also belongs to this group of studies showing how the prioritisation of climate change induced the EU to turn its attention to a technology that is associated with uncertain environmental and safety risks. Elina Brutschin (Chap. 10) and Jale Tosun (Chap. 12) contribute to the understanding of the *security-related aspects* of EU energy policy. In the case of Tosun’s chapter, security has a double meaning: on the one hand it refers to considerations about security of supply and on the other to public security and the protection of the environment.

Finally, the contribution by Stefan Bouzarovski and Saska Petrova (Chap. 7) helps to grasp the *social dimension* of EU energy policy, which has received only scant scientific attention so far. In this context, the authors focus on the issue of energy poverty, which the few existing studies show to be a real-existing phenomenon in Europe (see, e.g. Thomson and Snell 2013; Bouzarovski 2014; Schuessler 2014). While this topic is certainly an emerging one, Chap. 7 compellingly shows that there is an intensified political debate about the social foundations and implications of energy policy. It is possible that these considerations will produce corresponding legislation in the future.

All in all, with regard to the development of EU energy policy, this edited volume has generated three key insights. First, in the last few years, energy issues did benefit from elevated levels of political attention, thus leading to an increased production of corresponding rules. By illustrating different paths and patterns of agenda shaping, the case studies of this volume have furthered our understanding of agenda shaping as the bottleneck for subsequent policy making in the EU. Second, EU energy policy has become more diverse and encompassing, now also including considerations about the affordability of energy. Third, even while representing a policy field that was just formalised by the Lisbon Treaty, EU energy policy has also been transferred to non-EU states through the Energy Community.

The remainder of this chapter addresses the research questions posed in Chap. 1: When are energy issues likely to be placed on the EU’s political agenda? Which actors are influential in agenda shaping and what are their strategies? When does agenda shaping lead to legislative action? The findings of the individual chapters contribute to answering these questions. In a final section, the chapter presents some ideas we deem worth to be taken into account by future studies.

13.2 The Entering of Energy Issues on the EU's Political Agenda

Most contributions to this book address the more specific phenomenon of *agenda-setting*, that is, the process of putting predominantly new topics onto the political agenda (Peters 1994). Agenda-setting is, for instance, very well illustrated by Jacobs and Fuchs as well as Cox and Dekanozishvili. Furthermore, the chapters by Biesenbender, Schulze and Alexandrova and Timmermans display a primary interest in the agenda-setting processes. This finding concurs with the prevalent perspective adopted by the research literature. Furthermore, it is plausible that among the three types of agenda shaping defined by Tallberg (2003), agenda-setting receives the highest scholarly attention. First, the process of placing an issue on the agenda is analytically intriguing because it provides insights into the power resources of individual actor groups. The other reason is more pragmatic and concerns the possibility to empirically observe agenda-shaping efforts in the real world, which gives the purposeful and visible agenda-setting attempts an advantage over the other, more subtle or less visible forms of agenda shaping. Nevertheless, some contributions in this volume also captured agenda structuring and agenda exclusion.

Attempts of *agenda exclusion* are illustrated by the contributions of Ciambra and Solorio, Bouzarovski and Petrova as well as Tosun. One of the most interesting insights is provided by Ciambra and Solorio as they assign the United Kingdom the power to practice agenda exclusion at the European level. According to the analysis, the United Kingdom fought to keep the issue of energy-market development off the agenda during the 1970s since it did not correspond to its national preferences. The other two case studies (see Chaps. 7 and 12), by contrast, highlight the Commission's power to exclude issues from the decision agenda and the strategy the Commission applies to seek agenda exclusion.

Processes that correspond to *agenda structuring* are described in the contributions by Herweg and Brutschin. In both cases, issues that were already around for a while became re-emphasised and associated with different images. What these two contributions manage to show is that the redefinition of issue images is essential for facilitating agenda structuring. This became particularly clear in the chapter by Brutschin, which associates the making of the third gas directive with a successful redefinition of the issue from an emphasis on competition to a question of foreign policy in the wake of the EU's eastern enlargement. In addition to this, Herweg's analysis shows how the concept of agenda structuring can be seminally studied from the perspective offered by Kingdon's (1984) multiple streams approach.

Altogether, we can state that all three forms of agenda shaping advanced by Tallberg (2003)—agenda-setting, structuring and exclusion—could be observed in the present collection of studies. This suggests that Tallberg's approach is indeed based on real-life patterns of agenda shaping. By adopting this differentiation, the causal processes underlying agenda shaping could be even better understood by empirical research.

When are energy issues likely to be placed on the political agenda of the European Union? In the introductory chapter, we stated that the literature assigns external events an important role for the definition of the EU energy policy agenda. A number of case studies in this volume illustrated the consequences that external events have had for agenda shaping. What is remarkable about these events in the context of EU energy policy is the fact that in most cases they concern issues of energy security related to a dependence on imports of energy or fossil fuels from third states (see chapters by Brutschin, Cox and Dekanozishvili as well as Tosun) or to the diversification of the energy mix and energy efficiency (see chapter by Jacobs). This observation is perfectly in line with the argument put forward by Buchan (2010), who posits that security-related issues most likely end up on the political agenda because of certain events.

Some case studies also pointed out that the EU's energy policy agenda is influenced by broader policy goals, especially by the EU's ambitions to combat climate change. This goal was able to bring the issues of renewable energy promotion (see Chaps. 6 and 9) and carbon capture and storage (see Chap. 11) on the EU energy policy agenda. This finding corresponds well with the logic of neo-functionalist theories, which emphasise the idea of a progressive EU integration process as a result of endogenous interdependencies and spillovers (Schimmelfennig 2014, p. 327). Put differently, given the very nature of energy policy, agenda shaping is to a notable extent the result of decisions taken in adjacent policy fields. From this, one could conclude that the development of the energy agenda is based on a functional logic, that is, as a response to events or broader policy goals. Yet, the contributions by Herweg and Bouzarovski and Petrova show that this is not quite the case. In fact, Herweg discusses how the Commission managed to bring onto the agenda a 'problem' that was completely decoupled from any concrete event. In a similar vein, the issue of energy poverty almost incidentally ended up on the EU's political agenda in the context of the Third Energy Package.

All in all, we could indeed observe that the EU's political agenda regarding energy issues displays "a number of regularities and recurring dynamics" (Princen 2012, p. 207). These refer to the observation that agenda-setting—as a special type of agenda shaping—often occurs in response to external events, even though the concrete process can evolve in different ways and does not ensure that concrete action will follow (see Chaps. 2 and 3). And in such cases, it is often the European Council that sets the agenda. Moreover, the EU's energy policy agenda was found to be affected by functional considerations about a wide range of energy-related challenges. Finally, the energy policy agenda is rather dynamic because it is generally affected by decisions taken in other policy areas. Since energy policy reaches into many adjacent policy areas, agenda-setting via spillovers occurs quite regularly (see Tosun and Solorio 2011). Nonetheless, there is also something unintentional about how the EU's energy policy agenda is defined, which might best be explained by Kingdon's (1984) multiple streams approach.

13.3 The Actors and Their Strategies

In the EU polity, the Commission has the exclusive right of legislative initiative, which turns it into the most important formal agenda shaper as highlighted in the introductory chapter. The Commission however does not act in a vacuum and the formal right of initiative is no guarantee for a successful policy proposal (Tallberg 2006). In this regard, many studies stress the importance of the interaction between the Commission and the European Council (see, e.g. Alexandrova et al. 2012; Bocquillon and Dobbels 2014). The case studies presented in this book contribute to this research perspective in two ways. First, they provide insights into the framing strategies of the Commission. Second, the contributions directly address the relationship between the Commission and a range of other EU institutions and the government of the member states (for the latter, see, e.g. Alexandrova and Timmermans 2013).

13.3.1 Framing Strategies of the Commission

Overall, the agenda-shaping powers of the Commission are fundamentally linked to its political and legal mandate as well as its personnel resources available. The Single European Act has equipped the Commission with the necessary mandate to place energy policy on the EU's political agenda. At the same time, the administrative capacities of the Commission have considerably expanded over the last 25 years enabling the Commission to exert its agenda-shaping powers both autonomously and in response to the European Council and other actors that are entitled to approach the Commission to initiate legislation (see, e.g. Trondal 2012).

Even though the Commission makes constant use of its formal monopoly to put different energy topics on the European agenda, the strategies and their success vary over issues. The case studies show that the Commission's agenda-shaping success is largely related to the framing strategies employed and the ability to anticipate the interests of other EU institutions (such as the Council and the European Parliament) and the member states.

As Herweg in Chap. 5 observes, the liberalisation of the European gas market (i.e. the negotiations over the first gas directive) was proactively approached by the Commission and convincingly framed as an internal market or competition issue that should be addressed at the EU-level. One particularity of the Commission's agenda was that it anticipated the member states' national regulatory interests in the topic. The Commission was able to keep the issue on the EU energy agenda despite diverging political interests in the different institutions and member states. It chose a similar (that is, inclusive) approach when shaping the agenda and negotiating the third gas directive (see Chap. 10 by Brutschin). Following the enlargement of the EU, the Commission managed to take changed national interests and constellations into account. The reframing of the topic as both an internal market and a foreign policy issue in the negotiations enabled the Commission to successfully keep it on the European agenda across institutions. This finding stresses again how important the definition or re-definition of issues is to structure the already existing political agenda.

With regard to the regulation of renewable electricity, the framing of the topic as a competition issue was less straightforward and more reserved (see Chap. 6 by Jacobs). The variety of different national interests and approaches made it difficult for the Commission to advance its preferred policy solution or to reach consensus in the complex debate on financing mechanisms for renewable electricity with the member states. As a result, the Commission reduced both its agenda-setting and decision-making ambitions for this policy issue under the internal market frame. Instead of advancing a comprehensive European policy on renewable electricity, it started to focus on individual regulations that freed it from the need to reach consensus in the complex co-decision process (i.e. involving the Council and the European Parliament).

In sum, the European Commission has deliberately used different framing strategies and adjusted its regulatory ambitions to shape the European agenda with respect to the regulation of the European gas market and renewable electricity. In particular, the Chap. 2 by Biesenbender and the three case studies (Chaps. 5, 6 and 10) suggest that the Commission has so far predominantly relied on the internal market frame when making use of its formal monopoly to place and keep different topics on the EU's energy policy agenda. This perspective is also reflected in the design and functioning of the EU's external energy policy (see Chap. 4 by Schulze). What can be inferred from this finding is that the Commission tends to choose its strategies in accordance with its respective preferences. Also, the agenda-shaping powers of the Commission are truly encompassing, including agenda-setting, structuring and exclusion.

Even though the European Council has become more active in defining the EU's energy policy agenda, the actor that must and usually does act in a more strategic way is the Commission. The main instrument it can rely on is the definition and redefinition of issues by means of framing, which is perfectly in line with the more general theories of agenda shaping (see Baumgartner and Jones 1993; Baumgartner et al. 2006; Princen 2011, 2012; Engeli et al. 2012; Green-Pedersen and Walgrave 2014).

The picture is different in regard to the issues of energy poverty, carbon capture and storage or hydraulic fracturing that entered the European agenda under different frames. These cases show that the Commission has not always made use of its formal agenda-setting monopoly especially when the link with the internal market was weak. In some cases, the European Parliament has taken the lead in the subsequent shaping of the EU energy agenda (see Chaps. 7 and 12 by Bouzarovski and Petrova as well as Tosun). In other situations, attention for an issue has trickled away (see Chap. 11 by Fuchs). As the chapter by Bouzarovski and Petrova illustrates, the Commission has not (yet) tried to place the issue of energy poverty on the EU agenda by explicitly framing the topic as a European one. In the presence of growing problem perception however, the resulting vacuum has been filled by other policy actors (in this case the European Economic and Social Committee) that took the lead in bringing the issue onto the European agenda, which has since then been advanced further by the European Parliament.

The case of carbon capture and storage (see chapter by Fuchs) illustrates a similar passive approach of the Commission towards the policy. Even though the Commission was asked by the European Council to follow-up on the agenda by developing a legal framework, the Commission did not engage in serious and sustained agenda-shaping activities. Different from the case of energy poverty, the agenda-setting vacuum has not been filled so far at the European level.

The case study on hydraulic fracturing (chapter by Tosun) shows yet another agenda-setting case that was not dominated by the Commission. Right from the beginning (i.e. following the European Council meeting in 2011) the European Parliament became also active in this matter. The two institutions relied on competing framing strategies with the European Parliament stressing the potential environmental implications of the technology (which was well in line with previous framing strategies for energy policy; see chapter by Biesenbender). Despite converging preferences of the Commission and the Parliament, none of the involved actors managed to frame the topic as a 'European issue', which would have paved the way for ambitious European legislation on the issue (see also chapter by Jacobs).

These examples of agenda shaping beyond the competition or internal market frame illustrate the volatility of attention in European institutions for different energy policies. While the European Parliament has a tendency to engage in agenda shaping under the environmental or the sustainability frame (see chapters by Biesenbender and Tosun), the Commission has a focus on the internal energy market when considering the regulation of energy production (see chapter by Jacobs). This has important implications for the expansion or containment of the political conflict and may explain the variation in the success of the agenda-shaping efforts (see Engeli et al. 2012 and Schulze in Chap. 4).

13.3.2 Competitive Cooperation Between European Institutions

Most case studies have highlighted the role of the Commission or the 'competitive cooperation' between Commission and the European Council (see Bocquillon and Dobbels 2014). With regard to the latter, no contribution to this book could really confirm that both EU institutions compete against each other regarding agenda shaping. Even if the European Council brings issues onto the agenda, the Commission was found to approach them in ways that are close to its own preferences (see chapter by Biesenbender). However, what should not be overlooked is the role of the European Parliament here, which has indeed helped to keep issues on the agenda. Furthermore, it should be noted that the governments of the individual member states—as for example Germany or the United Kingdom—can also influence the agenda (see chapters by Ciambra and Solorio as well as Cox and Dekanozishvili). This finding is in line with the well-established literature on Europeanisation (see, e.g. Börzel 2002; Radaelli 2003, 2008).

In their instructive article, Princen and Rhinard (2006) expect that it makes a difference whether issues are placed on the agenda via the high-politics or the low-politics route. While this reasoning is well plausible in the case of energy policy, most of the case studies in this volume addressed the high-politics route. In fact, it seems there are only very few cases in which energy issue entered the agenda via the low-politics route. According to Princen and Rhinard (2006) the low-politics route is characterised by evolvement of an issue in a close circle of policy experts, which then leads to a set of specific, expertise-driven proposals. A case that approximates this scenario best is the proposal on carbon capture and storage (see chapter by Fuchs). The predominance of the high-politics venue in EU energy policy suggests that energy issues (probably given the far-reaching social, economic and political implications of their regulation) are not as easily placed on the European agenda through the low-politics venue as might be the case for other topics that are of less cross-sectoral nature. An alternative interpretation is that an improved understanding of the low-politics route requires an entirely different research design as indicated below. In any case, agenda shaping in EU energy policy as illustrated here is mostly a process where the issues are placed on the agenda by political actors and not groups of policy experts.

13.4 Agenda Shaping and Legislative Action

The observed agenda-shaping dynamics as illustrated in this volume are also found to have different consequences or impacts on the subsequent legislative processes (see chapters by Brutschin, Herweg, Biesenbender and Schulze). In fact, the evidence presented by the individual chapters suggests that agenda shaping most likely leads to legislative action when it has been initially triggered by the European Council and if the Commission accepts the European Council's call to act.

The chapter by Tosun has shown that there are instances when the Commission is—at least initially—hesitant to propose legislation. In such cases, agenda shaping primarily leads to the commissioning of (scientific) evidence and reports, which not only help to gain a better understanding of the issue concerned, but also help to extend the time frame for the Commission's activities. In fact, considering numerous efforts made to create a basis for the regulation of shale gas extraction by means of hydraulic fracturing, the eventual outcome of the whole policy-making process was very humble. A similar finding is presented by Biesenbender's chapter: the Commission has been active in issuing preparatory acts and non-binding policy documents in the field of renewable energy, but binding regulatory output on these issues was rather limited. With the regulation of electricity or gas, the picture is quite different.

There are two possible interpretations of the Commission's varying commitment to end the policy-making process with legislation. One interpretation is that the issues concerned fail in attracting sufficiently high levels of interest among their promoters. As a consequence, given the perpetual emergence of new topics, issues that fail to generate enough attention (or if the attention generated subsides) run the risk of being replaced by other ones.

The second view is that some issues fail to be addressed by binding rules because of opposing interests. One possibility is that the Commission itself is not interested (anymore) in addressing the issue. For example, all case studies of the internal energy market suggested that this represents an overarching goal for the Commission. Conversely, the Commission will abstain from policy measures that put the meeting of this target at risk. Another possibility refers to the Commission's anticipation of resistance from the member states (see, e.g. Häge and Toshkov 2011). It is plausible that the Commission evaluates the chances of realising its legislative proposals before proposing them formally, which may explain the variation in the outcomes of the agenda-shaping processes. Finally, it might turn out the findings of reports and scientific evidence suggest that no action needs to be taken or perhaps even cannot be taken and so the Commission abstains from initiating the legislative process.

Which additional factors matter for agenda shaping to culminate in the formulation of legally-binding rules? Based on the studies by Ciambra and Solorio, Cox and Dekanozishvili, Jacobs as well as Fuchs, we can state that the availability of a national model seems to support the success of agenda shaping. There are two possible reasons for this. The first one is that the existence of a national model reduces the transaction costs for policy drafting and also increases the other member states' acceptance for an EU-wide policy measure. The second reason is that national models are promoted by the corresponding member states, which suggests that the success of agenda shaping is in fact a consequence of effective lobbying by the government of that state. Both reasons are plausible. But empirically, it is challenging to pinpoint which of them holds true.

It is interesting that energy poverty was placed on the European agenda, but failed then to result in the adoption of legislation because the United Kingdom has indeed a model policy for this problem in place. In other cases, the United Kingdom or Germany did indeed serve as example for EU-wide rules. All this suggests that the availability of a national model is at best a facilitating factor for the success of agenda-shaping efforts—but it must be analysed in combination with other variables.

Other important determinants of agenda shaping and its success (i.e. when it actually leads to policy formulation) include the actors' preferences and the degree to which they concur. This point has been illustrated in particular by Tosun's chapter for the case of the European Parliament. Generally speaking, based on the findings presented in this book it is rather remarkable how scant attention existing agenda-shaping models—such as those put forward by Baumgartner and Jones 1993; Baumgartner et al. 2006; Princen 2011, 2012; Engeli et al. 2012; Green-Pedersen and Walgrave 2014—pay to the actors' preferences. Of course, actors are a central analytical category in these models, but questions about their preferences and their origins are only seldom asked. The consideration about the concurrence of the actors' preferences is closely associated with the veto player approach (Tsebelis 2002), which may be merged with other models of agenda shaping in fruitful ways.

13.5 Avenues for Future Research

We identify four ways in which this study offers a promising starting point for future research. The first way refers to the improved understanding the case studies have provided about how the Commission uses its agenda-shaping powers. The insights mainly concern the interaction between the Commission and other EU bodies and member states. To advance our understanding of the Commission's role, we recommend to zoom inside the Commission and to explore when the Commission becomes entrepreneurial. Second, this edited volume showed how pioneering member states and public demand for EU energy policy matters. This is only one side of the story. As a matter for fact, as EU energy policy develops further it becomes more contested (e.g. by reaching into neighbouring policy fields, see above Sects. 13.1 and 13.2). This may have repercussions on how the broad EU energy agenda, which subsumes different issue-specific agendas will look in the future. Third, many case studies highlighted how considerations about environmental protection and climate change have affected EU energy policy and diversified the opportunities for strategic framing of different actors and institutions (see, in particular, Sect. 13.3). In this context, one wonders how the EU's international image affects agenda shaping at the EU-level. Finally, this book illuminated the role of many different actors, but there is one that has not been addressed in a systematic fashion: the European Court of Justice. Consequently, future studies are encouraged to analyse what role this EU body plays in the building of the EU's energy agenda.

13.5.1 When Does the Commission Become Entrepreneurial?

There is a broad consensus among the contributions to this volume that the Commission is influential for building the European Union's energy agenda. Similar to most studies in the literature, we treated the Commission as an actor but did not pay attention to when exactly the Commission becomes entrepreneurial (see Bauer 2008: 693). This question might initially look unsubstantiated since some contributions (in particular Chaps. 5 by Herweg and 6 by Jacobs) identified the Commission as the policy entrepreneur that promoted an increased supranationalisation of EU energy policy (see also Maltby 2013). This finding is well in line with bureaucratic conceptualisations portraying the Commission as main promoter of supranationalisation, which is in turn expected to maximise its regulatory competencies (Wonka 2007, pp. 169–170; see also Majone 1996; Hooghe 2001). Yet, the study of Bouzarovski and Petrova (Chap. 7) has clearly shown that the Commission did not act in an entrepreneurial way for tackling energy poverty. As the authors showed, the Commission was willing to engage in a "fact-finding mission" but refused to take more consequential steps in the following. In fact, the Commission not only abstained from proposing legislation but even did not "consider it appropriate at this stage to propose a European definition of energy poverty or of vulnerable customers" (European Commission 2010, p. 11, cited in Chap. 7). Similarly, Tosun (Chap. 12) showed that the Energy Commissioner negated the need for adopting EU-wide rules for hydraulic fracturing (for further details see Sect. 13.3 above).

Two important questions emerge here: When does the Commission become entrepreneurial? Who are the entrepreneurs inside the Commission? The second question paraphrases the research interest of Bauer (2008). With regard to the first question, both organisation-level and individual-level factors seem to matter. At the organisation level, the study by Häge and Toshkov (2011) illustrates that the Commission is eager to anticipate resistance from the member states before proposing legislation. Bauer (2008: 694) adds to this point by arguing that "successful policy drafts are the currency of prestige and the 'capital' that returns in terms of career advancement, resource expansion or obtaining other interesting dossiers. Successful drafts reflect on the Commissioner in charge, the director-general, the director and down the line of organizational hierarchy". From this, one can infer that the Commission takes the chances of a successful agenda shaping (that is, one that leads to legislation) into account and reacts accordingly. This behaviour can therefore lead to all three types of agenda shaping, i.e. agenda-setting, agenda structuring or agenda exclusion.

The agenda entrepreneurship of the Commission can also be affected by the degree to which the Commissioner responsible for a field and the preferences of a national government concur. As shown by Wonka (2007), Commissioners are chosen in a careful manner to ensure that they reflect the policy preferences of the member states' governments. Thus, a Commissioner might turn entrepreneurial if this reflects the wish of his or her national government. Turning to the individual level, personal dispositions of the Commissioners (most importantly their preferences) might be important. Going one step further, one could—similarly to Hooghe (2005)—ask whether socialisation processes affect how entrepreneurial the individual Commissioners are.

Turning to the question about who is entrepreneurial within the Commission, the literature puts forward three candidates worth being studied in greater detail. The most obvious agenda entrepreneurs appear to be the individual Commissioners. However, then one must remember that the Commission does not act as a unitary actor when shaping the agenda (Hartlapp and Rauh 2013, p. 20). Taking the heterogeneity of the Commission into account, Bauer (2008, p. 692) draws attention to the role of the heads of unit within the Commission, who are important for delivering concrete policy drafts. Therefore, it is plausible to hypothesise that the success of agenda shaping eventually depends on the behaviour of the heads of unit.

Finally, following Trondal et al. (2008), the seconded national civil servants hired by short-term contracts play an important role. They are typically seconded from the administrations of EU member states, non-member states, the private sector and from other international organisations. According to the authors, they have a "double allegiance at the outset between their home organisation (who continue to pay their salaries) and the Commission under which they have to serve loyally" (ibid: 254). It is well possible that these actors bring in new ideas into the Commission and therefore also have an impact on it acting as an agenda entrepreneur. Of course, the Commission is a much more complicated political body and there are also many more aspects regarding the composition of the Commission and the politics inside the Commission than we could discuss here. For example, we did not touch upon the question whether decision making in the Commission is "partisan, national or sectoral" (see, e.g. Wonka 2008 on this point). Also, the relationship between the individual Commissioner and the College was not addressed. Acknowledging this flaw, we state that a promising avenue for future research is to zoom into the Commission and make use of insights provided by the literature on public administration. Furthermore, such a focus would allow for a more nuanced and systematic study of the low-politics route by showing how institutional agendas emerge from expert working groups (such as Commission Expert Groups in this case; Princen and Rhinard 2006).

13.5.2 Contestation of EU Energy Policy

In this book, we have provided insights into the motivations of some EU member states for pushing EU energy policy. However, it is also true that the governments of some member states also oppose energy policies, especially those relating to climate objectives. Poland is among the countries that are most sceptical about the EU's progress with regard to regulate the production and use of energy. One of the main reasons why Poland actively blocks the EU's effort to make further progress in combating climate change is arguably the country's heavy reliance on coal. The government of Donald Tusk has in fact stated that "Poland will fulfill its EU 20-20-20 climate change commitments but no more as reducing the country's emissions further would raise electricity prices and slow economic growth".[1] Remarkably, the very issue of energy poverty—which is not addressed at the EU-level so far if we remember the account given by Chap. 7—is used in this statement to oppose climate policy. From this, it follows that the relationship between measures aimed at combating climate change and energy policy is much more complex than one would have initially thought (see also Chap. 6 by Jacobs). In fact, it appears that considerations about the security and social dimensions of energy policy can be

[1] Information retrieved from the following website: http://www.europeanenergyinnovation.eu/LatestNews/WeeklyNewsRoundup/15thSeptember2013.aspx (last accessed 13 October 2014).

used to shape the EU's political agenda in a way that leads to the initiation of less ambitious climate policies. This is an interesting perspective, and we invite scholars in EU energy policy to address it.

Yet, energy policy is not only contested by governments but also by the people in the member states and the European Citizens' Initiative provides them with an instrument to directly shape the agenda. In fact, on 1st November 2013 the initiative 'Suspension of the EU Climate and Energy Package' finished to collect signatures. The organisers want the 2009 EU Climate & Energy Package (excluding the energy efficiency clauses) and further climate regulations to be suspended until a climate agreement is signed by the major CO_2 emitters China, USA and India.[2] There are also other examples where citizens disapprove of EU energy rules, one of the best known ones being the gradual phase-out of incandescent light bulbs (see, e.g. Frondel and Lohmann 2011; Howarth and Rosenow 2014). Thus, one can expect that EU energy policy will become increasingly contested both politically and socially in the future. This could also lead to agenda-shaping activities that—in marked contrast to prior situations—aim for the dismantling of existing rules.

13.5.3 Climate Negotiations and Agenda Shaping

The EU has paid considerable attention to the development and implementation of climate change policies. Since 2009, the EU has adopted several climate and energy policies to reduce greenhouse gas emissions by 20 % before 2020 (Wettestad et al. 2012, p. 65, see also Chap. 2 by Biesenbender). The priority that the EU gives to climate change is also reflected by the establishment of the Directorate-General for Climate Action (DG CLIMA) in February 2010 (Massey and Huitema 2013, p. 341). Among many other tasks, DG CLIMA leads international negotiations, which represents the second arena in which the EU has acted in order to combat climate change. In fact, the EU has been one of the jurisdictions pushing for the establishment of the Kyoto Protocol to the United Nations Framework Convention on Climate Change (Schreurs and Tiberghien 2007, p. 19). In light of this achievement, a large but still growing body of literature attributes a leadership role to the EU in global climate change politics (Sbragia and Damro 1999; Gupta and Ringius 2001; Vogler 2005; Vogler and Stephan 2007; Biesbroek et al. 2010). The EU's leadership in climate change can be traced back to the role of a few individual member states, namely: Denmark, Germany, the Netherlands, Sweden and the United Kingdom (Schreurs and Tiberghien 2007, p. 19).

Existing studies have provided many important insights into the motivations of some EU member states for pushing for international negotiations in the area of climate change (see also Chap. 9 by Cox and Dekanozishvili). Yet, our knowledge

---

[2] Information retrieved from the following website: http://ec.europa.eu/citizens-initiative/public/initiatives/finalised/details/2012/000010 (last accessed 13 October 2014).

is limited about whether the EU's international commitment has implications for the EU's own energy agenda. In fact, Oberthür and Roche Kelly (2008) suggest that EU leadership in international climate policy should be reflected in EU-level initiatives for advancing energy policy. Buchan (2010) as well as Morata and Solorio (2012) also argue that there is an interdependency between the EU's ambition to be perceived as a leader in international climate policy and the advances in the environmental dimension of energy policy. While it is straightforward that the international image of the EU is likely to trickle down to actual policy making, it seems promising to address this process in greater detail. From such an analytical perspective, we can expect to gain an even better understanding of the role of the European Council and the Commission for agenda shaping. Important questions in this context include the following: Which of the two EU bodies initiates energy policy by referring to international climate negotiations? What is the role of the European Parliament given its focus on the environmental and climate-change implications of energy policy in the past?

Another potential line of future research relates to the framing strategies of the Commission and the European Council (see above Sect. 13.3.2). One can advance two expectations regarding the use of the climate change frame for motivating energy policies. One expectation is that this frame is used widely and perhaps even more often than necessary to legitimise the taking of legal action since the governments and the citizens of the EU member states become more accepting of it. The other expectation is the exact opposite, suggesting that this frame is not applied as widely as one might expect since climate change is a diffuse phenomenon with no readily available measures for combating it. Thus put more broadly, it seems promising to shed light on how EU policy-makers employ climate change for motivating energy-related measures.

13.5.4 Judicial Agenda Shaping

The Court of Justice of the EU has consistently played an important role in European integration and more specifically for EU energy policy (see, e.g. Pointvogl 2009). In this regard, Börzel (2010, p. 199) stresses that it was the Court of Justice's "dynamic interpretation of the Treaties in its case law" that helped to further EU policies beyond negative integration.

For example, the European Court of Justice's 2001 ruling on case C-379/98 PreussenElektra AG versus Schleswag AG showed that feed-in tariffs are compatible with EU state-aid and competition rules (Wüstenhagen and Bilharz 2006, p. 1687; Muñoz et al. 2007, p. 3104). This ruling was important for promoting the generation of renewable energy through feed-in tariffs (see Jacobs in Chap. 6 and Cox and Dekanozishvili in Chap. 9). There are further examples where Court rulings were influential for at least facilitating agenda-shaping activities by the other EU bodies by interpreting EU law. In the past, the Commission made an instrumental use of the Court of Justice to press for reforms in the field of energy policy.

As Eberlein (2008, p. 76) points out, some EU scholars argue that liberalisation of the energy market could be realised because the "member states preferred negotiated (and contained) liberalisation to uncontrolled liberalisation under potential Court rulings that the Commission threatened to trigger".

While the Court of Justice clearly is an important player in EU politics, the contributions to this edited volume did not address its role in a systematic fashion. This represents a limitation of this book but at the same time a rewarding avenue for future research. Agenda shaping could be seminally studied by expanding the analytical focus to more areas of EU energy policy than the liberalisation of the gas and energy market. More broadly, one can ask how the Commission strategically uses the 'threat' of Court ruling to make sure that its proposals will become binding laws (see Pollack 2003). In this context, it would be particularly interesting to see whether there is variation in the different types or targets of EU energy policy. Does the Commission announce to take legal recourse to the Court of Justice more often, when the economic or the internal market aspects of EU energy policy are concerned? A comparative approach to the study of the Commission's announcement to invoke the Court of Justice could therefore help to improve our understanding of agenda-shaping processes in EU energy policy in many ways.

References

Alexandrova, P., Carammia, M., & Timmermans, A. (2012). Policy Punctuations and Issue Diversity on the European Council Agenda. *Policy Studies Journal, 40*(1), 69–88.

Alexandrova, P., & Timmermans, A. (2013). National interest versus the common good: The Presidency in European Council agenda setting. *European Journal of Political Research, 52* (3), 316–338.

Bauer, M. W. (2008). Diffuse anxieties, deprived entrepreneurs: Commission reform and middle management. *Journal of European Public Policy, 15*(5), 691–707.

Baumgartner, F. R., & Jones, B. D. (1993). *Agendas and Instability in American Politics*. Chicago: University of Chicago Press.

Baumgartner, F. R., Green-Pedersen, C., & Jones, B. D. (2006). Comparative Studies of Policy Agendas. *Journal of European Public Policy, 13*(7), 959–974.

Biesbroek, G. R., Swart, R. J., Carter, T. R., Cowan, C., Henrichs, T., Mela, H., et al. (2010). Europe adapts to climate change: Comparing national adaptation strategies. *Global Environmental Change, 20*(3), 440–450.

Börzel, T. A. (2002). Pace-setting, foot-dragging, and fence-sitting: member state responses to Europeanization. *Journal of Common Market Studies, 40*(2), 193–214.

Börzel, T. (2010). European governance: negotiation and competition in the shadow of hierarchy. *Journal of Common Market Studies, 48*(2), 191–219.

Bocquillon, P., & Dobbels, M. (2014). An elephant on the 13th floor of the Berlaymont? European Council and Commission relations in legislative agenda setting. *Journal of European Public Policy, 21*(1), 20–38.

Bouzarovski, S. (2014). Energy poverty in the European Union: landscapes of vulnerability. *Wiley Interdisciplinary Reviews: Energy and Environment, 3*(3), 276–289.

Buchan, D. (2010). Energy Policy: Sharp Challenges and Rising Ambitions. In H. Wallace, W. Wallace, & M. Pollack (Eds.), *Policy-Making in the European Union* (pp. 357–380). Oxford: Oxford University Press.

Eberlein, B. (2008). The Making of the European energy market: The interplay of governance and government. *Journal of Public Policy, 28*(1), 73–92.
Engeli, I., Green-Pedersen, C., & Larsen, L. T. (2012). Theoretical Perspectives on Morality Politics. In I. Engeli, C. Green-Pedersen, & L. T. Larsen (Eds.), *Morality Politics in Western Europe* (pp. 5–26). Basingstoke: Palgrave Macmillan.
European Commission (2010). *Commission Staff Working Paper: An Energy Policy for Consumers*. Brussels: European Commission.
Frondel, M., & Lohmann, S. (2011). The European Commission's light bulb decree: Another costly regulation? *Energy Policy, 39*(6), 3177–3181.
Green-Pedersen, C., & Walgrave, S. (2014). Political Agenda Setting: An Approach to Studying Political Systems. In C. Green-Pedersen & S. Walgrave (Eds.), *Agenda Setting, Policies, and Political Systems: A Comparative Approach* (pp. 1–18). Chicago: University of Chicago Press.
Gupta, J., & Ringius, L. (2001). The EU's climate leadership: Reconciling ambition and reality. *International Environmental Agreements, 1*(2), 281–299.
Häge, F., & Toshkov, D. (2011). Anticipating Resistance: The Effect of Member State Preferences on the European Commission's Agenda-Setting Activity. University of Limerick PPA Working Papers.
Hartlapp, M., & Rauh, C. (2013). The Commission's internal conditions for social re-regulation: Market efficiency and wider social goals in setting the rules for financial services in Europe. *European Journal of Government and Economics, 2*(1), 25–40.
Hooghe, L. (2001). *The European Commission and the Integration of Europe. Images of Governance*. Cambridge: Cambridge University Press.
Hooghe, L. (2005). Several roads lead to international norms, but few via international socialization: A case study of the European Commission. *International Organization, 59*(04), 861–898.
Howarth, N. A., & Rosenow, J. (2014). Banning the bulb: Institutional evolution and the phased ban of incandescent lighting in Germany. *Energy Policy, 67*, 737–746.
Kingdon, J. W. (1984). *Agendas, alternatives, and public policies*. Boston: Little, Brown.
Majone, G. (1996). The European Commission as a regulator. In G. Majone (Ed.), *Regulating Europe* (pp. 61–82). London: Routledge.
Maltby, T. (2013). European Union energy policy integration: A case of European Commission policy entrepreneurship and increasing supranationalism. *Energy Policy, 55*, 435–444.
Massey, E., & Huitema, D. (2013). The emergence of climate change adaptation as a policy field: the case of England. *Regional Environmental Change, 13*(2), 341–352.
Morata, F., & Solorio, I. (2012). *European Energy Policy: An Environmental Approach*. Cheltenham: Edward Elgar.
Muñoz, M., Oschmann, V., & David Tàbara, J. (2007). Harmonization of renewable electricity feed-in laws in the European Union. *Energy policy, 35*(5), 3104–3114.
Oberthür, S., & Roche Kelly, C. (2008). EU leadership in international climate policy: achievements and challenges. *The International Spectator, 43*(3), 35–50.
Peters, G. (1994). Agenda-setting in the European community. *Journal of European Public Policy, 1*(1), 9–26.
Pointvogl, A. (2009). Perceptions, realities, concession. What is driving the integration of European energy policies? *Energy Policy, 37*(12), 5704–5716.
Pollack, M. (2003). *The Engines of European Integration. Delegation, Agency and Agenda Setting in the EU*. New York: Oxford University Press.
Princen, S. (2011). Agenda-Setting Strategies in EU Policy Processes. *Journal of European Public Policy, 18*(7), 927–943.
Princen, S. (2012). Agenda-setting. In A. Jordan & C. Adelle (Eds.), *Environmental Policy in the EU: Actors, institutions and processes* (pp. 191–208). London/New York: Routledge.
Princen, S., & Rhinard, M. (2006). Crashing and Creeping: Agenda-Setting Dynamics in the European Union. *Journal of European Public Policy, 13*(7), 1119–1132.
Radaelli, C. M. (2003). The Europeanization of Public Policy. In K. Featherstone & C. M. Radaelli (Eds.), *The Politics of Europeanization* (pp. 27–55). Oxford: Oxford University Press.

Radaelli, C. M. (2008). Europeanization, policy learning, and new modes of governance. *Journal of Comparative Policy Analysis, 10*(3), 239–254.
Sbragia, A. M., & Damro, C. (1999). The changing role of the European Union in International Environmental Politics: Institution building and the politics of climate change. *Environment and Planning C: Government and Policy, 17*(1), 53–68.
Schimmelfennig, F. (2014). European integration in the euro crisis: the limits of postfunctionalism. *Journal of European Integration, 36*(6), 321–337.
Schuessler, R. (2014). *Energy Poverty Indicators: Conceptual Issues-Part I: The Ten-Percent-Rule and Double Median/Mean Indicators*. ZEW-Centre for European Economic Research Discussion Paper.
Schreurs, M. A., & Tiberghien, Y. (2007). Multi-Level reinforcement: Explaining European Union Leadership in climate change mitigation. *Global Environmental Politics, 7*(4), 19–46.
Tallberg, J. (2003). The agenda-shaping powers of the EU Council Presidency. *Journal of European public policy, 10*(1), 1–19.
Tallberg, J. (2006). *Leadership and Negotiation in the European Union*. Cambridge: Cambridge University Press.
Thomson, H., & Snell, C. (2013). Quantifying the prevalence of fuel poverty across the European Union. *Energy Policy, 52*(1), 563–572.
Tosun, J., & Solorio, I. (2011). Exploring the Energy-Environment Relationship in the EU: Perspectives and Challenges for Theorizing and Empirical Analysis. *European Integration online Papers, 15*(7), http://eiop.or.at/eiop/texte/2011-007a.htm.
Trondal, J. (2012). On bureaucratic centre formation in government institutions: lessons from the European Commission. *International Review of Administrative Sciences, 78*(3), 425–446.
Trondal, J., Van den Berg, C., & Suvarierol, S. (2008). The compound machinery of government: the case of seconded officials in the European Commission. *Governance, 21*(2), 253–274.
Tsebelis, G. (2002). *Veto Players: How Political Institutions Work*. Princeton: Princeton University Press.
Vogler, J. (2005). The European Contribution to global environmental governance. *International Affairs, 81*(4), 835–850.
Vogler, J., & Stephan, H. R. (2007). The European union in global environmental governance: Leadership in the making? *International Environmental Agreements, 7*(4), 389–413.
Wettestad, J., Eikeland, P. O., & Nilsson, M. (2012). EU Climate and Energy Policy: A Hesitant Supranational Turn? *Global Environmental Politics, 12*(2), 67–86.
Wonka, A. (2007). Technocratic and independent? The appointment of European Commissioners and its policy implications. *Journal of European Public Policy, 14*(2), 169–189.
Wonka, A. (2008). Decision-making dynamics in the European Commission: partisan, national or sectoral? *Journal of European Public Policy, 15*(8), 1145–1163.
Wüstenhagen, R., & Bilharz, M. (2006). Green energy market development in Germany: effective public policy and emerging customer demand. *Energy policy, 34*(13), 1681–1696.

Lightning Source UK Ltd.
Milton Keynes UK
UKOW06n0811170816

280877UK00013B/278/P

9 781447 166443